Spiritual Fetichism

Spiritual Fetichism
A study of West African Culture, Witchcraft, Magic & Demonology
Author: Robert Hamill Nassau

Original title: *Fetichism in West Africa* (1904)
Cover image: *African Mask* (Stock)
Lay-out: www.burokd.nl

ISBN 978-94-92355-18-8

VAMzzz Publishing
P.O. Box 3340
1001 AC Amsterdam
The Netherlands
www.vamzzz.com
contactvamzzz@gmail.com

SPIRITUAL FETICHISM

A study of West African Culture, Witchcraft, Magic & Demonology

Robert Hamill Nassau

VAMzzz PUBLISHING

Robert Hamill Nassau
Pennsylvania, October 11, 1835 – Pennsylvania, May 6, 1921

contents

Preface

ON THE 2D OF JULY, 1861, I sailed from New York City on a little brig, the "Ocean Eagle," with destination to the island of Corisco, near the equator, on the West Coast of Africa. My first introduction to the natives of Africa was a month later, when the vessel stopped at Monrovia, the capital of the Liberian Republic, to land a portion of its trade goods, and at other ports of Liberia, Sinoe, and Cape Palmas; thence to Corisco on September 12.

Corisco is a microcosm, only five miles long by three miles wide; its surface diversified with every variety of landscape, proportioned to its size, of hill, prairie, stream, and lake. It is located in the eye of the elephant-head shaped Bay of Corisco, and from twelve to twenty miles distant from the mainland. Into the bay flow two large rivers,—the Muni (the Rio D'Angra of commerce) and the Munda (this latter representing the elephant's proboscis).

The island, with adjacent mainland, was inhabited by the Benga tribe. It was the headquarters of the American Presbyterian Mission. On the voyage I had studied the Benga dialect with my fellow-passenger, the senior member of the Mission, Rev. James L.

Mackey; and was able, on my landing, to converse so well with the natives that they at once enthusiastically accepted me as an interested friend. This has ever since been my status among all other tribes.

I lived four years on the island, as preacher, teacher, and itinerant to the adjacent mainland, south to the Gabun River and its Mpongwe tribe, east up the Muni and Munda rivers, and north to the Benito River.

In my study of the natives' language my attention was drawn closely to their customs; and in my inquiry into their religion I at once saw how it was bound up in these customs. I met with other white men—traders, government officials, and even some missionaries—whose interest in Africa, however deep, was circumscribed by their special work for, respectively, wealth, power, and Gospel proclamation. They could see in those customs only "folly," and in the religion only "superstition."

I read many books on other parts of Africa, in which the same customs and religion prevailed. I did not think it reasonable to dismiss curtly as absurd the cherished sentiments of so large a portion of the human race. I asked myself: Is there no logical ground for the existence of these sentiments, no philosophy behind all these beliefs? I began to search; and thenceforward for thirty years, wherever I travelled, wherever I was guest to native chief, wherever I lived, I was always leading the conversation, in hut or camp, back to a study of the native thought.

I soon found that I gained nothing if I put my questions suddenly or without mask. The natives generally were aware that white men despised them and their beliefs, and they were slow to admit me to their thought if I made a direct advance. But, by chatting as a friend, telling them the strange and great things of my own country, and first eliciting their trust in me and interest in my stories, they forgot their reticence, and responded by telling me of their country. I listened, not critically, but apparently as a believer; and then they vied with each other in telling me all they knew and thought.

That has been the history of a thousand social chats,—in canoes by day, in camp and but by night, and at all hours in my own house, whose public room was open at any hour of day or evening for any visitor, petitioner, or lounger, my attention to whose wants or wishes was rewarded by some confidence about their habits or doings.

In 1865 I was transferred to Benito, where I remained until the close of 1871. Those years were full of travels afoot or by boat, south the hundred miles to Gabun, north toward the Batanga region, and east up the Benito for a hundred miles as a pioneer, to the Balengi and Boheba tribes,—a distance at that time unprecedented, considering the almost fierce opposition of the coast people to any white man's going to the local sources of their trade.

After more than ten uninterrupted years in Africa, I took a furlough of more than two years in the United States, and returned to my work in 1874.

I responded to a strong demand on the part of the supporters of Foreign Missions in Africa, that mission operations should no longer be confined to the coast. Unsuccessful efforts had been made to enter by the Gabun, by the Muni, and by the Benito.

On the 10th of September, 1874, I entered the Ogowe River,

at Nazareth Bay, one of its several embouchures into the Atlantic, near Cape Lopez, a degree south of the equator. But little was known of the Ogowe. Du Chaillu, in his "Equatorial Africa" (1861), barely mentions it, though he was hunting gorillas and journeying in "Ashango Land," on the sources of the Ngunye, a large southern affluent of the Ogowe.

A French gunboat a few years before had ascended it for one hundred and thirty miles to Lembarene, the head of the Ogowe Delta, and had attached it to France. Two English traders and one German bad built trading-bouses at that onehundred-and-thirty-mile limit, and traversed the river with small steam launches in their rubber trade. Besides these three, l was the only other white resident. They were living in the Galwa tribe, cognate in language with the Mpongwe. l settled at a one-hundred-and-flfty-mile limit, in the Akele tribe (cognate with the Benga), building my house at a place called Belambila.

Two years later l abandoned that spot, came down to Lembarene, and built on Kângwe Hill. There l learned the Mpongwe dialect. l remained there until 1880, successful with school and church, and travelling by boat and canoe thousands of miles in the many branches of the Ogowe, through its Delta, and in the lake country of Lakes Onange and Azyingo. In 1880 l took a second furlough to the United States, remaining eighteen months, and returning at the close of 1881.

My prosperous and comfortable station at Kangwe was occupied by a new man, and l resumed my old role of pioneer. l travelled up the Ogowe, one hundred and fifty miles beyond Lembarene, ascending and descending the wild waters of its cataracts, and settled at Talaguga, a noted rock near which was subsequently established the French military post, Njoli, at the two-hundred-mile limit of the course of the river. There I was alone with Mrs. Nassau, my nearest white neighbors the two French officers five miles up river at .the post, and my successors at Kângwe, seventy miles down river. The inhabitants were wild cannibal Fang, just recently emerged from the interior forest. It was a splendid field for original investigation, and I applied myself to the Fang dialect.

I remained at Talaguga, until 1891, when I took a third furlough to the United States, and stayed through 1892, during which time the Mission Board transferred my entire Ogowe work, with its two stations and four churches and successful schools, to the French Paris Evangelical Society.

In March, 1893, at the request of the Rev. Frank F. Ellinwood, D.D., LL.D., I wrote and read, before the American Society of Comparative Religions, a forty-minute essay on Bantu Theology.

At the wish of that Society I loaned the manuscript to them, for their use in the Parliament of Religions at the Chicago Exposition; but I carried the original draft of the essay with me on my return to Africa in August, 1893, where I was located at Libreville, Gabun, the Mission's oldest and most civilized station. There I found special advantage for my investigations. Though those educated Mpongwes could tell me little that was new as to purely unadulterated native thought, they, better than an ignorant tribe, could and did give me valuable intelligent replies to my inquiries as to the logical connection between native belief and act, and the essential meaning of things which I had seen and heard elsewhere. My ignorant friends at other places had given me a mass of isolated statements. My Mpongwe friends had studied a little grammar, and were somewhat trained to analyze. They helped me in the collocation of the statements and in the deduction of the philosophy behind them. It was there that I began to put my conclusions in writing.

In 1895 Miss Mary H. Kingsley journeyed in West Africa, sent on a special mission to investigate the subject of freshwater fishes. She also gratified her own personal interest in native African religious beliefs by close inquiries all along the coast.

During her stay at Libreville in the Kongo-Frangais, May-September, 1895, my interest, common with hers, in the study of native African thought led me into frequent and intimate conversations with her on that subject. She eagerly accepted what information, from my longer residence in Africa, I was able to impart. I loaned her the essay, with permission to make any use of it she desired in her proposed book, "Travels in West Africa." When that graphic story of her African wanderings appeared in 1897, she made courteous acknowledgment of the use she had made of it in her chapters on Fetich.

On page 395 of her "Travels in West Africa," referring to my missionary works, and to some contributions I had made to science, she wrote: "Still I deeply regret he has not done more for science and geography. . . . I beg to state I am not grumbling at him . . . but entirely from the justifiable irritation a student of fetich feels at knowing that there is but one copy of this collection of materials, and that this copy is in the form of a human being, and will disappear with him before it is half learned by us, who cannot do the things he has done."

This suggestion of Miss Kingsley's gave me no new thought; it only sharpened a desire I had hopelessly cherished for some years.

In my many missionary occupations—translation of the Scriptures, and other duties—I had never found the strength, when the special missionary daily work was done, to sit down and put into writing the mass of material I had collected as to the meaning and uses of fetiches. Nor did I think it right for me to take time that was paid for by the church in which to compile a book that would be my own personal pleasure and property.

Impressed with this idea, on my fourth furlough to America in 1899, I confided my wish to a few personal friends, telling them of my plan, not indeed ever to give up my life-work in and for Africa, but to resign from connection with the Board; and, returning to Africa under independent employ and freed from mission control, but still working under my Presbytery, have time to gratify my pen.

One of these friends was William Libbey, D. Sc., Professor of Physical Geography and Director of the E. M. Museum of Geology and Archaeology in Princeton University. Without my knowledge he subsequently mentioned the subject to his university friend, Rev. A. Woodruff Halsey, D.D., one of the Secretaries of the Board of Foreign Missions. Dr. Halsey thought my wish could be gratified without my resigning from the Board's service.

In November, 1899, the following action of the Board was forwarded to me: "November 20th, 1899. In view of the wide and varied information possessed by the Rev. Robert H. Nassau, D.D., of the West Africa Mission, regarding the customs and traditions of the tribes on the West Coast, and the importance of putting that knowledge into some permanent form, the Board requested Dr. Nassau to prepare a volume or volumes on the subject; and it directed the

West Africa Mission to assign him, on his return from his furlough, to such forms of missionary work as will give him the necessary leisure and opportunity."

On my return to Africa in 1900, I was located at Batanga, one hundred and seventy miles north of Gabun, and was assigned to the pastorate of the Batanga Church, the largest of the twelve churches of the Corisco Presbytery, with itineration to and charge of the sessions of the Kribi and Ubenji churches.

During intervals of time in the discharge of these pastoral duties my recreation was the writing and sifting of the multitude of notes I had collected on native superstition during the previous quarter of a century. The people of Batanga, though largely emancipated from the fetich practices of superstition, still believed in its witchcraft aspect. I began there to arrange the manuscript of this work. There, more than elsewhere, the natives seemed willing to tell me tales of their folk-lore, involving fetich beliefs. From them, and also from Mpongwe informants, were gathered largely the contents of Chapters XVI and XVII.

And now, on this my fifth furlough, the essay on Bantu Theology has grown to the proportions of this present volume. The conclusions contained in all these chapters are based on my own observations and investigations.

Obligation is acknowledged to a number of writers on Africa and others, quotations from whose books are credited in the body of this work. I quote them, not as informants of something I did not already know, but as witnesses to the fact of the universality of the same superstitious ideas all over Africa.

By the courtesy of the American Geographical Society, Chapters IV, V, X, and XI have appeared in its Bulletin during the years 1901-1903.

I am especially obligated to Professor Libbey for his sympathetic encouragement during the writing of my manuscript, and for his judicious sug estions as to the final form I have given it.

– Robert Hamill Nassau
Philadelphia, March 24 1904

Map of the West African Coasts

CHAPTER I
Constitution of Native African Society–Sociology

THAT STREAM OF THE NEGRO RACE which is known ethnologi-
cally as "Bantu," occupies all of the southern portion of the African
continent below the fourth degree of north latitude. It is divided
into a multitude of tribes, each with its own peculiar dialect. All
these dialects are cognate in their grammar. Some of them vary only
slightly in their vocabulary. In others the vocabulary is so distinctly
different that it is not understood by tribes only one hundred miles
apart, while that of others a thousand miles away may be intelligible.

In their migrations the tribes have been like a river, with its
windings, currents swift or slow; there have been even, in places,
back currents; and elsewhere quiet, almost stagnant pools. But they
all—from the Divala at Kamerun on the West Coast across to the
Kiswahile at Zanzibar on the East, and from Buganda by the Victoria
Nyanza at the north down to Zulu in the south at the Cape—have a
uniformity in language, tribal organization, family customs, judicial
rules and regulations, marriage ceremonies, funeral rites, and religious beliefs and practice. Dissimilarities have crept in with mixture
among themselves by intermarriage, the example of foreigners, with

some forms of foreign civilization and education, degradation by foreign vice, elevation by Christianity, and compulsion by foreign governments.

As a description of Bantu sociology, I give the following outline which was offered. some years ago, in reply to inquiries sent to members of the Gabun and Corisco Mission living at Batanga, by the German Government, in its laudable effort to adapt, as far as consistent with justice and humanity, its Kamerun territorial government to the then existing tribal regulations and customs of the tribes living in the Batanga region. This information was obtained by various persons from several sources, but especially from prominent native chiefs, all of them men of intelligence.

In their general features these statements were largely true also for all the other tribes in the Equatorial Coast region, and for most of the interior Bantu tribes now pressing down to the Coast. They were more distinctly descriptive of Batanga and the entire interior at the time of their formulation. But in the ten years that have since passed, a stranger would find that some of them are no longer exact. Foreign authority has removed or changed or sapped the foundations of many native customs and regulations, while it has not fully brought in the civilization of Christianity. The result in some places, in this period of transition, has been almost anarchy,— making a despotism, as under Belgian misrule in the so-called Kongo "Free" State; or commercial ruin, as under French monopoly in their Kongo-Français; and general confusion, under German hands, due to the arbitrary acts of local officials and their brutal black soldiery.

I. The Country

The coast between 5° and 4° N. Lat. is called "Kamerun." This is not a native word: it was formerly spelled by ships' captains in their trade "Cameroons." Its origin is uncertain. It is thought that it came from the name of the Portuguese explorer Diego Cam. The tribes in that region are the Divala, Isubu, Balimba, and other lesser ones.

The coast from 4° to 3° N. Lat. has also a foreign name, "Batanga." I do not know its origin.

The coast from 3° to 2° N. Lat. is called, by both natives and foreigners,"Benita"; at 1° N., by foreigners,"Corisco," and-by natives, "Benga." The name "Corisco" was given by Spaniards to an island in the Bay of Benga because of the brilliant coruscations of lightning so persistent in that locality. The Benga dialect is taken as the type of all the many dialects used from Corisco north to Benita, Bata, Batanga, and Kamerun.

From 1° N. to 30° S. is known as the "Gabun country," with the Mpongwe dialect, typical of its many congeners, the Orungu, Nkâmi (miscalled "Camma"), Galwa, and others.

From 3° S. to the Kongo River, at 6° S., the Loango tribe and dialect called "Fyât" are typical; and the Kongo River represents still another current of tribe and dialect.

In the interior, subtending the entire coast-line as above mentioned, are the several clans of the great Fang tribe, making a fifth distinctly different type, known by the names "Osheba," "Bulu," "Mabeya," and others. The name "Fang" is spelled variously: by the traveller Du Chaillu, "Fañ" by the French traveller, Count de Brazza,

"Pahouin" by their Benga neighbors, "Pangwe"; and by the Mpongwe, "Mpañwe." These tribes all have traditions of their having come from the far Northeast.

Before foreign slave-trade was introduced, and subsequently the ivory, rubber, palm-oil, and mahogany trades, the occupations of the natives were hunting, fishing, and agriculture. They subsisted on wild meats, fish, forest fruits and nuts, and the cultivated plantains, cassava, maize, ground-nuts, yams, eddoes, sweet potatoes, and a few other vegetables.

II. The Family

The family is the unit in native sociology. There is the narrow circle of relationship expressed by the word "ijawe," plural "majawe" (a derivative of the verb "jaka" = to beget), which includes those of the immediate family, both on the father's as well as on the mother's side (*i.e.*, blood-relatives).. The wider circle expressed by the word "ikaka" (pl."makaka") includes those who are blood-relatives, together with those united to them by marriage.

In giving illustrative native words I shall use the Benga dialect as typical. All the tribes have words indicating the relationships of father, mother, brother, sister. A nephew, while calling his own father "paia," calls an uncle who is older than himself "paia-utodu"; one younger than himself he calls "paia-ndembe." His own mother be calls "ina," and his aunts "ina-utodu" and "ina-ndembe," respectively, for one who is older or younger than himself.

A cousin is called "mwana-paia-utodu," or "-ndembe," as the case may be, according to age. These same designations are used for both the father's and the mother's side. A cousin's consanguinity is considered almost the same as that of brother or sister. They cannot marry. Indeed, all lines of consanguinity are carried farther, in prohibition of marriage, than in civilized countries.

Family Responsibility

Each family is held by the community responsible for the misdeeds of its members. However unworthy a man may be, his "people" are to stand by him, defend him, and even claim as right his acts, however unjust. He may demand their help, however guilty he may be. Even if his offence be so great that his own people have to acknowledge his guilt, they cannot abjure their responsibility. Even if he be worthy of death, and a ransom is called for, they must pay it: not only his rich relatives, but all who are at all able must help.

There is a narrower family relationship, that of the household, or "diyâ" (the hearth, or fireplace; derivative of the verb "diyaka" to live). There are a great many of these. Their habitations are built in one street, long or short, according to the size of the man's family.

In polygainy each wife has a separate house, or at least a separate room. *Her* children's home is in that house. Each woman rules her own house and children.

One of these women is called the "head-wife" ("konde"=queen). Usually she is the first wife. But the man is at liberty to displace her and put a younger one in her place.

The position of head-wife carries with it no special privileges except that she superintends; but she is not herself excused from work. In the community she is given more respect if the husband happens to be among the "headmen" or chiefs.

Each wife is supplied by the husband, but does not personally own her own house, kitchen utensils, and garden tools. She makes her own garden or "plantation" ("mwanga").

There is no community in ownership of a plantation. Each one chooses a spot for himself. Nor is there land tenure. Any man can go to any place not already occupied, and choose a site on which to build, or to make a garden; and he keeps it as long as be or some member of his family occupies it.

Family Headship
It descends to a son; if there be none, to a brother; or, if he be dead, to that brother's son; in default of these, to a sister's son. This headship carries with it, for a man, such authority that, should he kill his wife, be may not be killed; though her relatives, if they be influential, may demand some restitution.

If an ordinary man kills another man, he may himself be killed. For a debt he may give away a daughter or wife, but he may not give away a son or a brother. A father rules all his children, male and female, until his death.

If adult members of a family are dissatisfied with family arrangements, they can remove and build elsewhere; but they cannot thereby entirely separate themselves from rule by, and responsibility to and for the family.

A troublesome man cannot be expelled from the family village.

A woman can be, but only by her husband, for such offences as stealing, adultery, quarrelling; in which case the dowry money paid by him to her relatives must be returned to him, or another woman given in her place.

Marital Relations

Marriages are made not only between members of the same tribe but between different tribes. Formerly it was not considered proper that a man of a coast tribe should marry a woman from an interior tribe. The coast tribes regarded themselves as more enlightened than those of the interior, and were disposed to look down upon them. But now men marry women not only of their own tribe but of all inferior tribes.

Polygamy is common, almost universal. A man's addition to the number of his wives is limited only by his ability to pay their dowry price.

He may cohabit with a woman without—paying dowry for her; but their relation is not regarded as a marriage ("diba"), and this woman is disrespected as a harlot ("evove").

There are few men with only one wife. In some cases their monogamy is their voluntary choice; in most cases (where there is not Christian principle) it is due to poverty. A polygamist arranges his marital duties to his several wives according to his choice; but the division having been made, each wife jealously guards her own claim on his attentions. A disregard of them leads to many a family quarrel. [1]

---

1   Gen. xxx. 15-16.

If a man die, his brothers may marry any or all of the widows; or, if therp be no brothers, a son inherits, and may marry any or all of the widows except his own mother.

It is preferred that widows shall be retained in the family circle because of the dowry money that was paid for them, which is considered as a permanent investment.

Ante-ceremonial sexual trials (the ancient German "bundling") are not recognized as according to rule; but the custom is very common. If not followed by regular marriage ceremony, it is judged as adultery.

While a man may go to any tribe to seek a wife, he does not settle in the woman's tribe; she comes to him, and enters into his family.

Arrangements for Marriage

On entering into marriage a man depends on only the male members of his family to assist him. If the woman is of adult age, he is first to try obtain her consent. But that is not final; it may be either overridden or compelled by her father. The fathers of the two parties are the ultimate judges; the marriage cannot take place without their consent, after the preliminary wooing. The final compact is by dowry money, the most of which must be paid in ad-vance. It is the custom which has come down from old time. It is now slightly changing under education, enlightemment, and foreign law., The amount of the dowry is not prescribed by any law. Custom alters the amount, according to the social status of the two families and the pecuniary ability of the bridegroom.

The highest price is paid for a virgin; the next, for a woman who has been put away by some other man; the lowest price for widows. It is paid in instalments, but is supposed to be completed in one or two years after the marriage.

But the purchase of the woman by dowry does not extinguish all claim on her by her family. If she is maltreated, she may be taken back by them, in which case the man's dowry money is to be returned to him. Not only the woman's father, but her other relatives, have a claim to a share in the dowry paid for her. Her brothers, sisters, and cousins may ask gifts from the would-be husband.

If a husband die, the widow becomes the property of his family; she does not inherit, by right, any of his goods because she herself, as a widow, is property. Sometimes she is given something, but only as a favor.

If she runs away or escapes, her father or her family must return either her or the dowry paid for her.

On the death of a woman after heir marriage, a part of the money received for her is returned to, the husband as compensation for his loss on his investment. If she has borne no children, nothing is given or restored to the husband.

If a woman deserts her husband, her family is required to pay back the dowry. If the man himself sends her away, the dowry may be repaid on his demand and after a public discussion.

There is no escape from marriage for a woman during her life except by repayment of the money received for her.

Two men may exchange wives thus: each puts away his wife, sending her back to her people and receiving in return the money paid for her. With this money in hand each buys again the wife the other has put away; and all parties are satisfied.

A father can force his daughter to marry against her will; but such marriages are troublesome, and generally end in the man putting the woman away.

A daughter may be betrothed by her parents at any time, even at birth. The marriage formerly did not take place until she was a woman grown of twenty years; now they are married at fifteen or sixteen, or earlier.

Marriage within any degree of consanguinity is forbidden. Marriage of cousins is impossible. Disparity of age is no hindrance to marriage: an old man may take a young virgin, and a young man may take an old woman.

There are no bars of caste nor rank, except the social eminence derived from wealth or free birth.

Only women are barred from marrying an inferior. That inferiority is not a personal one. No personal worth can make a man of an inferior tribe equal to the meanest member of a superior tribe.

All coast tribes reckon themselves superior to any interior tribe; and, of the coast tribes, a superiority is claimed for those who have the largest foreign commerce and the greatest number of white residents.

A man may marry any woman of any inferior tribe, the idea being that be thus elevates her; but it is almost unheard of that a woman shall marry beneath her.

As a result of this iron rule, women of the Mpongwe and a few other small "superior" coast tribes being barred from many men, of their o wn tribe by lines of consanguinity, and unable to marry beneath themselves, expect to and do make their marriage alliances with the white traders and foreign government officials. Their civilization has made them attractive, and they are sought for by white men from far distant points.

Younger sons and daughters must not be married before the older ones.[2]

Courtship and Wedding

The routine varies greatly according to tribe; and in any tribe, according to the man's self-respect and regard for conventionalities. A proper outline is: First, the man goes to the father empty-handed to ask his consent. The second visit he goes with gifts, and the father calls in the other members of the family to witness the gifts. On the third visit he goes with liquor (formerly the native palm wine, now the foreign trade gin or rum), and pays an instalment on the dowry; on the fourth visit with his parents, and gives presents to the woman herself. On a fifth occasion the mother of the woman makes a feast for the mother and friends of the groom. At this feast the host and hostess do not eat, but they join in the drinking. Finally, the man goes with gifts and takes the woman. Her father makes return gifts as a farewell to his daughter.

On her arrival at the man's village they are met with rejoicing, and a dance called "nkanjo"; but there is no further ceremony, and she is his wife.

---

2   Gen. xxix. 26.

For three months she should not be required to do any hard work, the man providing her with food and dress. Then she will begin the usual woman's work, in the making of a garden and carrying of burdens.

Weddings may be made in any season of the year. Formerly the dry season, or the latter part of the rainy, was preferred because of the plentifulness of fish at these periods, and the weather being better for outdoor sports and plays.

The man is expected to visit his wife's family often, and to eat with them. Her mother feasts him, and he calls her parents to eat at his house.

Dissolution of Marriage

By death of the husband. Formerly, in many tribes one or more of the widows were put to death, either that the dead might not be without compamonship in the spirit world, or as a punishment for not having cared better for him in the preservation of his life.

Formerly the women mourned for six months; now the mourning (i.e., the public wailing) is reduced to one month. But signs of mourning are retained for many months in dark, old, or scanty dress, and an absence of ornament.

The mourning of both men and women begins before the sick have actually died. The men cease after the burial, but the women continue.

All the dead man's property goes to his male relatives. On the death of a wife the husband is expected to make a gift to pacify her relatives. Formerly the corpse was not allowed to be buried until this gift was made. The demand was made by the father, saying, "Our child died in your hands; give us!" Now they make a more quiet request, and wait a week before doing so. Something must be given, even if the husband bad already paid her dowry in full.

Marriage can be dissolved by divorce at almost any time, and for almost any reason, by the man,—by a woman rarely. The usual reasons for divorce are unfaithfulness, quarrelling, disobedience, and sometimes chronic sickness. There are many other more private reasons. In being thus put away the woman has no property rights; she is given nothing more than what the man may allow as a favor. If the woman has children, she has no claim on them; they belong to the father. But if she has daughters who are married, she can ask for part of the money which the husband received for them. The man and the divorced woman are then each free to marry any other parties.

Illegitimate Marital Relations

These are very common, but they are not sanctioned as proper. The husband demands a fine for his wife's infidelity from the co-respondent. Cohabitation with the expected husband previous to the marriage ceremonies is common; but it is not sanctioned, and therefore is secret.

The husband of a woman who is mother of a child begotten by another man takes it as his own. If it be a girl, he (and not the real father) is the person who gives her in marriage and retains the dowry.

Domestic Life

No special feast is made for the birth of either a son or a daughter, but there is rejoicing. During the woman's pregnancy both she and her husband have to observe a variety of prohibitions as to what they may eat or what they may do. They cohabit up to the time of the child's birth; but after that not for a long period, formerly three years. Now it is reduced to one and a half years, or less. This custom is one of the reasons assigned by men for the alleged necessity of a plurality of wives.

During the confinement and for a short time after the birth, the wife remains in the husband's house, and is then taken by her parents to their house.

Deformed and defective children are kept with kindness as others; but monstrosities are destroyed. Formerly in all tribes twins were regarded as monstrosities and were therefore killed,—still the custom in some tribes. In the more civilized tribes they are now valued, but special fetich ceremonies for them are considered necessary.

In the former destruction of twins there were tribes that killed only one of them. If they were male and female, the father would wish to save the boy and the mother the girl; but the father ruled. A motherless new-born infant is not deserted; it is suckled by some other woman.

A portion of the wearing apparel and other goods are placed in the coffin with the corpse. The greater part of a man's goods are taken by his male relatives. Formerly nothing was given to his widow; now she receives a small part. And the paternal relatives of the dead man give something to his maternal relatives.

The corpse is buried in various ways,—on an elevated scaffold, on the surface of the ground, or in a shallow grave, rarely cremated.

Formerly the burial could be delayed by a claim for settlement of a debt, but this does not now occur.

No coast tribe eats human flesh. The Fang and other interior tribes eat any corpse, regardless of the cause of death. Families hesitate to eat their own dead, but they sell or exchange them for the dead of other families.

The name given a child is according to family wish. There is no law. Parents like to have their own names transmitted; but all sorts of reasons prevail for giving common names, or for making a new one, or for selecting the name of a great person or of some natural object. A child born at midday may be called "Joba" (sun), or, at the full moon, "Ngânê" (moon). A mother who had borne nine children, all of whom had died, on bearing a tenth, and hopeless of its surviving, named it "Botombaka" (passing away).

Circumcision is practised universally by all these tribes. An uncircumcised native is not considered to be a man in the full sense of the word,—fit for fighting, working, marrying, and inheriting. He is regarded as nothing by both men and women, is slandered, abused, insulted, ostracized, and not allowed to marry.

The operation is not performed in infancy, but is delayed till the tenth year, or even later. The native doctor holds cayenne pepper in his mouth, and, on completing the operation, spits the pepper upon the wound. Then seizing a sword, he brandishes it with a sbout as a signal to the spectators that the act is completed. Then the crowd of men and women join in singing and dancing, and compliment the lad on being now "a real man."

As natives have no records of births, they cannot exactly tell the ages of their children, or the time when a youth is fit to marry or assume other manly rights; but by the eighteenth or nineteenth year he is regarded with the respect due a man. He can marry even as early as fifteen or sixteen. There are no tests to which be is subjected as proof of his manhood.

A woman may speak in a court of trial, for defence of herself or friends. She may also be summoned as a witness, but she has no political rights.

Aged persons are not put to death, to escape the care of them; they are reasonably well provided for.

III. Succession to property and authority

Only men inherit. The children of sisters do not inherit unless all the children of the brothers are dead.

Slaves do not inherit.

"Chieftains" (those chosen to rule) and "kings" (those chosen to the office) inherit more than their brothers, even though the ruling one be the younger.

A woman does not inherit at any time or under any circumstances, nor hold property in her own right, even if she has produced it by her own labor.

There is no supremacy in regard to age in the division of property. The things to be inherited are women (the widows), goods, house, and slaves. An equal division, as far as it is possible, is made of all these.

The dead man's debts are to be paid by the heirs out of their inheritance, each one paying his part. There is no written will, but it is common for a man to announce his intention as to the division while still living.

IV. Political organization

The coast tribes and some of the interior have so-called "kings," who are chosen by their tribe to that office.

There are family cliques for the accomplishment of a desired end, but these are overruled by the tribal king.

There are headmen in each village with local authority; but they too are subject to the king, they having authority only in their own village.

Quarrels and discussions, called "palavers," are very common. (A palaver need not necessarily be a quarrel; the word is derived from a Portuguese verb = "to speak." It comes from the old days of slavery; it was the "council" held between native chiefs and white slave traders, in the purchase of a cargo of slaves.)

The headmen settle disputes about marriage, property rights, murders, war, thefts, and so forth. Their decisions may be appealed from to a chief, or carried further to the king, whose decision is final. Any one, young and old, male and female, may be present during a discussion. Usually only chosen persons do the speaking.

Instead of a question being referred to a chief or king, a committee of wise men is sometimes chosen for the occasion. Public assemblages are gathered by messengers sent out to summon the people. The meeting is presided over by the king.

V. Servants

The domestic servants are slaves. Prisoners of war are also made to do service; but on the making of peace male prisoners are returned to their tribe; the female prisoners are retained and married. Slaves were bought from interior tribes. If a male child was born to slave parents, be was considered free and could marry into the tribe. If the slave mother died, the widower could marry into the tribe. If the slave father died, the widow was married by some man of the family who owned him. There are—no slaves bought or sold now, but there is a system of "pawns,"—children or women given as a pledge for a debt and never redeemed. Their position is inferior, and they are servants, but not slaves.

Also, if a prominent person (e.g., a headman) is killed in war, the people who killed him are to give a daughter to his family, who may marry her to any one they please.

A pawn may be sent away by the bolder to some other place, but he cannot be sold or killed; but the holder may beat him if he be obstreperous.

During slavery days anything earned by a slave was taken to his master, who would allow him a share; also, at other times, the master would give the slave gifts. The slave could do paid labor for foreigners or other strangers, and was not necessarily punished if he did not share his wages with the master, but he would at least be rebuked for the omission. Women ruled their female slaves. For a slave's minor offences, such as stealing, the master was held responsible; for grave offences, such as murder, the slave himself was killed.

Certain liberty was allowed a slave; be could attend the village or tribal, palavers and take part in the discussion. If a slave was unjustly treated by some other person, his owner could call a council and have the matter talked over, and the slave could be allowed to plead his case.

A slave man could hold property of his own; and if be were a worthy, sensible person, he could inherit.

In a slave's marriage of a woman the custom of gifts, feasts, and so forth was the same as for a free man.

If ill treated, he could run away to another tribe (not to any one of his own tribe), and would there be harbored, but still as a slave, and would not be given up to his former owner. A slave could become free only by his master setting him free; be could not redeem himself.

VI. Kingship

Kingship has connected with it the great honor that a son may inherit it if he is the right kind of man; but it is possible for him to be set aside and another chosen. A son may lose his place by foolishness and incompetency.

Attempts to rule independently of the king are sometimes made by cliques composed of three or four young persons of the same age, who make laws or customs peculiar to themselves. There is no national recognition of them, nor are they given any special privilege.

Kings have very little power over the fines or property of others. These are held, each man for himself; nor have they the right of 'taxation; but they. have power to declare war, acting in concert with their people in declaring it and waging it. They administer justice as magistrates, decide palavers according to the unwritten law of custom, summon offenders, and inflict the punishment due.

Their dwellings differ but little from those of other persons of like wealth and personal ability.

When a palaver is called, the king sits as ruler of the meeting and does most of the talking. He provides food for those who come from a distance.

A king may be blamed if a war he has declared ends disastrously. While a king's son expects to inherit the title and power, there is no invariable rule of succession; he cannot take the position by force. He must be chosen; but the choice is limited to the members of one family, in which it is hereditary.

If the chosen person be a minor, another is selected (but of the same family) to act as regent. The "incompetency" which could bar a man from kingship, even though in regular succession, would be lack of stamina in his character. The king-elect must make a feast, to which he is to call all the people to eat, drink, and play for twenty days.

There are no higher state forms among the coast tribes, as in civilized lands; no union among tribes; no feudal power nor vassals;

no monarchy, nothing absolute; no taxation, no monopoly. Some of the interior tribes formerly had tributes and kingly monopoly of certain products.

VII. Fetich doctors

They still exist, but it can scarcely be said that they are a class. They have no organization; they have honor only in their own districts, unless they be called specially to minister in another place. They have power to condemn to death on charge of causing sickness. In their ceremonies they send the people to sing, dance, play, and beat drums, and they spot their bodies with their "medicines." Any one may choose the profession for himself; fetich doctors demand large pay for their services.

VIII. Hospitality

A stranger is entertained hospitably. He is provided with a house and food for two weeks, or as much longer as he may wish to stay. On departing be is given a present. His host and the village headman are bound to protect him from any prosecution while he is their guest, even if he be really guilty.

Fetich Magician.
(With horns, wooden mask, spear, and sword; dress of leaves of palm and plantain.)

IX. Judicial System

Such a system does not exist. Whatever rules there are are handed down as tradition, by word of mouth. There are persons who are familiar with these old sayings, proverbs, examples, and customs, and these are asked to be present in the trial of disputed matters.

Courts

In the righting of any wrong the head of the family is to take the first step. If the offenders fail to satisfy him, he appeals to the king, who then calls all the people, rehearses the matter to them, and the majority of their votes is accepted by the king as the decision. The offenders will not dare to resist.

There is no regular court-house. In almost all villages there is a public shed, or "palaver-house," which is the town-ball, or public reception room. But a council may be held anywhere,—in the king's house, in the house of one of the litigants, on the beach, or under a large shady tree.

The council is held at any time of day,—not at night. There are no regular advocates; any litigant may state his own case, or have any one else do it for him. There are no fees, except to the king for his summoning of the case. There is sometimes betting on the result; though no stakes are deposited, the bets are paid. There is not much form of court procedure. All the people of a village or district, even women and children, according to the importance of the case, assemble. While women are generally not allowed to argue in the case, yet their shouts of approval or protest have influence in the decision, and encourage the parties by outspoken sympathy.

If an accused. person does not come voluntarily to court, the king's servants are sent to bring him. In the court the accused does not need to have some one plead for him, he speaks for himself. Accusers speak first, then the accused; the accusers reply, the accused answers; and the king and his aged counsellors decide. Witnesses are called from other places. As theie is no writing among untaught tribes, the depositions are by word of mouth.

Formerly the accused was subjected to the poison ordeal; indeed, the accuser also had to take the poison draught as a proof of his sincerity, and that his charge was not a libel. But this custom is no longer practised on the coast.

There is no substitution of any kind, except in rare cases. A guilty person must bear his own punishment in some way.

Oaths are common, and are used freely and voluntarily in the course of the discussion. A man who utters false testimony or bears false witness is expected to be thrust out of the assembly, but it is not always done.

When an oath is required, there is no escape from it; he who refuses to swear is considered guilty. Sometimes, under bravado, he will demand to be given "mbwaye" (the poison test), hoping that his demand will not be complied with. When the test is produced, be may seek to escape it by refusing that particular kind and demanding another not readily obtainable. But his attempt at evasion is generally regarded as a sign of guilt.

In court, parties are not obstinate in their opinion; they ask for and take advice from others.

Punishment

If it be capital, the accusers are the executioners. Death is by various modes,—formerly very cruel, *e.g.*, burning, roasting, torturing, amputation by piecemeal; now it is generally by gun, dagger, club, or drowning. For a debt that a creditor is seeking to recover, securities may be accepted. But if the accused then runs away, the person giving the security is tried and punished.

A creditor does not usually attach the property of the debtor, though often, in the interior tribes, a woman is seized as hostage. If a long time elapses in deciding the matter, the debtor may be held as prisoner until the debt is paid. Formerly it was very common for the debtor's family's property, or even their persons, to be seized as security; and it still is common for a person of the debtor's tribe to be caught by the creditor's tribe, and detained until he is redeemed by his own people.

The king of the prisoner's tribe is called to help release him. If the king himself become a captive, his people combine to collect goods for the payment, and meanwhile give other persons in his place to secure his immediate release. Sometimes differences are settled in a fight, by a hand-to-hand encounter.

Blood Atonement and Fines

Revenge, especially for bloodshed, is everywhere practised. It is a duty belonging first to the "ijawe" (blood-relative), next to the "ikaka" (family), next to the "etomba" (tribe).

The murdered man's own family take the lead,—in case of a wife, her husband and his family, and the wife's family; sometimes the whole "ikaka"; finally, the "etomba."

A master seeks revenge for his slave or other servants. Formerly it was indifferent who was killed in revenge, so that it be some member of the murderer's tribe. Naturally that tribe sought to retaliate, and the feud was carried back and forth, and would be finally settled only when an equal number had been killed on each side,—a person for a person: a woman for a man, or vice versa; a child for a man or woman, or vice versa. A woman (wife of the man killed) does not take the lead in the revenge; his family must take the lead, her family must join in. They would be despised and cursed if they did not do so. The woman herself does not take part in this killing for revenge.

The avenger of blood may not demit his duty until some member of the other tribe has been killed. If a thief has been killed for his theft, blood may be taken for his death.

But when that one other life is taken, the matter is considered settled; it is not carried on as a feud.

For a life taken by accident, a life is not required; but some penalty must be paid, *e.g.*, a woman may be given as a wife. But, practically, in former times it was not admitted that "accidents" occurred; any misfortune was adjudged a fault.

Formerly even the plea of self-defence was not accepted. Even idiotic or otherwise irresponsible persons were held responsible, though sometimes they were ransomed by payment of a woman and goods.

At present blood is not always required, but formerly no money would have been accepted as a sufficient penalty. A man would have been despised for accepting it. There was no way of settlement except by bloodshed,—a life for a life,—except that, for the life of a woman, a woman and goods of a certain amount and kind might be accepted. When a woman was thus given for a murdered one, the living woman must not be old, but one capable of bearing children. Among the acceptable goods were sheep, goats, and pottery.

A wound or a broken limb is paid for in goods. These must come not solely from him who caused the injury; his family, as fellow offenders, must assist in paying.

The man who obtains the woman who is given for a woman killed, retains with her also part of the goods given with her, and part he shares with the family of the murdered one. If, in giving a woman for a murdered one, the offending family is unable to furnish also the required goods, they must sell another of their women in order to obtain those goods. The point is that they must give a woman and goods; two women will not suffice.

The ceremonies in settlement of a blood-feud are as follows: The woman is paid in presence of both parties; then the goods are given, counted, and received. Then both parties retire. In the course of a week the parties receiving the woman and the goods call the other party, and produce a goat and kill it in their presence. It is divided equally, and given half to each party; and the feud is settled, as by a covenant of peace, over the divided goat (Gen. xv. 10). The woman thus given in settlement will be married to some one.

The customs in her marriage are the same as for any other woman. Subsequently those whp paid her as a fine may come and ask a portion of goods for her as a wife. Not that they have any claim on her as their daughter; but the man who has married her will give the goods they ask for, under the common belief that, unless he does so, the children born by her will die early, or at least will not come to years of maturity.

All misdeeds and offences, even capital ones, may be condoned by a fine in goods, excepting only the murder of a man. This murderer must forfeit his life. These fines are paid with foreign goods, each offence having its own regulation price as a punishment.

In general, the punishment for an injury is the same, whether the injured one be rich or poor. A man's "majawe" are held responsible if he refuses to make restitution. If they also refuse, the offended party await a suitable opportunity, and then seize some one and hold him as a hostage until he is redeemed, for the price of the original offence, every mite of it being then exacted.

There is no right of asylum to any offender within the limit of his own tribe. In case of a man visiting, for any reason whatever, in the limits of another tribe one of whose members is a fugitive from justice into the limits of the visitor's tribe, this visitor may be seized, and his countrymen asked to extradite the criminal staying in their midst.

Corporal punishment is administered publicly, the townspeople being called to witness it, so as to operate on their fears and cause them to dread the doing of deeds which may bring on them such a penalty.

Punishable Acts

A person is punishable only for an iujury committed intentionally, not by accident.

For damages by cattle, the animal may be killed if the damage be considerable. The injured party may keep and eat the carcass, and the owner cannot recover for it. In this respect animals are treated as human beings, their lives being forfeit; and the owner's majawe are held responsible along with him.

Punishments are rated according to the degree of the crime, in the order theft, adultery, rape, murder. Insults are not punishable by law; the insulted insults in return. If a fight results, and wounds are made during the fight, no fine is required.

Kidnapping, incest, and abortion are not known.

Under the slight duty owed to kings, treason can scarcely be said to exist. Its equivalent, the betrayal of tribal interests, is publicly rebuked, and a curse laid on the offender. If he be a servant, he is beaten and sent away.

The disturber of the peace of a wedding is expected to express regret, but no calamity will follow because of the disturbance. The offence is not common.

X. Territorial Relations

The tribes have fixed settlements wherever foreign governments have not taken possession. Each man may choose for a garden a place that has not been already occupied. The land is common property for the tribe. But each ijawe may choose a separate place for itself.

No man of a tribe has any claim on the soil other than is common to any other man of that tribe. He has, however, a claim greater than any stranger.

Tenure

Land is held as common property; it is not bought or sold, to a fellow-tribeman. It may be bought from the confines of another tribe, and it is sold to foreigners. A hunter is free to go anywhere, even into the territory of an adjacent tribe. If he kills game there, he does not have to divide. Bee trees and honey are free to any one. The sea is free for fishing only to the coast tribes.

Every woman has a separate garden; even the wives of polygamists do not have gardens in common.

Soil is free. A family, however, may settle in a limited district, and claim it as theirs as long as they live there; or, leaving it temporarily, if they return after a reasonable time, they may still claim it. They temporarily mark their places by trees or stones, as boundary lines. But there is nothing permanent. They prove their right to it by residing on it or making a garden from time to time. But their claim may be lost if the entire family leave it and go elsewhere. Such a place being vacated, and some one else wishing to occupy it, permission may be granted on formal application to the king. But if an occupant has deserted a place, and no one else has applied for it, he can resume it as his even after the lapse of years.

Dwellers on any ground have right to all the trees of fruitage on it, *e.g.*, palm-nuts, and other natural wild edible nuts. Wells are never dug. People depend on springs and streams. Springs are free, even though they be on land claimed by others.

A man assists his wife in the clearing of the forest for a garden plot; but she and her servants attend to the planting, weeding, and other working of the garden itself.

Rights in Movables

The tenant dweller on any particular lot of ground owns everything on it, except the ground itself. If a foreigner buy a piece of ground, he may or may not buy the houses, and so forth, according to agreement. The movables on any ground are houses, trees, and any vegetables planted.

XI. Exchange Relations

There is no coin or metal currency, except among the coast tribes, where foreign governments have introduced it. Foreign trade-goods are everywhere the medium of purchase and exohange. But there is a sort of currency, in the shape of iron spear-heads and other forms resembling miniature hatchets, a certain number of which are given by interior tribes in the purchase of a wife. They are used only for this purpose, and are exchanged by the parties themselves for the foreign goods required in the dowry.

They are manufactured by any village blacksmith from imported iron. They are not received or recognized by white traders.

Formerly cowry shells were used, even by foreign traders, as a currency; and they are still so used in the Sudan. But in all coast tribes purchase and sale are effected by foreign-made calico prints, pottery, cutlery, guns, powder, rum, and a great variety of other goods.

The natural products of the country—ivory, rubber, palm-oil, dyewoods—and many other native unmanufactured articles are exchanged for these goods. The natural products belong to the men.

If a woman should find ivory, she cannot sell it; it belongs to her husband to barter it.

Contracts are confirmed in various ways in different tribes. A common mode is to eat and drink together, as a sign that the bargain is closed; and it will not be broken. A contract cannot be broken after the price is agreed upon, even if only a part of the price is paid; the remainder is to be paid in instalments.

If one overreaches another in a trade, he must take back the imperfect article or add to it. This is true, according to native law, among themselves. Any amount of overreaching and deception is practised toward foreigners in a trade, or to members of another tribe; and many foreigners are just as guilty in their dealings with the natives.

Loans of trade-goods are constantly made, but the taking of interest therefor is not known. If a borrowed article, such as a canoe, is broken or lost, a new canoe must be given in its place. If the canoe is only injured and had been in want of repair, the borrower, on returning it, must repair it and also pay some goods. One going as surety for goods is held responsible.

Pawning of goods is commonly practised everywhere.

People are generous in making gifts to friends, or donations to the needy; but if a man who has been helped in time of distress subsequently increases in wealth, the one who helped him may demand a return of the original gift.

English Trading-House, Gabun.

XII. Religion

Religion is intimately mixed with every one of these aforementioned sociological aspects of family, rights of property, authority, tribal organization, judicial trials, punishments, intertribal relations, and commerce.

Mr. R. E. Dennett, residing in Loango, has made a careful and philosophic investigation into the religious ideas of the Ba-Vili or Fyât nation and adjacent tribes bordering on the Kongo. The result of his research shows that the native tribal government and religious and social life are inseparably united. He claims to have discovered a complex system of "numbers" and "powers" showing the Loango people to be more highly organized politically than are the equatorial tribes, and revealing a very curious co-relation of those "numbers," governing the physical, rational, and moral natures, with conscience and with God.

Some traces of the"numbers with meanings" are found in Yoruba, where, as described by Mr. Dennett, the division of the months of the year, the names of lower animals typical of the senses, and the powers of earth that speak to us represent religious ideas and relations. They err, therefore, who, as superficial observers, would brush away all these native views as mere superstition. They are more than mere superstition; though indeed very superstitious, they point to God.

The particular exponent of religious worship, the fetich, governs the arrangements of all such relations. It will be discussed as to its origin and the details of its use in the subsequent chapters.

CHAPTER II
The Idea of God–Religion

Theology, Religion, Creed, Worship — Source of the Knowledge of God; outside
of us; comes from God; Evolution of Physical Species — Materialism; Knowledge
of God not evolved — Superstition in all Religions — Dominant in African
Religion — No People without a Knowledge of at least the Name of God —
Testimony of Travellers and Others

MISSIONARY PAUL OF TARSUS, in the polite exordium of his great
address to the Athenian philosophers on Mars Hill, courteously tells
them that be believes them to be a very"religious" people,—indeed,
too much so in their broad-church willingness to give room for an
altar to the worship of any new immanence of God; and then, with
equal courtesy, he tells them that, with all their civilization, with all
their eminence in art and philosophy, they were ignorant of the true
character of a greater than any deity in their pantheon.

Modern missionaries, also, in studying the beliefs and forms
of worship of the heathen nations among whom they dwell, while
they may be shocked at the immoralities, cruelties, or absurdities of
the special cult they are investigating, have to acknowledge that its
followers, in their practice of it, exhibit a devotion, a persistence, and
a faithfulness worthy of Christian martyrs. They are very "religious."
Verily, if the obtaining of heaven and final salvation rested only on
sincerity of belief and consistency of practice, the multitudinous
followers of the so-called false religions would have an assurance
greater than that of many professors of what is known as Christian-

ity, and much of the occupation of the Christian missionary would be gone.

I say much; but not all, by any means. For the feeling with which I was impressed on my very first contact with the miseries of the sociology of heathenism, entirely aside from its theology and any question of salvation in a future life, has steadily deepened into the conviction that, even if I were not a Christian, I still ought to, and would, do and bear and suffer whatever God has called or allowed me to suffer or bear or do since 1861—in my proclamation of His gospel, simply for the sake of the elevation of heathen during their present earthly life from the wrongs sanctioned by or growing out of their religion. Distinctly is it true that "Godliness is profitable unto all things, "not only for the life" which is to come," but also for "the life that now is." Those in Christian lands who have no sympathy for, or who refuse to take any interest in, what are known as "Foreign Missions," err egregiously in their failure to recognize the indisputable fact that they themselves are debtors for their possession of protected life, true liberty, and unoppressed pursuit of personal happiness, not to civilization as such, but to the form of religious belief called Christianity, which made that civilization possible. And by just so much as divine law has ordained us each our brother's keeper, we are bound to share the blessings of the gospel with those whom God has made of one blood with us in the brotherhood of humanity.

A pursuit of this line of thought would lead me into an argument for the duty of foreign missions. That is not the direct object of these pages. True, I pray that, as a result of any reader's following me in this study of African superstition, his desire will be deepened to give to Africa the pure truth in place of its falsity. But the special object of my pen, in following a certain thread of truth, is to show how degradingly false is that falsity, in its lapse from God, even though I accord it the name of religion.

For my present purpose it is sufficiently accurate to define theology as that department of knowledge which takes cognizance of God,—His being, His character, and His relation to His Cosmos. Whenever any intelligent unit in that Cosmos looks up to Him as something greater than itself, under what Schleiermacher describes as "a sense of infinite dependence," and utters its need, it has expressed its religion. It may be weak, superstitious, and mixed with untruth; nevertheless, it is religion.

When a study of God and the thoughts concerning Him crystallize into a formula of words expressing a certain belief, it is definitely a creed. When, under a human necessity, a creed clothes itself in certain rites, ceremonies, and formulas of practice, it is a worship. That worship may be fearful in its cruelty or ridiculous in its frivolity; nevertheless, it is a worship. Worship is essential to the vitality of religion; without it religion is simply a theory.

Theology differentiates itself from other departments of knowledge, as to its source and its effects. For instance, in the study of geography, as to its effects, it is comparatively a matter of indifference whether we believe that the earth is flat or globular, like Booker T. Washington's teacher who in his district school was prepared to teach either, "according to the preference of a majority of his patrons"; or, in astronomy, whether we believe that the sun is the stationary centre of our planetary system, or whether, with the late

Rev. John Jasper, we assert that the sun "do move" around our earth.

But in theology it matters enormously for this present life, whether we believe the supreme object of our worship to be Moloch, and infinitely for our future life, whether Jesus be to us the Son of God.

As to the source of theological knowledge, all our other knowledge is evolved, systematized, and developed by patient experiment and investigation. The results of any particular branch of human knowledge are cumulative, and are enlarged and perfected from generation to generation. But the source of our knowledge of God is not in us, any more than our spiritual life had its source in ourselves. It came *ab extra*. God breathed into the earthly form of Adam the breath of life, and be became a living creature, essentially and radically different from the beasts over which he was given dominion. Knowledge of God was thus an original, donated, component part of us. It grew under revelations made during the angelic communications before the Fall. Revelation was continued by the Logos along thousands of years, until that Logos himself became flesh and dwelt among us in visible form in His written word, and by His Comforter, who still reveals to us.

I do not feel it necessary here to discuss, or even to express an opinion as to the evolution of the physical species. I know, simply because God says so,—and am satisfied with this knowledge,—that "in the beginning God created." As to *when* that "beginning" was, there may be respectable difference of opinion; for it is only a human opinion that asserts *when*. Assertion may have apparently very reliable data; but these data often are like the bits of glass, factors in the geometric figures of a kaleidoscope, whose next turn in scientific discovery dislocates and relocates in an apparently reliable proof of the existence of another figure.

As to what it was that God created in that beginning, there may be also respectable difference of opinion. Whether, like Minerva, full armed from the head of Jove, Adam sprang into his perfect physical, mental, and moral manhood on the sixth of consecutive days of twenty-four solar hours each; or whether, created a weakling, he slowly grew up to perfect development; or whether life began only in protoplasm, and gradually differentiated itself into the forms of beasts, and finally into that of man,—back of all was a great First Cause that "created" in the "beginning." It is all a subject fearfully wonderful.

"My substance was not hid from Thee when I was made in secret, and curiously wrought in the lowest parts of the earth. Thine eyes did see my substance, yet being unperfect; and in Thy book all my members were written, which in continuance were fashioned, when as yet there was none of them."

But all such assertion, discussion, and attempt at proof I allow only to what is physical and finite, and is therefore a legitimate subject of assertion on merely physical data; for I do not desire to discuss, beyond simple mention, the Spencerian doctrine of evolution, that materialism which would make thought and soul only successions in a series (even if the highest and best) of evoluted developments. To account for the religious nature in man by evolution I regard as a thing that cannot be done. It is a tenable position held by evolutionists such as Dana, Winchell, and the late Professor

Le Conte of California, that "at the creation of man the divine fiat asserted itself, and 'breathed into man the breath of life, and man became a living soul.' Immortality cannot be evolved out of mortality. If Spencerian evolution is true, either everything is immortal or nothing is immortal; man and vermin in this hypothesis go together."

Man's soul came to him direct from God, a part of His own infinite life, in His "image," and like Him in His holiness. Man's thoughts of God were holy. The expression of them in words and acts was his practical religion, the visible, audible link that "bound" (ligated) him to God. In this there could be no evolution, unless that, in the many forms and ceremonies used in the expression of religious thought (which ceremonies constitute worship), there could be, and were, variation, change, development, or retrogression.

Therefore I cannot accept the conclusions of those who in their study of ethnology claim to find that the religious beliefs of the world, and even the very idea of a Supreme Being, have been evolved by man himself *ab intra*. They claim that this evolution has been by primitive man, from low forms of beliefs in spiritual beings, through polytheism and idolatry, up to the conception of monotheism and its belief in the one living God. This process they claim to be able to follow on lines racial and national, under the civilizations of Chaldee, Greek, Roman, Teutonic, and other stocks.

"Until some human being can be found with a conception of spiritual existences without his having received instruction on that point from those who went before him, the claim . . . that primitive man ever obtained his spiritual knowledge or his spiritual conceptions from within himself alone, or without an external revelation to him, is an unscientific assumption in the investigation of the origin of religions in the world."[3]

The rather I find, in my own ethnological observations during these more than forty years in direct contact with aboriginal peoples, that the initial starting-point of man's knowledge of God was by revelation from Jehovah himself. This knowledge was to be conserved by man's conscience, God's implanted witness,—a witness that can be coerced into silence, that may be nursed into forgetfulness, that may be perverted by abuse, that may be covered up by superimposed falsities, that may be discolored by the blackness of foul degradation, but which can never be utterly destroyed; which on occasions, like the Titans, arouses itself with volcanic force; which at God's final bar is to be His sufficient proof for the verities and responsibilities of at least natural religion ("natural" religion, a recognition of certain attributes of God as revealed in the works of nature). This knowledge of God, a treasure hid in earthen vessels, rightly used and cherished, was to grow and develop under subsequdnt divine revelation, so that man might become more and more like his divine original; or, if abused, neglected, or perverted, it would carry him even farther away from God.

"Not alone those who insist on the belief that there was a gradual development of the race from a barbarous beginning, but also those who believe that man started on a higher plane, and in his degradation retained vesticres of God's original revelation to him, are finding profit in the study of primitive Myths, and of aboriginal

---

3   Trumbull, Blood Covenant, p. 311.

rites and ceremonies all the world over." [4]

I do not impeach the sincerity of those students of primitive thought who teach that man in his religious beliefs has reached his present monotheism by progressive growths from polytheism, or that he has attained his present conception of the very existence of a Supreme Being by a gradual emergence from a state of ignorance in which even the idea of such a being did not exist; but I do discount the competency of many of the witnesses on whose testimony they base their conclusions.

Whatever may be proved in a complete investigation by science into the arcana of nature,—of archæology and other channels of research,—a reverent comparison of these results of finite intelligence will find them not inconsistent with the statements of God's infinite Word. Indeed, that Word was not written to make any definite statement on astronomy or geology, or any other human science. The only science of the Bible is that of man's relation to his divine Father; its only history a history of redemption, as promised to Eve and her seed, the Jewish nation, and as fulfilled in the Lion of the Tribe of Judah. Apparent conflicts of the Bible with science are not always real; too often a claim is set up, based on a single observation, perbaps hastily made, and not verified by a comparison of the variable factors in that observation.

I suppose that it is true that in the theology of even the worst forms of religion there is more or less truth, and almost equally true that in the theology of the best forms there may be somewhat

---

4   Trumbull, Blood Covenant, p. 4.

of superstition. This is so because, as I believe, all religions bad but one source, and that a pure one. From it have grown perversions varying in their proportion of truth and error.

In this study of the African theologic ideas I shall endeavor to separate these two—the false and the true—into two divisions: First, Beliefs in God more or less true, which have had their birth in tradition of some divine revelation, which find at least faint echoes in human conscience, and which among exalted nations would be formulated into confessions, creeds, and articles of faith. Second, Animism or beliefs in vague spiritual beings, which, being almost pure superstitions, cannot, from their very nature, be accurately formulated, they being the outgrowth of every individual's imagination, and varying with all the variances of time, place, and human thought.

Eliminating from any theology its superstitious element, we shall find the highest and truest religion. But if you eliminate from the theology of the Bantu African its superstition, you will have very little left; for, among the religions of the world, it comes nearest to being purely a superstition. So nearly is this true that travellers and other superficial observers and theorists have asserted that the religious beliefs of some degraded tribes were simply superstitions, destitute of reference to any superior being.

I can readily see how the reports of some travellers—even of those who had no prejudice against the Negro, the precepts of the Bible, or missionary work—could be made in apparent sincerity, when they state that native Africans have confessed of themselves that they had no idea of God's existence; also, their belief that some pygmy and other tribes were too destitute of intelligence to possess that idea,—that it either must be given them ab extra by the posses-sors of a superior civilization, or must be developed by themselves as they rise in civilization.

The difficulty about the testimony of these witnesses in this matter is that, being passers-by in time, they were unable—by rea-son of lack of ability to converse fluently, or absence of a reliable interpreter, or of being out of touch with native mode of thought or speech—to make their questionings intelligible.

On the heathen side, also, the obsequious natives, unaccus-tomed to analytic thought, will answer vaguely on the spur of the moment, and often as far as possible in the line of what they sup-pose will best please the questioner. All native statements must be discounted, must be sifted.

I am aware that some missionaries are quoted as having said or written that the people among whom they were laboring "had no idea of God." Even Robert Moffat is reported to have held this opin-ion. If so, it must have been in the earlier days of his ministry, under his first shock at the depth of native degradation, before he bad become fluent in the native language, and before he had found out all the secrets of that difficult problem, an African's native thought. Such an unqualified phrase could be uttered by a missionary in an hour of depression, in the presence of some great demonstration of heathen wickedness, and in an effort to describe how very far the heathen was from God. That the heathen had no correct idea of God is often true.

Arnot, who among modern African missionaries has lived most closely and intimately with the rudest tribes in their veriest hovels, writes:[5] "Man is a very fragile being, and be is fully conscious that be requires supernatural or divine aid. Apart from the distinct revelation given by God in the first chapter of Romans, there is much to prove that the heathen African is a man to whom the living God has aforetime revealed himself. But he had sought after things of his own imagination and things of darkness to satisfy those convictions and fears which lurk in his breast, and which have not been planted there by the Evil One, but by God. Refusing to acknowledge God,[6] they have become haters of God.[7] The preaching of the gospel to them, however, is not a mere beating of the air; there is a peg in the wall upon which something can be hung and remain. Often a few young men have received the message with laughter and ridicule, but I have afterwards heard them discuss my words amongst themselves very gravely. I heard one man say to a neighbor, 'Monare's words pierce the heart.' Another remarked that the story of Christ's death was very beautiful, but that he knew it was not meant for him; he was a 'makala' (slave), and such a sacrifice was only for white men and princes."

Lionel Declè,[8] Who certainly is not prejudiced toward missionaries or the Negro, writes of the Barotse tribe in South Africa and their worship of ancestors: "They believe in a Supreme Being, Niambe, who is supl)osed to come and take away the spiritual part

---

5   Garenganze, p. 79.

6   Rom. i. 28, margin.

7   Rom. i. 30.

8   Three Years in Savage Africa, p. 74.

of the dead." This name "Niambe," for the Deity, is almost exactly the same as "Anyambe," in Benga, two thousand miles distant.

Illustrative of traveller Declè's baste or inexactitude in the use of language, he apparently contradicts himself on page 153, in speaking of a tribe, the Matabele, adjacent to the Barotse: "The idea of a Supreme Being is utterly foreign, and cannot be appreciated by the native mind. They have a vague idea of a number of evil spirits always ready to do harm, and chief among these are the spirits of their ancestors; but they do not pray to them to ask for their help if they wish to enter on any undertaking. They merely offer sacrifices to appease them when some evil has befallen the family."

Perhaps he and other cursory travellers, in making such hasty assertions, mean that the native has no idea of the true character of God; in that they would be correct.

The accounts which some travellers have given of tribes without religion I either set down to misunderstanding, or consider them to be insufficient to invalidate the assertion that religion is a universal feature of savage life.

However degraded, every people have a religion. But they are children, babes in the woods, lost in the forest of ignorance, dense and more morally malarious than Stanley's forest of Urega. In their helplessness, under a feeling of their "infinite dependence," they cry out in the night of their orphanage, "Help us, O Paia Njambe!" Their forefathers wandered so far from him that only a name is left by which to describe the All-Father, whose true character has been utterly forgotten,—so forgotten that they rarely worship him, but have given such honor and reverence as they do render literally to the supposed spiritual residents in stocks and stones. "Lo! this only have I found, that God hath made man—upright; but they have sought out many inventions."

Offering in the following pages a formulation of African superstitious beliefs and practice, I premise that I have gathered them from a very large number of native witnesses, very few of whom presented to me all the same ideas. Any one else, inquiring of other natives in other places, would not find, as held by every one of them, all that I have recorded; but parts of all these separate ideas will be found held by separate individuals everywhere.

After more than forty years' residence among these tribes, fluently using their language, conversant with their customs, dwelling intimately in their huts, associating with them in the varied relations of teacher, pastor, friend, master, fellow-traveller, and guest, and, in my special office as missionary, searching after their religious thought (and therefore being allowed a deeper entrance into the arcana of their soul than would be accorded to a passing explorer), I am able unhesitatingly to say that among all the multitude of degraded ones with whom I have met, I have seen or heard of none whose religious thought was only a superstition.

Standing in the village street, surrounded by a company whom their chief has courteously summoned at my request, when I say to him, "I have come to speak to your people," I do not need to begin by telling them that there is a God. Looking on that motley assemblage of villagers,—the bold, gaunt cannibal with his armament of gun, spear, and dagger; the artisan with rude adze in hand, or hands soiled at the antique bellows of the village smithy; women who have hasted from their kitchen fire with hands white with the manioc dough or still grasping the partly scaled fish; and children checked in their play with tiny bow and arrow or startled from their dusty street pursuit of dog or goat,—I have yet to be asked, "Who is God?"

Under the slightly varying form of Anyambe, Anyambie, Njambi, Nzambi, Anzam, Nyam, or, in other parts, Ukuku, Suku, and so forth, they know of a Being superior to themselves, of whom they themselves inform me that he is the *Maker* and *Father*. The divine and human relations of these two names at once give me ground on which to stand in beginning my address.

If suddenly they should be asked the flat question, "Do you know Anyambe?" they would probably tell any white visitor, trader, traveller, or even missionary, under a feeling of their general ignorance and the white man's superior knowledge, "No! What do we know? You are white people and are spirits; you come from Njambi's town, and know all about him!" (This will help to explain, what is probably true, that some natives have sometimes made the thoughtless admission that they "know nothing about a God.") I reply, "No, I am not a spirit; and, while I do indeed know about Anyambe, I did not call him by that name. It's your own word. Where did you get it?" "Our forefathers told us that name. Njambi is the One-who-made-us. He is our Father." Pursuing the conversation, they will interestedly and voluntarily say, "He made these trees, that mountain, this river, these goats and chickens, and us people."

That typical conversation I have had hundreds of times, under an immense variety of circumstances, with the most varied audiences, and before extremes of ignorance, savagery, and uncivilization, utterly barring out the admission of a probability that the tribe, audience, or individual in question bad obtained a previous knowledge of the name by hearsay from adjacent more enlightened tribes. For the name of that Great Being was everywhere and in every tribe before any of them had become enlightened; varied in form in each tribe by the dialectic difference belonging to their own, and not imported from others,—for, where tribes are hundreds of miles apart or their dialects greatly differ, the variation in the name is great, *e.g.*, "Suku," of the Bihe country, south of the Kongo River and in the interior back of Angola, and "Nzam" of the cannibal Fang, north of the equator.

But while it is therefore undeniable that a knowledge of this Great Being exists among the natives, and that the belief is held that he is a superior and even a supreme being, that supremacy is not so great as what we ascribe to Jehovah. Nevertheless, I believe that the knowledge of their Anzam or Anyambe has come down-clouded though it be and fearfully obscured and marred, but still a revelationfrom Jehovah Himself. Most of the same virtues which we in our enlightened Christianity commend, and many of the vices which we denounce, they respectively commend and denounce. No one of them praises to me theft or falsehood or murder. They speak of certain virtues as "good," and of other things which are "bad," though, just as do the depraved of Christian lands, they follow the vices they condemn. True, certain evils they do defend, *e.g.* (as did some of our New England ancestors) witchcraft executions, justifying them as judicial acts; and polygamy, considering it (as our civilized Mormons) a desirable social institution (but, unlike the Mormons, not claiming for it the sanction of religion); and slavery, regarded (as only a generation ago in the United States) as necessary for a certain kind of property. But theft, falsehood, and some other sins, when committed by others, their own consciences condemn,—closely covered up and blunted as those consciences may be,—thus witnessing with and for God.

While all this is true, their knowledge of God is almost simply a theory. It is an accepted belief, but it does not often influence their life. "God is not in all their thought." In practice they give Him no worship. God is simply "counted out."

Resuming my street-preaching conversation: Immediately after the admission by the audience of their knowledge of Anzam as the Creator and Father, I say, "Why then do you not obey this Father's commands, who tells you to do so and so? Why do you disobey his prohibitions, who forbids you to do so and so? Why do you not worship him?" Promptly they reply: "Yes, he made us; but, having made us, be abandoned us, does not care for us; he is far from us. Why should we care for him? He does not help nor harm us. It is the spirits who can harm us whom we fear and worship, and for whom we care."

Another witness on this subject is the Rev. Dr. J. L. Wilson.[9] Speaking of Africa and its Negro inhabitants, he says: "The belief in one great Supreme Being is universal. Nor is this idea held imperfectly or obscurely developed in their minds. The impression is so deeply engraved upon their moral and mental nature that any

---

9 Western Africa, p. 209.

system of atheism strikes them as too absurd and preposterous to require a denial. Everything which transpires in the natural world beyond the power of man or of spirits, who are supposed to occupy a place somewhat higher than man, is at once and spontaneously ascribed to the agency of God. All the tribes in the country with which the writer has become acquainted (and they are not few) have a name for God; and many of them have two or more, significant of His character as a Maker, Preserver, and Benefactor. (In the Grebo country Nyiswa is the common name for God; but He is sometimes called Geyi, indicative of His character as Maker. In Ashanti He has two names: viz., Yankumpon, which signifies 'My Great Friend,' and Yemi, 'My Maker.') The people, however, have no correct idea. of the character or attributes of the Deity. Destitute of (a written) revelation, and without any other means of forming a correct conception of His moral nature, they naturally reason up from their own natures, and, in consequence, think of Him as a being like themselves.

"Nor have they any correct notion of the control which God exercises over the affairs of the world. The prevailing notion seems to be that God, after having made the world and filled it with inhabitants, retired to some remote corner of the universe, and has allowed the affairs of the world to come under the control of evil spirits; and hence the only religious worship that is ever performed is directed to these spirits, the object of which is to court their favor, or ward off the evil effects of their displeasure.

"On some rare occasions, as at the ratification of an important treaty, or when a man is condemned to drink the 'redwater ordeal,' the name of God is solemnly invoked; and, what is worthy of note, is invoked *three times* with marked precision. Whether this involves the idea of a Trinity we shall not pretend to decide; but the fact itself is worthy of record. Many of the tribes speak of the 'Son of God.' The Grebos call him 'Greh,' and the Amina people, according to Pritchard, call him 'Sankombum.'"

The following testimony I gather from conversations with the late Rev. Ibia j'Ikenge, a native minister and member of the Presbytery of Corisco, who himself was born in heathenism. He stated:

That his forefathers believed in many inferior agencies who are under the control of a Superior Being; that they were therefore primitive monotheists. Under great emergencies they looked beyond the lower beings, and asked help of that Superior; before doing so, they prayed to him, imploring him as Father to help;

That the people of this country believed God made the world and everything in it; but be did not know whether they had had any ideas about creation from dust of the ground or in God's likeness;

That they believed in the existence, in the first times, of a great man, who had simply to speak, and all things were made by the word of his power. As to man's creation, a legend states it thus: Two eggs fell from on high. On striking the ground and breaking, one became a man and the other a woman. (Apparently there is no memory of any legend indicating the name, character, or work of the Holy Spirit.)

That there is a legend of a great chief of a village who always warned people not to eat of the fruit of a certain tree. Finally, he himself ate of it and died;

That there was no legend, but, among a few persons, a vague tradition of a once happy period, and of a coming time of good; but he knew of nothing corresponding to the story of Cain and Abel;

That there is a fable that a woman brought to the people of her village the fruit of a forbidden tree. In order to hide it she swallowed it; and she became possessed of an evil spirit, which was the beginning of witchcraft;

That there was some tradition of a Deluge (he was not aware of any about the Dispersion at the Tower of Babel);

That all men believed they were sinners, but that they knew of no remedy for sin;

That sacrifices are made constantly, their object being to appease the spirits and avert their anger;

That many of the tribes are, and probably all, before they emerged on the seacoast, were cannibal (of the origin of cannibalism he did not know, but he was certain it had no religious idea associated with it);[10]

That there was a legend that a "Son" of God, by name Ilongo ja Anyambe, was to come and deliver mankind from trouble and give them happiness; but as he had not as yet come, the heathen were no longer expecting him;

That there was a division of time, six months, making an "upuma," or year, and a rest day, which came two days after the new moon, and was called Buhwa bwa Mandanda,—it was a day for dancing and feasting;

That the dead were usually buried; but persons held in superstitious reverence, as twins, Udinge, etc., were not buried, but

---

10   I am strongly disposed to think that, in its origin, there was a sacrificial idea connected with cannibalism.—R. H. N.

left at the foot of a ceiba, or silk-cotton tree, or other sacred tree;

That burial-places are regarded with a mixed feeling of reverence and awe;

That the immortality of the soul is believed in, but that there is no tradition of the resurrection of the body;

That they believe God gave law to mankind, and that, for those who keep this law, there is reserved in the future a "good place," and for the bad a "bad place," but no definite ideas about what that "good" or that "bad" will be, or as to the locality of those places;

That they believe in a distinction of spirits,—that some are demons, as in the old days of demoniacal possession, this distinction following the Jewish idea of diaboloi and daimonai.

CHAPTER III
Polytheism–Idolatry

Religion and Civilization — Worship of Natural Objects — Polytheism —
Idolatry — Worship of Ancestors — Fetichism

CIVILIZATION AND RELIGION do not necessirily move with equal pace. Whatever is really best in the ethics of civilization is derived from religion. If civilization falls backward, religion probably has already weakened or will also fall. The converse is not necessarily true. Religion may halt or even retrograde, while civilization steps on brilliantly, as it did in Greece with her Parthenon, and in Rome the while that religion added to the number of idols in the pantheon. Egypt, too, had her men learned in astronomy, who built splendid palaces and hundred-pillared Thebes the while they were worshipping Osiris. The dwellers before the Deluge had carried their civilization to a knowledge of arts now lost, while their wickedness and utter wanderings from God's worship caused the earth to cry out for a cleansing Flood.

Whatever therefore may be true in the history of civilization—whether man was gifted, *ab initio*, with a large measure of useful knowledge which he had simply easily to put into practice; or whether, as a savage, primitive man had slowly and painfully to find out under pressure the use of fire, clothing, weapons of defence and offence, tools, and other necessary articles and arts—is not important here to be discussed. From whatever point of vantage, high or low, Adam's sons started, we know that they bad at least tools for agriculture[11] and for the building of houses;[12] and that a few generations later, their knowledge of arts had grown from those which aided in the acquisition of the bare necessaries of life into the æstheties of music and metallic ornamentation.[13]

But religion did not wait that length of time for its growth. To the original pair in Eden, Jehovah had given a knowledge of Himself. They felt His character, they were told His will; and when they had disobeyed that will, they were given a promise of salvation, and were instructed in certain given rites of worship, *e.g.*, offerings and sacrifice. They knew[14] the significance of atoning blood, and the difference between a simple thank-offering and a sin-offering. All this knowledge of religion was not a possession which man had attained by slow degrees. He started with it in full possession, while yet he was clothed only in the skins of beasts[15] and before he knew how to make musical instruments or to fashion brass and iron. His religion was in advance of his civilization. Subsequently his civilization pushed ahead.

What were the gradual steps before the Deluge, in the di-

---

11   Gen iv. 2.

12   Gen iv. 17.

13   Gen. iv. 21, 22.

14   Heb. xi. 4.

15   Gen. iii. 21.

vergence of man's worship of God, is not difficult to imagine if we look at the history of the Chaldees, of the Hittites, and of the Jews themselves. Subsequent to the Deluge, from the grateful sacrifice of the seventh animal by Noah, to Abraham's typical offering of Isaac, it is not a very far cry to the butchery of Jephthah's daughter or the immolations to Moloch. A well-intended Ed[16] may readily become a schismatic Mecca. An altar of Dan is soon furnished with its golden calf.

With this as a starting-point, viz., that the knowledge of himself was directly imparted to man by Jehovah, and that certain forms of worship were originally directed and sanctioned by Him, I wish in subsequent pages to follow that line of light through the labyrinths of man's wandering from monotheism into polytheism, idolatry, and even into crass fetichism.

Abstract faith is difficult. It is so much easier to believe what we see, to have faith assisted by sight. Even such faith is not without its blessing, but"blessed are they that have not seen, and yet have believed."[17] Memory is assisted by visible signs; whence the art of writing,-in its usefulness so far beyond the Indian's wampum belts. Merely oral law is apt to be forgotten, or its requisitions and prohibitions become hazy.

As the years passed by, and nations, after the dispersion from the tower on the plain of Shinar, diverged more and more, not only in speech and writing but also in customs, their religious thought

---

16   Joshua xxii. 34.

17   John xx. 29.

began to vary from the simple standard of Adam and Noah. Between those small beginnings of variation and the gulf-like depth of the fetich, there are three successive steps.

First, retaining the name of and belief in and worship of Jehovah, mankind added something else. They associated with Jehovah certain natural objects. This, it is readily conceivable, they could do without feeling that they were dishonoring Him. They could not see Him; in their expression of their wants in prayer they were speaking into vague space and heard no audible response. The strain on simple unassisted faith was heavy. The senses asked for something on which they could lean. Very reasonable, therefore, it was for the pious thought, in speaking to the Great Invisible, to associate closely with His name the great natural objects in which His character was revealed or illustrated the,—sun, shining in strength and beneficently giving life to plants and the comfort of its warmth to all creation; the moon, benefiting in a similar though less prominent way; the sky, from which spake the thunder; the mountain, towering in its solemn majesty; the sea, spread out in its inscrutable immensity. All these illustrating some of Jehovah's attributes,—His power, goodness, infinity,—without impropriety associated themselves in man's thought of God, were named along with His name, and were looked upon with same of the sarne reverence which was ac corded to Him. In all this there was no conscious departure from the worship of the one living and true God. The position to which these great natural objects were gradually elevated relatively to God, in the thought of the worshipper, was not as yet blasphemous, or in any intentional way derogatory to Him. But the evil in this elevation of nature into prominence with God was that there was no limit to the number of objects or the degree of their elevation. From the dignified use of sun, moon, sky, and sea, by unconscious degradations animals became the objects of worship-the bull, the serpent, and the cat (each illustrative of some attribute), and thence finally objects that were frivolous, ridiculous, or disgusting, which nevertheless were each the exponent of some principle. Even the indecencies of Phallic worship had found their dignified beginning in an attempt to honor the great principle of life in nature's procreative processes.

But there came a time, in the multiplying of the objects illustrative of God's attributes, when they, by their very numbers, minimized divine dignity. Their constant, visible, tangible presence to the senses begaii not simply passively to represent God, but actively to personify Him, and Jehovah was subdivided. He was still the great God; but these others were given riot only a naine, but a personality which shadowed Him and dishonored Him, by admitting them to fellowship with Him, and regmaling Him as no longer alone the, great I Am. Though supreme, His supremacy was not exclusive; it was comparative. He was over others, who also were gods, with whom He shared His power, and to whom was to be given somewhat of His worship. He was not indeed denied, but He was dishonored. He became only one of the many gods along with Baal and Ashtaroth. But the worship of Him was not abandoned. He was worshipped along with these others, as One among many. And finally polytheism had become the belief of the world, except of the many scattered small communities which, with their priests of the Most High God, like Melchisedek and Job, held the true light from extinction. "Jehovah" became a name for the Deity of a nation; each nation, while reverencing its own god, not denying power to that of another nation. Man's little thought was trying to localize the Deity in its own small tribal limits.

Philistia worshipped its Dagon, but it feared and made trespass offerings to Jehovah of the Ark of Israel's Covenant.[18]

Nebuchadnezzar, startled by a vision of a Son of God in the flame of his fiery furnace, in an hour of repentance could decree that the God of Shadrach, Meshacb, and Abednego should not be spoken against.[19] This was the second step in religion's retrograde movement. The personified natural objects were actually worshipped. No longer considered simply as *representatives* of God, they were actually given a part of God's place, and were worshipped as God. The prayer was not, "Jehovah, bear us, for the sake of Baal , through whom we plead!" nor "O Baal, present our petition to Jehovah!" but, flatly and directly,"O Baal, hear us!"

Having reached in their religious thought this position of a belief in many gods, it was a natural and logical result that worship was to be rendered to them all. The sacrifices that had been offered to Jehovah alone were divided for service to other gods. But it was the same religious sentiment, in both monotheist and polytheist, that prompted the rendering of prayer, sacrifice, and other service. The same sense of an "infinite dependence" that had led arms of weak faith to lay hold for help on that which was nearest and most

---

18   I Sam. vi. 3.

19   Dan. iii. 29.

obvious, operated with the heathen who had wandered from God, in his petition to his many gods, just as it had operated originally with the worshipper of the true God. The sentiment was right, the principle was good; only, its application was wrong,—sometimes fearfully wrong. Man's religious nature is a force. There are other forces in nature that belong to other domains than religion. They are good forces if well applied; they become engines of destruction if misapplied or applied in excess.

In all history no misapplied force has wrought more fearful evil than the religious. It made holy even the atrocities of the Inquisition; it ordained a Te Deum for the massacre of St. Bartholomew's Day.

Similarly mankind found not only justification but propriety in the human sacrifices to Moloch, and in the holocausts of the Aztec civilization. If in giving a gift of thanks, tribute, admiration, or fear to a human friend, ruler, or employer, we choose that which is good and best in our own eyes, so as to win the favor of the being to whom it is given, much more would we strive to please the god in whose power lies our life, health, and prosperity. It was a logical result, therefore, in choosing for sacrifice on great emergencies, to select the bestbeloved child. Moloch would be pleased and propitiated by such a valuable gift. The more that the human love was renounced in the agony of the parents' view of their child's dying struggle, the more favorable would be the response to the worshipper. Under this misapplied religious force an Iphigenia is logical, and the Hindu infant cast to Gunga's wave a fitting offering in the agonized mother's eyes. But how fearfully mistaken! The religion that recognizes and directs such abuse is a "false religion," as compared with Christianity; not in the sense that it has nothing good in it, but in the falsity of the objects of its worship and—in the cruelty of the rites employed in that worship. In the genera of the sciences there is only one species of religion, but that one species has many varieties. In this sense Calvin is correct if, in speaking of the "immense welter of errors" in which the whole world outside of Christianity is immersed,"he regards his own religion as the true one and all the others were false." The function of a comparative study of religions is to point out the connecting line of truth running through the mass of error. Back of all the cruelty and error and falsity in polytheism lie the proper sense of need, the natural feeling of helplessness in the great emergencies of life, and the commendable desire to honor the Being known under different names as Jehovah, Moloch, Jupiter, Allah, Budh, Brahm, Odin, or Anyambe; to which Being His children all over the world looked up as the All-Father. But the *descensus Averni* from the One living and true God soon multiplied gods, dividing among many the attributes that had been centred in the One, and finally carried man's religious thoughtso far from God that only His name was retained, while the trust which had belonged to Him alone was scattered over a multitude of objects thatwere not even dignified with the name "gods." Worship of ancestors was established. Great human benefactors, heroic human beings, were deified and canonized. The whole air of the world became peopled with spiritual influences; literally"stocks and stones" became animated with demons of varying power and disposition; and fetichism erected itself as a kind of religion.

I see nothing to justify the theory of Menzies[20] that primitive man or the untutored African of to-day, in worshipping a tree, a snake, or an idol, originally worshipped those very objects themselves, and that the suggestion that they represented, or were even the dwelling-place of, some spiritual Being is an after-thought up to which he has grown in the lapse of the ages. The rather I see every reason to believe that the thought of the Being or Beings as an object of worship has come down by tradition and from direct original revelation of Jehovah Himself. The assumption of a visible, tangible object to represent or personify that Being is the after-thought that human ingenuity has added. The civilized Romanist claims that he does not worship the actual sign of the cross, but the Christ who was crucified on it; similarly, the Dahondan, in his worship of a snake.

Rev. J. L. Wilson, D.D.,[21] says of the condition of Dahomy fifty years ago, that in Africa "there is no place where there is more intense heathenism; and to mention no other feature in their superstitious practices, the worship of snakes at this place [Whydah] fully illustrates this remark. A house in the middle of the town is provided for the exclusive use of these reptiles, and they may be seen here at any time in very great numbers. They are fed, wid more care is taken of them than of the human inhabitants of the place. If they are seen straying away, they must be brought back; and at the sight of them the people prootrate themselves on the ground and do them all possible reverence. To kill or injure one of them is to incur the penalty

---

20 History of Religion, pp. 129 et seq.

21 Western Africa, p. 207.

of death. On certain occasions they are taken out by the priests or doctors, and paraded about the streets, the bearers allowing them to coil themselves around their arms, necks, and bodies. They are also employed to detect persons who have been guilty of witchcraft. If, in the hands of the priest, they bite the suspected person, it is sure evidence of his guilt; and no doubt the serpent is trained to do the will of his keeper in all such cases. Images, usually called 'gregrees,' of the most uncouth shape and form, may be seen in all parts of the town, and are worshipped by all classes of persons. Perhaps there is no place in Africa where idolatry is more openly practised, or where the people have sunk into deeper pagan darkness."

Also, of the people on the southwest coast at Loango:

"The people of Loango are more addicted to idol worship than any other people on the whole coast. They have a great many carved images which they set up in their fetich houses and in their private dwellings, and which they worship; but whether these images represent their forefathers, as is the case among the Mpongwe (at Gabun), is not certainly known." [22]

Having thus followed the religious thought of mankind in its divagation from monotheistic worship of the true God, down through polytheism and idolatrous sacrifices, to the worship of ancestors, we have reached a third stage, where the worship of God is not only divided between Him and other objects, but, a step beyond, God Himself is quietly disregarded, and the worship due Him is transferred to a multitude of spiritual agencies under His power,

---

22 Wilson.

but uncontrolled by it.

The details of this stage in the religious worship known as fetichism will be considered in the following chapters.

CHAPTER IV
Spiritual Beings in African Religion

THE BELIEF IN SPIRITUAL BEINGS opens an immense vista of the purely superstitious side of the theology of Bantu African religion.

All the air and the future is peopled with a large and indefinite company of these beings. The attitude of the Creator (Anyambe) toward the human race and the lower animals being that of indifference or of positive severity in having allowed evils to exist, and His indifference making Him almost inexorable, cause effort in the line of worship to be therefore directed only to those spirits who, though they are all probably malevolent, may be influenced and made benevolent.

I. Origin

The native thought in regard to the origin of spirits is vague; necessarily so. An unwritten belief that is not based upon revelation from a superior source nor on an induction from actual experience and observation, but that is added to and varied by every individual's fancy, can be expressed in definite words only after inquiry among many as to their ideas on the subject. These, I find, coincide on a few lines; just as the consensus of opinion on any subject in any community win find itself running in certain channels, influenced by the utterances of the stronger or wiser leaders.

1. It appears, therefore, that some of the spirits seem to have been conterminous with the life of Paia-Njambi in the eternities. An eternity past, impossible as it is for any one to comprehend, is yet a thing thinkable even with the Bantu African, for be has words to express it, "peke-na-jome," ever-and-beyond, "tamba-na-ngama," unknown-and-secret.

Away back in that unknown time existed Paia-Njambi. Whence or how, is not asked by the natives; nor have I had any attempt even of a reply to my own inquiries. He simply existed. They are not sufficiently absurd to say that He created Himself. To do that He would need to antedate Himself. I have met none who thought sufficiently on the subject to worry their minds, as we in our civilization often do, in effort to go back and back to the unthinkable point in time past when God was not. Indeed so little is the native mind in the habit of any such research that I can readily perceive how their "We don't know" could easily be misunderstood by a foreign traveller, scientist, or even missionary, as a confession that "they did not know God,"—a statement which is true, but not the equivalent of, or synonymous with, that traveller's assertion that the native had no idea of a God. The native thought, wiser than ours, simply and unreasoningly says, "He is, He was." Conterminous with Him in origin there may have been some other spirits. This has been said to me by a very few persons with some hesitation. But if those spirits were indeed equal in existence with Njambi, they were in no respect equal to Him in character or power, and had no hand in the creation of other beings. In the Mpongwe tribe at Gabun one writer, Rev. J. L. Wilson, D.D., fifty years ago, thought the belief existed that "next to God in the government of the world are two spirits, one of whom, Onyambe, is hateful and wicked. The people seldom speak of Onyambe, and always evince displeasure when the name is mentioned in their presence. His influence over the affairs of men, in their estimation, does not amount to much; and the probability is that they have no very definite notions about the real character of this spirit." His character would be indicated by his name, O-nya-mbe (He-who-is-bad). This name has sometimes been used by missionaries to translate our word "devil." Perhaps the idea of the word itself came from long-ago contact of this coast tribe with foreigners.

2. A second and more recognized source of supply to the company of spirits is original creation by Njambi. While this origin is named by some, I have not found it believed in to any very great extent. Even those whom I did find believing it had very vague ideas as to the mode or object of their creation. Of the Creation of mankind, and even of the Fall, almost all of the tribes have legends, more or less distinct, and with a modicum of truth, doubtless derived from traditions coinciding with the Mosaic history; but of a previous creation of purely spiritual beings I have found no legend nor well-defined story. If such specially created spirits exist at all, their relation to Njambi is

of a very shadowy kind; they are, indeed, inferior to Him, and are in theory under His government in the same sense that human beings are. But Njambi, in His far-off indifference in actual practice, does not interfere with or control them or their actions. They are part of the motley inhabitants of "Njambi's Town," the place of the Great Unknown, as also are all the other living beasts and beings of creation. They also have their separate habitat, and pursue their own devices, generally malevolent, with the children of men.

3. But the general consensus of opinion is that the world of spirits is peopled by the souls of dead human beings. This presupposes a belief in a future life, the existence of which in the native mind some travellers have doubted. I have never met that doubt from the native himself. While I do not impute to the travellers referred to any desire, in their efforts at describing the low grade of intelligence or religious belief of certain tribes, to misrepresent, I fully believe they were mistaken, their mistake arising from misunderstanding. It is not probable that they met, in the course of their few years, what I have not met with in a lifetime. It is probable that natives had expressed to them a doubt, or even ignorance, of a general resurrection, and may have said to them, as a few have said to me, "No, we do not live again; we are like goats and dogs and chickens,—when we die that is the end of us." Such a statement is indeed a denial of the resurrection of the body, but it is not a denial of a continued existence of the soul in another life. The very people who made the above declaration to me preserved their family fetich, made sacrifices to the spirits of their ancestors, and appealed to them for aid in their family under-

takings. The few who have expressed a belief in transmigration did not consider that the residence of a human spirit in the body of a beast was a permanent state; it was a temporary condition, assumed by the spirit voluntarily for its own pleasure or convenience, and terminable at its own will, precisely as human spirits during their mortal life are, everywhere and by all, believed capable of temporarily deserting their own human body and controlling the actions of a beast. This belief in transmigration, though not general, has been found among individuals in almost all tribes.

It being thus generally accepted that all departed human souls become spirits of that future that is all around us, there is still a difference in the testimony of intelligent witnesses as to who and what, or even how many, of these souls are in one human being. (1) Ordinarily, the native will say in effect, "I am one, and my soul is also myself. When I die, it goes out somewhere else." (2) Others will say, "I have two things,—one is the thing that becomes a spirit when I die, the other is the spirit of the body and dies with it." (This "other" may be only a personification of what we specify as the animal life.) But it has frequently occurred that even intelligent natives, standing by me at the side of a dying person, have said to me, "He is dead." The patient was indeed unconscious, lying stiff, not seeing, speaking, eating, or apparently feeling; yet there was a slight heartbeat. I would point out to the relatives these evidences of life. But they said: "No, he is dead. His spirit is gone, he does not see nor hear nor feel; that slight movement is only the spirit of the body shaking itself. It is not a person, it is not our relative; he is dead." And they began to prepare the body for burial. A man actually came to me on

Corisco Island, in 1863, asking me for medicine with which to kill or quiet the body-spirit of his mother, whose motions were troubling him by preventing the funeral arrangements. I was shocked at what I thought his attempt at matricide, but subsequently found that he really did believe that his mother was dead and her real soul gone.

Such attempt to distinguish between soul-life and body-life has not infrequently led to premature burial. The supposed corpse has sometimes risen to consciousness on the way to the grave. A long-protracted sickness of some not very valuable member of the village has wearied the attendants; they decide that the body, though mumbling inarticulate words and aimlessly fingering with its arms, is no longer occupied by its personal soul; *that* has emerged. "He is dead"; and they proceed to bury him alive. Yet they deny that they have done so. They insist that *he* was not alive; only his body was "moving." Proof of premature burial has been found by discoveries made in the practice of a custom which is observed when a village has been afflicted with various troubles after the death of one of its members. The villagers, after ineffectual efforts to drive away the evil influences that are supposed to cause these troubles, decide that the spirit of some dead relative is dissatisfied about something, and order the grave to be opened and the bones rearranged or even thrown into the river or sea. On opening the grave, corpses that had been buried in a recumbent position have been found in a sitting position. It is possible for one thus prematurely buried to change posture in a dying struggle; for, mostly, heathen graves are shallow, and are hastily and not always completely filled in.

3. Another set of witnesses will say that, besides the personal soul and the soul of the body, there is a third entity in the human unit, namely, a drearn-soul. That it is which leaves the body on occasions during . sleep, and, wandering off, delights itself by visiting strange lands and strange scenes. On its return to the body its union with the material blunts its perceptions, and the person, in his efforts to remember or tell what be has seen, relates only the vagaries of a dream,—a psychological view which, under the manipulation of a ready pen, could give play to fantasies pretty, romantic, not unreasonable, and not impossible.

Some who are only dualists, nevertheless, believe in the wanderings of this so-called dream-soul, but say that it is the personal soul itself that has gone out and has returned. Both dualists and trinitarians add that sometimes in its wanderings this soul loses its way and cannot find its body, its material home; should it never return, the person will sicken and die.

4. A fourth entity is vaguely spoken of by some as a component part of the human personality, by others as separate but closely associated from birth to death, and called the life-spirit. Some speak of it as a civilized person speaks of a guardian angel. Regarded in that light, it should not be considered as one of the several kinds of souls, but as one of the various classes of spirits (which will be discussed in a subsequent chapter). To it worship is rendered by its possessor as to other spirits,—a worship, however, different from that which is performed for what are known and used as "familiar spirits." Others speak of the vague life-spirit as the "heart." The

organ of our anatomy which we designate by that name, they call by a word which variously means "heart" or "feelings," much like our old English "bowels," the same word being employed equally to designate a physical organ and a mental state. Considering the organic heart as the seat (or a seat) of life, the natives believe that by witchcraft a person in bealth can be deprived of his life-soul, or "heart"; that he will then sicken; that the wizard or witch feasts in his or her magic orgy on this "heart," and that the person will die if that heart is not returned to him.

II. Number

But whatever this human soul may be, whether existing in unity, duality, trinity, or quadruplicity, all agree in believing that it adds itself, on the death of the body, as another to the multitudinous company of the spirit-world. That world is all around us, and does not differ much in its wants and characteristics from this earthly life, except that it is free from some of the limitations to which material bodies are subject. In that spirit-world they require the same food as when on earth, but consume only its essence; the visible substance remains. They are possessed of all their human passions, both bad and good. Men expect to have their wives with them in that future, but I have never beard the idea even named, that there is procreation by spirits in that after-world. Not having believed during this life in a system of reward and punishment, they have no belief in heaven or hell. All the dead go to Njambi's Town, and live in that new life together, good and bad, as they lived together on earth. The "hell" spoken of by some of my informants, I believe, is not a native thought; it was probably engrafted on the coast tribes by the Portuguese Roman Catholic missionaries of three hundred years ago.

If therefore the spirits consist almost entirely of the souls of departed human beings, how immense their number! Equal in number with all the dead that have passed from this life in the ages gone by, excepting those who have gone permanently into the bodies of new human beings. That form of metempsychosis is believed in. Occasional instances of belief of transmigration into the body of a lower animal do not necessarily include the idea of a permanent residence there, or that the departed soul has lost its personality as a human being and has become the soul of a beast.

But the idea of reappearance in the body of a newly born child was formerly believed in, especially in regard to white people. Thirty years ago I wrote:[23] "Down the swift current of the Benita, as of other rivers on the coast, are swept floating islands of interlaced rushes, tangled vines, and waterlilies that, clinging to some projecting log from the marshy bank, had gathered the sand and mud of successive freshets, and gave a precarious footing for the pandanus, whose wiry roots bound all in one compact mass. Then some flood had torn that mass away, and the pandanus still waving its long, bayonet-like leaves, convolvuli still climbing and blooming, and birds still nesting trustfully, the floating island glided past native eyes down the stream, out over the bar, and on toward the horizon

---

23   Crowned in Palmland, p. 234.

of broad ocean. What beyond? Native superstition said that at the bottom of the 'great sea' was 'whiteman's land'; that thither some of their own departed friends found their happy future, exchanging a dusky skin for a white one; that there white man's magic skill at will created the beads, and cloth, and endless wealth that came from that unknown land in ships, in whose masts and rigging and sails were recognized the transformed trees and vines and leaves of those floating islands. When on the 12th of July, 1866, a few with bated breath came to look on my little new-born Paull, the only white child most of the community had seen, and the first born in that Benita region, the old people said, 'Now our hopes are dead. Dying, we had hoped to become like you; but verily ye are born as we.'"

Not long after I had arrived at Corisco Island in 1861 I observed among the many people who came to see the new missionary one man who quietly and unobtrusively but very steadily was gazing at me. After a while he mustered courage and addressed me: "Are you not my brother,—my brother who died at such a time, and went to White Man's Land?" I was at that time new to the superstitions of the country; his meaning had to be explained to me. His thought of relationship was not an impossible one, for many of the Bantu Negroes have somewhat Caucasian-like features. I have often seen men and women at the sigbt of whom I was surprised, and I would remark to a fellow-missionary: "How much this person reminds me of So-and-so in America!" This recognition of resemblance of features to white persons living in America was the third step in my acquaintance with native faces. At first, all Negro faces looked alike. Presently I learned differences; and when I had reached the third step, I felt that my acquaintance with African features was complete.

III. Locality

The locality of these spirits is not only vaguely in the surrounding air; they are also localized in prominent natural objects,—eaves, enormous rocks, hollow trees, dark forests,—in this respect reminding one of classic fauns and dryads. While all have the ability to move from place to place, some especially belong to certain localities which are spoken of as having, as the case might be, "good" or "bad" spirits. It is possible for a human soul (as already mentioned in this chapter) to inhabit the body of a beast. A man whose plantation was being devastated near Benita by an elephant told me, in 1867, he did not dare to shoot it, because the spirit of his lately deceased father bad passed into it. Also a common objurgation of an obstreperous child or animal is, "O na nyemba!" (Thou hast a witch.)

Their habitats may be either natural or acquired. Natural ones are, for the spirits of the dead, in a very special sense, the villages where they had dwelt during the lifetime of the body; but the presence of the spirits of the dead is not desired. It is one of the pitiable effects of African superstition that its subjects look with fear and dread on what the denizens of civilization look with love and tender regret. We in our Christian civilization cling to the lifeless forms of our dead; and when necessity compels us to bury them from our sight, we bid memory call up every lineament of face and tone of voice, and are pleased to think that sometimes they are near us.

But it is a frequent native practice that on the occasion of a death, even while a portion of the family are wailing and to all appearances passionately mourning the loss of their relative, others are firing guns, blowing trumpets, beating drums, shouting and yelling, in order to drive away from the village the retently disembodied spirit. On consideration, it can be seen that these two diverse demonstrations are sincere, consistent, and, to the natives, reasonable. With natural affection they mourn the absence of a tangible person who, as a member of their family, was helpful and even kind; while they fear the independent existence of the invisible thing, whose union with the physical body they fail to recognize as having been a factor in that helpfulness and kindness. This departed spirit, joining the company of other departed spirits, will indeed become an object of worship,—a worship of principally a deprecatory nature; but its continued presence and immediate contact with its former routine are not desired. In Mashonaland the native fears death by accident or human enmity. "But a greater dread than this is of a visitation of evil by the spirit of a departed friend or relative whom be may have slighted while living."

A village in Nazareth Bay, the embouchure of one of the mouths of the Ogowe River, is called "Abun-awiri" ("awiri," plural of "ombwiri," a certain class of spirits, and "abuna," abundance).

Large, prominent trees are inhabited by spirits. Many trees in the equatorial West African forest throw out from their trunks, at from ten to sixteen feet from the ground, solid buttresses continuous with the body of the tree itself, only a few inches in thickness, but in width at the base of the tree from four to six feet. These buttresses are projected toward several opposite points of the compass, as if to resist the force of sudden wind-storms. They are a noticeable forest feature and are commonly seen in the silk-cotton trees. The recesses between them are actually used as lairs by small wild animals. They are supposedly also a favorite home of the spirits.

Caverns and large rocks have their special spirit inhabitants. At Gabun, and also on Corisco Island, geological breaks in the horizontal strata of rock were filled by narrow vertical strata of limestone, between which water action has worn away the softer rock, leaving the limestone walls isolated, with a narrow ravine between them. These ravines were formerly reverenced as the abodes of spirits.

When I made a tour in 1882, surveying for a. second Ogowe Station, I came some seventy miles up river from my well-established first station, Kingwe, at Lambarene, to an enormous rock, a granite boulder, lying in the bed of the river. The adjacent hillsides on either bank of the river were almost impassable, being covered with boulders of all sizes, and a heavy forest growing in among and even on them. This great rock had evidently in the long past become detached by torrential streams that scored the mountainside in the heavy rainy season and had plunged to its present position. The swift river current swirled and dashed against the huge obstruction to navigation, making the ascent of the river at that point particularly difficult. Superstition suggested that the spirits of the rock did not wish boats or canoes to pass their abode. Nevertheless, necessities of trade compelled; and crews in passing made an ejaculatory prayer, or doffed their bead coverings, in respect, but with the fear that the "ascent" in that part of the journey might be for "woe," whence they called the rock "Itala-ja-maguga," which, contracted to "Talagua," I gave as a name to my new station, erected in 1882 in the vicinity of the rock. During my eight subsequent years at the station I did, indeed, meet with some "woe," but also much weal. And the missionary work of Talaguga, carried on since 1892 by the hands of the Société Évangelique de Paris, has met with signal success.

Capes, promontories, and other prominent points of land are favorite dwelling-places of the spirits. The Ogowe River, some one hundred and forty miles from its mouth, receives on its left bank a large affluent, the Ngunye, coming from the south. The low point of land at the junction of the two rivers was sacred. The riverine tribes themselves would pass it in canoes, respectfully removing their bead coverings; but passage was forbidden to coast tribes and other foreigners. Portuguese slave-traders might come to the point; but, stopping there, they could trade beyond only through the bands of the local tribe (evidently superstition had been invoked to protect a trade monopoly). A certain trader, Mr. R. B. N. Walker, agent for the English firm of Hatton & Cookson, headquarters at Libreville, Gabun, in extending his commercial interests some forty years ago, made an overland journey from the Gabun River, emerging on the Ogowe, on its right bank, *above* that sacred point. Ranoke, chief of the Inenga tribe, a few miles below, seized him, his porters, and his goods, and kept them prisoners for several months. Mr. Walker succeeded in bribing a native to carry a letter to the French Commandant at Libreville, who was pleased to send a gunboat to the rescue. Incidentally it furnished a good opportunity to demonstrate

France's somewhat shadowy claim to the Ogowe. After the rescue a company from the gunboat proceeded to the Point and lunched there, thus effectually desecrating it. Mr. Walker made peace with his late captor, and established a trading-station at the Inenga village, Lambarene. For years afterward, natives still looked upon that Point with respect. My own crew in 1874 sometimes doffed their hats; but before I left the Ogowe in 1891, a younger generation had grown up that was willing to camp and eat and sleep there with me, on my boat journeys.

Graveyards, of course, are homes of spirits, and therefore are much dreaded. The tribes, especially of the interior, differ very much as to burial customs. Some bury only their chiefs and other prominent men, casting away corpses of slaves or of the poor into the rivers, or out on the open ground, perhaps covering them with a bundle of sticks; even when graves are dug they are shallow. Some tribes fearlessly bury their dead under the clay floors of their houses, or a few yards distant in the kitchen-garden generally adjoining. But, by most tribes who do bury at all, there are chosen as cemeteries dark, tangled stretches of forest, along river banks on ground that is apt to be inundated or whose soil is not good for plantation purposes. I bad often observed, in my earlier African years, such stretches of forest along the river, and wondered why the people did not use them for cultivation, being conveniently near to some village, while they would go a much longer distance to make their plantations. The explanation was that these were graveyards. Such stretches would extend sometimes for a mile or two. Often my hungry meal hour on a journey happened to coincide with our passing just such a piece of forest, and the crew would refuse to stop, keeping themselves and myself hungry till we could arrive at more open forest.

In Eastern Africa it is believed that "the dead in their turn become spirits under the all-embracing name of Musimo. The Wan-yamwezi hold their Musimo in great dread and veneration, as well as the house, but, or place where their body has died." [24]

Beyond the regularly recognized habitats of the spirits that may be called "natural" to them, any other location may be *acquired* by them temporarily, for longer or shorter periods, under the power of the incantations of the native doctor (uganga). By his magic arts any spirit may be localized in any object whatever, however small or insignificant; and, while thus limited, is under the control of the doctor and subservient to the wishes of the possessor or wearer of the material object in which it is thus confined. This constitutes a "fetich," which will be more fully discussed in another chapter.

IV. Characteristics

The characteristics of these spirits are much the same as those they possessed before they were disembodied. They have most of the evil human passions, *e.g.*, anger and revenge, and therefore may be malevolent. But they possess also the good feelings of generosity and gratitude; they are therefore within reach of influence, and may be benevolent. Their possible malevolence is to be deprecated, their

24

anger placated, their aid enlisted.

Illustration of malevolence in their character has already been seen in the dread connected with deaths and funerals. The similar dread of graveyards in our civilized countries may rest on the fear inspired by what is mysterious or by those who have passed to the unknown, simply because it and they are unknown. But, to superstitious Africa, that unknown is a certainty, in that it is a source of evil; the spirit of the departed has all the capacity for evil it possessed while embodied, with the additional capacity that its exemption from some of the limitations of time and space increases its facilities for action. Being unseen, it can act at immensely greater advantage for accomplishing a given purpose. Natives dying have gone into the other world retaining an acute memory of some wrong inflicted on them by fellow-villagers, and have openly said, "From that other world I will come back and avenge myself on you!"

In any contest of a human being against these spirits of evil be knows always that whatever influence he may obtain over them by the doctor's magic add, or whatever limitations may thus be put on them, they can never, as in the case of a human enemy, be killed. The spirits can never die.

Sometimes the word "dead" is used of a fetich amulet that has been inhabited by a spirit conjured into it by a native doctor. The phrase does not mean that its spirit is actually dead, but that it has fled from inside of the fetich, and still lives elsewhere. Then the native doctor, to explain to his patient or client the inefficacy of the charm, says that the cause of the spirit's escape and flight is that the wearer has failed to observe all the directions which bad been

given, and the spirit was displeased. The dead amulet is, nevertheless, available for sale to the curio-hunting foreigner.

CHAPTER V
Spirituel Beings in Africa
– their classes and functions –

INEQUALITIES AMONG THE SPIRITS themselves, though they are so great, indicate no more than simple differentiations of character or work. Yet so radical are these varieties, and so distinct the names applied to them, that I am compelled to recognize a division into classes.

I. Classes and functions

Inina, or Ilina

A human embodied soul is spoken of and fully believed in by all the tribes. It is known in the Mpongwe tribes of the Gabun country as inina (plural, "anina"); in the adjacent Benga tribe, as "ilina" (plural, "malina"); in the great interior Fang tribes, as "nsisim."

This animating soul, whether it be only one, or whether it appear in two, three, or even four forms, is practically the same, that talks, hears, and feels, that sometimes goes out of the body in a dream, and that exists as a spirit after the death of the body. That it has its own especial materiality seems to be indicated by the fact that in the Fang, Bakele, and other tribes the same word "nsisim" means not only soul but also shadow. The shadow of a tree or any other inanimate object and of the human body as cast by the sun is "nsisim."

In my first explorations up the Ogowe River, in 1874, as in my village preaching I necessarily and constantly spoke of our soul, its sins, its capacity for suffering or happiness, and its relation to its divine Maker, I was often at a loss how to make my thoughtless audience understand or appreciate that the nsisim of which I was speaking was not the nsisim cast by the sun as a darkish line on the ground near their bodies. Even to those who understood me, it was not an impossible thought that that dark narrow belt on the ground was in some way a part of, or a mode of manifestation of, that other thing, the nsisim, which they admitted was the source of the body's animation. So far defined was that thought with some of them that they said it was a possible thing for a human being to have his nsisim stolen or otherwise lost, and still exist in a diseased and dying state; in which case his body would not cast a shadow. Von Chamisso's story of Peter Schlemelil,"the man who lost his shadow," in actuality!

So few are the special activities by which to distinguish anina from other classes of spirits, that I might doubt whether they should properly be considered as distinct, were it not true that the anina are all of them embodied spirits; none of them are of other origin. As disembodied spirits, retaining memory of their former human relationships, they have an interest in human affairs, and especially in the affairs of the family of which they were lately members.

Ibambo (Mpongwe; plural,"abambo")

There are vague beings, "abambo," which may well be described by our word "ghosts." Where they come from is not certainly known, or what locality they inhabit, except that they belong to the world of spirits. Why they become visible is also unknown. They are not called for, they are only occasionally worshipped; their epiphany is dreaded, not reverenced.

"The term 'Abambo' is in the plural form, and may therefore be regarded as forming a class of spirits instead of a single individual. They are the spirits of dead men; but whether they are positively good or positively evil, to be loved or to be hated, or to be courted or avoided, are points—which no native of the country can answer satisfactorily. Abambo are the spirits of the ancestors of the people of a tribe or race, as distinguished from the spirits of strangers. These are the spirits with which men are possessed, and there is no end to the ceremonies used to deliver them from their power." [25]

The ibambo may appear anywhere and at any time and to anybody, but it has no message. It rarely speaks. Its most common effect on human lives is to frighten. It flits; it does not remain in one spot, to speak or to be spoken to. Indistinctly seen, its appearances are reported as occurring mostly in dark places, in shadows, in twilight, and on dark nights. The most common apparitions are on lonely paths in the forest by night.

To all intents and purposes these abambo are what superstitious fears in our civilization call "ghosts." The timid dweller in

---

25   J.L. Wilson.

civilization can no more tell us what that ghost is than can the ignorant African. It is as difficult in the one case as in the other to
argue against the unreal and unknown. What the frightened eye or
ear believes it saw or heard, it persists in believing against all proof.
Nor will ridicule make the belief less strongr. However, the intelligent
child in civilization, under the hand of a judicious parent or other
friend, and relying on love as in expounder, can be led to understand
by daylight, that the white bark of a tree trunk shimmering in uncertain moonlight, or a white garment flapping in the wind, or a white
animal grazing in the meadow, was the ghost whose waving form
had scared him the night before. His superstition is not so ingrained
by daily exercise but that reason and love can divest him of it. But to
the denizen of Fetich-land superstition is religion; the night terror
which he is sure he saw is too real a thing in his life to be identified
by day as only a harmless white-barked tree or quartz rock.

Ombwiri

A third class of spirits is represented by the name *Ombwiri*. The
"ombwiri" (Mpongwe; plural, "awiri") is certainly somewhat local,
and in this respect might be regarded as akin to the ancient fauns
and dryads, with a suggestion of alikeness to the spirits resident in
the dense oak groves and the massive stones of the Druid Circle.
But the awiri are more than dryads. They are not confined to their
local rock, tree, bold promontory, or point of land, trespass on which
by human beings I they resent. The traveller must go by silently, or
with some cabalistic invocation, with bowed or bared head, and with
some offering,—anything, even a pebble. On the beach, as I bend to

pass beneath an enorinous tree fallen across the pathway, I observe the upper side of the log covered with votive offerings,—pebbles, shells, leaves, etc.,—laid there by travellers as they stooped to pass under. Such votive collections may be seen on many spots along the forest paths, deposited there by the natives as an invocation of a blessing on their journey.

"The derivation of the word 'Ombwiri' is not known. As it is used in the plural as well as in the singular form, it no doubt represents a class or family of spirits. He is regarded as a tutelar or guardian spirit. Almost every man has his own ombwiri, for which he provides a small house near his own. All the harm that he has escaped in this world, and all the good secured, are ascribed to the kindly offices of this guardian spirit. Ombwiri is also regarded as the author of everything in the world which is marvellous or mysterious. Any remarkable feature in the physical aspect of the country, any notable phenomenon in the heavens, or extraordinary events in the affairs of men are ascribed to Ombwiri. His favorite places of abode are the summits of high mountains, deep caverns, large rocks, and the base of very large forest trees. And while the people attach no malignity to his character, they carefully guard against all unnecessary familiarity in their intercourse with him, and never pass a place where he is supposed to dwell except in silence. He is the only one of all the spirits recognized by the people that has no priesthood; his intercourse with men being direct and immediate."[26]

These spirits are sometimes spoken of with the nkinda and

_____

26   L. Wilson.

olâgâ (Mpongwe; plural,"ilâgâ"). They all come from the spirits of the dead. These several names indicate a difference as to kind or class of spirit, and a difference in the work or functions they are called upon to exercise. The ilâgâ are spirits of strangers, and have come from a distance.

While the ombwiri is indeed feared, it is with a respectful reverence, different from the dread of an ibambo. Ombwiri is fine and admirable in aspect, but is very rarely seen; it is white, like a white person. Souls of distinguished chiefs and other great men turn to awiri. The fear with which the native regards massive rocks and large trees—the ombwiri homes—need not be felt by white people, who are themselves considered awiri, without its being clearly understood whether their bodies are inhabited by the departed spirits of the Negro dead, or whether some came from other sources.

The awiri are generally favorably disposed, especially to their former human relatives; but it is necessary to gratify them with religious services constituting an ancestral worship. While some of them reside in great rocks or trees, others dwell in rivers, lakes, and seas.

Awiri, if they love a person and desire to favor him or her, have the special power to grant a gift desired by most Africans, viz., the birth of children. The awiri live mostly in the region of their own former human tribe. It is possible,.however, for them to go everywhere; but they usually remain within their old tribal limits. If, however, a tribe should remove or become extinct, their awiri would still remain in that region, and would affiliate with the new people who might come to occupy the deserted village sites.

Awiri have a period of inactivity, the cold dry season of four months (in western Equatorial Afriea), May to September. At that time they become very small, inactive, and almost lifeless (a condition of hibernation, soniewhat like that of bears; or of inertia,—is when a snake casts its skin?).

Nkinda

There is another class of spirit, called *Sinkinda* (singular, "nkinda"), some of whom are the spirits of people who in the ordinary stations of life were "common," or not distinguished for greatness or goodness. Others of these sinkinda are of uncertain origin, perhaps demons whom Njambi had created, but to whom He had never given bodily existence.

Almost all sinkinda are evilly disposed. They come to the villages on visits to warm themselves by the kitchen fires or out of curiosity to see what is going on, and sometimes, temporarily, to enter into the bodies of the living, especially of their own family. The entrance of a nkinda into a human body always sickens the person. It may enter any one, even a child. If many of them enter a man's body, he becomes crazy.

Sometimes the nkinda, when asked who he is, says:"I am a spirit of a member of your own family, and I have come to live with you. I am tired of living in the forest with cold and hunger. I wish to stay with you."

Often when people are sick with fever or cold, the diagnosis is inade that some nkinda has come on a visit. If it is of the same family as those whom it is visiting, it comes and goes from time to time, to please itself; but it is never, like an uvengwa, visible.

Sometimes these sinkinda are called "ivâvi" (sing."ovâvi," messenger). They come from far and bring news, *e.g.*, "An epidemic of disease is coming," or "A ship is coming with wealth." Sometimes the news thus brought proves true. (Is this our modern spiritualism?) In such cases the coming of the nkinda is regarded as a blessing, in that it warns the living of evil or brings them wealth. The information is always carried by the mouth of some living member of the family. If these sinkinda are asked by a non-possessed member of the family,"Where do you live?" the reply is, "Nowhere in particular. But at evenings we gather about your town, to see you and join in your dances and songs. We see you, though you do not see, us."

Mondi

There are beings, "myondi" (Benga; singular, "mondi"), who are agents in causing sickness or in either aiding or hindering human plans. These spirits are much the same as those of the fourth class, except that in power they seem to be more independent than other spirits. But they are not always simply passive in the hands of the doctor; they are often active on their own account, or at their own pleasure, generally to injure. They are worshipped almost always in a deprecatory way. They often take violent possession of human bodies; and for their expulsion it is that ilâgâ, sinkinda, and awiri are invoked. They are invoked especially at the new moons, but also at other times, particularly in sickness. The native oganga decides whether or no they be myondi that are afflicting the patient. When the diagnosis has been made, and myondi declared to be present in the patient's body, the indication is that they are to be exorcised.

A slight doubt must be admitted in regard to these myondi, whether they really do constitute a distinct class, or whether any spirit of any class may not become a myondi. The name in that case would be given them, not as a class, but as producers of certain effects, at certain times and under certain circumstances.

The powers and functions of the several classes of spirits do not seem to be distinctly defined. Certainly they do not confine themselves either to their recognized locality or to the usually understood function pertaining to their class. These powers and functions shade into each other, or may be assumed by members of almost any class, But it is clearly believed that spirits, even of the same class, differ in power. Some are strong, others are weak. They are limited as to the nature of their powers; no spirit can do all things. A spirit's efficiency runs only on a certain line or lines. All of them can be influenced and made subservient to human wishes by a variety of incantations.

II. Special manifestations

There are other names which, while they belong to spirits, apparently indicate only peculiarities in spiritual manifestations, and not representatives of a class.

1. There may enter into any animal's body (generally a leopard's) some spirit, or, temporarily, even the soul of a living human being. The animal then, guided by human intelligence and will, exercises its

strength for the purposes of the temporary human possessor. Many murders are said to be committed in this way, after the manner of the mythical German wehr-wolf or the French loup-garou,

This belief in denioniacal possession of a lower animal must not be confounded with the equally believed transmigration of souls. The former is widespread over at least a third of the African continent. In Mashona-land "they believe that at times both living and dead persons can change themselves into animals, either to execute some vengeance, or to procure something they wish for; thus, a man will change himself into a hyena or a lion to steal a sheep and make a good meal off it; into a serpent to avenge himself on some enemy. At other times, if they see a serpent, it is one of the Matotela tribe or slave tribe, which has thus transformed himself to take some vengeance on the Barobse." [27]

2. Another manifestation is that of the uvengwa. It is claimed to be not simply spiritual, but tangible. It is the self-resurrected spirit and body of a dead human being. It is an object of dread, and is never worshipped in any manner whatever. Why it appears is not known. Perhaps it shows itself only in a restless, unquiet, or dissatisfied feeling. It is white in color, but the body is variously changed from the likeness of the original human body. Some say that it has only one eye, placed in the centre of the forehead. Some say that its feet are webbed like an aquatic bird. It does not speak; it only wanders, looking as if with curiosity.

---

27   Declè.

My little cottage at Batanga is a mile and—a half from the three chief dwellings of the station. One afternoon in 1902 went to the station, leaving my cook and his wife in charge of the cottage. When I returned late at night, he asserted that an uvengwa had come there. A few yards in front of the door of the house is a mango tree with its very dense dark foliage. The trunk is divided a few feet from the ground. The light from the open door streamed into a part of the front yard, leaving the tree trunk in dark shadow. The woman going out of the door had started back, screaming to her husband that she saw an uvengwa standing in the crotch of the tree and peering around one of the branches. The husband went to the door. He asserted to me that he also had seen the form. In their terror, neither of them made any investigation. Possibly a chalk-whitened thief had taken advantage of my absence to prowl about. But the two witnesses rejected such a suggestion; they were sure it was a visitor from some grave.

3. Other spiritual manifestations are spoken of as the personal guardian-spirit and the family guardian-spirit. These do not constitute a separate class, but are the special modes of operation adopted by the ancestral spirit or spirits in the protection of their family. Its description belongs properly to a later chapter under the name of the Family Yâkâ fetich.

The manner of invocation of all these five classes of spirits, in the case of obscure diseases, is very much the same now as what Dr. Wilson described fifty years ago. What he saw on the Gabun River tallies with what I also saw thirty years ago at Benita, and subsequently in the Ogowe. Even at Gabun, in the present day, though the Mpongwe have been enlightened, the same ceremonies are kept up by other tribes, the Shekani and Fang, who have emerged on the coast at Libreville.

"Sick persons, and especially those that are afflicted with nervous disorders, are supposed to be possessed by one or the other of these spirits. If the disease assumes a serious form, the patient is taken to a priest or a priestess, of either of these classes of spirits. Certain tests are applied, and it is soon ascertained to which class the disease belongs, and the patient is accordingly turned over to the proper priest. The ceremonies in the different cases are not materially different; they are alike, at least, in the employment of an almost endless round of absurd, unmeaning, and disgusting ceremonies which none but a heathenish and ignorant priesthood could invent, and none but a poor, ignorant, and supenstitious people could ever tolerate.

"In either ease a temporary shanty is erected in the middle of the street for the occupancy of the patient, the priest, and such persons as are to take part in the ceremony of exorcism. The time employed in performing the ceremonies is seldom less than ten or fifteen days. During this period dancing, drumming, feasting, and drinking are kept up without intermission day and night, and all at the expense of the nearest relative of the invalid. The patient, if a female, is decked out in the most fantastic costume; her face, bosom, arms, and legs are streaked with red and white chalk, her head adorned with red feathers, and much of the time she promenades the open space in front of the shanty with a sword in her hand, which she brandishes in a very menacing way against the bystanders. At the same time she assumes as much of the maniac in her looks, actions, gestures, and walk as possible. In many cases this is all mere affectation, and no one is deceived by it. But there are other cases where motions seem. involuntary and entirely beyond the control of the person; and when you watch the wild and unnatural stare, the convulsive movements of the limbs and body, the unnatural posture into which the whole frame is occasionally thrown, the gnashing of the teeth, and foaming at the mouth, and supernatural strength that is put forth when any attempt is made at constraint, you are strongly reminded of cases of real possession recorded in the New Testament.

"There is no reason to suppose that any real cures are effected by these prolonged ceremonies. In certain nervous affections the excitement is kept up until utter exhaustion takes place; and if the patient is kept quiet afterwards (which is generally the case), she may be restored to better health after a while; and, no matter how long it may be before she recovers from this severe tax upon her nerves, the priest claims the credit of it. In other cases the patient may not have been diseased at all, and, of course, there was nothing to be recovered from.

"If it should be a case of undissembled siekness, and the patient become worse by this unnatural treatment, she is removed, and the ceremonies are suspended, and it is concluded that it was not a real possession, but something else. The priests have certain tests by which it is known when the patient is healed, and the whole transaction is wound up when the fees are paid. In all cases of this kind it is impossible to say whether the devil has really been cast out or merelya better understanding arrived at between him and the person he has been tormenting. The individual is required to build a little house or temple for the spirit near his own, to take occasional offerings to him, and pay all due respect to his character, or to be subject to renewed assaults at any time. Certain restrictions are imposed upon the person who has recovered from these satanic influences. He must refrain from certain kinds of food, avoid certain places of common resort, and perform certain duties; and, for the neglect of any of these, is sure to be severely scourged by a return of his malady. Like the Jews, in speaking of the actions of these demoniaes, they are said to be done by the spirit, and not by the person who is possessed. If the person performs any unnatural or revolting act,—as the biting off of the head of a live chicken and sucking its blood,—it is said that the spirit, not the man, has done it.

"But the views of the great mass of the people on these subjects are exceedingly vague and indefinite. They attend these ceremonies on account of the parade and excitement that usually accompany them, but they have no knowledge of their origin, their true nature, or of their results. Many submit to the ceremonies because they are persuaded to do so by their friends, and, no doubt, in many cases in the hope of being freed from some troublesome malady. But as to the meaning of the ceremonies themselves, or the real influence which they exert upon their bodily diseases, they probably have many doubts, and when called upon to give explanation of the process which they have passed through, they show that they have none but the most confused ideas."[28]

---

28   Wilson, Western Africa.

CHAPTER VI
Fetichism – its philosophy –
a physical salvation – charms and amulets

Monotheism — Polytheism — Animism — Fetichism. The Salvation Sought: its
Kind, Physical; its Source, Spirits; its Reason, Fear. The Means used: Prayer,
Sacrifices, Charms; Vocal, Ritual, Material, Fetiches. Articles used in the Fetich —
Mode of Preparation: A Fitness in the Quality of the Object for the End desired;
Efficiency depends on the Localized Spirit; Misuse of the Word "Medicine";
Native "Doctors"; Connection of Fetich with Witchcraft.

EVEN DURING THE WHILE that man was still a monotheist, as seen
in a previous chapter, be had eventually come to the use of idols
which he did not actually worship, by the making of images simply
to represent God; be had not yet become an idolater.

Subsequently, in his farther lapse away from God, when he
began to render worship to beings other than God, fashioned images
to represent them also, and actually worshipped them, he became a
polytheist and an idolater.

When he had wandered still farther, and God was no longer
worshipped, the knowledge of Him being reduced to a name, a multitude of spiritual beings were substituted in place of God, and religion
was only animism.

Farther on, when it seemed desirable to provide local residence for these spirits, as had been done for God Himself in temples
and costly images, the material objects used for that residence were
no longer matter of value and choice; anything and any place was
sufficient for a spirit's habitat. Neither dignity, beauty, nor strength

was any longer a factor in the selection. For these objects did not represent the deities in any way whatever. They were simply local residences. As such, a spirit could live anywhere and in anything. This is bald fetichism. The thing itself, the material itself, is not worshipped. The fetich worshipper makes a clear distinction between the reverence with which he regards a certain material object and the worship he renders to the spirit for the time being inhabiting it. For this reason nothing is too mean or too small or too ridiculous to be considered fit for a spirit's *locum tenens*; for when for any reason the spirit is supposed to have gone out of that thing and definitely abandoned it, the thing itself is no longer reverenced, and is thrown away as useless.

The selection of the article in which the spirit is to reside is made by the native "uganga" (doctor), who to the Negro stands in the office of a priest. The ground of selection is generally that of mere convenience. The ability to conjure a free wandering spirit into the narrow limits of a small material object, and to compel and subordinate its power to the aid of some designated person or persons and for a specific purpose, rests with that uganga.

Over the wide range of many articles used in which to confine spirits, common and favorite things are the skins and especially the tails of bush-cats, horns of antelopes, nut-shells, snail-shells, bones of any animal, but especially human bones; and among the bones are specially regarded portions of skulls of human beings and teeth and claws of leopards. But, literally, anything may be chosen,—any stick, any stone, any rag of cloth. Apparently, there being no limit to the number of spirits, there is literally no limit to the number and character of the articles in which they may be localized.

It is not true, as is asserted by some in regard to these African tribes and their degraded form of religion, that they worship the actual material objects in which the spirits are supposed to be confined. Low as is fetichism, it nevertheless has its philosophy, a philosophy that is the same in kind as that of the higher forms of religion. A similar sense of need that sends the Christian to his knees before God to ask aid in time of trouble, and salvation temporal and spiritual, sends the fetich worshipper to offer his sacrifice and to ejaculate his prayer for help as he lays hold of his consecrated antelope horn, or as he looks on it with abiding trust while it is safely tied to his body. His human necessity drives him to seek assistance.

The difference between his act—and the act of the Christian lies in the kind of salvation he seeks, the being to whom he appeals, and the reason for his appealing. The reason for his appeal is simply fear; there is no confession, no love, rarely thanksgiving.

The being to whom he appeals is not God. True, he does not deny that He is; if asked, he will acknowledge His existence. But that is all. Very rarely and only in extreme emergencies, does he make an appeal to Him; for he thinks God so far off, so inaccessible, so indifferent to human woes and wants, that a petition to Him would be almost in vain. He therefore turns to some one of the mass of spirits which he believes to be ever near and observant of human affairs, in which, as former human beings, some of them once had part.

As to the character of the salvation sought, it is not spiritual; it is a purely physical salvation. A sense of moral and spiritual need is lost sight of, although not eliminated. This is an index of the distance the Negro has travelled away from Jehovah before he finally reached the position of placing his trust in a fetich. By just so much as he seems to himself living in a world crowded with unseen but powerful spiritual beings (with whom what a Christian calls "sin" has no reprehensible moral quality), by just so much he seems to have lost sight of his own soul and its moral necessities.

The future is so vague that in the thought of most tribes it contains neither heaven nor hell; there is no certain reward or rest for goodness, nor positive punishment for badness. The future life is to each native largely a reproduction, on shadowy and intangible lines, of the works and interests and passions of this earthly life. In his present life, with its savagery and oppression and dominance of selfish greed and right of might, goodness has no reward. It is badness which in his personal experience makes the largest gains. From this point of view, while some acts are indeed called "good" and some "bad" (conscience proving its simple existence by the use of these words in the record of language), yet conscience is not much troubled by its possessor's badness. There is little sense of the sinfulness of sin. There is only fear of possible human injury by human or subsidized spiritual enemies. This is all the salvation that is sought.

It is sought by prayer; by sacrifice, and by certain other ceremonies rendered to the spirit of the fetich or to other non-localized spirits; and by the use of charms or amulets.

These charms may be vocal, ritual, or material.

(1) The vocal are the utterance of cabalistic words deprecatory of evil or supplicatory of favor, which are supposed in a vague way to

have power over the local spirits. These words or phrases, though sometimes coined by a person for himself or herself (and therefore like our slang having a known meaning), are often archaisms, handed down from ancestors and believed to possess efficiency, but whose meaning is forgotten. In this list would be included long incantations by the magic doctors and the Ibâtâ-blown blessing.

(2) Certain rites or ceremonies are performed for almost every child—at some time during his or her infancy or youth, or subsequently as occasion may demand, in which a prohibition is laid upon the child in regard to the eating of some particular article of food or the doing of some special act. It is difficult to get at the exact object for this "orunda." Certainly the prohibited food or act is not in itself evil; for all but the inhibited individual may eat of the food or commit the act as they please. Most natives blindly follow the "custom" of their ancestors, and are unable to give me the *raison d'être* of the rite itself. But I gather from the testimony of those best able to give a reason that the prohibited article or act is literally a sacrifice, ordained for the child by its parents and the, magic doctor, as a gift to the governing spirit of its life. The thing prohibited thus becomes removed from the child's common use and is made sacred to the spirit. It is therefore a sacrament. Any use of it by the child will thenceforth be a sacrilege which would draw down the spirit's wrath in the form of sickness or other evil, and which can be atoned for only through expensive ceremonies and by gifts to the magician interceding for the offender.

Anything may be selected for an orunda. I do not know the

ground for a selection. Why one child, perhaps a babe too young to have eaten of the to-be—prohibited thing, should be debarred forever from eating a chicken, or the liver or any other particular part, or any portion at all, of a goat or an ox: or any other animal, I do not know. But that orunda is thenceforth faithfully complied with, even under pangs of hunger. It is like a Nazarite's vow.

I have a strong suspicion that where the orunda laid on a woman is a matter of meat, superstition has played into the hands of masculine selfishness, and denies to women the choice meat in order that men may have the greater share. My suspicion rests on almost positive evidence in the case of some prohibitions to the women of the Bulu and other Fang tribes of the interior.

On a boat journey in the Ogowe River, about 1818, I camped on the edge of a forest for the noon meal. My crew of four, members of the Galwa and Nkâmi tribes, had no meat. They needed it, for they had rowed hard and well. For myself, I had only a small chicken. I was satisfied with a portion of it, and gave the rest to the crew. It would make at least a tasty morsel for each, with their manioc bread. Three of them thanked me; the fourth did not touch his share. I felt slightly vexed, thinking my favor was not appreciated, and I asked the cause of his apparent sullenness. He said he did not dare to eat of the fowl, as it was orunda to him.

On another journey, in 1876, a young man whom I had picked up as extra hand in my boat's crew, when at the noon mealtime we stopped under the shade of a spreading tree by the river's bank, instead of respectfully leaving me alone with my lunch in the boat, and going ashore where the others were eating, wanted to remain in the boat, his orunda being that when on a journey by water his food should be eaten only over water.

Two Ogowe obiefs, near whose villages was anchored the small river steamer "Pioneer," on which I was passenger, in 1875, came aboard, and in drinking a glass of liquor with the captain, one of them held up a piece of white cloth before his mouth, in order that strangers' eyes might not see him swallow. That was his orunda, probably. Perhaps also, the hiding of his drinking'may have bad refer. ence to the common fear of another's "evil eye."

The other, having taken a mouthful, wet his finger in his mouth, drew the wet finger across his throat, and then blew on a fetich which he wore as a ring on a finger of the other hand. I do not know the significance of his motion across his throat. The blowing was the Ibâtâ-blessing,—an ejaculatory prayer for a blessing on his plans, probably of trade.

This word "orunda," meaning thus originally *prohibited from* human use (like the South Sea "taboo"), grew, under missionary bands, into its related meaning of *sacred* to spiritual use. It is the word by which the Mpongwe Scriptures translate our word "holy." I think it an unfortunate choice; for the missionary has to stop and explain that orunda, as used for God, does not mean the orunda used by mankind. In the translation of the Benga Scriptures the word "holy" was transferred bodily, and we explain that it means some- thing better than good. To such straits are translators sometimes reduced in the use of heathen languages!

(3) The charms that are most common are material, the fet- ich,—so common, indeed, that by the universality of their use, and

the prominence given to them everywhere, in houses and on the person, they almost monopolize the religious thought of the Bantu Negro, subordinating other acknowledged points of his theology, dominating his almost entire religious interest, and giving the departmental word "fetich" such overwhelming regard that it has furnished the name distinctive of the native African religious system, viz., fetichism. "Fetich" is an English word of Portuguese origin. "It is derived from feitico, 'made,' 'artificial' (compare the old English fetys, used by Chaucer); and this term, used of the charms and amulets worn in the Roman Catholic religion of the period, was applied, by the Portuguese sailors of the eighteenth century, to the deities they saw worshipped by the Negroes of the West Coast of Africa.

"De Brosses, a French savant of the last century, brought the word 'fetichism' into use as a term for the type of religion of the lowest races. The word has given rise to some confusion, having been applied, by Comte and other writers, to the worship of the heavenly bodies and of the great features of Nature. It is best to limit it to the worship of such natural objects as are reverenced, not for their own power or excellence, but because they are supposed to be occupied each by a spirit." [29]

The native word on the Liberian coast is "gree-gree" in the Niger Delta, "ju-ju"; in the Gabun country, "monda"; among the cannibal Fang, "biah"; and in other tribes the same respective dialectic by which we translate "medicine." To a sick native's thought the adjuvant medicinal herb used by the doctor, and its associated ef-

---

29   Menzies, History of Religion, p. 33.

ficiency-giving spirit invoked by that same doctor, are inseparable. In the heathen Negro's soul the fetich takes the place, and has the regard, which an idol has with the Hindu and the Chinese.

"A fetich, strictly speaking, is little else than a ebarm or amulet, worn about the person, and set up at some convenient place, for the purpose of guarding against some apprehended evil or securing some coveted good." In the Anglo-African parlance of the Coast fetiches are called by various names, but all signify the same thing. Fetiches may be made of anything of vegetable, animal, or metallic nature "and need only to pass through the consecrating hands of a native priest to receive all the supernatural powers which they are supposed to possess. It is not always certain that they possess extraordinary powers. They must be tried and give proof of their efficiency before they can be implicitly trusted."[30]

A fetich, then, is any material object consecrated by the "oganga," or magic doctor, with a variety of ceremonies and processes, by virtue of which some spirit becomes localized in that object, and subject to the will of the possessor.

Anything that can be conveniently carried on the person may thus be consecrated,—a stone, chip, rag, string, or bead. Articles most firequently used are snail-shells, nut-shells, and small horns of gazelles or goats. These are used probably because of their convenient cavities; for they are to be filled by the oganga with a variety of substances depending, in their selection, on the special work to be accomplished by the fetich. Its value, however, depends not on

---

30   Wilson, Western Africa, p. 212.

itself, nor solely on the character of these substances, but on the skill of the oganga in dealing with spirits.

There is a relation between these selected substances and the object to be obtained by the fetich which is to be prepared of them,—for example, to give the possessor bravery or strength, some part of a leopard or an elephant; to give cunning, some part of a gazelle; to give wisdom, some part of a human brain; to give courage, some part of a heart; to give influence, some part of an eye; and so on for a multitude of qualities. These substances are supposed to lure some spirit (being in some way pleasing to it), which thenceforward is satisfied to reside in them and to aid the possessor in the accomplishment of some one specific wish.

In preparing a fetich the oganga selects substances such as he deems appropriate to the end in view,—the ashes of certain medicinal plants, pieces of calcined bones, gums, spices, resins, and even filth, portions of organs of the bodies of animals, and especially of human beings (preferably eyes, brain, heart, and gall-bladder), particularly of ancestors, or men strong or renowned in any way, and very especially of enemies and of white men. Human eyeballs (particularly of a white person) are a great prize. New-made graves have been rifled for them.

These are compounded in secret, with the accompaniment of drums, dancing, invocations, looking into mirrors or limpid water to see faces (human or spiritual, as may be desired), and are stuffed into the hollow of the shell or bone, or smeared over the stick or stone.

If it be desired to obtain power over some one else, the oganga must be given by the applicant, to be mixed in the sacred compound, either crumbs from the food, or clippings of finger nails or hair, or (most powerful!) even a drop of blood of the person over whom influence is sought. These represent the life or body of that person. So fearful are natives of power being thus obtained over them, that they have their hair cut only by a friend; and even then they carefully bum it or cast it into a river. If one accidentally cuts himself, he stamps out what blood has dropped on the ground, or cuts out from wood the part saturated with blood.

Sitting one day by a village boat-landing in the Benita region, about 1866, while my crew prepared for our journey, I was idly plucking at my beard, and carelessly flung away a few hairs. Presently I observed that some children gathered them up. Asking my Christian assistant what that meant, he told me: "They will have a fetich made with those hairs; when next you visit this village, they will ask you for some favor, and you will grant it, by the power they will thus have obtained over you."

The water with which a lover's body (male or female) is washed, is used in making a philter to be mingled secretly in the drink of the loved one.

While, as I have already stated, it is true that anything portable may be used either as the receptacle in which the spirit is to be located or as the substance or "medicine" to be inserted in it, I wish to insist that in the philosophy of fetich there is always a reason in the selection of all these articles,-a reason which it is often difficult for a foreigner to discover,—an apparent fitness for the end in view.

Arnot[31] refers to this: "Africans believe largely in preventive measures, and their fetich charms are chiefly of that order. In passing through a country where leopards and lions abound, they carefully provide themselves with the claws, teeth, lips, and whiskers of those animals, and hang them around their necks, to secure themselves against being attacked. For the same purpose the point of an elephant trunk is generally worn by elephant hunters. The bones from the legs of tortoises are much valued as anklets, in order to give the wearers endurance, reminding one of the fable of the tortoise. The lower jaw-bone of the tortoise is worn by certain tribes as a preventive against toothache. The spine bones of serpents are strung together with a girdle as a cure for back-ache."

A recent visitor to the Gabun country, in the "Journal of the African Society," makes this criticism: "When a white man or woman wears some trinket strung about them, they call it an amulet or charm. They ascribe to it some virtue, and regard it as a sacred (?) thing; but when an African native wears one, white men call it 'fetich,' and the wearer a savage or heathen." This defence of the Negro is gratifying, but the criticism of the white man, is not quite just. There is this radical difference: to the African the "fetich" is his all, his entire hope for his physical salvation; he does not reckon on God at all. The civilized man or woman with a "mascot" is very foolish in his or her belief in luck, but their mascots never entirely take God's place.

I met at Gabun about 1895 the same criticism from the mouth of a partly educated Sierra Leone Negro, who, though a professing

---

31   Garenganze, p. 237.

Christian, evidently was wearing Christianity hypocritically. His well-educated Mpongwe wife was a member of my church. It was discovered that she bad a certain fetich suspended in her bedroom. It was necessary to summon her before the church session; she explained that it was not hers, but her busband's, and disclaimed belief in it. She was rebuked for allowing it in her room. The husband, hearing of the rebuke, wrote me an angry letter justifying his fetich. He said in substance:

You white people don't know anything about black man's 'fashions.' You say you trust God for everything, but in your own country you put up-an iron rod over your houses to protect yourselves from death by lightning; and you trust in it the while that you still believe in God; and you call it 'electricity' and civilization. And you say it's all right. I call this thing of mine—this charm—'medicine'; and I hung it over my wife's bed to keep away death by the arts of those who hate her; and I trust in it while still believing in God. And you think me a heathen!" It was explained to him that in the use of the lightning-rod white men reverently recognized God in His own natural forces, but that his fetich dishonored God, ignored Him, and was a distinct recognition of a supposed power that was claimed to be able to act independently of God; that I trusted to the lightning-rod under God, while he trusted to his fetich outside of God.

For every human passion or desire of every part of our nature, for our thousand necessities or wishes, a fetich can be made, its operation being directed to the attainment of one specified wish, and limited in power only by the possible existence of some more powerful antagonizing spirit.

This, hung on the plantation fence or from the branches of plants in the garden, is either to prevent theft or to sicken the thief; hung over the doorway of the house, to bar the entrance of evil; hung from the bow of the canoe, to insure a successful voyage; worn on the arm in hunting, to assure an accurate aim; worn on any part of one's person, to give success in loving, hating, planting, fishing, buying, and so forth, through the whole range of daily work and interests.

Some kinds, worn on a bracelet or necklace, are to ward off sickness. The new-born infant has a health-knot tied about its neck, wrist, or loins. Down to the day of oldest age, every one keeps on multiplying or renewing or altering these life talismans.

If of the charge at Balaklava, it was said, "This is magnificent, but it is not war," I may say of these heathen, "Such faith is magnificent, though it be folly." The hunter going out, certain of success, returns empty-handed; the warrior bearing on his breast a fetich panoply, which he is confident will turn aside a bullet, comes back wounded; every one is some day foiled in his cherished plan. Do they lose their faith? No, not in the system,—their fetichism; but in the special material object of their faith—their fetich—they do. Going to the oganga whom they had paid for concocting that now disappointing amulet, they tell him of its failure. He readily replies: "Yes, I know. You have an enemy who possesses a fetich containing a spirit more powerful than yours, which made your bullet miss its mark, which caused your opponent's spear to wound you. Yours is no longer of use; it's dead. Come, pay me, and I will make you a charm containing a spirit still more powerful."

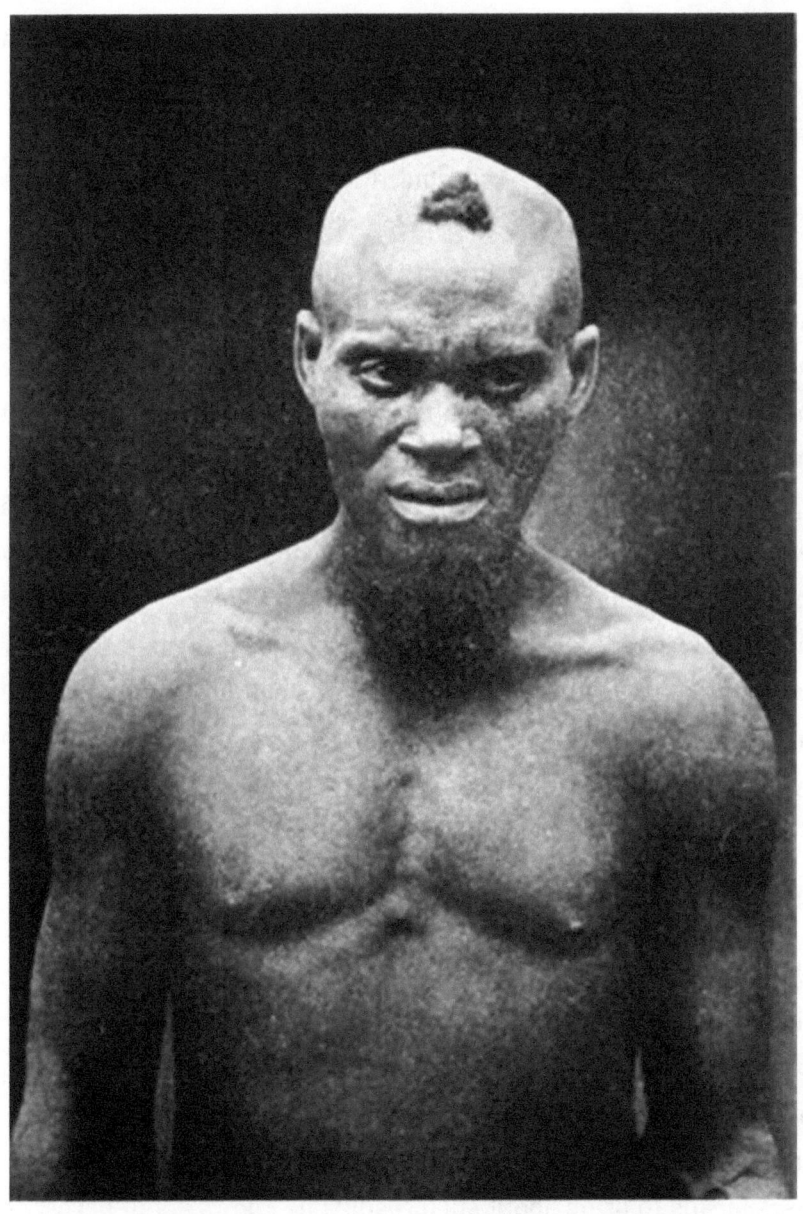

Fetich Doctor. (The triangular patch of hair is the professional tonsure.)

The old fetich hitherto jealously guarded, and which would not have been sold for any consideration, is now thrown away or sold to the foreign curio-hunter.

A native heathen Akele chief, Kasa, my friend and host in the Ogowe, in 1874, showed me a string of shells, bones, borns, wild-cat tails, and so forth, each with its magic compound, which be said could turn aside bullets. In a friendly way he dared me to fire at him with my sixteen-repeater Winchester rifle. I did not believe he meant it; but, on his taking his stand a few paces distant, he did not quail under my steady aim, nor even at the click of the trigger. I, of course, desisted, apparently worsted. Two years later, Kasa was charged by an elephant he had wounded, and was pierced by its tusks. His attendants drove off the beast; the fearfully lacerated man survived long enough to accuse twelve of his women and other slaves of having bewitched his gun, and thus causing it only to wound instead of killing the elephant. On that charge four of the accused were put to death.

Both men and women may become aganga on voluntary choice, and after a course of instruction by an oganga.

"There is generally a special person in a tribe who knows these things, and is able to work them. He has more power over spirits, than other men have, and is able to make them do what he likes. He can beal sickness, be can foretell the future, he can change a thing into something else, or a man into a lower animal, or a tree, or any-thing; he can also assume such transformations himself at will. He uses means to bring about such results; he knows about herbs, he has also recourse to rubbing, to making images of affected parts of the body, and to various other arts. Very frequently he is regarded as inspired. It is the spirit dwelling in him which brings about the wonderful results; without the spirit be could not do anything."[32]

Though these magicians possess power, its joy has its limitations; for, becoming possessed by a familiar spirit, through whose aid they make their invocations and incantations and under whose influence they fall into cataleptic trances or are thrilled with Delphic rages, if they should happen to offend that "familiar," it may destroy them by "eating" out their life, as their phrase is. On Corisco Island, in 1863, a certain man had acquired prominence as a magic doctor; he finally died of consumption. His friends began a witchcraft investigation to find out who had "killed" him. A post-mortem being made, cavities were found in the lungs. Ignorant of disease, they thereupon dropped the investigation, saying that his own "witch" had "eaten" him.

Captain Guy Burrows, a British officer, formerly in the service of the Kongo Free-State, left it unwilling to be a participant in the fearful atrocities allowed by the King of Belgium; and he 'has recently made a scathing exposure of the doings of Belgian agents that have made the Kongo a slave-ground of worse horrors than existed in the old days of the export slave-trade. He thus jocularly describes what he saw of fetich at the town of Matadi on the Kongo, where there is an English Baptist Mission: "Outside the small area, under the direct influence of the mission, there is but one deity,—the fetich. The heathen in his blindness, in bowing down to wood and stone,

---

32   Menzies, History of Religion, p. 73.

bows, as Kipling says, to 'wood for choice.' He carves a more or less grotesque face; and the rest is a matter of taste. I came across one figure whose principal ornament consisted of a profusion of tenpenny nails and a large cowrie shell.[33] But anything will do; an old tin teapot is another favorite fetich decoration. I have generally found that the uglier they are, the more they seem to be feared and reverenced.

"The fetich is sometimes inclined to be a nuisance. On one occasion I wanted to build an out-house at the far end of a plantation, where tools and other implements might be stored. I was told by the chief, however, that this was fetich ground, and that terrible misfortunes would follow any attempt to build on it. I tried to get some closer idea of the fetich, but could get no more material information than a recital of vague terrors of the kind that frighten children at night. So I began building my out-house, during the course of which operation some monkeys came and sat in the trees, highly interested in the proceedings. In some indefinite way I gathered that the fetich power was regarded as being invested in these monkeys, or that they were the embodiment of the fetich idea, or anything else you please. But I could not have my work interfered with by the ghosts of a lot of chattering apes, and the fears of those big children the natives; so I witch-doctored the monkeys after an improved recipe of my own-I shot the lot. Thereafter the spell was supposed to be

---

33   Those nails were not mere "ornaments." They were the records of the number of persons who had been transfixed by death or disease under the power of that fetich idol. A similar custom is known in the West Indies and in the southern United States. For every pin stuck into a wax figure intended to represent the person to be injured, some sickness or other evil will fall on him. Wilkie Collins also utilized this superstition in his novel, "I say, No."—R. H. N.

lifted, and no farther objections were raised; but the empty cartridge cases were seized upon by the men as charms against any further manifestations in the same place. I am glad to say none occurred; the spell I had used was too potent!"

Captain Burrows was probably an efficient administrator. But, like many foreigners, he evidently chose to ride, rough shod, over natives' prejudices, regarding them as idle superstitions, and unable or unwilling to investigate their philosophy. I see, however, from his story, that he had gotten hold of a part of the truth. That ground on which he desired to build was probably an old graveyard. The native chief very naturally did not wish it to be disturbed. Monkeys that gather on the trees in the vicinity of a graveyard are supposed to be possessed by the spirits of those buried there. An ordinary individual would have been forcibly prevented had he attempted what Captain Burrows did. He had a foreign government at his back, and the natives submitted. Their dead and their monkeys, sacred pro tempore, had succumbed to the superior power of the white man's cartridges. Their only satisfaction was to retain the empty shells as souvenirs.

CHAPTER VII
The Fetich – a Worship

WORSHIP IS AN EMINENT PART of every form of religion, but it is not essential to it. True, most religions have some form of worship. But a belief would still be a religion, even if it were so insignificant or so degraded or so indifferent as not to care to express itself in rites or ceremonies.

Fetichism, whose claim to a right to be reckoned as a religion some have been disposed to dispute, expresses itself by most of the visible and audible means used in the cults of other forms of religion.

The motives also that prompt to the performance of religious rites are not to enter into the question whether the beliefs associated with them are worthy to be dignified by the name "religion." Motives may vary widely, *e.g.*, love in an evangelical Christian, pride in a Pharisee, sensual lust in a follower of Islam and in a Mormon, and fear in the fetich worshipper. Those motives, mixed perhaps with other considerations, are the dominant factor in the government of the religious life of each.

We have already seen in the previous chapter that the religious thought of the believer in fetichism does not concern his soul or its future. The evils he would escape are not moral or spiritual. The sense of a great need that makes him look for help outside of himself is not based on a desire to obey God's will, but on his and some spirit's co-relation to the great needs of this mortal life.

The salvation sought being a purely physical one, tho thoughts that direct the use of means to that end are limited to physical needs, and largely to physical agencies. But not entirely: for one of these agencies, as already mentioned in the previous chapter, is prayer; other agencies are sacrificial offerings, and the use of amulet charms, or talismans, known as fetiches.

I. Sacrifice and other Offerings

Sacrifice is an element in all real worship, if by sacrifice, in the widest sense, may be understood the devoting of any object from a common to a sacred use, and this irrespective of the actual value of the gift (as is the case also with Chinese paper imitation money scattered around the grave, in Chinese funerals). The intention of the giver ennobles it; the spirit being supposed in some vague way to be gratified by the respectful recognition of itself, and even to be pleased sometimes by the gift itself.

(1) Thus the stones heaped by passers-by at the base of some great tree or rock, the leaf cast from the passing canoe toward a point of land on the river, though intrinsically valueless, and useless to the ombwiri of the spot, are accepted as acknowledgments of that

ombwiri's presence.

"All day we kept passing trees or rocks on which were placed little heaps of stones or bits of wood; in passing these, each of my men added a new stone or bit of wood, or even a tuft of grass. This is a tribute to the spirits, the general precaution to insure a safe return. These people have a vague sort of Supreme Being called Lesa, who has good and evil passions; but here (Plateau of Lake Tanganyika), as everywhere else, the Musimo, or spirits of the ancestors, are a leading feature in the beliefs. They are propitiated, as elsewhere, by placing little heaps of stones about their favorite haunts. At certain periods of the year the people make pilgrimages to the mountain of Fwambo-Liamba, on the sununit of which is a sort of small altar of stones. There they deposit bits of wood, to which are attached scraps of calico, flowers, or beads; this is to propitiate Lesa.

"After harvest, for instance, they make such an offering. So when a girl becomes marriageable, she takes food with her, and goes up to the mountain for several days. When she returns, the other women lead her in procession through the villages, waving long tufts of grass and palms."[34]

(2) Other gifts are supposed to be actually utilized by the spirit in some essential way. In some part of the long single street of most villages is built a low hut, sometimes not larger than a dog-kennel, in which, among all tribes, are hung charms; or by which is growing a consecrated plant (a lily, a cactus, a euphorbia, or a ficus). In some

---

34 Declè.

tribes a rudely carved human (generally female) figure stands in that hut, as an idol. Idols are rare among most of the coast tribes, but are common among all the interior tribes. That they are not now frequently seen on the Coast is, I think, not due to a lack of faith in them, but perhaps to a slight sense of civilized shame. The idol has been the material object most denounced by missionaries in their sermons against heathenism. The half-awakened native hides it, or be manufactures it for sale to curio-hunters. A really valued idol, supposed to contain a spirit, he will not sell. He does not always hide his fetich charm worn on his person; for it passes muster in his explanation of its use as a "medicine."

That idol, charm, or plant, as the case may be, is believed for the time to be the residence of a spirit which is to be placated by offerings of some kind of food. I have seen in those sacred huts a dish of boiled plantains (often by foreigners miscalled "bananas") or a plate of fish. This food is generally not removed till it spoils. Sometimes, where the gift is a very large one, a feast is made; people and spirit are supposed to join in the festival, and nothing is left to spoil. That it is of use to the spirit is fully believed; but just how, few have been able to tell me. Some say that the "life" or essence of the food has been eaten by the spirit; only the form of the vegetable or flesh remaining to be removed.

(3) Blood sacrifices are common. In any great emergency a fowl with its blood is laid at that low hut's door. In time of great danger, an expected pestilence, a threatened assault by enemies, or some severe illness of a great man or woman, a goat or sheep is sacrificed.

At the entrance to a village the way is often barred by a temporary light fence, only a narrow arched gateway of saplings being left open. These saplings are wreathed with leaves or flowers. That fence, frail as it is, is intended as a bar to evil spirits, for from those arched saplings hang fetich charms. When actual war is coming, this street entrance is barricaded by logs, behind which real fight is to be made against human, not spiritual, foes. The light gateway is sometimes further guarded by a sapling pinned to the ground horizontally across the narrow threshold. An entering stranger must be careful to tread over and not on it.

In an expected great evil the gateway is sometimes sprinkled with the blood of a sacrificed goat or sheep. The flesh is not wasted; it is eaten by the villagers, and especially by the magic doctor. Does not this look like a memory of a tradition of the Passover and its paschal lamb? And does it not suggest some thought of a blood atonement?

(4) I have not actually seen, or even heard of human sacrifices in the tribes I have personally visited. But on the adjacent Upper Guinea Coast, until ten years ago, there were human sacrifices to the sacred crocodiles of the rivers of the Niger Delta. In the oil rivers of that same coast there was, until recently, an annual sacrifice (as in the ancient Nile days) of a maiden to the river spirits of trade, for success in foreign commerce.

Treaties with foreign civilized nations have now prohibited this sacrifice, but the maiden has not gained much in the change. Instead of one being sacrificed to a brute crocodile to please the spirit of trade,hundreds are prostituted to please brutal, dissolute foreigners.

The thousands of captives butchered at the "annual custom" of Dahomey were claimed by its successive kings, in their answer to the protests of the ambassadors from civilized nations, to be required as offerings to the safety of the nation, the omission of which would be punished by the loss of the king's own life. Fearful as that annual barbarity was, I do not think that those kings should properly be called "bloodthirsty." It was their religion. All the more dreadful the religion that called for such deeds!

Here, again, the question presents itself whether Africa has gained much in the substitution of wicked white representatives of civilization for the heathen black representatives of fetichism. The Kongo River was rescued from the cruelties and loss of life in the foreign slave-trade, only to be subjected to greater cruelties, in its miscalled "Free State," under the control of Belgium, at the hands of men like Major Lothaire.

The following remarks of Menzies[35] on the use of sacrifice by primitive man are descriptive of the interior tribes of Africa to-day: "Sacrifice is an invariable feature of early religion. Wherever gods are worshipped, gifts and offerings are made to them of one kind or another. It is in this way that, in antiquity at least, the relation with the deity was renewed, if it had been slackened or broken, or strengthened and made sure. Sacrifice and worship are, in the ancient world, identical terms. The nature of the offering and the mode of presenting it are infinitely various, but there is always sacrifice

---

35   History of Religion, pp. 65, 69.

in one form or another. Different deities of course receive different gifts; the tree has its roots watered, or trophies of battle or of the chase are hung upon its branches; horses are thrown into the sea. But of primitive sacrifice generally we may affirm that it consists of such food and drink as men themselves partake of. Whether it be the fruit of the field or the firstlings of the flock that is offered at the sacred stone, whether the offering is burnt before the god or set down and left near him, or whether he is sum moned to come down from the sky or to travel from the far country to which he may have gone, it is of the materials of the meal that the sacrifice consists. In some cases it appears to be thought that the god consumes the offering, as when Fire is worshipped with offerings which he burns up, or when a fissure in the earth closes upon a victim; but in most cases it is only the spirit or finer essence that the god enjoys; the rest he leaves to men. And thus sacrifice is generally accompanied by a meal. The offering is presented to the god whole, but the worshippers help to eat it. The god gets the savor of it which rises in the air towards him, while the more material part is devoured below."

The testimony of travellers in other parts of Africa, distant thousands of miles from the West Coast, show that the practice of offerings is almost identical all over the southern third of the continent, the lines of latitude of Bantu tribes being conterminous with their language and their religion.

Arnot [36] says that in South Africa, "when going to pray, the Barotse make offerings to the spirits of their forefathers under a

---

36   Garenganze, p. 77.

tree, bush, or grove planted for the purpose; and they take a larger or a smaller offering, according to the measure of their request. If the offering be beer, they pour it upon the ground; if cloth, it is tied to a horn stuck in the ground; if an ox be slaughtered, the blood is poured over the horn, which, in fact, is their altar." (Ps. cxviii. 27.)

In that same region, among the Barotse, "Nothing of importance can be sanctified without a human sacrifice, in most cases a child. First the fingers and toes are cut off, and the blood is sprinkled on the boat, drum, house, or whatsoever may be the object in view. The victim is then killed, ripped up, and thrown into the river."

Declè also[37] describes the religious habits of the Barotse tribes of Southern Central Africa: "They chiefly worship the souls of their ancestors. When any misfortune happens, the witch doctor divines with knuckle-bones whether the ancestor is displeased, and they go to the grave and offer up sacrifice of grain or honey. . . . They also bring to the tombs cooked meats, which they leave there a few minutes and then eat. When they go to pray by a grave, they also leave some small white beads. Whilst an Englishman was journeying to Lialui, he passed near a little wood where there lay a very venerated chief. The boatmen stopped, and having sacrificed some cooked millet, their headman designated a man to offer up a prayer, which ran thus: 'You see us; we are worn out travellers, and our belly is empty; inspire the white man, for whom we row, to give us food to fill our stomachs.'"

Among the Wanyamwezi, "Every chief has near his hut a

---

37   Three Years in Savage Africa

Musinio hut, in which the dead are supposed to dwell, and where sacrifices and offerings must be made. Meat and flour are deposited in the Musimo huts, and are not, as with many other peoples, consumed afterwards. The common people also have their Musimo huts, but they are smaller than that of the chief, and the offerings they make are, of course, not so important as his."

The Wanyamwezi being great travellers, they have numberless ways of propitiating the Musimo. "The night before starting they put big patches of moistened flour on their faces and breasts. On the way, if by chance they are threatened with war or any other difficulty, some of them go on ahead in the early morning for about a hundred yards along the path over which they are about to travel. Then they place a hand on the ground,and throw flour over it in such a manner as to leave the impression of a hand on the soil. At the same time they 'wish' hard that the journey may go off well. On the march, from time to time each of them will deposit in the same spot a twig of wood or a stone in such a way that a great heap gets collected. If they halt in the midst of high grass each will plait a handful of grass, which they tie together so as to make a kind of bower.[38] In the forest, if they are pressed for time, each will make a cut with a blow of a hatchet in a tree; but if they have time, they will cut down trees, lop off the branches, and place these poles against a big tree; in certain places I have seen stacks of hundreds of them around a single tree. Sometimes they will strip pieces of bark from the trees, and stick them on the branches, and at others they,will place a pole

---

38   I saw the same on the Ogowe.—R. H. N.

supported by two trees right over the path. On it they will bang up a broken gourd, or an old box made of bark. On some occasions they will even erect a little hut made of straw to the Musimo on the road itself; but this is usually done when they are going on a hunting expedition, and not on a journey. Near the villages, where two roads meet, are usually found whole piles of old pots, gourds, and pieces of iron.[39] When a hunter starts for the chase, he prays to the Musimo to give him good luck. If he kills any big game, he places before the hut of his Musimo the head of the beast he has killed, and inside a little of the flesh."[40]

II. Prayer

Just as worship is an eminent part of religion, prayer is usually a chief part of religious worship. But in fetichism, though it undeniably has a part, it is not prominent, and not often formal or public. It plays a less obvious and less frequent part than either sacrifices or the use of charms.

"Prayer is the ordinary concomitant of sacrifice; the worshipper explains the reason of the gift, and urges the deity to accept it and to grant the help that is needed. The prayers of the earliest stage are offered on emergencies, and often appear to be intended to attract the attention of the god who may be engaged in another

---

39   These piles I have found at almost every village I have visited.—R, H. N.

40   Declè, p. 346.

direction. The requests they contain are of the most primary sort. Food is asked for, success in hunting or fishing, strength of arm, rain, a good harvest, children, and so forth. They have a ring of urgency; they state the claims the worshipper has on the god, and mention his former offerings as well as the present one; they praise the power and the past acts of the deity, and adjure him by his whole relationship to his people (and also to his enemies) to grant their requests." [41]

Fetich prayer may be and is offered without restriction by any one, young or old, male or female; but to my knowledge it is seldom used by the young. A very intelligent woman, a member of my Batanga church, tells, me that when she was a child she possessed a fetich supposed to be very valuable, whicli sbe had inherited from her father. She says that when she would be going into the forest or where she expected difficulty or danger or trouble or was anxious for success, she would hold the fetich in her hand, and with eye and thought directed toward it and the spirit it was supposed to contain, would utter a short petition for aid and protection.

But practically formal prayer is rarely made. Ejaculatory prayer, however, is made constantly, in the uttering of cabalistic words, phrases, or sentences adopted by or assigned to almost every one by parent or doctor. They are uttered by all ages and both sexes at any time, as a defence from evil, on all sorts of occasions,—*e.g.*, when one sneezes, stumbles, or is otherwise startled, etc.

The prayers which I have heard were of adults. On a journey, about 1876, stopping for a night in a village on the Ogowe River, I

---

41 Menzies.

saw the venerable chief stand out in the open street. He addressed the spirits of the air, begging them, "Come not to my town!" He recounted his good deeds—praising himself as just, honest, and kind to his neighbors—as reason why no evil should befall him, and closed with an impassioned appeal to the spirits to stay away.

At another time, about 1879, in another Ogowe village, where a man's son had been wounded, and a bleeding artery which had been successfully closed had just broken open again, and the hemorrhage, if not promptly checked, would probably be fatal, the father ran out of the hut, wildly gesticulating towards the sky, saying, "Go away! go away! O ye spirits! why do you come to kill my son?" And be continued for some time in a strain of alternate pleading and protestation.

In another case I saw a woman who rushed into the street objurgating the spirits, and in the next breath humbly supplicating them, who, she said, were vexing her child that was lying in convulsions.

Observe that while these were distinctly prayers, appeals for mercy, pathetic, agonizing protestations, there was no praise, no love, no thanks, no confession of sin,—only a long, pitiful deprecation of evil.

There are also prayers of blessing. Parents in farewells to their children, or a chief to his parting guest, or any grateful recipient of a valued gift, will take the head or hand of the child, guest, or donor, and saying, "Ibâtâ!" (blessing), or adding a cabalistic ejaculation, will sometimes "blow" a blessing. From this custom has arisen the statement in some books of travel that it was an African mode of honoring a guest to spit on his hand. It is true that the sudden and violent expulsion of the breath in "blowing" the "Ibâtâ" from the tip of the tongue is apt to be followed by an ejection of more or less saliva, but the kernel of the custom lies in the prayer of blessing accompanying the act.

In auguries made by the mfumu, or witch-doctor, among the Wanyamwezi, "the mfumu holds a kind of religious service; he begins by addressing the spirits of their forefathers, imploring them not to visit their anger upon their descendants. This prayer be offers up kneeling, bowing and bending to the ground from time to time. Then he rises, and commences a hymn of praise to the ancestors, and all join in the chorus. Then, seizing his little gourds, he executes a *pas seul*, after which he bursts out into song again, but this time singing as one inspired." [42]

III. The use of charms or "fetiches"

The third mode of worship has been already mentioned in a previous chapter, viz., the use of charms or fetiches. This is the mode most frequently used; and to the descriptions of their forms of preparation and manner, universality, and the various effects of their use, the following chapters are devoted.

---

42   Declè

The Fetich – Witchcraft
– A White Art – Sorcery

A passively Defensive Art — Professedly of the Nature of a Medicine —
Distinction between a Fetich Doctor and a Christian Physician — Manner of
Performance of the White Art — The Medicinal Herbs used sometimes Valuable
— Strength of Native Faith in the System

HUNDREDS OF ACTS AND PRACTICES in the life of Christian households in civilized lands pass muster before the bar of æsthetic propriety and society, and even of the church, as not only harmless and allowable, but as commendable, and conducive to kindness, good-will, and healthful social entertainment; but in the doing of these acts few are aware of the fact that some of them in their origin were heathenish and in their meaning idolatrous, and that long ago they would have brought on the doer church censure.

Norse legends and Celtic and Gaelic folk-lore abound in superstitions that were held by our forefathers in honor of false gods and demons. Their Christian descendants, to the present generations in Great Britain and the United States, delight our children with the beautifully printed fairy tale, forgetting, or not even. knowing, that once, long ago, that tale was a tale of sin. The superstitious peasant of Germany, Ireland, and other European countries, while as at least a nominal son of the church the worships God, fears the machinations of trolls and the "good little people," and wards off their dreaded influence by vocal and material charms,—a practice for—which the African Negro just emerging from heathenism is debarred church-membership. The practice is common to the three,— the untaught heathen, the ignorant peasant, and the enlightened Christian,—but its significance differs for each. To the Christian it is only a national or household tradition, without religious or moral significance, and his belief in the power of the cliarm is seldom seriously held. To the peasant the practice is also a tradition; it is not his religion, but be thinks that somehow under the divine Providence, in whom he believes and whom he worships in the church, it will be conducive to his physical well-being. But to the heathen it is a part of his religion, and leads to the exclusion of the true God, whom he does not know, or at least does not worship.

In our Christian homes, around the Christmas tree, with all its holy, happy thoughts, we decorate with the holly bush and we hang the mistletoe bough, never thinking that the December festival itself was originally a heathen feast, and that our superstitious forefathers spread the holly as a guard against evil fairies, and hung the mistletoe as part of the ceremonies of a Druid's human sacrifice.

The superstitious African Negro does precisely the same thing to-day, because be believes in witchcraft; the holly bush not growing in his tropical air, he has substituted the cayenne pepper bush. The witch or wizard whom he fears can no more pass over that pepper leaf with its red pods than the Irish fairy can dare the holly leaf with its red berries. Superstitious acts are thus rooted in us all, heathen and Christian, the world over; only with this great difference,—that to the Christian they bear no religious or even moral significance; to the heathen their entire *raison d'être* is that they are his religion, or rather part of his worship in the practice of his religion.

In emerging from his heathenism and abandoning his fetichism for the acceptance of Christianity, no part of the process is more difficult to the African Negro than the entire laying aside of superstitious practices, even after his assertion that they do not express his religious belief. From being a thief, he can grow up an honest man; from being a liar, he can beconie truthful; from being indolent, he can become diligent; froin being a polygamist, he can become a niouogamist; froin a status of ignorance and brutality, he can develop into educated courtesy. And yet in his secret thought, while he would not wear a fetich, he believes in its power, and dreads its influence if possibly it should be directed against himself.

Some church-members thus believing and fearing, do wear fetiches, claiming that their use is simply defensive. In their moral thought they make a distinction, which to them is clear and satisfactory in the present stage of the enlightenment of their conscience, between the defensive and the offensive use of the fetich,—the latter is a black art; the former is a white art. Only the heathen and non-Christian element of the community practise the black art. They ignore not God's existence, but deny that He plays any part in the economy of human life. They believe in evil spirits, and that they themselves can have association with them, by which they may obtain power for all purposes; they use enchantments to obtain that power; and having it, or professing to have it, they exercise it for the gratification of revenge or avarice, or in other ways to injure other persons. They become, in heart, murderers; and if occasion serve, by poison or other means, are willing to become actual murderers.

The community regards them as criminals, and executes them as such when it is proved that they used black art to accomplish the death of some one who has recently died.

The Christian, of course, will practise none of the black arts, but believing in their existence and power as permitted to the Evil One under the divine government, he is willing to allow himself to use, as a counter-influence, a fetich of the white art in self-defence.

The discussion of the morality of this white art is often a difficult question in the church sessions in the discipline of some offending church-member. Few of the natives have emerged so far into the light as to stand squarely and fully with the missionary in his civilized attitude toward this question of the allowability of a fetich charm under any circumstances. Even the missionary, if he is wise and would not be unjust, will look with the leniency of charity on an offence of this kind in the case of a convert only lately come out of heathenism, which he would not or should not exercise toward a fortune-teller or hoodoo practitioner under the broad light of civilization.

In electing men as ruling elders in the church session, or accepting candidates for the gospel ministry, while a certain degree of intellectuality is desired, and a certain amount of education required, we look first and always for the quality of their moral fibre, whether or not it be untrammelled by the fetich cult.

A rare and noble example of utter freedom from any such superstitious bias was the late Rev. Ibia ja Ikenge. From his youth, believing in, using, and practising fetich white art, when he became a Christian his conversion was so clear and decided that he was soon made a ruling elder, was accepted as a candidate, grew up to licensure as a probationer, subsequently reached ordination to the ministry, and finally became pastor of the Corisco church of his own Benga tribe. Honored during his ministerial life by all classes, foreigners and natives, he died regretted by all, even by the heathen whose sins he had unsparingly denounced. But there are few so morally clear as be.

A few years ago, while I was in charge of the Gabun church, in the Mpongwe tribe, at the oldest station and outwardly the most civilized part of the mission, I was surprised by a charge of witch-craft practice laid against a very lady-like woman who was one of my intimate native friends. I had known her from her childhood; had admired her intelligence, vivacity, and purity; had unfortunately helped her into a disastrous marriage from which, as her pastor, I afterwards rescued her with legal grounds for divorce; and subse-quently she had married a Sierra Leone man who professed to be a Christian. It was discovered that she had hanging over the doorway in her bedroom a fetich regularly made and bought from a fetich doctor. On trial of the case, she denied that it was hers, stated that it was her husband's, admitted that she knew of its existence and use, that she allowed it to be placed in the usual spot for warding off evil spirits, and was not clear in denial of belief that it might be of some use to her in that way.

My three ruling elders looked on the case more lightly than even I was charitably disposed to do, and my own duty as a judge was obscured by my friendship for the accused. It was a great pain for me to have even to rebuke a lady I had so loved and trusted.

She kept her anger wonderfully under control while in the session meeting; but she resented the rebuke, broke our friendship, and subsequently sought to injure me by slander. If there was any doubt about her complicity with the fetich, there was no doubt about the fact of her effort to injure me. I did not prosecute her (as I would have done had she slandered any one else), lest I be suspected of making-my position of session moderator an engine for personal revenge. She subsequently made a noble reparation. She still affirms that she does not believe in fetich, and remains in "good standing" in the church, while occasionally hanging a charm on. her garden fence for its "moral effect" on trespassers.

Lately a fellow missionary told me that in a conversation with certain natives, professed Christians, they admitted their fear lest their nail-clippings should be used against them by an enemy, and candidly acknowledged that when they pared their nails they threw the pieces on the thatch of the low roof of their house.

The missionary was surprised, and, perhaps with a little suspicion or perhaps as a test, turning to a man present who had remained silent during the discussion, said, "And you—what do you do with your parings?" He honestly replied, "I throw them on the roof!" And this man is an elder, and had been advanced to be a local preacher. There is no expectation of his ordination, for though he can preach a good sermon, he is lacking in all other abilities desirable in a minister. He is probably fifty years of age, and for forty years has been in mission employ of some kind, and living in the mission household much of that time. But this mission association has not been to him the benefit it would have been to almost any one else; for, being of slave origin, he seemed to prefer to keep aloof from the free-born, grew up without companionship, and is extremely secretive. Though a Christian and a good man, be bad not opened his inner life to all the ennobling influences of the light.

A difficulty, admitted by the missionary in judging of the morality of the use of a fetich charm, is the explanation offered by the natives, even by some professedly Christian, that the charm is of the nature of a "medicine," and, generally, actually has medicines in it. It is known to the native that civilized and Christian therapeutics recognize a great variety of medicinal articles, solid and liquid, and that they are employed in a variety of ways,—as lotions, ointments, and powders; and that some are drunk, some are rubbed into the skin, and some are worn on the body,—*e.g.*, a sachet of sulphur in skin diseases, or of pungent essential oils to fend off insects,—and that certain herbs whose scent is attractive to fish are rubbed on the fisherman's hook. The missionary knows, too, that certain native medicinal plants are used, and with efficiency, in precisely these ways and with precisely these reasons as, at least in part, the ground for their use.

Truth gains nothing by an indiscriminate denunciation of all native "medicine"; for the native knows by the personal experience of himself and his observation of others that a given "medicine" has helped or cured himself and others. His belief in this case is not a mere theory; it is actual fact. The missionary loses in the native's respect, and in the native's trust in his judgment or the value of his word, if he asserts unqualifiedly that "native medicine" is "foolishness," especially if, as was the case before the desirability of medical missionaries was as generally recognized by the church as it now is, the missionary was able to give him no substitute for the magic doctor. The native Christian's sense of justice was aggrieved at being disciplined for the use of a medicine in sickness, which experience told him had been of benefit and in place of which the missionary offered him no other.

The native's error in his judgment of the case and the missionary's justification of bis position lay in the idolatrous ceremonies that are associated with the administration of the medicine. In the native's ignorant mind, and in the distress of his disease, he was unable to see a distinction between the therapeutic action of a drug and the mode of its administration. In fact, to him that mode may be as important a factor contributive to the desired result as the drug itself. In the heathen belief of the native doctor it is admittedly true that the administration, not the drug, is the important factor, both mode of administration and the drug itself deriving all their efficiency from a spirit claimed by the magician to be under his control, which is in some vague way pleased to be associated with the particular drug and those special ceremonies. The native doctor does not understand therapeutics as such. Some one of his ancestors happened to observe that a certain leaf, bark, or root exhibited internally proved efficient in cases where the symptoms indicated a certain disease which he had failed to cure by his dances, drums, auguries, and other enchantments. Not knowing the *modus operandi* of the drug itself, he had jumped to the conclusion that he had finally happily found the adjuvant herb necessary to please the spirit for whom he had been making enchantments, without which herb the spirit had hitherto withheld its assistance. And ever afterward the secret of this particular drug was guarded by his family, the knowledge of its tree being handed down as an heirloom, the secret kept as jealously and carefully as the recipe for the proprietary medicine of any quack in civilized lands. In his medical ethics there was no *quæ prosunt omnibus*.

The dividing line of morality between the fetich doctor and the Christian physician is a narrow but deep chasm. The latter knows that, with all his skill in physiology and the infallibility of his drug's indication, results lie in the hand of God, with whom are the issues of life and death, who has sovereignly and beneficently endowed certain plants or minerals with properties befitting certain pathological conditions. The former ignores God, and firmly believes that his own encbantments have subsidized the power of a spirit, so that the spirit itself is to enter into the body of the patient, and, searching through his vitals, drive out the antagonizing spirit, which is the supposed actual cause of the disease. The etiology of disease is to the native obscure. His attempts at explanation are somewhat inconsistent; the sickness is spoken of as a disease, and yet the patient is said to be sick because of the presence of an evil spirit, which being driven out by the magician's benevolent spirit the patient will recover.

The drug exhibited with the ceremonies by which the friendly spirit is induced to enter the body is entirely secondary and adjuvant, and is not supposed to be any more efficient in producing a cure than was the Old Testament incense of the Temple ritual in obtaining an answer to prayer.

But the drug is often a really valuable medicine, and does cure the patient. Yet the native Christian must be forbidden to submit to its use, because of the invariably associated heathen ceremonies. The magician alone knows from what plant the drug came, and he positively refuses to administer it unless its associated ceremonies are carefully observed. For the Christian to consent to do that, is to "kiss the calves"[43] of idolatrous Israel, or to partake of the "meats offered to idols."[44]

The manner of practising the white art by the magic doctor may be purely ritual without his making or the patient's wearing any material amulet, but the performance is none the less fetich in its character.

According to the usual procedure an article is prepared with incantations referring to spiritual influences to be wom by the applicant either as a cure for an actually existing disease or any other expected danger, or, irrespective of disease, for the attainment of a desired object or for success in some cherished plan. Its application may be as limitless as the entire range of human desire.

The first step in the process is the selection of an object in which to enclose the various articles deemed necessary to attract and please the spiritual being whose aid is to be invoked. In this selection it is not probable that superstitious or other moral consideration enters. It is simply a matter of taste as to shape or availability or convenience. The article usually chosen is a horn of a gazelle or young antelope, or of a goat. The ground for the choice is availa-

---

43   Hosea xiii. 2.

44   Acts xv. 29.

bility; those animals are common. The horns are preserved and are therefore always at hand. They are small, light, and easily carried. They are durable, not liable to rust and decay, as would be an article of vegetable origin, and they have a convenient cavity.

The next step in the process is the selection of the substances which are to be packed into the hollow of the horn. These are of both animal and vegetable origin, but mostly vegetable. They may be very absurd to our civilized view, they may be disgusting and even filthy; but they are all ranked as "medicine," have actually some fitness to the end in view, as described in the previous chapter, and are to be as carefully regarded as are the ingredients of a physician's prescription by a druggist. Their absurdity must not militate against the view of them as "medicine," even to a civilized mind. We are not to forget that, all superstitious and fetich ideas aside, our own pharmacopoeia one hundred years ago contained animal products of supposed therapeutic value that were clumsy, annoying, and even disgusting. Indeed, it is only in very modern medicine that the profession have thought it worth while to regard the matter of agreeable look and pleasant taste. Homceopathy, even if we do not all believe in it, must be given credit for at least eliminating nauseous taste from the attributes of a good medicine, even of an emetic.

From the wide range of substances, mineral, animal, and vegetable, the magic doctor takes generally some plant. Indeed, so associated is the doctor's thought of a tree and some spirit belonging to it, that an educated and very intelligent native chief at Gabun who still clings to many heathen practices, of whom recently I asked an explanation of fetich from the native point of view, said sententiously, "A principle of fetich comes from trees." This carried to me very little meaning. I asked him to explain at length. He did so. He said that in the long ago, while still his ancestors knew of God and had not entirely forgotten to give him some kind of worship, their medicine men were botanists, and, like Solomon, "spake of trees." The herbs and barks they used were employed solely for their own intrinsically curative qualities. But as people became more degraded and "like people, like priest," the medicine men added a ritual of song, dances, incantations, and auguries by which to dignify their profession with mystery. As they grew in power, they added claims of spiritual influence, by which to impress their patients with fear and to exact obedience even from kings, until finally the idea of a spirit as the efficient agent in the cure was substituted for that of the drug itself, and fetich belief dominated all.

The reason for the choice of one tree rather than another in a given case of sickness is almost impossible to find out. Perhaps there is a vague tradition of the fact that it was used long ago by those who first happened to discover that it bad real medicinal quality, and the present generation continues to use it, though having forgotten what that quality was, or even that it had any intrinsic quality of its own, their etiology of disease assigning as the cause of all sickness the antagonistic presence of an evil spirit.

The laity, heathen and Christian, positively do not know from what particular tree the leaf or piece of bark was obtained, and they would not be able to recognize it even if they were allowed to see it. They see only the dry powder or ashes. Even if the heathen laity were able to tell me, they will not do so. Even if they were bribed, I would have no certainty that they were showing me the plant that was actually used; for they would know that I would have no means of comparing specimens or of proving their deception. The native will tell foreigners many things for friendship or for regard, and he enjoys conversation with us; but superstition slams his heart's door shut when he is asked to reveal secrets of the spirits. His prompt thought is: "White man's knowledge has given him power. There is little left of land, authority, women, or wealth in my country that he has not seized. Shall I add to his power by telling him the secrets of my spirits?" Of course the magic doctor will not tell. That would be giving himself entirely away.

Even Christian men and women who have inherited from a parent knowledge of some plant, and who use it rationally for its purely medicinal quality without any reference whatever to spiritual influences, can barely be induced to tell me of it. The fee they obtain is part of their means of living. They make honest "medicine" in the circle of their acquaintances for certain sicknesses for which their drug happens to be fitted. Of a cure for any other sickness they know nothing, and must themselves go to some one else who happens to possess the knowledge.

Even by me my native friends—though with their personal respect or affection for me they would be willing to do much—do not like to be asked. They know that I, in asking for information, expect to utilize it in letters or lectures or books. Their secret would not be safe even with me, and it may die with them. One of the noblest of my native female friends at Gabun, a Christian, well educated, with only a minimum of superstition remaining, and no belief at all in fetich, inherited from her mother much botanical and medicinal knowledge. I observe her decocting a medicine for a sick friend, and I ask her, "What medicine is that?" She turns away her usually frank eyes and simply says, "Sijavi" (leaves). "Yes, I see they are leaves. But I asked you what they are. Where do you get them?" With eyes still turned away, she only says, "Go-iga" (in the forest). "Exactly; of course it's a plant. But is it a tree or a vine or a shrub, or what?" And she looks at me steadily, and quietly says, "Mi amie" (I don't know). I have long ago learned that "mi amie," though only sometimes true, is not always a lie. It is equivalent to our conventional "Not at home, "or a polite version of, "Ask me no questions and I'll tell you no lies." From my friend it is a kind notification that the conversation had better be changed. It having reached this acute stage, the pursuance of it would be worse than useless. I talk about something else, and immediately she resumes her wonted cordiality.

Probably the particular herb selected by the fetich-man does possess some therapeutic value (for cures are effected) of which he does not himself know. He knows that that plant was said by his ancestors to be the proper one to use in case of a certain sickness, but knowledge of the *raison d'user* has been lost.

The use of drugs in decoctions is less likely to be merely superstitious. The fresh leaves and barks are recognized. There is not likely to be a secret about them. Whatever of fetich is introduced in the case will be in the mode of administration.

The next step, the admixture of the ingredients, is secret. They are ground or triturated, or reduced to ashes, and only the ash or charcoal of their wood is used. Among the common ingredients are colored earths, chalk, or potter's blue clays. Beyond the usual constituents constantly employed, there are other single ones, which vary according to the end to be obtained by the user of the fetich,—for one end, as elsewhere already mentioned, some small portion of an enemy's body; for another, an ancestor's powdered brain; for another, the liver or gall-bladder of an animal; for another, a finger of a dead first-born child; for another, a certain fish; and so on for a thousand possibilities. These ingredients are compounded in secret, and with public drumming, dancing, songs to the spirit, looking into limpid water or a mirror, and sometimes with the addition of jugglers' tricks, *e.g.*, the eating of fire.

The ingredients having been thus properly prepared, and the spirit, according to the magician's declaration, having associated itself lovingly with these mixed articles, they and it are put into the cavity of the selected horn or other hollow thing (a gourd, a nut-shell, and so forth). They are packed in firmly. A black resin is plastered over the opening. Perbaps also a twine is netted tightly on the top of it. A red paint—triturated red-wood mixed with palm or other oil—is daubed on it. While the resin is still soft, the red tail-feathers of the gray African parrot are stuck into it. This description is typical. It would be equally true if the chosen material object had no cavity, e.g., if it were a pebble or a piece of bark; in which case the sacred ingredients plastered on it would be held in situ by the twine netting. A hole is bored in the apex of the horn, and it is hung by a string from the neck, arm, waist, or ankle of the purchaser, or from his door, roof, or garden fence; or from the prow of his canoe; or from any one of a hundred other points, according to the convenience of the owner or the object to be obtained by its use.

Those objects may be, all of them, not only desirable, but commendable, even from a Christian point of view. In the exercise of the white art there is no ill-will to or malice against any other known person. The owner of the fetich amulet is only using, from his point of view, one of the known means of success in life,—somewhat as a business man in civilized lands uses his signs and tricks of trade to attract and influence customers.

It is true that our native convert, in abjuring fetich and refraining from the white art, is at a disadvantage, humanly speaking, alongside of his heathen fellow, just as the honest grocer who does not adulterate his foods is somewhat at a disadvantage with the man who does.

The heathen, armed with his fetich, feels strong. He believes in it; has faith that it will help him. He can see it and feel it. He goes on his errand inspired with confidence of success. Confidence is a large part of life's battle. If he should happen to fail, be excuses the failure by remembering that he had not obeyed all the minute "orunda" directions that the magician told him to follow. It is entirely in his power carefully to obey all directions next time; and then be cannot possibly fail! The Christian convert is weak in his faith. He would like to have something tangible. He is not sure that he will succeed on his errand. He goes at it somewhat half-hearted, and probably fails. His not very encouraging explanation is that God is trying his faith. That explanation is perhaps not the true one, but it is sufficient as his explanation. But it does not nerve him for the next effort; only the strong rise to overcoming faith. The weak ask the missionary whether they may not be allowed to carry a fetich only f or "show." That "show" is for effect on a heathen competitor; for the moral effect on that competitor's mind,—that he should not think that the convert, in becoming a Christian, was at a disadvantage as to chances of success in the race with him. But that would be allowing even the "appearance of evil."

It was actually true, in the early days of mission effort, that converts were oppressed by heathen under the idea that, as the gospel proclaimed by the missionary was a message of peace, all the "peace" was to be on the Christian's side, and that he dared not strike a blow even in self-defence. But we did not understand the angels' song of good-will as explained by the followers of George Fox, and by precept and example we allowed the use of force in the defence of right.

As to the use of fetich by those who did not really believe in it, it was true that some Europeans, non-Christian men in their trade with the natives, seeing what a power the fetich was in the native thought, and knowing that it was exercised against themselves, deemed it a matter simply of sharp praetice to adopt a fetich themselves, and play the native at his own game. To my knowledge this was done by an Englishman now dead. I was intimately acquainted with him; and though his morals were objectionable and his religion agnosticism, I enjoyed his society. He was a gentleman in manners, intelligent, well-read, interested, in common with myself, in African philology and ethnology, and his river steamers often generously helped me in my itinerations. His trade interests were large; he spoke the native language well, was practically acquainted with native customs and native mode of thought. He was a good hater and a firm friend, strict with subordinates to the point of severity, but on occasions free-handedly generous. Naturally such a character, while it made for him many friends, developed some enemies. A few hated him, most liked him, even while all feared him. To checkmate them on their own ground and to carry prestige in dealing with the heathen chiefs of wild tribes, he caused to be made for himself, and allowed it to be known in advance that he carried, a powerful fetich. The effect was very decided in increasing his power, influence, and trade success, so successful that I am not sure but that he grew himself to have some faith in it,—an illustration of the oft-noted fact in moral philosophy that non-Christian credulity often leads men's beliefs further than does Christian faith. The after history of my trader friend is a sad illustration of the wings that ill-gotten wealth develops. His fetich assisted in amassing a fortune several times over, but it did not retain it for him. He died in pitiful want.

Practice of this white art holds all over South Africa and among all its tribes. "They believe in charms, fetiches, and witchcraft. The latter is the source of great dread to a Mashona, who fears that death or accident may overtake him through the instrumentality of some fellow-being who may perchance hold against him a grudge. For the purpose of avoiding these calamities, charms are worn about the person, usually around the neck. Divining bones or blocks of wood called 'akata' are thrown by the witch-doctors to discover a witch or evil spirit, and they are also employed to ascertain the probable results of a journey, a hunt, or a battle,—in short, any and all of the events of life."[45]

"The tribes we have passed through seem to have one common religion, if it can be called by that name. They say there is one great spirit, who rules over all the other spirits; but they worship and sacrifice to the spirits of ancestors, so far as I can learn, and have a mass of fetich medicines and enchantments. The hunter takes one kind of charm. with him; the warrior another. For divining they have a basket filled with bones, teeth, finger-nails, claws, seeds, stones, and such articles, which are rattled by the diviner till the spirit comes and speaks to him by the movement of these things. When the spirit is reluctant to be brought up, a solemn dirge is chanted by the people. All is attention while the diviner utters a string of short sentences in different tones, which are repeated after him by the audience."[46]

---

45 Brown, On the South African Frontier, p. 113.

46 Arnot, Garenganze, p. 106.

CHAPTER IX
The Fetich – Witchcraft – A Black Art – Demonology

Distinction as to the Object aimed at in the White Art and in the Black Art
— Black Art actively Offensive — The Black Art distinctively "Witchcraft"
— Witchcraft Executions; claimed to be Judicial Acts — Hoodoo Worship —
Christian Faith and Fetich Faith Compared — Deception by Fetich Magicians —
Clairvoyance — Demoniacal Possession

THE DISTINCTION SOUGHT to be made by the half-civilized Negro between a white art and a black art, as a justification of his practice of fetich enchantments, lies in the object to be obtained by their use, He vainly tries to find a parallel to them ia Christian use of fire-arms,—proper for defence, improper for unprovoked assault. The black art he admits is wrong, its object being to kill or injure some one else; the white he thinks allowable, because with it he acts simply on the defensive. He wishes to ward off a possible blow of an unseen foe aimed at himself. He professes his intention not to strike or take otherwise active measures to injure any known person. After every allowance made, the distinction between the arts as moral and immoral is not a clear one. They differ only in their degree of immorality. The means both use are immoral, not justified by the possible goodness of the desired end, and not sanctified by the intention of the user. Both use fetiches. Fetich, if it has power at all, is not of God; if it is powerless, it is folly. Thus, in every and any case, it dishonors God.

But whatever doubt there might have been as to the allowability of white art practice, there is no doubt as to the immorality of black art. It always contemplates a possible taking of life.

The term "witchcraft," which attaches itself to all fetichism, localizes itself in the black art practice, which is thus pre-eminently known as "witchcraft." Its practitioners are all, "wizards" or "witch-es." The user of the white is not so designated. He or she does not deny the use; it is open and without any sense of criminality in the eyes of the community, however much he or she may endeavor to suppress the fact from the knowledge of church officers. But a prac-titioner of the black art denies it and carries on his practice secretly.

The above distinction is observed by travellers in other parts of Africa, as will be seen by the following quotations, which give also an interesting exposition of the ceremonies and practices of the black art in different regions:

"Among the Matabele of South Africa," says Declè, "it is well understood that there were two kinds of witchcraft. One was prac-tised by the witch-doctors and the king, such as, for instance, the 'making of medicine' to bring on rain, or the ceremonies carried out by the witch-doctors to appease the spirits of ancestors.[47] The other witchcraft was supposed to consist of evil practices pursued to cause sickness or death.

"According to native ideas, all over Africa, such a thing as death from natural causes does not exist. Whatever ill befalls a man or a family, it is always the result of witchcraft, and in every case the witch-doctors are consulted to find out who has been guilty

_____

47   This would be what I have denominated the "white art."—R, H. N.

of it. In some instances the witch-doctors declare that the evil has been caused by the angry spirits of ancestors; in which case they have to be propitiated through the medium of the witch-doctors. In other cases they point out some one or several persons as having caused the injury by making charms; and whoever is so accused by the witchcraft doctor is immediately put to death, his wife and the— whole of his family sharing his fate. To bewitch any one, according to Matabele belief, it is sufficient to spread medicine on his path or in his hut. There are also numerous other modes of working charms; for instance, if you want to cause an enemy to die, you make a clay figure that is supposed to represent him. With a needle you pierce the figure, and your enemy, the first time he comes in contact with a foe, will be speared.

"The liver and entrails of a crocodile are supposed to be most powerful charms, and whoever becomes possessed of them can cause the death of any man he pleases. For that reason, killing a crocodile is a very heinous crime. [48]

"While I was in Matabele-land, a crocodile was one day found speared on the bank of a river. The witch-doctors were consulted in order to find out who had been guilty of the deed; and six people were denounced as the offenders and put to death with their families.

"Of witch-doctors there are two kinds.[49] The first deliver oracles by bone-throwing. They have three bones carved with different signs; these they throw up, and according to the position they

---

48 In that part of Africa.—R. H. N.

49 Really, only a difference in admistration.—R. H. N.

assume when falling, and the side on which they fall, they make the prediction. The other kind deliver their oracles in a slow and very shrill chant. Both are supposed to be on speaking terms with spirits. They are in constant request, but are usually poorly paid. Their influence, however, is tremendous; and in Lo-Bengula's time their power was as great as, if not greater than, the king's. Lo-Bengula always kept two or three of them near him. Chief among their works was that of rain-making; this was done with a charm made from the blood and gall of a black ox. No witch-doctors, however, could make rain except by the orders of the king. It was a risky trade; for they were put to death if they failed in their endeavors to produce rain. Dreams are considered of deep significance by the witch-doctors. Madmen are supposed to be possessed of a spirit, and were formerly under the protection of the king.

"One of the most remarkable ceremonies that used to be performed by the witch-doctors was that of l smelling out the witches (wizards?). On the first moon of the second month of the year all the various regiments gathered at Buluwayo, and held a bip, dance in which the king took part; usually, from 12,000 to 15,000 warriors assembled for this ceremony. After the dance the smelling of witches began. The various regiments being formed in crescent shape, the king took his stand in front surrounded by the doctors, usually women. Then began a slow song accompanied by a dance; they carried in their hand a small wand. Gradually the song and the dance became quicker; they seemed to be possessed. They rushed madly about, passing in front of the soldiers, pretending to smell them. All of a sudden they stopped in front of a man, and touching him with their wands, began howling like maniacs; the man was immediately removed and put to death. In this way hundreds of people were killed every year during the big dance. No one, however high his position, was protected against the mandate of the witch-doctors, usually the tools of the king, who found in this a way of getting rid of his enemies, or of doing away with those in high station whose loyalty he had reason to doubt. Other crimes are few except the ever-present witchcraft. To bewitch an enemy on the Tanganika plateau, you scatter a red powder round his hut and a white one near his door; this never fails to kill.

"Ordeal by muavi is, of course, flourishing; with the enlightened modification. that, if the accused does not die, he can recover damages from the accuser. In the Mambwe district the muavi is made of a poisonous bean." [50]

The same "medicines," the same dances, the same enchantments used in the black art, are used in the professedly innocent white art; the chief difference being in the mission that the utilized spirit is entrusted to perform.

Similarity in witchcraft practices is one of the several grounds held by ethnologists, as proving identity in origin of the African Negro and the Australian black. To quote from Dr. Carl Lumholtz's book, "Among Cannibals": "In the various [Australian] tribes are so-called wizards, who pretend to communicate with the spirits of the dead and get information from them. They are able to produce sickness or death whenever they please, and they can produce or

---

50   Declè, Three Years in Savage Africa, pp. 152, 154, 294.

stop rain and many other things. Hence these wizards are greatly feared. Attention is called to the influence of this fear of witchcraft upon the character and customs of the natives. It makes them blood-thirsty, and at the same time darkens and embitters their existence. An Australian native is unable to conceive death as natural except as the result of an accident or of old age; while diseases and plagues are always ascribed to witchcraft and to hostile blacks. In order to practise his arts against any black man, the wizard must be in possession of some article that has belonged to him. On Herbert River the natives need only to know the name of the person in question, and for this reason they rarely use their proper names in addressing or speaking of each other, but simply their class names. I once met a black man who told me that he personally had been the victim of strange wizards, and that ever since that time he had been a sufferer from headache. One afternoon many years ago, two wizards had captured and bound him; they had taken out his entrails and put in grass instead, and had let him lie in this condition till sunrise. Then he suddenly recovered his senses and became tolerably well; a result for which he was indebted to a wizard of his own tribe, who thus proved himself more powerful than the two strangers. The blacks call an operation of this kind kobi, and a man who is able to perform it, as a matter of course, is very much respected and feared."

"The Ovimbundu race," says Arnot, "of Bibe and the country to the west are most enterprising traders and imitators of the Portuguese. They seem, however, to retain tenaciously their superstitions and fetich worship.

"In Chikula's yard there is a small roughly cut image, which I believe represents the spirit of a forefather of his. One day a man and woman came in and rushed up to this image, dancing, howling, and foaming at the mouth, apparently mad. A group gathered round, and declared that the spirit of Chikula's forefather had taken possession of this man and woman, and was about to speak through them. At last the 'demon' began to grunt and groan out to poor Chikula, who was down on his knees, that he must hold a hunt, the proceeds of which must be given to the people of the town; must kill an ox, provide so many pots of beer, and proclaim a great feast and dance. Furthermore, all this was to be done quickly. The poor old man was thoroughly taken in, and in two days' time the hunt was organized.

"Thus I find, as among the Barotse, that divining and prophesying, with other religious and superstitious means, are resorted to in order to secure private ends and to offer sacrifice to the one common god, the belly.

"At another time a man came to Senhor Porto's to buy an ox. He said that some time ago he had killed a relation by witchcraft to possess himself of some of his riches, and that now he must sacrifice an ox. to the dead man's spirit, which was troubling him. This killing by witchcraft is a thing most sincerely believed in; and on hearing this man's coldblooded confession of what was at least the intent of his heart, it made me understand why the Barotse put such demons into the fire.

"Among the Ovimbundu, old and renowned witches (wizards?) are thrown into some river, though almost every man will confess that he practises witchcraft to avenge himself of wrong done and to punish his enemies. One common process is to boil together certain fruits and roots, with which the wizard daubs his body, in order to enlist the aid of the demons; and the decoction is then thrown in the direction of the victim, or laid in his path, that he may be brought under the bewitching spell."[51]

We quote again from Dr. J. L. Wilson, "Western Africa": Witchcraft, and the use of fetiches as a means of protection against it, is carried to a greater extent here [Southern Guinea] than in Northern Guinea, owing, no doubt, to the greater imaginativeness of the people. The marvels performed by those who are supposed to possess this mysterious art transcend all the bounds of credulity. A man can turn himself into a leopard, and destroy the property and lives of his fellow-men. He can cause the clouds to pour out torrents of rain, or hold back at his pleasure.

"A different article is used here for the detection of witchcraft from that used in Northern Guinea. The root of a small shrub, called akazya, is employed, and is more powerful than that used in the other section of the country. A person is seldom required to drink more than half a pint of the decoction. If it acts freely as a diuretic, it is a mark of innocence; but if as a narcotic, and produces dizziness and vertigo, it is a sure sign of guilt. Small sticks are laid down at the distance of eighteen inches or two feet apart, and the suspected person, after he has swallowed the draught, is required to walk over them. If he has no vertigo, he steps over them easily and naturally; but, on the other hand, if his brain is affected, he imagines they rise up before him like great logs, and in his awkward effort to step

---

51   Arnot, Garenganze, p. 115.

over them, is apt to reel and fall to the ground. In some cases this draught is taken by proxy; and if a man is found guilty, he is either put to death or heavily fined, and banished from the country. In many cases post-mortem examinations are made with the view of finding the actual witch; I have known the mouth of the aorta to be cut out of a corpse, and shown as unanswerable proof that the man had the actual power of witchcraft.[52] No one expects to resent the death of a relative under such circumstances. He is supposed to have been killed by his awkward management of an instrument that was intended for the destruction of others; and it is rather a cause of congratulation to the living that he is caught in a snare of his own," and that his own "witch" has killed him.[53]

Not every one who uses white art is able also to use the black. Any one believing in fetich can use white arts, and not subject himself to the charge of being a wizard. Those who desire to go beyond the arts of defence, and gratify their revenge or any other passion by killing or injuring some one else, have generally to purchase the agency of a doctor or some one skilled in the black art. Should the means thus employed be efficient in causing a death (or seemingly so, by the coincidence of their use and the death itself) and the facts become known, both the doctor and the man who employed him would probably be put to death. Yet, inconsistently, the very men who would execute them have themselves used, or will some day

---

52   And, similarly, I have known the fimbriated extremities of the fallopian tubes in a woman held up as a proof of her having been a witch. The ciliary movements of these fimbriæ were regarded as the efforts of her "familiar" at a process of eating. The decision was that she had been "eaten" to death by her own offended familiar.—R. H. N.

53   Wilson, Western Africa, p. 398.

use, these same black arts for the same murderous purpose, and the native doctors will continue in their risky business.

And yet, again, inconsistently, every man and woman in the community dreads such a charge, and looks askance on those who are suspected of belonging to the Witchcraft Company. For there is such a society, not distinctly organized. It has meetings at which they plot for the causing of sickness or even the taking of life. These meetings are secret; preferably in a forest, or at least distant from a village. The hour is near midnight. An imitation of the hoot of an owl, which is their sacred bird, is their signal call. They profess to leave their corporeal body lying asleep in their huts, and claim that the part which joins in the meeting is their spirit-body, whose movements are not hindered by walls or other physical objects. They can pass with instant rapidity through the air, over the tree-tops. At their meetings they have visible, audible, and tangible communication with evil spirits. They partake of feasts; the article eaten being the "heart-life" of some human being, who, in consequence of this loss of his "heart," becomes sick, and will die, unless it be restored. The early cock-crowing is a warning for them to disperse; the advent of the morning star they fear, as it compels them to hasten back to their bodies. Should the sun rise upon them before they reach their corporeal "home," their plans would fail, and themselves would sicken. They dread cayenne pepper. Should its bruised leaves or pods have been rubbed over their body-home by any one during their absence, they would be unable to re-enter it, and would die or miserably waste away.

The attitude of all missionaries toward executions on a charge

of being a witch or a wizard has uniformly been distinctly in opposition to them. We characterize them as murder. The European
governments which have taken possession of Africa also put down
witchcraft, medicine-making, and execution of supposed witchcraft
murderers with a strong hand. The natives submit under pressure of
force, but unwillingly. Each man or woman is glad of the strong foreign power that protects himself or herself from being put to death
on a witchcraft charge; but they each complain that the government
does not execute, nor will allow them to execute, others against
whom they make the same charge. It is undeniably true that were
the European governments that have partitioned Africa to withdraw
to-day, the witch-doctors, with poison ordeal and fetich killing and
witchcraft execution, would promptly re-establish themselves and
soon would become rampant again. The Christian churches and communities already established would barely hold their own, and would
not have an influence extensive enough to restrain the forces of evil.

I quote from a recent issue of a Freetown, Sierra Leone,
newspaper, edited by a Negro, an article written by a Negro on this
subject: "The subject of 'witchcraft' has been agitating of late the
minds of this community, and much sense and more nonsense has
been heard from those who take upon themselves to elucidate the
matter. It is a very difficult and delicate question to tackle at all times,
especially when knowledge, which is always the foundation of elo-
quence, is absent. From the statement of Holy Scriptures we know
that there is such a thing as witchcraft, and the theory is confirmed
by the records of English history. It will be a most desirable thing if
any person guilty of witchcraft could be convicted by means that

would be convincing in the legal investigation of other crimes; it will save the community from many heart-burnings and mistakes.

"A writer in a local journal recently made the assertion that in any case of poisoning in the cities of Europe, steps are taken to trace the poison by eminent physicians and detectives employed to hunt up the accused, but in our opinion the cases are not analogous. In the case of suspected poisoning post-mortem examinations by competent authorities will disclose the fact whether the deceased died of poisoning; unfounded, and in some instances gratuitous, assertions are not without proofs allowed to cloud the life of individuals. A *prima facie* case once established, the suspect is pursued with the utmost vigor of the law.

"In this colony [Sierra Leone] most deaths are attributed to the influence of witches, and accusation of witchcraft is at once made against individuals without attempt at obtaining evidence.

"How can it be proved that there is a band of these wicked ones, so as to attach credence to the confession of a consciences-tricken member who implicates also a number of coadjutors? The problem is an intricate one, and requires thoughtful investigation."

The slaves exported from Africa to the British possessions in the West Indies brought with them some of the seeds of African plants, especially those they regarded as "medicinal," or they found among the fauna and flora of the tropical West Indies some of the same plants and animals held by them as sacred to fetich in their tropical Africa. The ceiba, or silk-cotton tree, at whose base I find in Africa so many votive offerings of fetich worship, they found flourishing on Jamaica. They had established on their plantations the fetich doctor, their dance, their charm, their lore, before they had learned English at all. And when the British missionaries came among them with school and church, while many of the converts were sincere, there were those of the doctor class who, like Simon Magus, entered into the church-fold for sake of whatever gain they could make by the white man's new influence, the white man's Holy Spirit! Outwardly everything was serene and Christian. Within was working an element of diabolism, fetichism, there known by the name of Obeah, under whose leaven some of the churches were wrecked. And the same diabolism, known as voodoo worship, in the Negro communities of the Southern United States has emasculated the spiritual life of many professed Christians.

It must be admitted, as to this whole matter of witchcraft belief and witchcraft murder and witchcraft execution, however wrong the Negro belief, his sense of justice is aggrieved by the attitude of the foreign missionary and the foreign government. Something should be allowed to that sense of justice. Both missionary and government err sometimes, in their judgment of individual or tribal crime and in their punishment of it, by arbitrarily following only civilized law and the civilized point of view; ignoring or not giving proper weight, in the make up of their judgment, to the degree to which the fetich enters as a factor in native motives and acts, and the power with which it influences native thought.

In Matabele-land, South Africa, after the defeat and death of the king Lo-Bengula, and the occupation of his country by Great Britain, there was an outbreak, the cause of which was not fully appreciated until it was traced to the witchdoctors, who seized the occasion of the ravages of the rinderpest, which was at that time devastating the cattle of South Africa, to make use of their power." Naturally they must have felt, more than anybody else, the occupation of Matabeleland by the whites, as it meant the disappearance of their former power. When the rinderpest broke out, they probably persuaded the natives, who understood nothing about an epidemic and attributed whatever ill befalls them to witchcraft, that it was the spirit of Lo-Bengula, which was dissatisfied with them and which caused their cattle to die. To appease Lo-Bengula's spirit, it was necessary to fight the whites. They, the witch-doctors, would make medicine to turn the bullets of the white men into water, so that the Matabele could not be hurt by them."[54]

Similarly Great Britain with difficulty has suppressed several risings of the Ashantees, and the late so-called "HutTax" rebellion in Sierra Leone. The actual force of the natives, in organization, arms, and skill, was almost ridiculous in its inferiority as compared with the thoroughly armed and disciplined troops of the British Empire; but the final result, though never doubtful, was attained with much loss of men and funds. The fetich doctor and fetich belief were a *vis a tergo* with the native horde. Its value as a factor in the contest had not been reckoned on by the foreigner. Whatever motives influenced the native in the contest, in patriotism, cupidity, revenge, bravery, they were minor. The grand influence that nerved his arm and made him perfectly fearless in his assaults against weapons of precision, was his deep conviction, more complete than Christian faith, that he

---

54   Brown, On the South African Frontier.

would win. Had not the fetich doctor told him so? Though there had been some apparent failures, in his belief they were only apparent. The real failure was in his own self, his not having followed minutely all the fetich directions. Those directions followed rightly in the next battle, he could not fail.

The faith of a Christian does not assure him, in any emergency of life, that he will be successful in his plan; it only certifies him that, whatever be the result, success or failure, of any single act or series of acts in life's drama, his own will must be subordinated to God's, who, if not granting his specific wish to-day, will overrule everything in the final denouement for his best spiritual good.

Similarly the heathen fetich, mixed with the fatalism of Islam, is an explanation of the splendid recklessness with which the followers of the Mahdi flung themselves against the sabres and maxims of General Kitchener's army at Omdurman.

Faith in fetich is a power as long as its devotee believes in its infallibility. When that is gone, his flight or conquest is instant. Fetich power therefore cannot be invariably relied upon as a motive to action. It may sometimes be magnificent. Only Christian faith or civilized discipline can be sublime, as compared with it.

But a fetich devotee who has lost his faith in his fetich could never have stood with Christian martyrs who knew perfectly well that within an hour they would be torn to pieces in the arena. Their sublime faith looked beyond that arena to the eternal promise. A fetich soldier who has lost his faith in his fetich could never have gone with those who stood head erect before certain death in the Alamo fort or who rode in the charge at Balaklava. Their elevated motives of patriotism, implicit soldierly obedience to order, and the sweet scent of human glory made them discount the value of their own blood. These were motives not only powerful in force, but great in character. The Negro's fetich faith is powerful, but never great.

Something cognate to this in the comparison of the power and the greatness of a motive will explain the persistent fatuity of the Boer in protracting his contest with Great Britain. From the very first, whatever the world may have thought of essential right or justice in the case, the world knew that England would win. The Boer would have been wise to have accepted defeat earlier and made terms with a conqueror who generally has been magnanimous and rarely cruel, rather than invite, by guerilla warfare, measures severer, harsher, and possibly exterminative. The Boer is a Christian, but his faith was of the Mosaic kind that expected the God of battles to interfere visibly in his behalf. The president of the republic had preached that he would do so. The Boer looked on the president as a prophet, and believed him. But his faith was an unreasonable one; it was fatuous. His bravery, patriotism, marksmanship, and endurance could not avail. These all tell well for a martyrdom, if martyrdom were desirable or necessary, but they did not tell well for assertion of success.

France, overcome by Germany, still was brave and patriotic; but she was wise in accepting the inevitable,—wiser than the Negro or the Boer. France believed in God; so did Germany. But the faith of neither was of the fetich kind. Nevertheless, the fetich faith is magnificent, even if it be fatuous.

For the apparently cruel side of the black art, viz., the killing of those guilty of witchcraft, there is some allowance to be made.

To the believer in fetich the killing is a judicial act. He does not call it a murder, but an execution; and he tries to justify it by an argument which even the missionary has to admit is correct if the Negro's premises in the argument are admitted. As we do not admit both of them, his argument falls. But it is difficult to show him that his second premise is wrong, and be is unconvinced.

I have several times been thoroughly worsted in my discussion with native chiefs on this matter of witchcraft executions. In the early years of my missionary life, while resident on Corisco Island, I followed the practice of my predecessor, the Rev. J. L. Mackey, in the effort to prevent such executions, which were then (about 1863) common. We directed the native Christians to notify us of any death, and we would at once go to the village and endeavor to forestall the almost invariable witchcraft investigation. The headman, Komben-yamango, of an adjacent village, was a large, strong, influential, cruel man. There was so little about him to command my respect that I had shown him but slight deference. Having thus his *amour propre* wounded, he was unfortunately not on very good terms with me. His aged mother had been failing in health for a long time, and finally had died. Her position, as mother of a chief, had given her much respect in native eyes. The concourse of mourners gathered from a distance was large. Feeling for her death was deep; threats of vengeance for her taking off were loud. I was soon informed that one of her female slaves bad been seized under pure suspicion because of her proximity as the dead woman's servant. In her case as a means of finding whether or not she was guilty, there had been no ordeal test of drinking the inbundu poison. (On the Upper Guinea Coast it is sassa-wood; at Calabar, the Calabar bean; at the equator, the akazya leaf.) Under torture, being beaten and lacerated by thorn bushes, she had confessed herself guilty, was in chains, and was soon to be executed.

On such occasions, on arriving at the village, there was often an effort on the part of the chief to deceive the missionary. The chief would either assert that he had had no intention of making a witchcraft investigation, or would consent now, in deference to his white friend the missionary, to abandon his intention, and would forbid any execution. But it would be revealed to us afterwards that at that very moment a victim was in chains in that very village, and had subsequently been secretly put to death.

This day Kombenyamango, though receiving me with sufficient respect, was nonchalant. He did not lie. He promptly, in answer to my question, said, "Yes, I have a prisoner here, and I intend to put her to death." "Why?" "Because she has killed my mother!" I told him I did not believe his mother had died by unnatural means, and I preached to him the usual sermon on the Sixth Commandment. I was at that time young in my knowledge of native thought and fetich belief. I can see now that to every sentence of my address he could have said Amen, in his believing, as he did, that his mother had been murdered, and that this slave woman had broken the Sixth Commandment. But, after listening awhile, he became impatient, and said, "Look here! in your country, when a person kills your mother, don't you tie a rope about his neck and hang him up, and don't you say you are doing right in so doing?" "Yes." "Well, that's just what I am going to do to this woman, and I am right." "Yes, you would be right if she has killed your mother; but she has not. The bewitching with which you charge her is foolish." (As to the folly, I know now that that was a matter of opinion between him and me; and be had reason for his opinion.) He replied, "But she has confessed that she is guilty." "Quite possibly; but still a lie on her part, for she would say anything to obtain temporary relief from your torture." "But ask her yourself." "No use to do so in your presence; she is afraid of you, and she will not dare to speak to me or contradict you." "Well, then, I will bring her; and you take her off there among the plantains by yourself, and see what she will say." This sounded fair; but even so, I had my doubts, for she did not know me. Perhaps they would lie to her, and tell her I was confederate with her master, and would order her not to alter her confession. And she, in her dazed condition, was really not responsible for anything she might say. She was brought from a hut. She was in chains, and yet with her limbs free to walk. There was no possibility of her escape; nor of my being able to abduct her, had I been unwise enough to attempt it. I led her out of Kombenyamango's hearing, but still plainly in his sight, and kindly said to her, "Did you do this?" To my amazement, she said, "Yes." "But what did you do? If you say you killed her, how did you do it?" She described minutely how, being in attendance on the old woman, she was often vexed at her petulance, and had been beaten by her for small neglects; bow, in her anger, she had desired her mistress's death; had collected crumbs of her food, strands of her hair, and shreds of her clothing; how she had mixed these with other substances, and had sung enchantments with drum and dance, aided by others; had tied all these things together on a stick which she had secretly buried at the threshold of the old woman's door, desiring and expecting that she should thereby die. By an unfortunate coincidence the old woman had died a month or two later; and the slave believed that what she had done had been efficient to accomplish the taking of life.

Baffled, I returned to Kombenyamango, and admitted her confession. But I told him that, even so, both be and she were under a delusion; that what she had done had no efficiency for accomplishing a murder; that it was impossible. (Here again was a difference of opinion as to possibility; he believed his senses. In his life he had seen witchcraft mysteries; I had not.)

It was useless, even inconsistent, to plead for mercy; I retired heartsick. I was morally certain the old woman had died a natural death. Yet this poor slave woman had had murder in her heart, and had tried to make her murderous thought effective. She was, before God, guilty. She had confessed herself, before man's bar, guilty. (Well for the thousands of us who know ourselves guilty in thought, that we are not to be held by our fellow-sinners as guilty in act!) I knew that she was really innocent, but I could not prove it. She was taken to sea in a boat, and decapitated; her remains were thrown into the sea.

On another occasion, a year later, also on Corisco Island, a certain heathen headman of a village, Osongo, had died. A female slave who was suspected had fled. Her flight was regarded as proof positive of her guilt. Our mission premises had always been accorded by the native chiefs the right of sanctuary. A refugee for any offence could not be seized on our premises till we saw just reason for "extraditing" him. This slave woman had hidden herself in our jungle-thicket adjoining a forest; just where I did not know. Two freemen-my personal employees, good Christians—knew, and secretly at night with my connivance fed her. My school-girls also learned of it. Such a secret is difficult to hide. One of the girls,—a niece of Osongo, revealed it to another of my workmen, Matoku, a slave also of Osongo, and a professed Christian. He, with the traitorous cowardice that makes many slaves informers on each other as a means of enhancing their own safety with their masters, revealed it to Ajai, Osongo's brother. Ajai, with a retinue of servants, came to visit me in my study. He, with a wily talk about the sadness of his brother's death, detained me, while the servants broke into the mission premises, and, led by Matoku, captured the woman, faint with her days and nights of exposure. I discharged Matoku from my employ, and dismissed the niece from school. But the heathen regarded these punishments as slight; they had obtained their object. My attempts to plead with Ajai for the woman's life were met with undisguised admission of his fixed purpose to kill her. With a family as prominent on the island and as wedded to heathenism as was Osongo's, and in face of the current that set against the woman, the influences I was able to employ, and which had at other times resulted in saving some lives accused of witchcraft, proved ineffectual. I was privately told tbat she was to be put into a boat and carried out to sea so as to prevent any interference I might possibly attempt. With a spy-glass I saw a native boat shoot rapidly out from beyond a point of land half a mile distant. The rowers rested on their oars when they reached deep water. She was seized; her head held over the gunwale, her throat cut, and her lifeless body cast into the sea.

She had a son, a stout lad. Ajai, fearing that he might live to avenge his mother's death, had ordered him also to be killed as an accomplice with her in the bewitching of Osongo. The tragedy that was being enacted on the beach behind the point of land from which had issued the boat I did not see; but I was told that the lad was seized, his hands and limbs tied to a stake, where be was slowly burned to death. A crowd sat on the beach jeering him, and amused themselves by tying little packets of gunpowder to different parts of his body, enjoying the sight of his struggles as the packets exploded in succession.

Undeniably there is much jugglery and conscious deception on the part of the magic doctors. How much they really believe in what they say or do no one has been able to discover; they assert that they are under supernatural influences, and have power given from supernatural sources. Rarely are any of this priest class converted to Christianity. A few have professed conversion, and have made a general acknowledgment of sinfulness; but they did not like to talk, about their divinations; they called them "foolishness." But evidently there was something about those divinations of which they seemed ashamed and which they wished to forget. Only one have I met who would talk on the subject, and she believed she had been under satanic influence,—not simply as all wicked thoughts are satanic in their ebaracter and inspiration, but that she bad actually been under satanic possession, and was given by the devil more than mere human power. Certainly, if there is in civilized jugglery, fortune-telling, clairvoyance, divining, spirit-rappings, theosophy, *et id omne genus*, nothing more than sleight of hand, alert observation of facial expression, and mind-reading, the African conjurer almost equals the civilized professional. The native magician does and tells some wonderful things. In one of my congregations an educated woman, a widow, who had only one child, a son grown to young manhood, had subsequently lived in succession with four other men, three of whom were white, who had either died or deserted her; and she supposed herself past child-bearing. She contracted a secret marriage with a white gentleman, but of it positively nothing was known or even suspected by any one. She confessed to me that one day, being a visitor in a distant place where she was not known, she, out of mere curiosity, hired a magician to divine her future. He looked into his magic mirror, and, among many other things which be could shrewdly have guessed in a quick study of her character as revealed in her looks, manner, and language, surprised her by describing a white man (whom he had never seen) who, he asserted, was deeply attached to her, and by whom she would become the mother of two children. She suppressed her surprise, and told him that though married four times, she had borne no child in eighteen years. He nevertheless asserted, "I see them in your womb."

Within five years from that time she did have two untimely births by her white husband. She told me in her confession that he knew nothing of them, they being miscarriages. She had suppressed from him the fact of her pregnancy. When subsequently she united with the church, she made these revelations only to me as her pastor, to save herself from public rebuke.

At another time a woman in Gabun became very anxious about

a brother of hers who was trading on the Ogowe River, at a place at least three hundred miles distant; no news had come of him. Evil news always flies fast and is always spread publicly. She went to a magician. Divining, he said, "Your brother is dead." "But where? What? When did be die?" "Only recently. I see his body lying bleeding." And he described the wounds, the locality on the river, the time, and other details of a country where he had never been. Two months later news did come, and it agreed in time, place, and circumstances with the divination.

Such things occur in civilized lands. They are accounted for without any reference to, or belief in, demoniac or even supernatural causes or influences. We call such recondite knowledge telepathy, and leave it for psychologists to study its character and application. It has no religious significance or use. The most devout Christian may believe in it or be subject to its operation. Other cases of telepathy in Africa I have been told of, that had no fetich nor any divination of magic doctor connected with them; but the natives attributed them to some unknown spirit-influence.

An outcome of the witchcraft of fetichism, demonolatry, though not necessarily identical with demoniacal possession, intimately associates itself with it as a part of its development. For the Negro belief in such possession there is good basis. The Bible recognizes the possibility of human beings in their free agency making pacts with the devil, in virtue of which he was allowed, under divine administration, to share with them some of his supernatural power as prince of the power of darkness, and god of this world. Such pacts were condemned by Jehovah as unholy. Those who made them were called witches and wizards; such transgressors were directed to be destroyed. "Thou shalt not suffer a witch to live" [55] (a command that does not necessarily prove that the professed diabolical compact was always a real one. The mere professing to have satanic companionship and aid was an offence heinous to Jehovah's theocratic government of his people.)

But the witch of Endor[56] certainly was a reality; she did "bring up" real departed spirits; perhaps only on that one occasion, and then only by direct divine and not satanic power and will, and for a divine object. She herself seems to have been surprised[57] at the real success of divinations which formerly may have been, in her hands, only deceptions.

My native heathen chiefs have good precedent for their witchcraft executions. New England history cannot wipe out the fact of the Salem witchcraft trials.

Demoniac possessions in supposed lunatics are possible; they were actual and numerous in Palestine during the ministry of Christ. Satan was "loosed" with unusual power, that the Son of God in his contest with him could give to the world convincing proof of his divine origin and authority, even the devils being subject to him. If demoniacal possessions are possible during a term of years, they are equally possible for a few hours; they never were nor are made by Satan for a good purpose. God, in the days of Christ, for the

---

55   Ex. xxii. 18.

56   1 Sam. xxvii. 11-15.

57   Verse 12.

special purpose of the time, overruled them for the defence of his kingdom; since then, in the hearts of evil men, their advent is only for evil and by evil.

If in Christian lands the encbantments of the hoodoo are only jugglery and nothing else, it may be that Satan's power is limited under the broad light of Christianity. But in heathen lands, where for ages Satan's power has not only been accepted but also sought, I am disposed to believe that some apparent cases of lunacy are real possessions by Satan, in which cases both the physical disease and its associated mental aberration are the effect of the possession. In lunacy pure and simple the mental aberration is the effect of disease alone,—some mental or physical injury.

The possibility of a permanent possession by Satan being admitted, it is easily possible that the fetich doctors or priestesses may be temporarily entered into by satanic power, and that some wonderful things they do and say while endowed with that power are used by the devil to blind men's minds against the truth.

It may be, therefore, that the missionary in his contest with heathenism has literally to fight with the devil, with principalities and powers in high places, and needs weapons more subtle than Martin Luther's inkstand. If so, he puts his preaching and his work at a disadvantage in deriding the witchcraft side of fetichism, revealed in black art, as simply "folly," and reprehensible only as a superstition. It is more than that; it is wickedness,—spiritual wickedness in high places. While it is true that it has much that is mere jugglery and charlatanism, it is quite possible that it may have something that is diabolically real.

But all this does not fully justify my Negro chief in putting to death his slave, who may or may not have been more than self-deceived and deceiving, who may or may not have had a temporary satanic possession, who may or may not have been guilty of murder before the bar of God or man. That chief and all his assistants in the execution, and all other users of the black art, bad, in the beginning of their fetich life, been users of only the defensive white art; had inevitably grown into the use of the offensive black art, and in all probability at some time or other had used divinations, with and by the aid of witchcraft doctors, for the destruction of others in a similar way and under the same motives as those admitted by my poor slave woman.

My chief's argument syllogized would be: Whoever kills should be killed; this woman has killed; therefore she should be killed. His first premise stands; but neither be nor any of his people had a right to use it; consistently, be and all his should themselves have been at the same bar with the woman; they either had done, or would some day be doing, just what they were charging her with doing. His second premise may or may not have been true; certainly, the only one who could know whether it was true was the accused herself, and she may have been self-deceived; and her confession should have no standing in court, having been forced under torture. I could not therefore admit his conclusion; and I think that, had the Master stood visibly on Corisco Island that day, He would have said, "He that is without sin among you, let him first cast a stone at her."

CHAPTER X
Fetichism – A Government

Egbo, Ukuku, Yasi, and other Societies — Their Power either to protect or
oppress — Contest with Ukuku at Benita, and with Yasi on the Ogowe

IN CIVILIZATION, under governments other than autocratic, law
being made and executed, at least professedly, with the consent of
the governed, all enactments find not only their justification, but
also the possibility of their enforcement, in their support by public
opinion. It is the general consensus as to the need of an enactment
regarding certain conditions affecting the lives or happiness or rights
of the majority, that crystallizes opinions into a form of words, and
gives authority for the enforcement of the decisions expressed by
those words.

This is also partly true even under governments more or less
despotic, where the will of the ruler, not of the ruled, is made the
basis of law. Few despots are so utterly tyrannical as deliberately
to arouse opposition on the Part of their subjects. Even a Nero, who
would refuse a petition if it happened to run counter to his whim
or caprice of the day, would grant that same petition if it happened
to coincide with his own whim of another day. Even he thought it
desirable to pander to the public taste for the buteberies of the am-
phitbeatre, not simply because be himself enjoyed them. Though be

could initiate no measure for the real good of Rome, he recognized the necessity of responding to the cry, "panem et circenses."

In all governments fear is recognized as one of the grounds for the enforcement of law. In even the freest nations and under the highest form of civilization the public opinion that administers law makes its demand partly in the interest of essential right, partly with the instinct of self-preservation against the forces of evil, and partly for the punishment of wrong. Punishment in itself is not reformatory; it is retributive; it is deterrent; it plays upon fear.

In the native African tribal forms of government, while it would not be true to say that there is no justice in the customs they recognize, it is true that the only sentiment appealed to, in the enforcement and even in the enactment of supposed needed measures, is that of fear. Their religion being one of fear, it is therefore appealed to to lend its sanction and aid.

"Fetiches are set up to punish offenders in certain cases where there is an intention to make a law specially binding; this refers more particularly to crimes which cannot always be detected. A fetich is inaugurated, for example, to detect and punish certain kinds of theft; persons who are cognizant to such crimes, and who do not give information, are also liable to be punished by the fetich. The fetich is supposed to be able not only to detect all such transgressions, but has power, likewise, to punish the transgressor. How it exercises this knowledge, or by what means it brings sickness and death upon the offender, cannot, of course, be explained; but, as it is believed in, it is the most effectual restraint that can possibly be imposed upon evil-disposed persons."[58]

Among the Negro tribes of the Bight of Benin and the Bantu of the region of Corisco Island and of the Ogowe River, in what is now the Kongo-Frangais, there was a power known variously as Egbo, Ukuku, and Yasi, which tribes, native chiefs, and headmen of villages invoked as a court of last appeal, for the passage of needed laws, or the adjudication of some quarrel which an ordinary family or village council was unable to settle.

In those councils an offender could be proved guilty of a debt or theft, or other trespass, and when it was no longer possible for him by audacity or mendacity to persist in his assertion of innocence, he would yield to the decision of the great majority against him. But there was no central government to enforce that decision or exact from him restitution. The only authority the native chiefs possessed was based on respect due to age, parental position, or strength of personal character. If an offender chose to disregard all these considerations, an appeal was then made to his superstitious fear.

Egbo, Ukuku, Yasi, was a secret society composed only of men, boys being initiated into it about the age of puberty. Members were bound by a terrible oath and under pain of death to obey any law or command issued by the spirit under which the society professed to be organized. The actual, audible utterance of the command was by the voice of one of the members of the society chosen as priest for that purpose. This man, secreted in the forest, in a clump of bushes on the outskirts of the village, or in one of the rooms of the Coun-

---

58   Wilson, Western Africa, p. 275.

cil House, disguised his voice, speaking only gutturally. The whole proceeding was an immense fiction; they believed in spirits and in the power of fetich charms, and they made such charms part of the society's ceremonies; but, as to the decisions, all the members knew that the decision in any case was their own, not a spirit's. They knew that the voice speaking was that of their delegate, not of a spirit. Yet for any one of them, or for any woman, girl, or uninitiated boy, to assert as much would have been death. And those men who would not have submitted to the same decision if arrived at in open council of themselves as men, and known before the whole village to be speaking only as men, would instantly submit when once the case had been taken to Ukuku's Court. They carried out that fiction all their lives. Let a man order his wives and other slaves to clear the overgrown village paths, they might hesitate to obey by inventing some excuse that they were too much occupied with other work, or that they would do it only when other people who also used the same path should assist; or if under the sting of a kasa-nguvu (lash of hippopotamus hide or manatus skin) they started to do the work, they might do it only partly or very unsatisfactorily. But let the man call in the other men of the village and summon a meeting of the society, the recalcitrants would submit instantly, and in terror of Ukuku's voice; much as they might possibly have suspected it was a human voice, they would not dare whisper the suspicion. They helped to carry on a gigantic lie. They taught their little children, both girls and boys, that the voice belonged to a spirit which ate people who disobeyed him. When the society walked in procession to or from their appointed rendezvous, they were preceded by runners who, with a well-recognized cry and with kasa-nguvu in hand, warned all on the path of the coming of the spirit. Women and children hastened to get out of the way; or, if unable to hide in time, they averted their faces. The penalty when a woman even saw the procession was a severe beating; that, however, might be commuted to a fine.

About thirty-nine years ago, on the island of Corisco, the then headquarters of the Corisco Mission, there was a longstanding feud between the Benga tribe, inhabiting that island, and the Kombe tribe, dwelling at the mouth of the Eyo River, of the Benita country, fifty miles to the north. Benita was also a part of the mission field. The quarrel between the two tribes greatly obstructed our mission work. Missionaries were entirely safe in travel between the two places, respect being given them as foreigners, and their presence in a boat protected their crews; but it was often difficult to obtain a crew willing to go on the journey without the presence of a white man. The difficulties caused by the feud fell heavily also on the Benga people themselves. The island itself had no products for trade; ivory, dye-woods, and rubber came from the Benita mainland. Many Kombe women had married Benga men, and needed frequently to revisit their own country. Finally, to end the feud, it was agreed that the Kombe Ukuku Society, whose power was held in even greater fear than that of Benga, should come to Corisco and settle the affair.

It was a day of terror at the Girls' Boarding School, of which I was then superintendent. As the long, blood curdling yell of the forerunners on the public path, that ran only one hundred feet from the school dwelling, announced the approach of the procession, the girls fled, affrighted, to the darkness of the attic of the house.

After the procession had passed, they ran away secretly in byways to their own villages, feeling safer in the darkness of their mother's buts than in the mission-house; for it had been reported that Ukuku, besides settling the tribal feud, intended to attack the mission work that bad been successfully making converts among the Kombe, because any native who became a Christian immediately withdrew from membership in the society. It had therefore begun to feel a little anxious about its safety. I stood at my door and saw the procession pass; they saw me, but, because of my sex, they did not show any displeasure. They were painted with white and other colored chalks that gave a horrible expression to their faces; their look was defiant, and a hoarse, muttered cbant had, even on myself, a depressing effect. I could well imagine that to a superstitious native mind the *tout ensemble* would be terrifying.

The procession on its way chose to pass over a road that bad by use become somewhat public, but which was owned by the mission; it was only fifty feet past the front door of the house of the senior missionary, the Rev. James L. Mackey. Mrs. Mackey was standing at the door of the house; not being a Benga woman, she saw no reason why she should retire before Ukuku, and stood her ground. Ukuku went to their rendezvous in a rage, and the Kombe portion demanded the life of the woman who not only had not hidden her face in their presence, but had dared persistently to look upon them. This demand was modified by the Benga portion to a fine; its alternative, whipping, not even they daring to suggest for a white lady. This demand for a fine was actually brought to Mr. Mackey, who gave a dignified reply, pointing out that, as foreigners, white people were not subject to Ukuku; that Ukuku had trespassed on mission private property, and was itself responsible for being seen; that, as a Christian, in no case could he recognize the authority of Ukuku to order or fine him. In reply, Ukuku made the point that it was the government of the.country, and that even foreigners were bound to obey law. (Corisco actually belonged to Spain, but Spain in no way exercised any visible authority over it.)

They admitted their trespass on private property, but still demanded the fine. Mr. Mackey made no further reply; and of course, as a matter of conscience, refused to pay the fine. But it transpired afterwards that native friends, fearful lest matters should come to an ugly pass through his refusal, privately paid the fine themselves. The missionary, unaware of this, thought he had triumphed; really Ukuku bad, but not unqualifiedly, for it was a shock to its power that it should have been disputed at all, even by a white man.

About the same time a young slave man who was beginning to attend church with desire to become a Christian, was sitting in a village where was being held a meeting of the local Ukuku Society. The object of the meeting was to alarm and drive back to a more constant performance of fetich observances some of the villages on which heathenism was beginning to lose its hold. In the course of his oracular deliverances the Ukuku priest mentioned by name this young man. In his fresh zeal as a convert he made a protest; perhaps duty did not call for even that just at the time, but be even went beyond. As he was able to recognize the voice, though disguised, and knew who its owner was, be made a fatal mistake in saying, "You, such-a-one, I know who You are; you are only a man;

why are you troubling me?" He was promptly dragged to the seaside and decapitated.

While converts felt the propriety of abandoning their membership in the society and any participation in its ceremonies, the mission bad not required of them nor deemed it desirable that they— should make a revelation of its secrets. But it had occurred in the early history of the mission that one young man, Ibia, a freeman, member of a prominent family, had felt that in breaking awayfrom heathenism and becoming a Christian he should cast off the very semblance of any Connection with evil or even tacit endorsement of it. He knew the society was based on a great falsehood. As a lad be had believed Ukuku was a spirit; on his initiation he had found that this was not so; but loyal to his heathenism and to his oath, he had assented to the lie and had assisted in propagating it. He was known for the fearlessness of his convictions, and in his conversion be to a rare degree emerged from all superstitious beliefs. Few emerge so utterly as he. He therefore publicly began to reveal the ceremonies practised in the Ukuku meetings. At once his life was in danger. The two pioneer missionaries, Rev. Messrs. Mackey and Clemens, were men of exceptional strength of character and wise judgment, and had obtained a very strong hold on the respect and affection even of the heathen. Their influence, united with a small party of Ibia's own family and a few of the more . civilized chiefs, was able to save his life, he being guarded in the mission-house until the fierceness of heathen rage should abate. But, though his enemies presently ceased from open efforts to kill him by force, they proclaimed that they would kill him by means of the very witchcraft power he was despising. They said they would concoct fetich charms which would destroy the life of his child, and that they would curse the ground on which be trod so that it should sicken his feet. Not long afterwards his infant child did die, and one of his feet for more than a year had a painful ulcer. The coincidence was startling, and somewhat triumphant for the heathen; but infant mortality is large even among natives, and pbagedenic ulcers of the leg are very common. Ibia recognized his afflictions as a trial of his faith permitted by God. He came out of his fiery trial strong, and his life since has been that of a reformer, uncompromising with any evil, earning from his own people their ill-will by his scathing denunciations of anything that savored of superstition. He became the Rev. Ibia j'lkenge, member of Corisco Presbytery and pastor of the Corisco church; and Ukuka has long since ceased to exist as a power on the island.

Like all government intended for the benefit and protection of the governed, Ukuku, when it happened to throw its power on the side of right, was occasionally an apparent blessing. It could end tribal quarrels and proclaim and enforce peace where no individual chief or king would have been able to accomplish the same result. In this connection I quote from an editorial in a Sierra Leone newspaper:

"Much of the ideas of our western civilization as to native African institutions have been crude and uninformed, based on misconception and a predisposition to consider such institutions as an outcome of barbarism and savagery, to be treated with unmitigated contempt. But as the light of modern researches is reflected on the question by sympathetic students who have brought an unprejudiced mind to bear on the subject, if haply they might discover the hidden truths underlying the fabric which age, custom, and intellect have combined to construct into a national system, it is becoming more and more apparent to those who are interested in the material progress of Africa and the Africans and who are believers in the fact that native races have a civilization of their own capable of development and expansion on right lines, that the study of such questions should be intelligently and scientifically pursued, and with a purpose to help those concerned in their onward progress towards the attainment of moral, social, and intellectual liberty.

"That [some] native [governmental] institutions have wielded, and are wielding, a power for good in the several communities belonging to each distinctive tribe, is a fact that cannot be disputed or contested, in the past as well as in the present. The Aro of the Yorubas [in the Niger Delta], the Porroh of the Mendis [of Sierra Leone], and the Bondo of the mixed mass who inhabit Sherbro-land, have and exercise judicial functions exemplary and disciplinary in their effects. By their means law and order are observed to such an extent that many of the unrestrained and rowdy outbursts cowardly indulged in by so-called civilized communities and people are practically unknown.

"These institutions are connected with and govern the agencies that work in the sociology of all communities, such as the marriage laws; the relation of children to parents and of sex to sex; social laws; the position of eldership and the deference to be paid to age and worth; native herbs and medicines, and the duties of the native doctor to the other members of the community."

On one occasion in 1861 the Rev. William Clemens took a young

Benga man from Corisco Island to locate him as evangelist in the bounds of a mainland heathen tribe where there was some doubt as to the young man's safety. The village chief, though a heathen and entirely uninterested in the religious aspect of the case, was alive to the fact that the presence among his people of this young protégé of the white man would increase his tribal importance, and that his people themselves would derive a pecuniary benefit from even the small amount of money that would be spent on the evangelist's food. He therefore voluntarily offered to call an Ukuku meeting and have a law enacted that no one should machinate against the Benga's life by fetiches of any kind. Mr. Clemens declined the offer. If he accepted Ukuku's authority to defend him, he might some day be called on to submit to the same power as an authority to punish him. He wisely avoided an entangling alliance. He told the chief that he preferred to entrust his protégé to his care and to rely on his promise rather than on Ukuku's. This compliment put the chief on his mettle; the evangelist's protection became to him a case of *noblesse oblige*.

The power of this society was often used as a boycott to compel white traders as to the prices of their goods, using intimidation and violence after the manner of trades unions in civilized countries. This was true all along the West Coast of Africa wherever no white government had been established. It ceased at Libreville, in the Gabun country, after the establishment of a French colony in 1843, with a white governor, a squad of soldiers, police, and a gunboat. Also at other trade centres such as Libreville, Ukuku early lost its position, for the population was too heterogeneous and there were too many diverse interests. At the large trading-houses were gathered native clerks and a staff of servants as cooks, personal attendants, boatmen, etc., representing a score of tribes from distant parts of the coast. Whatever obedience they gave to similar societies in their tribes, they did not feel bound by the local one, to which they were strangers; and they were disposed, under a community of trade interests with their employers, to disregard the society of the local tribe, to many of whom they felt themselves socially superior.

But at Batanga, in what is now the Kamerun colony of the German Government, the Ukuku Society forty years ago carried itself with a high hand. Batanga was not then claimed by any European nation, and the number of white men were few. Its trade in ivory was one of the richest on the West Coast of Africa,—so rich that the Batariga people became. arrogant. Some of them disdained to make plantations of native food supply, and lived almost entirely on foreign imported provisions, taking in exchange for their abundant ivory barrels of beef, bags of rice, and boxes of ship's biscuit. It was a case of demand and supply. The native got what he wanted in goods, and the white man obtained the precious ivory. But in the competitions of trade, fluctuations in the market, and the growing demand of the natives for a higher price, there came days when some white man, seeing the margin of his per cent of gain becoming too narrow, refused the current price. Doubtless often the white men were arbitrary, not only in prices but also in other matters. Doubtless, also, the natives were often exorbitant in their demands.—When the differences became extreme, the native chiefs called in the aid of Ukuku. The phrase was to "put Ukuku" on the white man's house. The trader was boycotted. He stood as under a major excommunication. No one should buy from, or sell to him. No one should work for him. He was deserted by cook, steward, washerman, and all other personal attendants. Sentinels stood on guard to prevent food being brought to him, or even to prevent his lighting a fire in his own kitchen if he sbould'attempt to cook for himself.

The white trader generally succeeded in breaking down the interdict put upon him by these means, viz. (1) He had in his house a supply of canned goods and ship's biscuit, with which he would not starve. (2) His Negro mistress almost always remained faithfully with him, secretly assisting him, divulging to him the plans of her own people,—as in the history of Cortes and the conquest of Mexico. She dared to do this, being tacitly upheld by her own family. The position of "wife" to a white man was considered by the natives an honorable one, and was sought by parents for their daughters. It was an exceptional source of wealth for them. (3) If other means failed, the trader could almost always break the boycott by bribes of rum. Time was money to him; often, indeed, in a malarial country it was life to him. Though time was worth nothing to the natives, the rum they had learned to love became, a necessity to them. In cutting the white man from their ivory, they had cut themselves from the white man's rum. A judicious expenditure of demijohns in proper quarters generally enabled Ukuku to revoke his own law. Then, perhaps, the white man would make some slight concession.

I had an experience of this kind in the Benita. country in 1868. I had been there several years. There was growth in the desire for the good things that money can buy, but wages and prices had remained unchanged. I was obtaining all I needed of both labor and food without difficulty. Had I had any difficulty, I should naturally have offered more inducement. I was not aware that there was any discontent. None of my employees had asked for a rise, nor had people, in selling their produce, complained of the price I gave.

Elephants' Tusks and Palm-leaf Thatch. Two Hundred Miles up the Ogowe River.

Suddenly, one morning, a company of about twenty men, led by an ambitious heathen whose manner had always been dictatorial to me and to whom I had shown no favor, filed into the public meeting-room of our mission-house. I knew them all; none were in my employ, nor were any of them Christians. As if they thought it was hopeless to attempt to obtain anything from me by petition or respectful request, they seemed to have decided to stake all on a demand and threat. They suddenly and harshly began, "We've come to order you to change prices." Naturally I felt nettled and replied that I saw no reason why I should take orders from them. They rose in a rage and said, "Then we'll put Ukuku on you—(1) no one shall work for you; (2) no one shall sell you food or drink; (3) you shall not go yourself to your spring;" and with a savage yell they left the house. Instantly a great terror fell on the native members of my household. Those who were heathen dropped work and went to their villages. Those who were Christians came to me distressed, saying that they desired to obey me, but they feared the interdict. I relieved the situation for them by excusing them from further work "till I should call them," and refrained from ringing the call-bell at the usual work hour.

With me were Mrs. Nassau, our child's nurse, my sister Miss I. A. Nassau, and two native girls, members of another tribe. Nurse was a foreigner, a Christian Liberian woman, who was not amenable to the interdict. Some of my Christian employees, though not working, remained on the premises. A few visitors came in the afternoon,— some, as sincere friends, to sympathize; some in curiosity, to see how we were feeling; and some as spies, to see what we were doing. The interdict, except as an expression of ill-will and a possible check to my mission work, did not trouble me. As to food, I had an ample supply of canned provisions, sufficient for a long siege. In refusing to sell me their native products, the people would miss more than I should. As to work, the cleaning of the premises was not pressing and could safely be neglected. As to drinking-water, enough could be caught from the roof in the almost daily rains. Food and labor were their own, to refuse if they chose. But the spring was on my premises and belonged to me. To refrain from going to it might be deemed cowardice; at least it would be obeying an order of what Ukuku claimed was a spirit. An order from men I might submit to under compulsion; to submit to this spirit went against my conscience. After prayer and consideration overnight, Mrs. Nassau fully agreed with me that it was right I should make a demonstration at the spring. In parting with her next morning, as I took up a bucket to go to the spring, she knew I might not return alive. A sandy path led through low bushes to the spring, several hundred yards distant. I saw no one on the way nor at the spring. I filled the bucket and was turning homeward, when a spy, armed with a spear, jumped out of his ambush and ordered me to leave the water. As I did not do so, but started to walk over the path, he stabbed at my back. I thrust the spear aside and faced him, but walking backward all the time kept my eye steadily on his. He feared my eye (most native Africans cannot stand a white man's fixed look) and did not attempt to stab me in front, but tried to spill the water in the bucket and stab me from behind. But the bucket and its contents I guarded, as he struck at it from right to left, by rapidly changing it from left to right with one hand and warding off the spear with the other. Still walking backward, and keeping my eye on him, the bucket and I reached the house in safety.

He hastened to the native villages, whence soon I heard a great outcry. A company of Christian natives came in haste, saying that Ukuku was on his way to assault the house, and that they and other young men, even some who were not Christians, would fight for me against their heathen parents if I could provide them powder. I supplied them. Then they bade me hasten and fasten all doors and windows.

The mission dwelling consisted of two houses joined by a covered veranda,—one, a one-storied bamboo; the other framed of boards, one and a half story. Mrs. Nassau was in the latter, closing it. Before I had finished closing the former, the enemies came, and I was alone in the bamboo house. Shots rattled against the walls. Through the chinks I could see the young men were guarding all entrances and firing. I think that in this difficult situation, defending me against their own people, they purposely fired wide, for no one was even wounded. But their armed stand checked the enemies, who then soon retired. In after years these were ashamed of their assault, and tried to minimize it, when it was related to new missionaries, by representing that they did not intend to kill me. I accepted that as a kindly afterthought. Certainly the spy at the spring intended, and tried hard, to kill me. Certainly, also, their gunshots left their marks on the walls of the bamboo house, and, for aught they knew, had penetrated the thin walls and might have struck me.

That their interdict had been successfully broken, and that, too, by the aid of their own sons, was a great blow to the Ukuku party. It was the beginning of the end of its power. Four years later, while I was absent on my furlough, the number of the church-members having largely increased, two young men, themselves of strong character and imbued with the courage of my able sutcessor at Benita, Rev. Samuel Howell Murphy, deliberately determined to "reveal Ukuku." They walked through a village street openly shouting to the women that "Ukuku is only a man." At once their lives were demanded; but so many of their companions stood up for them, and said to their fathers, "The day you kill those two you will have to kill all of us, for we all say also that Ukuku is only a person," that Ukuku was amazed. Nevertheless the society met. But when the members looked in each other's faces, each one knew that in voting to put to death the other men's sons, he was voting also against his own son. The society could have dared to kill one or two, but to kill a score! They shrank from it. Every one thought of his own son thus involved, and the great lie was exposed and died.

In 1879, on the Ogowe River, at my interior station, Kângwe, near the town of Lambarene, one hundred and thirty miles up the course of the river, I had a similar experience with that same society, known there in the Galwa tribe by the name of Yasi.

In my new work on the Ogowe, I pursued toward that society the same course I had followed with Ukuku at Benita. I preached simply the gospel of Christ; but it is true that the gospel touches mankind in all their human relations. I therefore was not silent about such sins as slavery and polygamy, any more than I would be silent about the sins of drunkenness or theft. All these were practices the evil of which in serious moments most natives would admit, however much they chose still to persist in them. But witchcraft was their religion; they believed in it. To attack it openly would only offend, and I would lose the personal influence which I was able to exercise in quiet, private discussions. Yasi, though a falsehood, was their government. To attack it would have simply emptied my church of every heathen audit or, and would have debarred any women or children from receiving further instruction. I could afford to bide my time, for the entering wedge of Christian principles to overthrow what I could never have removed by direct onslaught. In conversations with my heathen friends, the native chiefs, in their own houses, when no women or children happened to be present, I would expostulate with them against such a mode of government. I told them I would render them respect and even obedience, if as persons they should enact laws affecting me as a person, but that I could give neither respect nor obedience to what they knew I knew was a lie. They looked troubled, and replied, "Yes, that's so, but don't tell it to the women." And I did not. Neverthe less, in my untrammelled, conversations in the mission-house with my own Christian male employees, I was not careful to be silent if our school-boys happened to be present; and these same employees in their own dormitories deliberately and intentionally told the boys of the falsities of their tribal super-stitions. They were right. This was Christian principle, working as I desired it should. Inevitably there grew up a generation of lads who began to deride Yasi, and said that they would never join the society. There came one day a delegation of them led by two Christian young men, Mâmbâ and Nguva, asking my permission to play a mock Yasi meeting. I asked them, Will you dare to play that same play in your own villages? "No, we would be afraid." "Then don't do here what you are unable to carry out elsewhere. I cannot defend you in your own villages. You are safe here; wait until you are stronger and more numerous. Just now your play will create confusion." Nevertheless they did play, with the result which I had foretold. The chiefs were deeply enraged. They "put Yasi" on my house, which meant that I was not to be visited nor sold any food. There was a report, also, that the mission premises were to be assaulted with guns. The loss of food supply was a serious difficulty. I did not need any for myself and sister, nor for the two young missionaries, both of them laymen who were visiting me from a sea-coast station, and who could not understand the case in all its aspects, for they had never met with the society's power; it did not exist at their station, having been broken before they came to Africa. But how was I to feed thirty hungry school-boys? I had to send most of them away to their distant homes down the river; and my canoes returned with a temporary food supply that they had been able to buy at places on the route where news of the interdict had not as yet been officially carried.

The dozen young men who remained with me I armed with guns obtained from a neighboring trading-house, and I posted sentinels every night to guard against sudden assault. I went to the native villages and met a council of several chiefs. They seemed desirous to keep on friendly terms with myself, but they were angry at their own children. They took me to task for my warlike preparations. These I told them were for defence, that I would use the guns only when they compelled me to do so. Then they complained that I had taught their children to disobey them. I denied, stating that one of the greatest of God's commands which I had taught them was to honor their parents. But I added that the Father in Heaven claimed priority even to an earthly parent; and how could children really honor parents who were persistently deceiving them about Yasi, who they knew was only a person? They winced, and looking towards some women who were passing by, said, "Don't speak so loud, the women will hear you." They made another complaint, viz., that I was trying to change their customs; they bade me leave them alone in their customs; I could keep my white customs, and they would keep theirs. I frankly told them that I would be pleased to see some of their customs which were evil changed, but that neither I nor any other missionary could compel them to change; that, nevertheless, these customs would be changed in their and my own lifetime. They were terribly aroused, and swore "Never! never! You can't change them." "No, not I; but they will be changed." "Never! Who can or who will do it?" "Your own sons." Then we will kill our own sons."

They seemed to transfer their anger against me to their own children. The interdict against my house was not formally removed, but it was not rigidly enforced. I no longer felt it necessary to post sentinels at night, and secretly, at night, a sister of one of these very chiefs sold me food for my family. But the heathen rage spread down the river to the villages of the disbanded school children and native Christians. One of these, Nguva, was seized, chained, and offered to Yasi "to be eaten." He was rescued by a daring expedition made by my two lay missionary visitors, who went in my six-oared gig with my twelve enthusiastic young native Christian workmen. They went fifteen miles down river, were secretly directed by one of the little school-boys to the village where Nguva was chained in stocks, assaulted the village at the mid-afternoon hour, when almost all the men were away, cut Nguva from the stocks, and brought him in triumph to my house. But in their retreat up the river they had for a distance of five miles been subjected to a fusillade of native guns from both sides of the river. The river was wide, and they kept in mid-stream, and no one was injured. But the consequences of that resort to arms made me much trouble after my visitors had safely returned to their seaside station. According to native law, I, and not my guests, was held as the responsible party, and the affair was not satisfactorily settled until some months afterward.

My prophecy came true; less than ten years later little children were playing Yasi as amusement in the village streets. Nguva became an elder in the church. He is now dead. His chain is a trophy in the Foreign Board's Museum, 156 Fifth Avenue, New York City.

Malmbâ still lives, working faithfully as a church elder and evangelist.

CHAPTER XI
The Fetich – Its relation to the family

The Family the Unit in the African Community — Respect for the Aged —
Worship of Ancestors — Family Fetiches; Yâkâ, Ekongi, Mbati

IN MOST TRIBES of the Bantu the unit in the constitution of the community is the family, not the individual. However successful a man may be in trade, hunting, or any other means of gaining wealth, he cannot, even if he would, keep it all to himself. He must share with the family, whose indolent members thus are supported by the more energetic or industrious. I often urged my civilized employees not to spend so promptly, almost on pay-day itself, their wages in the purchase of things they really did not need. I represented that they should lay by "for a rainy day." But they said that if it was known that they had money laid up, their relatives would give them no peace until they had compelled them to draw it and divide it with them. They all yielded to this,—the strong, the intelligent, the diligent, submitting to their family, though they knew that their hard-earned pay was going to support weakness, heathenism, and thriftlessness.

Not only financial rights, but all other individual rights and responsibilities, were absorbed by the superior right and duty of the family. If an individual committed theft, murder, or any other crime, the offended party would, if convenient, lay hold of him for punishment. But only if it was convenient; to this plaintiff justice in the case was fully satisfied if any member of the offender's family could be caught or killed, or, if the offence was great, even any member of the offender's tribe.

Families recognized this custom as proper, and submitted to it; for the family expected to stand by and assist and defend all its members, whether right or wrong. Each member relied upon the family for escape from personal punishment, or for help in their individual weakness or inability.

In getting a wife, for instance, no young man had saved up enough to buy one. His wages or other gains, year after year, beyond what he had squandered on himself, had been squandered on members of his family. The family therefore all contributed to the purchase of the wife. Though he thenceforth owned her as his wife, the family had claims on her for various services and work which neither he nor she could refuse.

If in the course of time he had accumulated other women as a polygamist, and, subsequently becoming a Christian, was required to put away all but one (according to missionary rule), it was difficult for him to do so, not because of any special affection for the women involved in the dismissal, nor for pity of any hardship that might come to the women themselves. True, they would be a pecuniary loss to him; but his Christianity, if sincere, could accept that. And the dismissal of the extra women does not, in Africa, impose on them special shame, nor any hardship for self-support, as in some other countries. The real trouble is that they are not his to dismiss without family consent. The family had a pecuniary claim on them, and the heathen members thereof are not willing to let them go free back to their people. If this man puts them away, he must give them to some man or men in the family pale who probably already are polygamists. The property must be kept in the family inheritance. Thus, though attempting to escape from polygamy himself, this man would be a consenting party in fastening it on others. His offence before the church therefore would still be much the same.

For such concentrated interests as are represented in the family, there naturally would be fetiches to guard those interests separate from the individual fetich with its purely personal interests.

Respect for the family fetich is cognate to the worship of the spirits of ancestors. Among the Barotse of South Africa, for this worship, "they have altars in their huts made of branches, on which they place human bones, but they have no images, pictures, or idols."

Among the Mpongwe tribes of Western Equatorial Africa, "the profound respect for aged persons, by a very natural operation of the mind, is turned into idolatrous regard for them when dead. It is not supposed that they are divested of their power and influence by death, but, on the contrary, they are raised to a higher and more powerful sphere of influence, and hence the natural disposition of the living, and especially those related to them in any way in this world, to look to them, and call upon them for aid in all the emergencies and trials of life. It is no uncommon thing to see large groups of men and women, in times of peril or distress, assembled along the brow of some commanding eminence or along the skirts of some dense forest, calling in the most piteous and touching tones upon the spirits of their ancestors.

"Images are used in the worship of ancestors, but they are seldom exposed to public view. They are kept in some secret corner, and the man who has them in charge, especially if they are intended to represent a father or predecessor in office, takes food and drink to them, and a'very small portion of almost anything that is gained in trade.

"But a yet more prominent feature of this ancestral worship is to be found in the preservation and adoration of the bones of the dead, which may be fairly regarded as a species of relic worship. The skulls of distinguished persons are preserved with the utmost care, but always kept out of sight. I have known the head of a distinguished man to be dissevered from the body when it was but partly decomposed, and suspended so as to drip upon a mass of chalk provided for the purpose. The brain is supposed to be the seat of wisdom, and the chalk absorbs this by being placed under the head during the process of decomposition. By applying this to the foreheads of the living, it is supposed they will imbibe the wisdom of the person whose brain has dripped upon the chalk."[59]

In the Benga tribe, just north of the equator, in West Africa, this family fetich is known by the name of Yâkâ. It is a bundle of parts of the bodies of their dead. From time to time, as their relatives die, the first joints of their fingers and toes, especially including their nails, a small clipping from a lobe of the ear, and perhaps snippings of hair are added to it. But the chief constituents are the finger ends.

---

59   Wilson, Western Africa, p. 393.

Nothing is taken from any internal organ of the body, as in the composition of other fetiches. This form descends by inheritance with the family. In its honor is sacredly kept a bundle of toes, fingers, or other bones, nail clippings, eyes, brains, etc., accumulated from deceased members of successive generations. This is distinctly an ancestor worship.

"The worship of ancestors is a marked and distinguishing characteristic of the religious system of Southern Africa. This is something more definite and intelligible than the religious ceremonies performed in connection with the other classes of spirits."[60]

What was described by Dr. Wilson as respect for the aged among the tribes of Southern Guinea forty years ago, is true still, in a large measure, even where foreign customs and examples of foreign traders and the practices of foreign governments have broken down native etiquette and native patriarchal government." Perhaps there is no part of the world where respect and veneration for age are carried.to a greater length than among this people. For those who are in office, and who have been successful in trade or in war, or in any other way have rendered themselves distinguished among their fellow-men, this respect, in some outward forms at least, amounts almost to adoration, and proportionately so when the person has attained advanced age. All the younger miambers of society are early trained to show the utmost deference to age. They must never come into the presence of aged persons or pass by their dwellings without taking off their hats and assuming a crouching gait. When seated

---

60   Ibid.

in their presence, it must—always be at a 'respectful distance'—a distance proportioned to the difference in their ages and position in society. If they come near enough to hand an aged man a lighted pipe or a glass of water, the bearer must always fall upon one knee. Aged persons must always be addressed as 'father' (rera, lale, paia) or 'mother' (ngwe, ina). Any disrespectful deportment or reproachful language toward such persons is regarded as a misdemeanor of no ordinary aggravation. A youthful person carefully avoids communicating any disagreeable intelligence to such persons, and almost always addresses them in terms of flattery and adulation. And there is nothing which a young person so much deprecates as the curse of an aged person, and especially that of a revered father."

The value of the Yâkâ seems to lie in a combination of whatever powers were possessed during their life by the dead, portions of whose bodies are contained in it. But even these are of use apparently only as an actual "medicine," the efficiency of the medicine depending on the spirits of the family dead being associated with those portions of their bodies. This efficiency is called into action by prayer, and by the incantations of the doctor.

"In some cases all the bones of a beloved father or mother, having been dried, are kept in a wooden chest, for which a small house is provided, where the son or daughter goes stately to bold communication with their spirits. They do not pretend to have any audible responses from them, but it is a relief to their minds in their more serious moods to go and pour out all the sorrows of their hearts in the ear of a revered parent.

"This belief, however much of superstition it involves, exerts a very powerful influence upon the social character of the people. It establishes a bond of affection between the parent and child much stronger than could be expected among a people wholly given up to heathenism. It teaches the child to look up to the parent, not only as its earthly protector, but as a friend in the spirit land. It strengthens the bonds of filial affection, and keeps up a lively impression of a future state of being. The living prize the aid of the dead, and it is not uncommon to send messages to them by some one who is on the point of dying; and so greatly is this aid prized by the living that I have known an aged mother to avoid the presence of her sons, lest she should by some secret means be despatched prematurely to the spirit world, for the double purpose of easing them of the burden of taking care of her, and securing for themselves more effective aid than she could render them in this world.

"All their dreams are construed into visits from the spirits of their deceased friends. The cautions, hints, and warnings which come to them through this source are received with the most serious and deferential attention, and are always acted upon in their waking hours. The habit of relating their dreams, which is universal, greatly promotes the habit of dreaming itself, and hence their sleeping hours are characterized by almost as much intercourse with the dead as their waking hours are with the living. This is, no doubt, one of the reasons of their excessive superstitiousness. Their imaginations become so lively that they can scarcely distinguish between their dreams and their waking thoughts, between the real and the ideal, and they consequently utter falsehood without intending, and profess to see things which never existed."[61]

All that is quoted above from Dr. Wilson is still true among tribes not touched by civilization. What be relates of the love of children for parents and the desire to communicate with their departed spirits is particularly true of the children of men and women who have held honorable position in the community while they were living. And it is also all consistent with what I have described of the fear with which the dead are regarded, and the dread lest they should revenge some injury done them in life. The common people, and those who have neglected their friends in any way, are the ones who dread this. The better classes, especially of the superior tribes, hold their dead in affectionate remembrance.

I have met with instances of the preservation of a parent's brains for fetich purposes, as mentioned above by Dr. Wilson. As honored guest, I have been given the best room in which to sleep overnight. On a flat stone, in a comer of the room, was a pile of grayish substance; it was chalk mixed with the decomposed brain-matter that had dripped on it from the skull that formerly had been suspended above. I then remembered how, on visiting chiefs in their villages, they frequently were not in the public reception-room on my arrival, but I was kept awaiting them. They had been apprised of the white man's approach, had retired to their bedrooms, and when they reappeared, it was with their foreheads, and sometimes other parts of their bodies, marked with that grayish mixture. The objects to be attained were wisdom and success in any question of diplomacy or

---

61   Wilson, Western Africa.

in a favor they might be asking of the white man.

Around the doctor and his power is always a cloak of mystery which I have not been able to solve entirely, and of which the natives themselves do not seem to have a clear understanding. The other factors in their fetich worship have to them a degree of clearness sufficient to make them able to give an intelligible explanation. It is plain, for instan that the component parts of any fetich are looked upon them as we look upon the drugs of our *materia medica*. It is plain, also, that these "drugs" are operative, not as on ours, by certain inherent chemical qualities, but by the presence of a spirit to whom they are favorite media. And it is also clear that this spirit is induced to act by the pleasing enchantments of the magic doctor. But beyond this, what? Whence does the doctor get his influence? What is there in his prayer or incantation greater than the prayer or drum or song or magic mirror of any other person? For, admittedly, he himself is subject to the spirits, and may be thwarted by some other more powerful spirit which for the time being is operated by some other doctor; or he may be killed by the very spirit he is manipulating, if he should incur its displeasure.

Belief in the necessity of having the doctor is implicit, while the explanation of his modus operandi is vague, and he is feared lest he employ his utilized spirit for revenge or other harmful purpose. A patient and his relatives who call in the services of a doctor are therefore careful to obey him, and avoid off ending him in any way.

The Yâkâ is appealed to in family emergencies. Suppose, for instance, that one member has secretly done something wrong, *e.g.*, alone in the forest, he has met and killed a member of another family, devastated a neighbor's plantation, or committed any other crime, and is unknown to the community as the offender. But the powerful Yâkâ of the injured family has brought disease or death, or some other affliction, on the offender's family. They are dying or otherwise suffering, and they do not know the reason why. After the failure of ordinary medicines or personal fetiches to relieve or heal or prevent the continuance of the evil, the hidden Yâkâ is brought out by the chiefs of the offender's family. A doctor is called in consultation; the Yâkâ is to be opened, and its ancestral relic contents appealed to. At this point the fears of the offender overcome him, and be privately calls aside the doctor and the older members of the clan. He takes them to a quiet spot in the forest and confesses what he has done, taking them to the garden he had devastated, or to the spot where he had hidden the remains of the person he had killed. If this confession were made to the public, so that the injured family became aware of it, his own life would be at stake. But making it to his Yâkâ, and to only the doctor and chosen representatives of his family, they are bound to keep his secret; the doctor on professional grounds, and his relatives on the grounds of family solidarity. The problem, then, is for the doctor to make what seems like an expiation. The explanation of this, as made to me, is vague. I am uncertain whether the Yâkâ of the injured family is to be appeased or the offender's own Yâkâ aroused from dormant inaction to efficient protection, or both. The Yâkâ bundle is solemnly opened by the doctor in the presence of the family; a little of the dust of its foul contents is rubbed on the foreheads of the members present; a goat or sheep is killed, and its blood sprinkled on them, the while they are praying audibly to the combined ancestor-power in the Yâkâ. These prayers are continued all the while the doctor, who makes his incantations long and varied, is acting. The sanctifying red-wood powder ointment is rubbed over their bodies, and the Yâkâ spirit having eaten the life essence of the sacrificed animal, its flesh is eaten by the doctor and the family. The Yâkâ bundle is tied up again, and again is hidden away in one of their buts, care being taken to add to it from the body of the member who next dies. The curse that had fallen on them is supposed to be wiped out, and the affliction under which they were lying is believed to be removed.

Recently (1901) a Mpongwe man bad gone as a trader into the Batanga interior. He was sick at the time of his going, one of his legs being swollen with an edematous affection, so much so that people in the interior, natives of that part of the country, and fellow-traders, wondered that he should travel so far from his home in that condition. He said he was seeking among different tribes for the cure he had failed to obtain in his own tribe. Later on, be died. He happened to die alone, while others who lived with him, one of them a relative, were temporarily out of the house. The suddenness of the death aroused the superstitious beliefs of the relative, and be rushed to the conclusion that it had been caused by black art machinations of some enemy. But of the whereabouts or the personality of that enemy be had not even a suspicion. He cut from the dead man's body the first joints of his fingers and all the toe-nails, put them in the hollow of a horn, and closed its opening, intending to add its contents to his family Yâkâ when he should return to Gabun. Then he waved the horn to and fro toward the spirits of the air, held it above his head, and struck it on the back of his own neck, uttering at the same time an imprecation that as his relative had died, so might die that very day, even as he had died, the unknown enemy who bad caused his death.

There is another family "medicine," still used in some tribes, that was formerly held in reverence by the Banâkâ. and Bapuku tribes of the Batanga country of the German Kamerun colony. It was called "Malanda." For description of it see Chapter XVI.

Another medicine similar to the Yâkâ in its family interest is called by the Balimba people living north of Batanga, "Ekongi." The following statement is made to me by intelligent Batanga people who know the parties, and who believe that what they report actually occurred.

At Balimba, in the German Kamerun territory, lived a man, by name Elesa. He possessed a little bundle containing powerful fetich medicines, so compounded that they constituted the kind of charm known as Ekongi. Like Aladdin's lamp, and almost as powerful, it warned him of danger, helped him in all his wishes, assisted him in his emergencies, and when he was away from it, as it was hidden in one of his chests in his house, caused him to be able to see and hear anything that was plotted against him. Only he could handle it aright; no one else would be able to manage it.

A brother-in-law of Elesa, husband of his sister, knew of this Ekongi, and asked Elesa to loan it to him in order that he also might be successful in some of his projects.

Now, the peculiarity of the Ekongi medicine is that it acts for and assists only the family of the person who owns it. Elesa refused his brother-in-law, telling him that as they did not belong to the same family, he would not know what to do with a strange Ekongi, nor would Ekongi be willing to answer a stranger.

The brother-in-law knew perfectly well that this was the manner of all Ekongi medicine; but be was so covetous and so foolishly determined that he hoped that in some way this Ekongi might be of use to him if only he could possess himself of it.

One day Elesa went off into the forest on a hunting trip, leaving his Ekongi safely locked in a chest in his house. The brother-in-law obtained a number of keys, and going secretly to Elesa's house, tried them on the various chests stored in the back room. Finally a key fitted, and a lock turned. Suddenly the lid flew up, and out of the now opened chest jumped the little Ekongi bundle, followed by all the goods that bad been packed in the chest; and these spread themselves at his feet, yards of cloth, and hats, and shirts, and coats, and a multitude of smaller articles. He rejoiced at the success of his effort. His covetousness overcamehim. He said to himself that he would put back Ekongi into the chest, would lock it, gather up all this wealth and carry it away; and no one would see them, or know that the chest had been opened by him.

He started to step forward, but his feet were held fast by some invisible power. He tried to stoop down to lay bold of some of the goods within reach, but his arms and back were held fast and stiff by the same invisible power. And he realized that he was a prisoner in Ekongi's hands.

Off in the forest Elesa, in his chase, was enabled by his Ekongi to see and know what was going on in his house. He saw his brother-in-law's attempt at theft, and that his unlawful eyes had looked on the sacred Ekongi. He abandoned the chase that day, and came back in great anger to his house. There was his brother-in-law rooted to the spot on which he stood, the chest open and empty, and the goods scattered on the floor.

Elesa controlled his anger, and at first said nothing. He quietly took a chair from the room out into the street and sat down on it, opposite to the doorway, as if on guard. Then he spoke: "So! now! You have looked on my Ekongi! And you have tried to steal! I will not speak of the shameful thing of stealing from a relative.[62] That is a little thing compared with the sin you have done of looking on what was not lawful for your eyes. We are of different families. I will punish you by taking away my sister, your wife. You shall stand there until you agree to deliver up your wife, and also an amount of goods equal to what you paid for her." The brother-in-law began to plead against the hard terms, and offered to put his father into Elesa's hand instead of the wife. But Elesa insisted.

The brother-in-law's father, at a distant village, possessed also his own family Ekongi, which enabled him to see and know what was being said and done at Elesa's house. He was angry at the hard terms demanded; according to native view, he would defend any one of his family, even if he were in the wrong. A native eye does not look at essential wrong or right; it looks at family interest. His son's attempt at theft did not disturb him. It was enough that Elesa had seized his son as prisoner. He snatched up his spear, and hasted

---

62   To a native African that is a much greater wrong than stealing from other people, particularly from foreigners.—R. H. N.

away to quarrel with his marriage relative Elesa.

On reaching the house, he saw his son still standing helpless, and Elesa seated, still pressing his hard terms on him. The father said to Elesa, "You are not doing well in this matter. Let my son go at once!"

Elesa refused, saying, "He wanted that which was sacred to me. He has looked upon it and has desecrated it. I will not agree that the angry Ekongi shall let him go free. He shall pay his ransom." After along discussion Elesa changed his terms, and demanded a money substitute of one thousand German marks in silver ($250). The father also receded from his demand that the son should be released unconditionally. And after further discussion the father, having saved both his son and himself from the first terms of the ransom, returned again to the question of a person instead of money, and offered his daughter in marriage instead of the $250.

Elesa accepted. He picked up the now satisfied Ekongi, and put it back into the chest; and all the scattered goods followed it, drawn by its power. And when the lid was again closed down and locked, the brother-in-law felt his limbs suddenly released from constriction, and was able to walk away.

This was gravely told me by my cook, a member of the Roman Catholic church, and was endorsed by a woman of my own church, who was present during the recital.

My friend the late Miss Mary H. Kingsley, on page 273 of her "Travels in West Africa," mentions an incident which shows that she had discovered one of these Yâkâ bundles, though apparently she did not know it as such and suspected it to be a relic of cannibalism.

It is true, however, that she did come in contact with cannibalism. She had been given lodging in a room of a house in a Fang village in the country lying between the Azyingo branch of the Ogowe River and the Rembwe branch of the Gabun River. On retiring at night, she had observed some small bags suspended from the wall. "Waking up again, I noticed the smell in the hut was violent, from being shut up, I suppose, and it had an unmistakably organic origin. Knocking the end off the smouldering bush-light that lay burning on the floor, I investigated, and tracked it to those bags; so I took down the biggest one, and carefully noted exactly how the tie-tie (rattan rope) bad been put around its mouth; for these things are important, and often mean a lot. I then shook its contents out in my bat for fear of losing anything of value. They were a human hand, three big toes, four eyes, two ears, and other portions of the human frame. The hand was fresh, the others only so-so and shrivelled. Replacing them, I tied the bag up, and hung it up again." It was well she noticed a peculiarity in the tying of the calamus-palm string or "tie-tie." A stranger would not have been put in that room of whose honesty or honor there was doubt. White visitors are implicitly trusted that they will neither steal nor desecrate.

Another family medicine in the Batanga region is known by the name of Mbati. An account of the mode of its use was given me in 1902 by a Batanga man, as occurring in his own lifetime with his own father. The father was a heathen and a polygamist, having several wives, by each of whom he had children. One day he went hunting in the forest. He observed a dark object crouching among the cassava bushes on the edge of a plantation. Assuming that it was a wild beast wasting the cassava plants, he fired, and was frightened by a woman's outcry, "Oh! I am killed!" She was his own niece, who had been stooping down, hidden among the bushes as she was weeding the garden. He helped her to their village, where she died. She made no accusation. The bloodshed being in their own family, no restitution was required, nor any investigation made. The matter would have passed without further comment had not, within a year, a number of his young children died in succession; and it began to be whispered that perhaps the murdered woman's spirit was avenging itself, or perhaps some other family was using witchcraft against them. A general council of adjacent families was called. After discussion, it was agreed that the other families were without blame; that the trouble rested with my informant's father's family, which should settle the difficulty as they saw best, by inflicting on the father some punishment, or by propitiation being made by the entire family. The latter was decided on by the doctors. They gathered from the forest a quantity of barks of trees, leaves of parasitic ferns, which were boiled in a very large kettle along with human excrement, and a certain rare variety of plantain, as small as the smallest variety of banana. To each member of the family present, old and young, male and female, were given two of these unripe plantains. The rind does not readily peel off from unripe plantains and bananas; a knife is generally used. But for this medicine the rinds were to be picked off only by the finger-nails of those handling them, and then were to be shredded into the kettle in small pieces, also only by their finger-nails. A goat or sheep was killed, and its blood also mixed in. This mess was thoroughly boiled. Then the doctor took a short bush having many small branches (a tradition of hyssop?), and dipping it into the decoction, frequently and thoroughly sprinkled all the members of the family, saying, "Let the displeasure of the spirit for the death of that woman, or any other guilt of any hidden or unknown crime, be removed! "The liquid portion of the contents of the kettle having been used in the propitiatory sprinkling, the more solid pottagelike debris was then eaten by all members of the family, as a preventive of possible danger. And the rite was closed with the usual drum, dance, and song. My informant told me that at that time, and taking part in the ceremonies, was his mother, who was then pregnant with him. The Mbati medicine seems to have been considered efficient, for he, the seventh child, survived; and subsequently three others were born. The previous six had died. Though two of those three have since died, in some way they were considered to have died by Njambi (Providence), *i.e.*, a natural death; for it is not unqualifiedly true that all tribes of Africa regard all deaths as caused by black art. There are some deaths that are admitted to be by the call of God, and for these there is no witchcraft investigation.

The father also is dead. My informant and one sister survive. They think the Mbati "medicine" was satisfactory, notwithstanding that the sister believes that their father was secretly poisoned by his cousins, they being jealous of his affluence in wives and children.

The last step in the Mbati rite is the transplanting of some plant. A suitable hole having been dug at one end, or even in the middle of the village street, each person takes a bulb of lily kind, probably a crinum or an amaryllis, such as are common on the rocky edges of streams, and pressing it against their backs and other parts of their body, and with a rhythmic swaying of their bodies plant it in the hole. Thereafter these plants are not destroyed. They are guarded from the village goats by a small enclosure, and should at any time thevillage remove, the plants are also removed and replanted on the new site. Such plants are seen in almost every village.

CHAPTER XII
The Fetich – Its relation to daily work and occupations and to the needs of Life

IN THE GREAT emergencies of life, such as plagues, famines, deaths, funerals, and where witchcraft and black art are suspected, the aid or intervention of special fetiches is invoked, as has been described in the Yâkâ and other public ceremonies. The ritual required in such cases is often expensive, as money is needed for the doctor's fee, for purchase of ingredients and other materials for the "medicine," and in the entertainment of the assemblage that always gather as participants or spectators.

There is also loss in time, little as the native African values time, and slow as he is in the expedition of any matter. Houses that should be erected and gardens that should be planted are neglected while the rite to be performed is in hand. It may require even a month. During that time either the favorable season for building or planting may have passed, or the work has only partly been completed. The division of the seasons into two rainy (of three months each) and two dry (a short hot and a long cool) make it desirable, as in the temperate zones, for certain work to be done in certain seasons.

But for the needs of life, day by day, with its routine of occupations, whose outgoings and incomings are known and expected, the Bantu fetich worshipper depends on himself and his regular fetich charms, which, indeed, were made either at his request by a doctor (as we would order a suit of clothes from a tailor), or by himself on fetich rule obtained from a doctor; and when paid for, the doctor is no longer needed or considered. The worshipper keeps these amulets and mixed medicines hanging on the wall of his room or hidden in one of his boxes. But he gives them no regular reverence or worship, no sacrifice or prayer, until such times as their services are needed. He knows that the utilized actual spirits (or at least their influence), each in its specific material object, is safely ensconced and is only waiting the needs of its owner to be called into action.

These needs come day by day. Almost daily some one in the village is hunting, warring, trading, love-making, fishing, planting, or journeying.

For Hunting

The hunter or hunters start out each with his own fetich hanging from his belt or suspended from his shoulder; or, if there be something unusual, even if it be not very great, in the hunt about to be engaged in, a temporary charm may be performed by the doctor or even by the hunters themselves. This is the more likely to be done if there is an organized hunt including several persons. Such ceremonies preliminary to the chase are described by W. H. Brown[63] as performed by an old witch-doctor among the Mashona tribe: "Fat

---

63   On the South African Frontier, p. 214.

of the zebra, eland, and other game was mixed with dirt and put into a small pot. Then some live coals were placed on the grease, which caused it to burn, so that clouds of thick smoke arose. The huntsmen sat in a circle around the pot, with the muzzles of their old flint-locks and cap-guns sticking into the smoke. In unison they bent over and took a smell of the fumes, and at the same time called out the name of the 'medicine' or spirit they were invoking, which was Saru, saying thus, 'Saru, I must kill game; I must kill game, Saru! Now, Saru, I must kill game!'

"After this performance was finished, each of the candidates in turn sat down near the doctor, to be personally operated upon by him. He placed a bowl of medicated water upon the huntsman's head, and stirred it with a stick while the latter repeated the names of all the kinds of game he wished to kill. This was to ascertain whether or not the hunt was to be successful. If any of the water splashed out and ran down over the patient's head and face, success was assured. If not a drop had left the bowl, then the huntsman might as well have laid aside his gun and assegai, for his efforts would have been doomed to failure."

Among the Matabele of Southeast Africa, "when they are about to start for the chase, they arrange themselves in a circle at sunset, and the doctor comes with the bark of a tree filled with medicine, and with his finger marks the chiefs on the forehead, in order to give them authority over the animals."

For Journeying
No journey of importance is made without preparation of a fetich, to which more forethought and time and care are given than to the

preparation of food, clothing, etc., for the way. Arnot[64] describes the process: "On behalf of a caravan to start for Bihe, Msidi and his fetich priests have been at work a whole month, preparing charms and so forth. The process in such a case is first to divine as to the dangers that await them; then to propitiate with the appointed sacrifices to forefathers (in this case two goats were killed); afterwards to prepare the charms necessary either as antidotes against evil or to secure good. The noma or fetich spear to be carried in front of the caravan, with charms secured to it, was thus prepared. The roots of a sweet herb were tied around the blade; then a few bent splinters of wood were tied on, like the feathers of a shuttle-cock. In the cage thus formed, there were placed a piece of human skin, little bits of the claws of a lion, leopard, and so forth, with food, beer, and medical roots; thus securing, respectively, power over their enemies, safety from the paws of fierce animals, food and drink, and finally health. A cloth was sewn over all, and finally the king spat on it and blessed it. After all these performances they set out with light hearts, each man marked with sacred chalk."

"Before starting on a journey a man will spend perhaps a fortnight in preparing charms to overcome evils by the way and to enable him to destroy his enemies. If he is a trader, he desires to find favor in the eyes of chiefs and a liberal price for his goods."

---

64   Garenganze, p. 207.

War Canoe. Calabar, West Africa.

For Warring

So implicit is African faith in signs, charms, and auspices, that when the sign before going into war is inauspicious, the natives' hopelessness of success sometimes makes them seem almost cowardly. Among the people of Garenganze in Southeast Africa, "when the chiefs meet in war, victory does not depend on merely strength and courage, as we should suppose, but on fetich 'medicines.' If some men on the side of the more powerful chief fall, they at once retire and acknowledge that their medicines have failed, and they cannot be induced to renew the conflict on any consideration." [65]

Among the Matabele, "before a war the doctors concoct a

---

65 Arnot.

special medicine, and taking some of the froth from it, mark with it the forehead of those who have already killed a man."

A native of Batanga recently described to me the war-fetich as formerly prepared by his people. The medicine for it is arranged for thus. A house is built at least several hundred yards from the village. There will be present no one but the doctor, who eats and sleeps there while be is arranging with the spirits and deciding on the medicine. After two days be tells the people that he has finished it, that his preparations are ready, and that they must assemble at his house. He tells them to bring with them a certain shaped spear with prongs. Men have already gathered in the village, to the number of several hundred, waiting for the war. The doctor chooses from among them some man whom he sends to the forest to get a certain ingredient, a red amomum pod. (It contains the "Guinea grains," or Mulaguetta pepper, which taste like cardamom seeds, which a century ago were so highly valued in Europe that only the rich could buy them.) Then the doctor and the man, leaving the crowd, go together to the forest with knife and macbete and basket. They may have to go several miles in order to find a tree called "unyongo-muaele." The doctor holds the chewed amomum seeds in his mouth,and blows them out against the tree, saying, "Pha-a-a! The gun shots! Let them not touch me!" The assistant holds the basket while the doctor climbs the tree and rubs off pieces of loose bark which are caught in the basket as they fall. They then go on into the forest to find another tree named "kota." There he blows the chewed seeds in the same way saying the same,—"Pha-a-a! Thou tree! Let not the bullets hit me!" And the assistant, with basket standing below, catches the bark scraped down as the doctor climbs this tree.

They return to the village and enter the doctor's house. No women or children may enter the house or be present at the ceremonies. The men bring into the house a very big iron pot, and the doctor says, "This is what is to contain all the ingredients of the medicine." Then the doctor, with two other men, takes that spear by night, leaving all the other men to occupy themselves with songs of war, while the townspeople are asleep; they go to the grave of some man who has recently died. They dig open the grave, and force off the lid of the coffin. The doctor thrusts the spear down into the coffin into the head of the corpse. He twirls the spear about in the skull, so as to get a firm grip on it with the prongs of the spear. He changes his voice, and speaking in a hoarse guttural manner says, "Thou corpse! Do not let any one hear what I say! And do not thou injure me for doing this to you!" When the spear is well thrust into the skull, he stoops into the grave, and with a machete cuts off the head. He goes away carrying the head on the spear-point. While doing all this, be wears not the slightest particle of clothing. They go back to the village to the doctor's house; and there they catch a cock, and in the presence of the crowd the doctor twists (not cuts) off its head. The blood of the cock is caught in a large fresh leaf. He takes the fowl to the big pot, and lets some of its blood drip into it. The head of the corpse is also put into the pot, with water, and all the other ingredients, including the spear. The bullets of the doctor's gun are also to go into the pot, which is then set over a fire.

After the water has boiled the doctor takes a furry skin of a bush-cat, and all the hundreds of men stand on one side in a line.

He dips the skin into the pot, and shakes it over them. As he thus sprinkles them, he lays on them a prohibition, thus: "All ye! this month, go ye not near your wives!" All that month is spent by them practising war songs and dances.

Then the doctor takes the blood that was collected on the leaf, and mixes it with powdered red-wood. This mixture is tied up with the human head in a flying-squirrel's skin. He hangs this bundle up in the house over the place where he sits. The body of the fowl next day is torn in pieces, not cut with a knife, and placed in a small earthen pot with njabi oil (the oil of a large pulpy forest fruit), and ngândâ (gourd) seeds. An entire fresh plantain bunch is cut, and successive squads of the men peel each man his small piece with his finger-nails. These also they shred with their nails, part into the pot, and part on a plantain leaf, is the pot is small, and all the pieces will be added as the contents of the pot are gradually reduced. The doctor himself lifts the pot from the fire, and first eats of the mess, and then gives each of the men, with his hand, a small share.

When all have finished eating, he opens the bundle that had been tied in the squirrel skin, and with the fibrous inner bark of a tree, kinibwa-mbenje (from which formerly was made the native bark-cloth), sponges the red rotten stuff on their breasts, saying, "Let no bullet come here!" Then, led by the doctor, they march in procession to the town. There he tells the people of the town to try to shoot him, explaining that he does not wish any one to be in doubt of the efficacy of the charm. As he leads the procession, he holds the bundle in his hand, shouting, "Budu! hah! hah! Budu! hah! hah!" The "hah" is uttered with a bold aspiration. This is to embolden his followers. ("Budu! hah!" does not inean anything; it is only a yell.) The people are terrified, though he is still shouting to them to fire at him. He is safe; for he leads the procession to where is stationed a confederate, who does fire at him point blank from a gun from which the bullets have been removed. It is a triumph for him! The crowd see that not only he does not fall dead, but he is not even wounded! The charm has turned aside the bullets!

The townspeople are then invited to join the procession. They stand up with the doctor and his crowd, and dance the war-dance. When the dancing is ended, he takes the bundle and anoints all the townspeople, even the women and children. And the men go to their war, sure of victory. But the doctor himself does not go; he remains safely behind, saying that it is necessary for him to watch the bundle in his house. Defeat in the war is easily explained by saying that some one in the crowd had spoiled the charm by not obeying some item in the ritual.

For Trading

One method is described to me by a Batanga native who had seen it used by a certain man of his tribe. This man obtained the head of a dead person who had been noted for his intelligence. This be kept hidden in his house, lying in a white basin. To assure himself that it should be seen by no one else, he built a small hut in the behu (kitchen-garden), detached from his dwelling, and into which none but himself and wife should enter. There he kept the head in its basin. When he had occasion to go to a white man's trading-house to ask for goods or any other favor, he first poured water into this basin, mixed it with the decomposed brain that had oozed from the skull, and washed his cheeks in this dirty water. He also took some brain-matter, mixed it with palm-oil, and rubbed it over his hands. Then, on his going to the trading-house, when the white man shakes hands with him and looks on his face, he will be pleased and generously disposed, and will grant any request made.

My informant told me that when he was a lad he assisted his father in using another method. His father was intimate with white men, trading extensively with them in ivory, To increase his credit, he set out to make a new fetich. He called the son to accompany him to the forest, and handed him a basket to carry. They searched among the trees until they found two growing near together, but bent in such a waytoward eachother that their trunks crossed incontact, and were rubbed smooth by abrasion; and when violently rubbing, in a storm, gave out a creaking sound. In that mysterious sound inhered the fetich power. He chose the trees, not for any value in their kind, but because of their singular juxtaposition and their weird sounds. He gathered bark from these trees, and the son carried the basketful back to their village. The father fixed the time of axrival and point of entrance so that they should not be seen as they came to their house. He then went out to the behu (kitchen-garden) and plucked four ripe plantains (mehole); and gathered leaves of a certain tree, by name "boka." An earthen pot containing water and pieces of the twin-tree bark was set over the fire, and into the pot were finely sliced the mehole and the boka.leaves. To these were added a certain kind of fish, by name "hume," a bottle of palm-oil, gourd seeds, and groundnuts. All these were thoroughly boiled together. When they were sufficiently boiled, he lifted off the pot from the fire, not by his hands, but by clasping its hot sides with his feet, as he sat on a low stool, and placed it on the ground. Sitting by it, he held his face over it, with a cloth thrown over his head, thus inhaling the steam. He remained in this steam bath for about an hour.

At food time he cut two pieces of leaves from plantains, spread them on the ground and sat on them, and ate the mess that was in the pot. While eating, he uttered into the pot adjurations, *e.g.*, "Let no one, not even a Mabeya tribesman, hinder me from the white man's good-will! When I go some day to make my request to the white man, let him grant it!" When he had finished eating, he told his son to carry the pot into an inner room and deposit it in a large box, which the father opened for that purpose. The pot was not washed; it still contained the remains of the pottage. He told his son to reveal to no one what they had done.

That very day he heard that his trade friend in the adjacent inferior Mabeya tribe had obtained an ivory tusk for him. He at once started out alone to meet his friend on the way, so as to be sure that it would not be earried to some one else; but not as on other ordinary journeys. He was to look neither to the right nor to the left (as if watchful of possibly ambushed enemies), nor to look back, even if called by name; but with eye straightforward, to walk steadily to the goal. Before starting, he had rubbed some of the pottage mess on his band and tongue. On reaching the Mabeya village, his friend did not hesitate or haggle about the price, but promptly told him to take the tusk. Before selling it to the white trader, he scraped some ivory flakes from the outside of the tusk, put them into a decanter with two bottles of rum (before foreign liquor was known, native plantain beer was used) and pieces of the twin-tree bark. When subsequently he had occasion to go to the trading-house, he first drank a little from this decanter.

Another Bwanga-bwa-lbâmâ, or trade medicine, is concocted as follows: A man who decides to make one for himself does not allow any one but his wife to know what he is about to do. He gathers from the forest leaves of a tree, by name "kota," the skin of a flying-squirrel (ngunye), from some dead person the nail from the fourth or little finger (of either hand), and the tip of the tongue, some drops of his wife's menses, a solution of red-wood powder, and the long tail-featbers of a forest bird, by name "kilinga." He then provides himself with an antelope's horn. Having burned the squirrel skin, he puts its ashes into the horn, mixed with the above-named articles, including the feather, whose end is allowed to stick out. Then, with the gum of the okume, or African mahogany tree, he closes the mouth of the horn, as with a cork, to prevent the liquid contents from escaping. This horn he suspends by a string from his neck or shoulder whenever be takes it with him on a journey. He uses it in his trade dealings with both whites and blacks. Before beginning a bargain or asking a white trader or another person for gifts of goods, he secretly pulls out the feather through the soft gum, and rubs a little of the liquid on the end of his nose. When this fetich is not in use, it is hidden in his bedroom or other private part of his house. But no one, not even his own family, is allowed to know where it is kept.

Among the Mpongwe tribes of the equator in West Africa there are trade medicines that involve actual murder. One of these is called "Okundu." Like modern spiritualism, it seeks to employ a human medium to communicate with the dead; but it is unlike spiritualism in that the medium must actually be killed before he can go on his errand.

In the case of a man who seeks to become wealthy in trade and goes to a magic doctor for that purpose, the doctor tells him of the different kinds of medicine, and some of the most important things required for each. The seeker, may choose what he is able and willing to do. For Okundu medicine it is required that the seeker shall name some one or more of his relatives who he is willing should die, and that their spirits be sent to influence white traders or other persons of wealth, and make them favorably disposed toward the seeker, so that they may employ him in positions of honor and profit. If the seeker hesitate to do the actual murder, the doctor, by his black art, is to kill the person nominated and send him on his errand. If the fear should occur to the seeker that perhaps the murdered relative, instead of devoting himself in the spirit-world to the trade interests of his murderer, should attempt to avenge himself, the subject is dismissed by the doctor's assurance that either the spirit shall not know that the death of its body was premature, or that he will overrule it for the desired purpose.

I know, personally, a Mpongwe man still living in Gabun who is believed to have done this Okundu. He is of prominent family, and had held lucrative service with white traders. His fortunes began to wane; he fell into debt, and white men began to doubt him and hesitated to entrust him. Though wearing the dress of a civilized gentleman, he is a heathen at heart. He had a little slave boy. The child suddenly and mysteriously disappeared. Those who asked questions received evasive and contradictory answers. A very reliable native told me that it was known that this man had been communicating with an Okundu doctor, and many believed that the child had been put to death. But no one dared to say anything openly, and there was not sufficient proof on which to lay an information before the French governor, only a mile distant.

Another Mpongwe trade medicine is Mbumbu (which means rainbow"). Old tradition said that the rainbow was caused by a forest vine which a great snake had changed to the form of the sun-colored arc. The seeker of wealth is aided by the doctor to obtain a piece of this rainbow, which he keeps in secret, and can carry hidden with him. By it he is able at any time to kill any one of his relatives whom be may choose (of course unknown to them) and send their spirits off to induce foreign traders to give him a store of goods (the children's pot of gold at the rainbow's end?).

For Sickness

Among the Mpongwe and adjacent tribes there are three kinds of spirits invoked, according to the character of the disease. These are Nkinda, Ombwiri, and Olâgâ.

It is clear that these, as explained in a previous chapter, are names of spirits, but the same names (as in the case of other fetich mixtures) are given to the medicines in whose preparation they are invoked. But my informants differed in their opinions whether these names indicate different kinds of spirits, or only a difference in the functions or works done by them. One very intelligent and prominent native at first seemed uncertain, but subsequently said that "Nkinda" indicated the spirits of the common dead; "Ombwiri" the spirits of distinguished dead, kings, and other prominent men; and "Olâgâ," a higher class, who had been admitted to an "angelic" position in the spirit-world. All, however, asserted that all these are spirits of former human beings. Which kind shall be invoked depends on the doctor's diagnosis of the disease.

Natives trading in Plantains and Bamboo Building Materials.—Gabun.

Take the case of some one who has been sick with an obscure disease that has not yielded to ordinary medication: the doctor begins his incantations with drum and dance and song. This is sometimes kept up all night, and in minor cases the patient is required to join in these ceremonies. But in the more mystic Nkinda, Ombwiri, and Olâgâ the sick person sits still, being required to do so as a part of the diagnosis. For if after a while the patient shall begin to nod his head violently, it is a sign that a spirit of some one of these three classes has taken possession of him. The doctor then takes him to a secret place in the forest, and asks the spirit what kind it is, and what the nature of the disease. The reply, though made by the patient, is not supposed to be his, but the spirit's who is using his mouth. Really the sick, dazed, submissive patient does not know what be is saying. After this diagnosis the doctor goes to seek plants suitable for the disease. By chance the patient may recover. If he does not, the doctor asserts that the spirit had misinformed him, and the ceremony must be performed again.

One of the physical signs indicating that Olâgâ, rather than Nkinda or Ombwiri, is the medicine to be used, is vomiting. Hemorrhages from the lungs would be included in the Olâgâ diagnosis.

"Among the Mashonas of South Africa a 'medicine' used is a small antelope horn called 'egona,' in which was a mixture of ground-nut oil and a medicinal bark known as 'unchanya.' The concoction is taken out on the end of a stick termed 'mutira,' and administered to the patient by dropping it into his ear. The doctor stated that it was a sure cure for headache.

"Another horn, four inches long, called 'mulimate,' was for the purpose of cupping and bleeding, and is used in this wise: An incision is made with a knife into the body, the large end of the horn is placed over the wound; then a vacuum is formed by the doctor's sucking the air out through an opening at the little end. The small hole is closed with wax, and the horn is left until it has become filled with clotted blood. This is the process of curing rheumatism and other maladies, which are supposed by the Mashonas to be literally drawn out with the blood. Bleeding is practised extensively; and I have seen natives bled from arms, legs, body, and head until they were so exhausted that weeks were required for their recovery.

"Another important instrument was a brush made of a zebra's tail, among the hairs of which were tied inany small roots and herbs possessing various medicinal properties. One of the remedies was known as 'gwandere,' and, taken internally, was a sure cure for worms, so the doctor stated. The brush was called 'muskwa,' this being the name of any animal's tail. The doctor demonstrated its use by operating upon a man in my presence. He placed some powdered herbs in a bowl of water, then dipped the brush in, and sprinkled the patient. Next, he performed several magic evolutions with the brush around the patient's body, at the same time repeating, 'May the sickness leave this person!' and so forth. The doctor told me that after this operation the patient was certain of recovery, unless some witch or spirit intervened to prevent it or to cause his death."[66]

For Loving

Love philtres are common, even among the civilized and professedly Christian portion of the community. Philtres are both male and female. If a woman says to herself, "My husband does not love me; I will make him love me!" or if any woman desires to make any man love her, she prepares a medicine for that purpose. This charm is

---

66   Brown, On the South African Frontier.

called "Iyele." The process is as follows: First, she scrapes from the role of her foot some skin, and lays it carefully aside. Next, when she has occasion to go to the public latrine at the seaside or on the edge of the forest, she washes her genitals in a small bowl of water, which she secretly carries to her house. Then, with a knife, she scrapes a little skin and mucous from the end of her tongue. These three ingredients she mixes in a bottle of water, which is to be used in her cooking.

The most attractive native mode of cooking fish and meat is in Jomba ("bundle"). The flesh is cut into pieces and laid in layers with salt, pepper, some crushed oily nut, and a little water. These all are tied up tightly in several thicknesses of fresh green plantain leaves, and the bundle is set on a bed of hot coals. The water in the bundle is converted into steam before the thick fleshy leaves are charred through. The steam, unable to escape, permeates the fibres of the meat, thoroughly cooking it without boiling or burning.

When the above-mentioned woman cooks for the man, her husband, or any other for whom she is making the philtre, the water she uses in the jomba is taken from that prepared bottle. This jomba she sets before him, and be eats of it (unaware, of course, of her intention, or of the special mode of preparation). It is fully believed that the desired effect is immediate; that, as soon as he has finished eating, all the thoughts of his heart will be turned toward this woman, and that be will be ready to comply with any wish of hers. No objection to her, or to what she says, coming from any other person in the village, male or female, will be regarded by him.

I know a certain Gabun woman who boasted of her power,

by the above-described means, to cause a certain white man whom she loved (but who was not her husband) to do anything at all that she bade him.

Also a small portion from that bottle may be poured (secretly) into the glass of liquor that is to be drunk by a favored guest. This is practised alike on visitors, white or black.

The process of making a love charm by a man is more elaborate. The ingredients are more numerous and require more time in their collection. Having fixed his desire on some woman, be decides in his heart, "I am going to marry such and such a woman in such and such a village!" But he keeps his intention entirely secret. He proceeds to make the male charm called "Ebâbi." (I do not know the origin of this word; it looks as if it belonged to the adjective "bobâbu" = soft, which is a derivative of the verb "babâkâ," to yield, to consent, to soften.) The first ingredient is coconut oil, which is poured into a flask made of a small gourd or calabash. Then, going to the forest, be gathers leaves of the borigom tree. Another day he will go again to the forest, and find leaves of the bokadi tree. Then he plucks some hairs from his arm-pits, and puts them and the bruised leaves, with some of his own urine, into the flask. This flask he then suspends from his kitchen roof above the itaka frame or hanging-shelf that in almost all kitchens is placed above the fire-hearth. It remains there in the smoke for ten days. Then taking it down, he inserts into it, tip downward, a long tail-feather of a large bird called "koka." He is ready then for his experiment. Any day that he chooses to go to seek the woman, be first draws out the feather, with whatever of the mixture clings to it, and wipes it on his hands. His hands he then rubs over his face rapidly and vigorously, saying, "So will I do to that woman!

He must immediately then start on his journey. This act of anointing his bands and face must have been his very last act before starting. And there are several prohibitions. He must have thought beforehand of all things needed to be done or handled, for after the anointing be must not touch any other thing. In taking the gourd-flask from above the hanging-shelf he must not touch the shelf. He must not rub or scratch his bead. He must not handle a broom. He must not shake hands with any one on the path to the woman's village. All these prohibitions are in order that the anointed mixture may not be rubbed off, or its effect counteracted by contact with anything else. When he reaches the woman's village, he goes directly to her, and clasping her on the shoulder, he rubs his bands downward on her arm, saying, "You! you woman! I love you!" Instantly the medicine is operative, and she is willing to go with him.

If it is only a love affair, she goes secretly. If he offers her marriage, there is first the amicable settlement by the council that is then held by the woman's family as to the amount of the dowry to be paid for her. Presents having, been given to her by him, the woman goes with the man without further objection. On reaching his house, he points out to her the gourd-flask hanging in the kitchen, and tells her, "Let that thing alone." But he does not inform her what it is; nor does she know or suspect that it is anything more than an ordinary fetich. Nor does any one else know; for no one had been allowed to see him perform any part of the several processes of the ritual in compounding the charm.

For Fishing

The prescription for making the fetich for success in fishing is as follows: Go in the morning early, while the rest of the villagers are asleep, to an adjacent marsh or pond. (Almost all African villages are built on or near the bank of some stream or lake.) Find a place where pond-lilies are growing. Wade into the pond, bend low in the water, and pluck three lily-pads. There are water-spiders, called "mbwa-ja-miba" (dogs of the water), generally running over the surface of the water at such places; catch four of them. Gather also leaves of another water-plant called "ngâma." All these articles leave in the village in a safe place. When other fishers come in from the sea, go to the beach to meet them; and if they have among their catch a certain fish called "bume," having three spines, beg or buy it. This you are to dry over the fire. Watch the daily fishing until some one has killed a shark; obtain its heart, which also is to be dried. Take also a plate full of gourd seeds (nganda) and some ground-nuts (mbenda); also five "fingers" of unripe plantains cut from the living bunch on the stalk, and a tumblerful of palm-oil. All these above-named ingredients are to be mixed in one pot (which must be earthen) and are to be cooked in it. While the mess is boiling, sit by, face over the pot, in the steam rising from it, and speak into the pot, "Let me catch fish every day! every day!" No people are to be present, or to see any of these proceedings. Take the pot off the fire, not with your hands, but by your feet, and set it on the ground. Take all your fish-hooks, and hold them in the steam arising from the pot. Take a banana leaf that is perfect and not torn bywind, and laying it on the ground, spread out the hooks on it. Then eat the stewed mess, not with a real spoon, but with a leaf twisted as a spoon. In eating, flic inedible portions, such as fish-bones, skins, rind, and so forth, are not to be ejected from the mouth on the ground, but must be removed by the fingers and carefully laid on the banana leaf. Having finished eating, call one of the village dogs, as if it was to be given liberty to eat the remains of the mess. As the dog begins to eat, strike it sharply, and as the aninial runs away howling, say, "So! may I strike fish!" Then kick the pot over. Take the refuse of food from the banana leaf, and the hooks, and lay them at the foot of the plantain stalk from which the five "fingers" were cut. Leave the pot lying as it was until night. Then, unseen, take it out into the village street, and violently dash it to pieces on the ground, saying, "So! may I kill fish!" It is expected that the villagers shall not hear the sound of the breaking of the vessel; for it must be done only when they are believed to be asleep. When the bunch of plantains from which those fingers were taken ripens, and is finally cut down for food by others, you are forbidden to eat not only of it, but of the fruit of any of its shoots that in regular succession, year after year (according to the manner of bananas and plantains), take the place of the predecessor stalk. You may never eat of their fruit.

For Planting

Planting is done almost entirely by women. If a woman says to herself, "I want to have plenty of food! I will make medicine for it!" she proceeds to gather the necessary ingredients. She takes her ukwala (machete), pavo (knife), short hoe (like a trowel), and elinga (basket), and goes to the forest. She must go very early in the morning, and alone. She gathers a leaf called "tube," another called "injenji," the bark of a tree called "bohamba," the bark also of elâmbâ, and leaves of bokuda. Hiding them in a safe place, she goes back to her village to get her earthen pot. Returning with it to the forest, she makes a fire, not with coals from the village, but with new, clean fire made by the two fire-sticks. These, used by natives before steel and flint were introduced, require often an hour's twirling before friction develops sufficient heat to cause a spark. The sparks are caught on thoroughly dried plantain fibre. Then she builds her fire. She goes to some spring or stream for water to put in the pot with the leaves and barks, and sets it on the fire. All this while she is not to be seen by other people. When the water has boiled, she sets the pot in the middle of the acre of ground which she intends to clear for her garden until its contents cool. In the meanwhile she goes to some creek and gets "chalk" (a white clay is found in places in the beds of streams). She washes it clean of mud and rubs it on her breast. Then she takes the pot, and empties its decoction by sprinkling it, with a bunch of leaves, over the ground, saying, "My forefathers! now in the land of spirits, give me food! Let me have food more abundantly than all other people!" Then she again sets the pot in the middle of the proposed plantation. She takes from it the tube leaves and puts them into four little cornucopias (ehongo), which she rolls from another large leaf of the elende tree. She sets these in the four corners of the garden. Whenever she comes on any other day to work in the garden, she pulls a succulent plant, squeezes its juice into the ehongo; and this juice she drops into her eye. To be efficient, this medicine has a prohibition connected with it, *viz.*, that during the days of her menses she shall not go to the garden.

When her plants have grown, and she has eaten of them, she must break the pot. Having done so, she makes a large fire at an end of the garden, and burns the pieces of earthenware so that they shall be utterly calcined. It is not required that she shall stay by the fire awaiting that result. She may, if she wishes, in the meanwhile go back to her village. She takes the ashes of the pot, mixes them with chalk in a jornba (bundle) of leaves, which she ties to a tree of her garden in a hidden spot where people will not see it.

Another strict prohibition is required of her by the medicine, viz., that she is not to steal from another woman's garden. If she break this law, her own garden will not produce. The jomba is kept for years, or as long as she plants at that place, and the chalk mixture is rubbed on her breast at each planting season. From time to time also, as the leaves of the jomba decay or break away, she puts fresh ones about it, to prevent the wetting of its contents by rain or its injury in any other way.

CHAPTER XIII
The Fetich – superstition in customs

THE OBSERVANCES OF FETICH WORSHIP fade off into the customs and habits of life by gradations, so that in some of the superstitious beliefs, while there may be no formal handling of a fetich
amulet containing a spirit, nor actual prayer or sacrifice, nevertheless spiritism is in the thought, and more or less consciously held.

In our civilization there are thousands of professedly Christian people who are superstitious in such things as fear of Friday,
No. 13, spilled salt, etc. In my childhood, at Easton, Pa., I was sent
on an errand to a German farmhouse. The kind-hearted Frau was
weeding her strawberry bed in the spring garden-making, and was
throwing over the fence into the public road superfluous runners. I
asked permission to pick them up to plant in my own little garden.
She kindly assented, and I thanked her for them, whereupon she
exclaimed, "Ach! nein! nein! Das ist no goot! You say, 'Dank you';
now it no can grow any more!" I was too young to inquire into the
philosophy of the matter. Surely she would not forbid gratitude. I
think the gist of what she thought my error was, that I had thanked
her for what she considered a worthless thing and had thrown away.

I do not think she would have objected to thanks for anything she valued sufficiently to offer as a gift.

The difference between my old Pennsylvania-Dutch lady and my "Number 13" acquaintances, and my African Negro friend is that to the former, while they are somewhat influenced by their superstition, it is not their God. To the latter it is the practical and logical application of his religion. Theirs is a pitiable weakness; his a trusted belief.

It would be impossible to enumerate all the thousands of practices dominated by the superstitious beliefs of the Bantu,—practices which sometimes erect themselves into customs and finally obtain almost the force of law. Many of these are prevalent all over Africa; others are local.

Rules of Pregnancy

Everywhere are rules of pregnancy which bind both the woman and her husband. During pregnancy neither of them is permitted to eat the flesh of any animal which was itself pregnant at the time of its slaughter. Even of the flesh of a non-pregnant animal there are certain parts—the heart, liver, and entrails—which may not be eaten by them. It is claimed that to eat of such food at such a time would make a great deal of trouble for the unborn infant. During his wife's pregnancy a man may not cut the tbroat of any animal nor assist in the butchering of it. A carpenter whose wife is pregnant must not drive a nail. To do so would close the womb and cause a difficult labor. He may do all other work belonging to carpentering, but he must have an assistant to drive the nails.

In my early years on Corisco Island, and while I was expecting to become a father, I was one day superintending the butchering of a sheep. It was not necessary that I should actually use the knife; that was done by the cook; but I stood by to see that the work was done in a cleanly manner, and that in the flaying the skin should be rolled constantly away, so that the hair should not touch the flesh. In the dissection I assisted, so that the flesh should not be defiled by a carelessly wounded entrail. My servant was amazed, and said my child would be injured. He was still more shocked when Mrs. Nassau herself came to urge haste and to secure the liver for dinner.

Among the station employees oil Corisco in 1864 was an ex-slave, a recent convert, whose freedom had been purchased by one of the missionaries. The native non-Christian freemen begrudged him his position as a mission employee; for his wages were now his own, and could no longer be claimed by his former master. Some of his fellow-servants, freemen, put off on him, as much as they could, the more menial tasks. It was incumbent, therefore, on the mission-aries to see that be was not oppressed by his fellows. Clearing of the graveyard was a task no one liked to have assigned to him; and it was often thrown on poor Evosa. One day a newly arrived mis-sionary, the Rev. George Paull, the noblest of my associates these forty years, who just then knew little of the language or of native thought or custom, ordered Evosa to take his hoe and clean the cemetery path. Evosa bluntly said, "Mba haye!" (I won't). "You won't! You refuse to obey me?" "Mba haye!" "Then I dismiss you." Evosa went away, much cast down. Some of his fellow-Cliristians came to me saying they were sorry for him, and asked me to interfere.

"But," I said, "he should obey; the work is not hard." "Oh! but be can't do it!" "Why not?" "Because his wife is pregnant." Immediately I understood. Evosa may not have believed in the superstition, but for all that, if he did the work and subsequently there should be anything untoward in his wife's confinement, her relatives would exact a heavy fine of him. We had not required our converts to disregard these prohibitions, if only they did not actually engage in any act of fetich worship. I was careful to say nothing to the natives that would undermine my missionary brother's authority; but privately I intiniated to Mr. Paull that I thought that if be had been fully aware of the state of the case, be would not have dismissed the man. He was just, and reversed the dismissal. Evosa was pardoned also for the bluntness of his refusal; it was a part of his slavish ignorance. In conclusion, I warned him that he should have explained to Mr. Paull the ground of his refusal, and should have asked for other work. He had not supposed that tlie white man did not know; wid the asking of excuse is a part of politeness tbat has to be taught. Almost every new missionary makes unwise or unjust orders and decisions before be learns on what superstitious grounds he is treading. Not all are willing to be rectified as was my noble brother Paull.

In the burial of a first-born infant the lid of the coffin is not only not allowed to be nailed down, but it must not entirely cover the corpse; a space must be left open (generally above the child's head); the superstition being that if the coffin be closed, the mother will bear no more children.

Omens on Journeys

Almost every traveller in Africa, in publishing his story, has much to say about the difficulties in getting his caravan of porters started on their daily journey. His detailed account of slowness, disobedience, and desertions is as monotonous to the reader as they were distressing to himself. Did he but know it, the fault was often largely his own. The man of haste and exactitude, that has grown up on railroad time-tables, demands the impossible of aborigines who never have needed to learn the value of time. Anglo-Saxon, Teutonic, and even Latin diligence expects too much of the happy-go-lucky African. The traveller fumes, and frets, and works himself into a fever. He would gain more in the end if he would *festina lente*. He would save himself many a quarrel or case of discipline (for which he earns the reputation of being a hard master; and for which, further on in the journey, he may be shot by one of his outraged servants) if he only knew that superstition had met his servant, as the angel "with his sword drawn" met Balaam's ass, "in a narrow place"; and that servant could no more have dared to go on in the way than could that wise ass who knew and saw what his angry master did not know.

Mr. R. E. Dennett, for many years a resident in Loango among the Bavili people, and author of "Seven Years among the Fjort," recognizes this in "A Few Signs and Omens," contributed recently to a Liverpool weekly journal, "West Africa." What he says of the Fyât (Fiot) tribes is largely true of all the other West African tribes. "They have a number of things to take into consideration, when setting out upon a journey, which may account for many of those otherwise inexplicable delays which so annoy the white man at times when anxious to start 'one time' for some place or other.

"The first thing a white man should do is to see that the Negro's fetiches are all in order; then, when on the way, he must manage things so that the first person the caravan shall meet shall be a woman; for that is a good sign, while to meet a man means that something evil is going to happen. Then, to meet the bird Kna that is all black is a bad sign; while the Kna that has its wings tipped with white is a good sign.

"The rat Benda running across your path from left to right is good; from right to left fairly good; should it appear from the left and run ahead in the direction you are going, 'Oh! that is very good!' but should it run towards you, well, then the best thing for you to do is to go back; for you are sure to meet with bad luck!

"See that your men start with their left foot first, and that they are 'high-steppers'; for if their left foot meet with an obstacle, and is not badly hurt, it is not a bad sign; but if their right foot knocks against anything, you must go back to town.

"See that you do not meet that nasty brown bird called Mvia, that is always crying out, 'Via, via'; for that means 'witch-palaver,' and strikes consternation into your people. Nobody likes to be reminded of his sins or witch deeds, and be condemned to be burnt in the fire; and that is what 'via' means.

"Then there is that moderately large bird with wings tipped with white called 'Nxeci,' also reminding one of 'witch-palaver,' and continuously crying out, 'Ke-e-e,' or 'No.' You had far better not start.

"Take care also to shoot the cukoo o Nkuku before it crosses your path; for if you allow it to pass, you had better return; it is a bad omen.

"Then, concerning owls: see that your camp at night is not disturbed by the cry of the Kulu (spirit of the departed), that warns you that one of you is going to die; or that of the Xi-futu-nkubu, which means that you may expect some evil shortly. On the other hand, let the Mampaulo-paulo hoot as much as it likes; for that is a good sign.

"Then look out that the snake Nduma does not cross your path; for that is a sign of death, or else of warning to you that you should return and see to the fetich obligations the iron bracelet Ngofu reminds you of. Examine your men, and ask those who wear the bracelet the following questions: Have you eaten the flesh of anything (save birds) on the same day that it was killed? Have you pointed your knife at any one? Did you know your wife on the Day of Rest (Nsâna, Sunday)? Have you looked upon a woman during a certain period of the month? Have you eaten those long 'chilli' peppers instead of confining yourself to the smaller kinds?

"You must send those who have not the bracelet, together with those who have not been true to ngofu, back to town, to set this 'palaver' right. Take great care of your fowls, and see that you have no ill-regulated cock to crow between 6 P.M. and 3 A.M., as that means that there is a palaver in town to which your men are called, so that it may be settled at once.

"Then, there is that large bird Knakna, whose cry warns your men that there is something wrong with the fetich Mabili ('the east wind,' on the gateway at the east entrance to each town), and this knowledge will hang as a dead weight on all their energies until they have just run back to town to see what the matter may be.

"Get your men to sleep early, lest they should see the 'falling stars '; for it means that one of their princes is about to die, and that is disquieting. Then don't let it thunder out of season; for that portends the death of an important prince.

"And if you determine to go out fishing, and meet the rat Benda (as above noted), go or not, as the signs command you. If you meet the bird Mbixi that sings 'luelo-elo-elo,' go on your way rejoicing; or when the little bird Nxexi, true to nature, sings 'xixexi,' all is well; but when it sings, 'tietie,' go back, for you will catch nothing.

"Then there is the wild dog Mbulu; well, that must not cross your path at starting. You laugh? Well, so did Nyambi, the brother of my headman, Bayona; and what bappened? Nyambi had come down from the interior with his master; and after a short stay was ordered back to his trading post, his master saying that he would follow him shortly. A friend handed him a son of his for him to educate, and to attend upon him; in fact, to be his 'boy.' Everything being ready, be set out from Loango; and the first thing they met on the road was the wild dog. Now Nyambi was a plucky Bantu and took no notice of this warning, but continued on his way. On reaching the forest country in Mayomba, the boy entrusted to him ran away. Nyanibi, true to his trust, came after him back to his town, to see that the boy was once more placed in the care of his father, and so to avoid any further complications. Then he once more started on his way, and, nearing the forest country again, was bitten severely on the foot by a snake. He tied a rag around his leg just under the knee, and another just above his ankle, and squeezed as much blood as he could from the wound itself. Then he hobbled into the nearest town, and waited

there for assistance from his family, to whom he had at once despatched a messenger. They sent men and women to bring him back
to Loango, where he arrived in a very weak condition, and with a
fearful sore on his foot,—an awful warning to all those who will not
take the omens sent to them in earnest! What! you still laugh? Well,
there is no hope for you; you are too persistent, and have not read
the story of the rabbit and the antelope, and of the trap laid for the
former.[67] And if you keep on laughing at these superstitions of the
natives, don't blame any one if they call you a 'rabbit,' and refuse to
follow you in your wanderings through their land. Most haste is very
often worst speed in Africa; and the white man who ignores all but
physical difficulties does well to stay his impatient hand when about
to strike his most provoking and apparently dilatory black carrier,
who is beset by endless moral obstacles retarding his progress as
no physical difficulties can."

When I was beginning my pioneering of the Ogowe River in
September-November, 1874, I had with me one Christian coast native. I completed my canoe's crew with four heathen Galwa, placed
myself under the patronage of the Akele chief Kasa, resided in his
village, and bought from him a site, Belambila, for my mission station, about a mile distant from him. Daily I went with my crew in the
canoe to work at the building of a temporary house on the Belambila
premises. One day a water-snake crossed the canoe's bow, and I
struck at it. The Christian looked serious, and the four heathen laid
down their paddles. It was sufficiently disastrous that the snake had

---

67   Tale 23, p. 93, my "Notes on the Folk-Lore of the Fiort."

crossed our path; l had made matters worse by attempting to injure it. They said, "You should not have done that." "Why?" "Because somewhere and sometime it will follow us and will bite us. Let us go back to Kasa's." l refused, and insisted on our proceeding with the day's work. l might better have yielded to their request. It was as if l were under an Ancient Mariner's curse. My snake was as bad as his albatross. My men either could not or would not. Everything went wrong. They worked without heart and under dread. What they built that day was done with so many mistakes that l had to tear it down. l did not fully appreciate at that time, but l do not now think that they were intentionally disobedient or recalcitrant. Just as well compel a crew of ignorant sailors to start their voyage on a Friday. The fear of ominous birds and other animals is over all Africa. In Garenganze, according to Arnot, "many have a superstitious dread of the horned night-owl. Its cry is considered an evil omen, which can only be counteracted effectually by possessing a whistle made out of the windpipe of the same kind of bird.

"Jackals, wild dogs" also are very much disliked. The weird cry of one of these animals will arouse the people of a whole village, who will rush out and call upon the spirit-possessed animal to be quiet and leave them, or to come into the village, and they will feed and satisfy it.

"When travelling, they are careful to notice the direction this animal may take. Should its cry come from the direction in which they are going, they will not venture a step farther until certain divinations have been performed that they may learn the nature of the calamity about to befall them."[68]

The chameleon is an object of dread to all natives wherever I have lived. I have never met, even among the most civilized, any man or woman who would touch one. For friendship, or to make a sale, they would bring it to me at the end of a long stick, in my various efforts at zodlogical and other collections.

Traveling by Canoe. Ogowe River.

The millepedes they also dread. I handle them with impunity, and my little daughter, on the Ogowe, in 1888 did so too, under my example. But her young Negro companions soon made her afraid. True, the adult millepede ejects a dark liquid which stained my hands

---

68   Arnot.

and which natives said was poisonous if taken internally. (That I never tested.)

A native friend, one of my Batanga female church-members, a sincere Christian, of bright mind but limited education, told me recently (1902) of her belief in the chameleon as a bad omen. She was visiting relatives a dozen miles north. Word was sent her to return, as another relative, a woman in my Bongaheli village, was dangerously ill. Her host told her to go, and advised her to gather on the way a certain fern, parasitic on trees, that is used medicinally in the disease of which the woman was sick. My friend started on her day's journey, came to the tree, and was about to pluck the ferns when she observed a chameleon clasping the tree; it stood still and looked at her. She instantly left the tree, abandoned the ferns, went back to tell her host that a chameleon was in possession of them and had stared at her, and that it was useless to gather the medicine, for she was sure their relative was dead. And she resumed her journey, coming back to Bongaheli in order to attend the mourning. It was true; the relative was dead, and the mourning had begun. Her belief was not shaken when I reminded her that that chameleon was only doing just what all chameleons do when they are not walking, and when confronted by any one. They all clasp the branch on which they happen to be, and stare at their supposed pursuer, if unable to escape.

Leopard Fiends

Formerly a strange superstition said that on him who should kill a leopard there would come an evil disease, curable only by ruinously expensive ceremonies of three weeks' duration, under the direction of the Ukuku (Spirit) Society. So the natives allowed the greatest ravages, until their sheep, goats, and dogs were swept away; and were aroused to self-defence only when a human being became the victim of the daring beast. The carcass of a leopard, or even the bones of one long dead, were not to be touched.

While I was living at Benita, about 1869, the losses by leopards became so great that, in desperation, some of the braver young men, under my encouragement, determined that the depredator should be caught. (Nothing was just then said about what should be done with it when caught.) A trap was built in one of the villages, and baited with a live goat. Soon a leopard was entrapped. What to do with it was then the question. Some favored leaving it alone till they could ask permission of Ukuku to kill it, even if they had to pay heavily for the permission. Others, who had heard me laugh at their super-stition, proposed that I should be asked to shoot it. They came at night; I willingly and promptly went with my Winchester repeating rifle, which could easily be thrust into the chinks between the logs of which the trap was built. When the animal was shot, came the question, Who should remove it? None would touch it.

Among my employees were two young men of another tribe with whom that superstition did not exist. With their aid I lifted the carcass upon a wheelbarrow, and took it to a place where I could comfortably skin it. Some objected to my retaining the skin. They wanted the whole animal put out of sight. But the majority agreed that the skin should be my compensation for my rifle's service. Then a deputation carefully followed me out on the prairie, to see that the spot where the skinning was to be done was not near any of their frequented paths. After the flaying was complete, what was best to do with the carcass? The majority objected to its being buried, fearing to tread over its grave. So I sent the two young men in a canoe, to sink the carcass out in the river's mouth toward the sea. Even then there were those who for two weeks afterward would eat no fish caught in the river.

With this fear of the leopard was united a superstition similar to that of the "wehr-wolf" of Germany, viz., a belief in the power of human metamorphosis into a leopard. The natives had learned, from foreigners who were ignorant of the fact that there are no tigers in Africa, to call this leopard fiend a "man-tiger." They got their fears still more mixed by a belief in a third superstition, viz., that sometimes the dead returned to life and committed depredations. This belief was not siniply that disembodied spirits (mekuku) returned, but that the entire person, soul and body (ilina na nyolo), rose temporarily from the grave, with a few changes (among the rest, that the feet were webbed). Such a being, as mentioned in a previous chapter, was called "Uvengwa." At one time, while I was at Benito, intense excitement prevailed in the community: doors and shutters were violently rattled at night; marks of leopard's claws scratched doorposts; their tracks lay on every path; women and children in lonely places saw their flitting forms, in the dark were knocked down by their spring, or heard their growl in the thickets. It was difficult to decide, in hearing these reports, whether it was a real leopard, a leopard fiend, or only an uvengwa. To native fear, th-ey were practically the same. I felt certain that the uvengwa was a thief disguised in a leopard skin. Under such disguise murders were sometimes committed. By bending my thumb and fingers into a semiclosed fist, I could make an impression in the sand that exactly resembled a leopard's track; and this confirmed my conclusions as to the real cause of the phenomenon.

The pioneer of the Gabun Mission, Rev. Dr. J. L. Wilson, in 1842, found the wehr-wolf superstition prevalent among all the tribes of Southern Guinea. The leopard "is invested with more terror than it otherwise would have, by a superstitious apprehension on the part of the natives, that wicked men frequently metamorphose themselves into leopards and commit all sorts of depredations, without the liability or possibility of being killed. The real leopard is emboldened by impunity, and often becomes a terrible scourge to the village be infests. I have known large villages to be abandoned by their inhabitants, because they were afraid to attack these animals on account of their supposed supernatural powers."

At Gabun, about 1865, there still remained a jungle on one side of the public road that constituted the one street of the town of Libreville, as it followed the curve of the bay for three miles. There were frequent alarms and occasional murders along lonely parts of that road. The natives believed that the leopard fiend was a beast; the French commandant believed it was a human being. He had the jungle cut away. Since then, no mangled bodies have been found there.

Among the Garenganze people, in 1884, Mr. Arnot often chid them "for their want of bravery in not hunting down the many wild animals that prey around their towns, carrying off the sick people, and frequently attacking and seizing solitary strangers. They excused themselves by explaining that these wild animals are really 'men of other tribes,' turned, by the magic power they possess, into the form of lions, panthers, or leopards, who prowl about to take vengeance on those against whom they are embittered. In defending this absurd theory, one man said it was not possible for a Luba and a Lamba man to go out into the country together without one stealing a march on his neighbor, getting out of sight, and returning again in the form of a lion or leopard, and devouring his travelling companion. Such things, they say, are of daily occurrence amongst them; and this foolish superstition leads them not only to tolerate the wild animals about, but almost to bold them sacred."

This particular superstition still exists extensively. As late as 1898, it is stated of the Barotse of Southeast Africa: "They believe that at times both living and dead persons can change themselves into animals, either to execute some vengeance or to procure something that they wish for: thus a man will change himself into a hyena or a lion in order to steal a sheep, and make a good meal off it; into a serpent, to avenge himself on some enemy. At other times, if they see a serpent, it is one of the 'Matotela' or slave tribe, which has thus transformed himself to take some vengeance on the Barotse."[69]

Luck

There exists a custom, even among the civilized, for the seller of an article to hold back a small portion after his price has been paid. When I first met with this custom, I was indignant at what seemed

---

69   Declè.

like stealing; and yet it was so open, and without any attempt at concealment, that I was amazed. One who brought for sale a bunch of plantains twisted off and took away one of its "fingers." Another who had just been paid for a peck of sweet potatoes deliberately picks off one tuber. Another who brought a gazelle for sale would not complete the bargain till I had consented that be might remove the gall-bladder and a portion of the liver. I learned that all these were for "luck": in order that the garden whence came that plantain bunch or potato should be blessed with abundance; and the hunter, that be might be successful in his next hunt. The gazelle is credited with being a very artful animal, the cunning being located especially in the liver.

One might ask why, if those pieces are so needed for luck, the owner did not take them before selling, and while they were still his own and under his entire control. I do not know their exact thought; but the statement was that the chances of good luck were greater if the pieces of plantain, potato, meat, etc. were abstracted after the article had actually passed out of the seller's possession.

On the Ogowe, at Lake Azyingo, in 1874, I was present at the cutting up of a fernale hippopotamus which a hunter had killed the night before. By favor of the native Ajumba, chief, Anege, I was allowed to see the ceremonies. They were many; of most of them I did not understand the significance; and the people were loath to tell me, lest I should in some way counteract them. Even my presence was objected to by the mother of the hunter (he, however, was willing).

After the animal had been decapitated, and its quarters and bowels removed, the hunter, naked, stepped into the hollow of the ribs, and kneeling in the bloody pool contained in that hollow, bathed his entire body with that mixture of blood and excreta, at the same time praying the life-spirit of the hippo that it would bear him no ill-will for having killed it, and thus cut it off from future maternity; and not to incense other hippopotami that they should attack his canoe in revenge. (Hippos are amphibians, but are generally killed in the water.) He kept choice parts of the flesh to incorporate into his luck fetich.

Mr. Arnot mentions the same custom in Garenganze:

One morning I shot a hyena in my yard. The chief sent up one of his executioners to cut off its nose and the tip of its tail, and to extract a little bit of brain from the skull. The man informed me that these parts are very serviceable to elephant hunters, as securing for them the cunning, tact, and power to become invisible, which the hyena is supposed to possess. I suppose that the brain would represent the cunning, the nose the tact, and the tip of the tail the vanishing quality." The stomach of the hyena is valued by the Ovimbundu (of Southwest Africa) as a cure for apoplexy.

Twins

Mr. Arnot states that in Garenganze "cases of infanticide are very rare. Twins, strange to say, are not only allowed to live, but the people delight in them." Though they are not regarded as monstrosities deserving death, as among the Calabar people on the West Coast, it is nevertheless considered necessary that certain preservative ceremonies should be performed on the infants and their parents.

Mr. Swan, an associate of Mr. Arnot, describes a ceremony be was unexpectedly made to share in while on a visit to the native king Msidi: "My attention was drawn to a crowd of folk, mostly women, who approached, singing and ringing a kind of bell. They formed in lines opposite to us. In front of the rest were a man and woman, each holding a child not more than a few days old. I learned that the little ones were twins, the man and woman holding them being the happy parents, who had come to present their offspring to the king. They wore nothing but a few leaves about their loins,—a hint to Msidi, I suppose, that they would like some cloth.

"After chanting a little, an elderly woman came forward, with a dish in her left hand and an antelope's tail in her right. When she reached Msidi, I was astonished at her dipping the tail in the dish and dashing the liquid over his face. Msidi's wife had a like dose. But my surprise increased when she came to us and gave us a share. What was in the dish I cannot say, but it struck me as possessing a very disagreeable odor. This discourteous creature was the Ocimbanda (fetich doctor). She did not cease her dousing work till she had favored all sitting around. The king then went into the house, and his wife came out with some cloth, which she tied around the mother's waist; and then a piece of cloth was given to the husband. The friends had brought some native beer; and when Msidi came out, he went to one of the pots, filled his mouth, spouting the beer in his wife's face; she did the same to him, after which the spouting became general.... They told me it was their custom to act thus when twins are born."

In the Benga tribe, thirty-five years ago, I observed that if one of a pair of twins died, a wooden image was substituted for it on the bed or in the cradle-box, alongside of the living child. I strongly suspected Animism in the custom; but some Christians explained that the image was only a toy, so that the living babe should not miss the presence of an object resembling its mate.

Names of twins are always the same, in the same cognate tribes. In Benga they are always Ivaha (a wish) and Ayenwe (unseen). These names are given irrespective of sex. But not every man or woman whom one may meet with these names is necessarily a twin. They may have inherited the name from ancestors who were twins.

All over Africa the birth of twins is a notable event, but noted for very different reasons in different parts of the country. In Calabar they are dreaded as an evil omen, and until recently were immediately put to death, and the mother driven from the village to live alone in the forest as a punishment for having brought this evil on her people.

In other parts, as in the Gabun country, where they are welcomed, it is nevertheless considered necessary to have special ceremonies performed for the safety of their lives, or, if they die, to prevent further evil.

In the Egba tribes of the Yoruba country they become objects of worship. As in other parts of Africa where twins are preserved, they are given twin names; which, of course, differ in different languages. Among the Egbas the firstborn is Taiwo, *i.e.*, "the first to taste the world," and the other Kehende, *i.e.*, "the one who comes last."[70] About eight days after their birth, or as soon as the parents have the money for the sacrificial feast, they invite all relatives on

---

70   See "Niger and Yoruba Notes."

both sides, neighbors and friends together. Various kinds of food are prepared, consisting chiefly of beans and yams. A little of each kind of food is set apart with some palm-oil thrown upon it, and the small native plates or basins containing it are set before the children in their cradle. They are then invoked to protect their mother from sickness, to pity their parents and remain with them, to watch over them at all times. I quote in this connection the following from a West African newspaper:

"After the ceremony an elderly man or woman who has been a twin is called upon to split the kola nuts, in order to find out whether the children will live or die. This is their way of asking the god or goddess to answer their requests (and it is singular that this throwing of kolas may be done repeatedly until the reply is favorable to the inquirer). Thus: if a kola nut is split into four parts in throwing it down, they say, "You Idol, please foretell if the children will live long or die.". If all the four pieces of the kola fall flat on their backs, or all flat with their faces to the ground, or if two of them fall with their faces downward and the other two upward, then in each of those cases the reply is favorable, and it means they will live long and not die. But if three pieces of the kola should turn their faces to the ground and only one fall flat on its back, or if the three pieces should turn their faces upward and only one downward, the reply is unfavorable, and it means that the children will die before long. In such cases they continue throwing the kola nut indefinitely until they obtain their wish; or, in rare cases of total failure, the subject of inquiry is reserved till a future time, when they hope the idol may speak more favorably. Thus, twin children are worshipped every month.

"In some cases, where the parents have the means, an invitation goes round to as many twins as they can get to partake of the sacrificial feasts. Of course, the people enjoy themselves at the feast.

"The twins have everything in common; they eat the same kind of food and wear the same dress. If one of them should die, the mother is bound to make a wooden image to represent the dead child. This kind of image is generally about a foot in length, and is made of Ire wood, which is flexible and durable. It is carved in such a manner as to represent the human anatomy."

These images, substitute for a dead twin, are used very extensively among all the tribes of Africa. Various reasons are given for their use: that the surviving twin shall not be lonely; that the departed one may be sure it is not forgotten; and other reasons. The images are retained as family fetiches, to ward off evil from the mother.

"If both children should die, the mother must have two wooden images, and regard them as her living children; she worships them every morning by splitting kola nuts and throwing down a few drops of palm-oil before them. Of course, the occasional feasts follow in their due course, and as oftentimes as she may happen to see them in her dreams.

"If they should live, and both are males, they make engagements and marry at the same time. If one is male, and the other is female, their dowry must be given the same day; the parents believe that if things done for them are not alike or do not go together, one will soon die."[71]

---

71   From a West African Newspaper.

Customs of Speech

Superstition mingles in customs of speech. There is the custom of Kombo, existing to-day. Something about the act of sneezing is considered uncanny. A phrase or a cabalistic word, intended as an adjuration or a protestation in the nature of a prayer for protection or blessing, is very commonly ejaculated by one who sneezes and sometimes when one stumbles. (In the old despotic days of native kings, in the Benito region, if a king, on first emerging from his house in the morning, should happen to stumble, be would order the nearest person in sight to be killed.) That word is uttered by an adult for himself, by a parent or other relative for an infant child. It may be an archaism whose meaning has been forgotten. Generally the Kombo is an epigrammatic phrase invented by the individual himself, and to be used only by him.

Sometimes, instead of a phrase, the single word "Kombo!" as representing the custom, is uttered.

Some forty years ago the ejaculation, before the invariable "Mbolo" salutation was uttered, that was used by visitors to the Mpongwe king on the south side of the Gabun estuary, was, "What evil law has God made?" The response was, "Death!" Little as the heathen natives liked to talk of death, their use of that word to their king was in the nature of a good wish that he might escape the universal law. And the "Mbolo!" (gray hairs) that followed was a wish that he might live to have gray hairs.

His son, an edueated man and a nominal Romanist, is now saluted quite as formally, but the ejaculation has been changed to a more respectful and Christian recognition of God.

Oaths

Blasphemy of the Divine name, so fearfully common in professedly Christian countries, is almost unknown to the African heathen.
Though the native name for God, Anyambe, is improperly used in
names of persons (which is not intended for disrespect), it is not
often actually blasphemed. An equivalent blasphemy, is occasionally
practised in the misuse of the name of their great and sacred spirit-society. In the Benga tribe "Saba?" and "Sabali?" used interroga-
tively, mean only "True?" "Is that so?"; but, used positively, they are
of the nature of an oath, especially when the society's name (Ukuk)
was added: "Saba n' Ukuku" (True! by Ukuk!).

On the Ogowe River, in the Galwa tribe, the name of that society was Isyoga, more commonly spoken of as Yasi. In the initiation
into it the neophytes were taught a long and very solemn adjuration,
that could be uttered only among the initiated, as an oath; but they
were allowed commonly to use simply its title "Yasi," the utterance of
that one word being accompanied by a downward sweep of the right
hand over the left arm from shoulder to hand. It was not permitted
to women to speak this word.

In no tribes with which I have lived was this "By-the-Spirit"
oath used so much as among the Galwa of the Ogowe. It became
monotonously frequent, in and out of season, in all conversations
and on the slightest assertion or the simplest excitement.

I became very tired of "Yasi! Yasi! Yasi!" and that sweep of the
right hand, for the doing of which the canoe paddle or a tool was
laid down. And, by the way, the more of a liar a man was, the more
frequent and vociferous was he in his persistent use of "By Yasi!"

Totem Worship

Totem worship is found in Africa, though nothing at all to the extent to which it existed among the Indian tribes of the United States, and especially Alaska.

In Southern Africa it exists among the Bechuanas (who, however, are not pure Bantu); not in the form of carving and setting up poles in their villages, but in the respect which different clans give to certain animals, *e.g.*, one clan being known as "buffalo-men," another as "lion-men," a third as "crocodile-men," and so forth. To each clan its totem animal is sacred, and they will not eat of its flesh. In some parts this sanctity is regarded as so great that actual prayer and sacrifice are made to it. But in most of the Bantu tribes this totem idea does not exist as a worship. Indeed, the animal (or part of an animal) is not sacred to an entire clan, but only to individuals, for whom it is chosen on some special occasion; and its use is prohibited only to that individual. Only in the sense that it may not be used for common purposes is it "sacred" or "holy" to him.

Taboo

Taboo" is a Polynesian term, and indicates that which man must not touch because it belongs to a deity. The god's land must not be trodden, the animal dedicated to the god must not be eaten, the chief who represents the god must not be lightly treated or spoken of. These are examples of taboo where the inviolable object or person belongs to a good god, and where the taboo corresponds exactly with the rule of holiness. But instances are still more numerous, among savages, of taboo attaching to an object because it is connected with a malignant power. The savage is surrounded on every side by such prohibitions; there is danger at every step that he may touch on what is forbidden to him, and draw down on himself unforeseen penalties."[72]

This idea exists very largely in the Gabun and Loango coasts: as described in a previous chapter, the custom is there called "orunda"; e.g., such and such an animal (or part of an animal) is "orunda," or taboo, to such and such a person.

The Portuguese Roman Catholic missionaries to the Kingdom of Kongo, more than two hundred and fifty years ago, found this custom "of interdicting to every person at their birth some one article of food, which they were not through life, upon any consideration, to put into their mouths. This practice was regarded [by those Roman Catholic priests] as specially heathenish, and was unconditionally" forbidden.

Explanation may here be found why a church which two hundred years ago had baptized members by the hundreds of thousands, with large churches, fine cathedrals, schools, colleges, and political backing, and no other form of Christianity to compete with it, shows in Kongo to-day no results in the matters of civilization, education, morality, or pure religion. Its baptism was only an outward one, the heathen native gladly accepting it as a powerful charm. For each and all his heathen fetiches the priest simply substituted a Roman Catholic relic. The ignorant African, while he learned to bow to the Virgin, kept on worshipping also fetich. The Virgin was only just

---

72 Menzies, History of Religion, p. 71.

another fetich. The Roman Catholic priests were to him only another set of powerful fetich doctors. They commanded that, instead of the orunda, "the parents should enjoin their children to observe some particular devotion, such as to repeat many times a day the rosary or the crown, in honor of the Virgin; to fast on Saturdays; to eat no flesh on Wednesdays; and such other things as are used among Christians."

A similar substitution was made in the case of a superstition of the Kongo country which exists universally among all African tribes to-day, *viz.*, "to bind a cord of some kind around the body of every new-born infant, to which were fastened the bones and teeth of certain kinds of wild animals." In place of this, the Roman Catholic records enjoin "that all mothers should make the cords with which they bound their infants, of palm-leaves that had been consecrated on Palm Sunday, and, moreover, guard them well with other such relies as we are accustomed to use at the time of baptism."

Thus the heathen, in becoming a baptized "Christian," left behind him only the name of his fetich ceremonies. Some new and professedly more powerful ones were given him, which were called by Christian names, but which very much resembled what he had been using all his life. His "conversion" caused no jar to his old beliefs, nor change in its practice, except that the new fetich was worshipped in a cathedral and before a bedizened altar.

Baptism
Forty years ago, on Corisco Island, I found the remains of a custom

which resembled baptism.[73] Before that time it was very prevalent in other parts of the Gabun country, whose people probably had derived it, like their circumcision, from East Africa and from Jewish traditions. As described at that time, "a public crier announces, the birth, and claims for the child a name and place among the living. Some one else, in a distant part of the village, acknowledges the fact, and promises, on the part of the people, that the new-born babe shall be received into the community, and have all the rights and immunities pertaining to the rest of the people. The population then assemble in the street, and the new-born babe is brought out and exposed to public view. A basin of water is provided, and the headman of the village or family sprinkles water upon it, giving it a name, and invoking a blessing upon it, such as, that it may have health, grow up to manhood or womanhood, have a numerous prog-eny, possess much riches, etc."[74] The circumcision of the child is performed some years later.

Spitting

The same Benga word, "tuwaka," to spit, is one of the two words which mean also "to bless." In pronouncing a blessing there is a vi-olent expulsiou of breath, the hand or head of the one blessed being held so near the face of the one blessing that sometimes in the act spittle is actually expelled upon him.

This blessing superstition exists among the Barotse of South

---

73   See an illustration of it on p. 102 of my "Crowned in Palm-Land"; an infant is lying on a plantain leaf in the street.

74   Wilson, Western Africa.

Africa (whose dialect is remarkably like the Benga). "Relatives take leave of each other with elaborate ceremony. They spit upon each other's faces and heads, or, rather, pretend to do so, for they do not actually emit saliva. They also pick up blades of grass, spit upon them, and stick them about the beloved head. They also spit on the bands: all this is done to warn off evil spirits. Spittle also acts as a kind of taboo. When they do not want a thing touched, they spit on straws, and stick them all about the object."[75]

Notice of Children
Recently (1903), in passing through a street of Libreville, I saw seven women sitting on the clay floor of the wide veranda of a house. In their arms or playing on the ground were a number of children. I was attracted by their gambols, and stopped on my way, and having saluted the mothers, I began to notice the children. The women knew me by sight, but I was a stranger to most of them. I thought they would be pleased by attention to their children. There were seven of them; and I exclaimed, "Oh! so many children!" And I began counting them, "One, two, three, four—" But I was interrupted by a chorus from the mothers, of "No! no! no! Stop! That is not good! The spirits will hear you telling how many there are, and they will come and take some away!" They were quite vexed at me. But I could not understand why, if spirits—can see, they would not know the number without hearing my count. Perhaps my enthusiastic counting brought the number more obviously to the attention of the surrounding spirits.

---

75 Declè.

CHAPTER XIV

Fetich – Its relation to the future life – ceremonies at deaths and funerals

Sickness, Death, Burial, Modes of Burial — Mourning, Treatment of Widows — Witchcraft Investigations — Places of Burial — Cannibalism — Family Quarrel as to Precedence in the Burying — Custom of "Lifting Up" of Mourners — Ukuku Dance for Amusement — Destination of the Dead — Transmigration

WHEN A HEATHEN NEGRO IS SICK, the first thing done, just as in civilized lands, is to call the "doctor," who is to find out what is the particular kind of spirit that, by invading the patient's body, has caused the sickness.

This diagnosis is not made by an examination and comparison of the physical and mental symptoms, but by drum, dance, frenzied song, mirror, fumes of drugs, consultation of relies, and conversation with the spirit itself. Next, as also in civilized lands, must be decided the ceremony particular to that spirit, and the vegetable and mineral substances supposed to be either pleasing or offensive to it. If all those cannot be obtained, the patient must die; the assumption probably being that some unknown person is antagonizing the "doctor" with arts of sorcery.

Fearing this, all the family relatives and friends come, having been informed by a messenger of the state of the case. They speak to and try to comfort the sick, as would be done in civilization. But to believers in fetich their coming means more than that. They have come from distant places as soon as the news had spread that their relative was seriously ill, without waiting for summons. Their coming is, indeed, a necessary mark of respect for the sick; but it may happen, too, in case of the sick man's dying, that it would be a proof for them of their innocence if a charge should come up of witchcraft as the cause of death. The neglect to make this prompt visit of condolence would be resented by the sick should he recover, or, in case of his death, in the days when witchcraft arts were more common, would have been held as a proof that the absentee had purposely absented himself, under a sense of guilt.

In the sick man's village there already has been a slight wailing the while that be is dying. Before life is extinct, and while yet the sick may still be conscious though speechless, a low wail of mourning is raised by the female relatives who have gathered in the room.

These visitors have sat quietly in the sick-room while the patient was still conscious. To a foreigner that quiet is very strange in its oppressive silence and in the stolidity of faces (at other times expressive), whose very reason for being present is supposed to be the expression of sympathy. Only a few assist in the making of food or medicine for the patient, even when the medicines are not fetich. All the others are spectators, smoking, lounging, dozing, or, if conversing, speaking in a low tone. At the first report that death has actually come, the women break into a louder wail.

But about a quarter of an hour is spent by some of the old members of the family, testing to see whether life is really extinct. When that fact is fully certified to the crowd in the street, the wailing breaks forth unrestrainedly from men, women, and children. The moment that death is declared, grief is demonstrated in screams, shrieks, yells, pitiful supplication, and extravagant praise by the entire village.

Shortly after this first frantic outburst quiet is ordered, and the arrangements for burial begin. The body is bathed and the limbs are straightened. The stomach is squeezed so as to make the contents emerge from the mouth in order that decomposition may be delayed and the body kept as long as possible. The time will vary according to the necessity of the case and the social position of the dead. Usually the corpse is retained only one day; but in case of a prominent person as many as five days, and in case of kings in some tribes, *e.g.*, of Loango, the rotting corpse, rolled in many pieces of matting, is retained for weeks.

When the washing and vomiting have been done, the corpse is dressed in its finest clothing. The bed-frame is often enlarged so that many of the chief mourners may be able to sit on it.

The body is generally taken from the bed and laid on a piece of matting on the floor. The chief female mourner is given the post of honor, to sit nearest to the dead, holding the head in her lap.

During the time until the burial the women keep bending the joints of the corpse to prevent the body becoming stiff. The day before the burial (but if in haste, on the very day of the death) the coffin is made. During the making the mourning which had been resumed is again bidden to cease, in order that the spirit may be pleased with the wooden house that is being constructed for it. For the same reason the wailing is again intermitted while the grave is being dug. Those who are digging it must not be called off or interrupted in any way. When begun, the job must be continued to completion.

After the grave is completed, when they leave it and go to arrange the coffin, they must put into the excavation some article, *e.g.*, a stick of wood, as a notice to any other wandering spirit not to occupy that grave.

When all these preparations are complete, the corpse is laid in the coffin, and some goods of the deceased, such as pieces of cloth and other clothing, are stuffed into it for his use in the other world. If the deceased was addicted to smoking, a pipe and tobacco are laid in the coffin, or if accustomed to spirituous drink, some liquor is often placed there, either native palm-wine or foreign rum.

Recently, while the Rev. F. S. Myongo, a native clergyman, was visiting on Corisco Island, be saw a mother put into a coffin a bundle of salt for her daughter to eat in the future world.

If the deceased was a rich man, the people of his mother's side do not allow him to be buried without their first being given a part of his property by the people of the father's side.

If there be a suspicion that he has been killed by witchcraft, and yet not enough proof to warrant a public charge and investigation, the relatives take amomum seeds (cardamom), chew them, and put them into the mouth of the dead, as a sign that the spirit shall itself execute vengeance on the murderer, and that the survivors will take no further steps. It is a *nolle prosequi* of a judicial case.

All being ready, the lid of the coffin is nailed down, except in the case of a first-born only child, as has been stated.

In former days, before coffins were used, the bamboo tatta of the bed-frame, the pandanus leaf mat, palm-fibre mosquito-net, and other bedding were all rolled about the corpse as it lay, and were buried with it.

While the corpse is being arranged in the coffin, the women have resumed their wailing. The coffin is lifted by strong men and hurriedly taken to the grave, the locality of which varies in different tribes,—sometimes in the adjacent forest, sometimes in the kitchen-garden of plantains immediately in the rear of the village houses, sometimes under the clay floor of the dwelling-house. With the men who are carrying the coffin may go some women as witnesses.

Formerly also slaves carried boxes of the dead man's goods, cloth, hardware, crockery, and so forth, to be laid by the body, which in those days was not interred, but was left on the top of the ground covered with branches and leaves.

In carrying the coffin to the grave it must not be taken through the village street but by the rear of the houses, lest the village be "defiled." As a result of such "defilement," all sorts of difficulties will arise, such as poor crops from the gardens and short supplies of fish.

The coffin is laid with the face of the dead looking eastward. During the interment people must not be moving about from place to place, but must remain at whatever spot they were when the coffin passed, until the burial is completed.

The digging of the grave, the carrying of the coffin, and the closing of the grave are all done only by men. When these have finished the work of burial, they are in great fear, and are to run rapidly to their village, or to the nearest body of water, river or lake or sea. If in their running one should trip and fall, it is a sign that he will soon die. They plunge into the water as a means of "purification" from possible defilement. The object of this purification is not simply to cleanse the body, but to remove the presence or contact of the spirit of the dead man or of any other spirit of possible evil influence, lest they should have ill-luck in their fishing, hunting, and other work.

During the time of these burial and other ceremonies the women have refrained from their mourning.

Women who have babes must not go along the route that was taken in the carrying of the coffin, lest their children shall become sick.

When all parties have returned from the grave, the wailing is resumed. They all mark their faces with ashes, and then begins the regular official kwedi (mourning). During the continuance of this, pregnant women and mothers with young children are not allowed to come near lest evil happen to them. To prevent any possibility of the just-departed spirit injuring any children of the village, leaves of a common weed, kâlâkâhi, are laid on their heads.

The day after the funeral a decoction is made of the bark of a well-known tree, bolondo. With it the doctor sprinkles the people, their houses, their utensils and weapons, and the two entrances to the village. During the ceremony the people are shouting an ejaculatory prayer, "Goods! Possessions! Wealth! Do not allow confusions to come to us!" this is distinctly a petition that the spirit should bring to them goods or help them to obtain wealth; "Let us have food!" and many other similar cries for good things. What remains in the vessel of the decoction of bolondo bark after the general sprinkling is carried to the ends of the village street, and emptied there, as a prevention against the entry of evil spirits.

Also there is made a mixture of scrapings of bolondo, powdered red-wood, and chalk. This is rubbed on the cheeks of the people to keep off the evil spirits. It is rubbed also, for that same purpose, on the walls of houses.

The cutlass (machete) and native hoe that was used in the digging of the grave are washed with the bolondo decoction after having been left exposed to rain over night.

Then one of the houses of the village is chosen as the ndabo ya kwedi (house of mourning). The mourners are to sit only in that house. If they should eat in any other house, the spirit of the dead would come and eat with them and would make them sick. During the days of kwedi the men go in the mornings to fish; while they are away at the work, the weeping is intermitted lest in some way it spoil the fishing.

The bedstead in the house of mourning must be constantly occupied, even during the daytime, by some persons sitting there, lest the spirit come to take any vacant space; and the house itself must not, by day or night, be without some occupant. The near relatives, when one has occasion to go out of that house, must not go unaccompanied, lest the spirit follow them and attempt to resume earthly companionship and thus injure them.

If it was a great man who has died, an occasional dance is held during the prescribed mourning time to please his spirit, which is supposed to be walking around and observing what is done.

The kwedi formerly lasted a month, or, for a prominent person, a month and a half.

People who while they were living were supposed to have witch power are believed to be able to rise in an altered form from their graves. To prevent one who is thus suspected from making trouble, survivors open the grave, cut off the head, and throw it into the sea,-or in the interior, where there is no great body of water, it is burned; then a decoction of the bolondo bark is put into the grave. (The bolondo is a poison; even a little of it may be fatal.)

When affairs are going wrong in the villages,and the people do not know the cause, offerings of food and drink are taken to the grave to cause the spirit to cease disturbing them, and pravers are made to it that it may the rather bless them.

If the deceased was (a very important person, the kwedi is interrupted on the fifth day, for the selection of his successor as chief or king. This ceremony is called "ampenda" (glories). The successor is placed on the vacant seat or "throne"; and songs are sung in his praise. But first, a herald is sent to the forest, or wherever the burial was made, to call the dead to come and dispute his right to the throne, if he be not really dead. The herald stands and calls on the dead by name", Such an one!" This he does slowly once, twice, thrice, until five times. He returns, and reports to the waiting assembly, "He is really dead. I called five times, and he did not answer." Then, this herald, standing in the street before all the people, praises the dead for all his good deeds, and blames for some of his bad ones. He turns to the chosen successor sitting on the throne, and asks pardon for the candor he is about to exercise: "To-morrow I will bow to you and take off my hat., but to-day I will tell the whole truth about you." Turning to the crowd, he says, "The man who is gone was good, and be has given us this new man. We hope that he too will be good. You all help me now to tell him his bad points." Then, addressing the new chief, he specifies, "You have a bad habit of so and so." And the crowd responds affirmatively, "Bad! cease it!" After this, when the herald has ended his own list of rebukes, any one else may call him aside and tell him of any other evil of which be knows, and ask him to direct the new king to reform it. This ceremony was particularly observed by the Mpongwe-speaking tribes of the Gabun country. In the presence of the domination by foreign governments, but little of it now exists there or in any other tribes to the north.

In the improvised songs and ejaculations of the kwedi period the goodness and greatness of the dead are recounted. The praise is fulsome, exaggerated, and often preposterously untrue. Some declare their hopelessness of ever again seeing any joy. Supplications are shrieked by others for the departed to come back and reanimate the dead body. By most the wailing is a song in moans. Men tear their garments; women dishevel their hair; all take off their ornaments, and disfigure their faces with ashes or clay. The female relatives reduce their clothing to a minimum of decency. In all tribes formerly, and in some interior tribes still, the wives are made naked, and compelled to remain so for months, especially if they were known not to have been as submissive as is expected in the slavery of savage African marriage.

During my early days in the Ogowe, about 1876, a native Akele chief, Kasa, who had been my patron at my first residence in the Ogowe, Belambila, died after I had removed to my second station, Kangwe. I made a ceremonious visit of respect and condolence about a month after his death, for Kasa, though a heathen and often cruel, to me had been true and helpful. His family appreciated the compliment of my visit. I looked around the room, and missed his wives. I did not know that they had been divested of all clothing. I asked for them. A man hastened to go out and call them. I wondered somewhat at the delay in their coming. I was afterward told that though they were accustomed to the disgrace of nakedness before native eyes, they did not wish to meet mine, for I had always treated them respectfully. A half-dozen of them sidled into the room, each carrying in their hands, as their only protection, a plate, and quickly huddled together in a corner of the room. I as quickly dismissed them, telling them I had not known of the rule under which they were living.

In the Batanga interior, among the Bulu-Fang tribe, where women at all times wear scarcely any clothing, most widows are still required to go perfectly naked, sometimes for a whole year.

All this wailing and mourning, while sincere on the part of some, is by most simply a yielding to the contagion of sympathy. By some it is a mere formality, and with many even a pretence.

In the older days, before Christianity had obtained any influence, or before foreign governments had exercised power to force away barbarous rites and compel civilized ones, when almost every death was regarded as due to the exercise of black art, and was always followed by a witchcraft investigation and by the putting to death of from one to ten socalled "witches" and "wizards" (in the case of kings, fifty to one hundred), no one, except the doctor and his secret councillors, knew on whom suspicion for the death might fall, and all were quick to be demonstrative in their grief, whether real or feigned, as a means of warding off the dreaded accusation against themselves.

Though those witchcraft executions have ceased wherever foreign power exists, the wailing is still as demonstrative, either as a sign of real grief or as a mere custom; and the mourning after burial continued for weeks (or even months) is an enormous evil. Wives and husbands abandoning their duties to their own villages; children either slighted at their own homes or idly helping to swell the confusion at the town of mourning; men neglecting their fishing, and women neglecting their gardens,—all these visitors are an expensive draft on the hospitality and resources of the town of kwedi, or on their other relatives who may happen to be living near. Inevitably there is not enough food for all, and they stanch their hunger by immoderate drinking of foreign alcoholic liquors.

After the first paroxysms of grief, in a few days the mourning is reduced to a perfunctory wail by the women for a short time each morning and evening. The remainder of the day is spent in idle talk, which always runs into quarrels; and the nights in dances, which generally end in dissolute revelry. A month of mourning lays up a list of assignations and intrigues that result in trials for adultery and broken marriage relations.

The feelings in the hearts of the mourners are very mixed. The outcry of affection, pleading with the dead to return to life, is sincere, the survivor desiring the return to life to be complete; but almost simultaneous with that cry comes a fear that the dead may indeed return, not as the accustomed embodied spirit, helpful and companionable, but as a disembodied spirit, invisible, estranged, perhaps inimical, and surrounded by an atmosphere of dread imparted by the unknown and the unseen. The many then ask, not that the departed may return, but that, if it be hovering near, it will go away entirely.

Few were those who during the life of the departed had not on occasions had some quarrel with him, or had done him some injustice or other wrong, and their thought is, "His spirit will come back to avenge itself!" So guns are fired to frighten away the spirit, and to cause it to go off to the far world of spirits, and not take up a residence in or near the town to haunt and injure the living.

Nevertheless, the kwedi is kept up, if for nothing else than to satisfy the self-complacence of the dead. It is believed that the dead, sometimes dissatisfied with the extent or character of the mourning ceremony, have returned and inflicted some sickness on the village, for the removal of which other ceremonies have to be performed.

Thus far acts which are dictated by natural feelings, good and otherwise, have been dealt with; but there are a multitude of other ceremonies, varied in different tribes and never the same in any one tribe, which are performed under the direct influence of religious duty as well as superstitious fear. What has been thus far described is especially true of the Mpongwe, Benga, and Batanga tribes of western Equatorial Africa, typical for most Bantu tribes of the continent. The following quotations afford a comparison of the burial customs of savages in other regions with those I have observed:

Lumholtz,[76] describing the burial customs of Australia, writes: "The natives in the neighborhood of Portland Bay, in the southwestern part of South Australia, cremate their dead by placing the corpse in a hollow tree and setting fire to it.... The natives of Australia have

---

76   Among Cannibals, pp. 278-279.

this peculiarity, in common with the savages of other countries, that they never utter the names of the dead, lest their spirits should hear the voices of the living and thus discover their whereabouts. There seems to be a widespread belief in the soul's existence independently of matter. On this point Fraser relates that the Kulie tribe (Victoria) believes that every man and animal has a muriep (ghost or spirit) which can pass into other bodies. A person's muriep may in his lifetime leave his body and visit other people in his dreams. After death the muriep is supposed to appear again, to visit the grave of its former possessor, to communicate with living persons in their dreams, to eat remnants of food lying near the camp, and to warm itself by the night fires. A similar belief has been observed among the blacks of Lower Guinea. On my travels I, too, found a widespread fear of the spirits of the dead, to which the imagination of the natives attributed all sorts of remarkable qualities. The greater the man was on earth, the more his departed spirit is feared.... An old warrior who has been a strong man and therefore much respected by his tribe, is, after his death, put on a platform made with forked sticks, cross-pieces, and a sheet or two of bark; he is hoisted up amidst a pandemonium of noise, howling, and wailing, besides much cutting with tomahawks, and banging of heads with nolla-nollas. He is laid on his back with his knees up, like the females, and the grass is cleared away from under and around. The place is now for a long time carefully avoided, till he is quite shrivelled, whereupon his bones are taken away and put in a tree.

"The common man is buried like a woman, only that logs are put over him, and his bones are not removed. Young children are put bodily into the trees.

"The fact that the natives bestow any care on the bodies of the dead is doubtless owing to the fear of the spirits of the departed. In some places I have seen the legs drawn and tied fast to the bodies, in order to hinder the spirits of the dead, as it were, from getting out to frighten the living. Women and children, whose spirits are not feared, receive less attention and care after death.

"In several tribes it is customary to bury the body where the person was born. I know of a case where a dying man was transported fifty miles in order to be buried in the place of his nativity. It has even happened that the natives have begun digging outside a white man's kitchen door, because they wanted to bury an old man born there. In Central Queensland I saw many burial-places on hills. Such are also said to be found in New South Wales and in Victoria. These burial grounds have been in use for centuries, and are considered sacred.

"In South Australia and in Victoria the bead is not buried with the body, for the skull is preserved and used as a drinking-cup. It is a common custom to place the dead between pieces of bark and grass on a scaffold, where they remain till they are decayed, and then the bones are buried in the ground.

"In the northern part of Queensland I have heard people say that the natives have a custom of placing themselves under these scaffolds to let the fat drop on them, and that they believe that this puts them in possession of the strength of the dead man.

"A kind of mummy dried by the aid of fire and smoke, is also found in Australia; male children are most frequently prepared in this manner. The corpse is then packed into a bundle, which is carried for some time by the mother. She has it with her constantly, and at night sleeps with it at her side. After about six months, when nothing but the bones remain, she buries it in the earth. Full-grown men are also sometimes carried in this manner, particularly the bodies of great warriors."

W. H. Brown, in "On the South African Frontier," describes a burial in Mashona-land: "When a member of the community dies, he or she, as the case may be, is usually buried under a shelf of rock in a reclining position, with arms folded and legs doubled up. In some districts, where heaps of rocks are scarce, I have seen graves made in large ant-heaps. As a rule, a small canopy or thatched roof is built over the grave, and under this it is common to see placed, as an offering, a pot of beer and a plate of sadza. The beer evaporates, and the ants eat the sadza; but, to the Mashona mind, the disappearance is due to supernatural causes. At the burial the near relatives of the deceased cry aloud. I was camping one night near a village where a child died. The obsequies took place next morning between dawn and sunrise. The mother cried loudly while the ceremony was proceeding, but her wailing ceased soon after the funeral, and there was no more noise made over it. I went into the village about two hours later, and saw some men, women, and children quietly sitting around the hut in which the death had taken place, and looking very solemn. The child was about two weeks old, and the cause of death was attributed by the Mashonas to the fact that the mother had not given beer to her grandfather when he wanted it at his death.

"If a woman's husband dies, and she afterwards procures another, the new man takes up his abode in the hut of the dead one, becomes owner of his assegais and battle-axes, and assumes his name. Whether or not the second husband is supposed to enter into possession of the spirit of the deceased, I could not discover. Some Mashonas have told me that they believe that the spirits of their departed relatives enter the bodies of animals, particularly those of lions.

"At the end of the lunar month during which a death has taken place, the surviving partner, man or woman, kills a goat, and its meat is cooked, as well as quantities of other food, and a large amount of Kaffir beer is brewed. The people gather from the neighboring kraals, and an all-night feast and dance ensue.

"Monthly 'dead-relative dances,' which are called 'machae' are very common; and if no one has been accommodating enough to die during the month, the feast and dance may be held in honor of some one who departed years before."

A similar dance is held in the Gabun region of West Africa, partly as a consolatory amusement for the living, near the close of whatever prescribed time of mourning. It is called "Ukukwe" (for the spirit), as if for the gratification of the hovering spirit of the dead; but in many places in that region this dance has lost all reference to or for the dead, or even any connection with a time of mourning, and has become simply a common amusement.

In the Bihe country of Southwest Africa,[77] "death is surrounded by many strange and absurd superstitions. It is considered essen-

_____

77   Arnot, Garenganze, p. 116.

tial that a man should die in his own country, if not in his own town. On the way to Bailundu, shortly after leaving Bihe territory, I met sorne men running at great speed, carrying a sick man tied to a pole, in order that be might die in his own country. I tried to stop them; but they were running, as fast as their burden would allow them, down a steep rocky bill. By the sick man's convulsive movements I could see that be was in great pain, perhaps in his death throes; hence the great haste. If a Bailundu man dies in Bibe, the Bibe people have to pay the Bailundu heavily for the shameful conduct of the Bihe demons in killing a stranger; and vice versa.

"When a man dies at home, his body is placed on a rude table, and his friends meet for days round the corpse, drinking, eating, shouting, and singing, until the body begins actually to fall to pieces. Then the body is tied in a fagot of poles and carried on men's shoulders up and down some open space, followed by doctors and drummers. The doctors demand of the dead man the cause of his death, whether by poison or witchcraft; and if by the latter, who was the witch? Most of the deaths I have known of in Negro-land were from pulmonary diseases, but all were set down to witchcraft. The jerking of the bier to and fro, causing the men bearing it to stumble hither and thither, is taken as the dead man's answer; thus, as in the case of spirit-rapping at home, the reply is spelled out. The result of this enquiry is implicitly believed in; and, if the case demands it, the witch is drowned."

Among the Barotse of South Africa[78] "funerals take place at

___

78   Deck, Three Years in Savage Africa, pp. 74-79.

night, and generally immediately after death, while the body is still warm. If the person, when alive, possessed the skin of an animal, they wrap the body in it, and also in a—plain mat, and then bury it near the hut. But death inspires them with a mortal terror, and thus the hut of the dead man is nearly always abandoned. Anything that has been used for the burial, such as the wood. on which the corpse was carried, is left near the grave. It is the fashion to display great external signs of grief, howls and cries of lamentation and the like. Formerly the graves of chiefs were distinguished by elephant tusks turned toward the east. All cattle belonging to the deceased are killed; and any animal of which he was particularly fond, such as the cow whose milk he drank, is killed first. They bury in the kraal itself those who died in the kraal; but whenever it is possible, the dying are taken out and laid in the fields or forest. There are two reasons for this: first, they think that away from other people is a better chance of the invalid making a recovery; and, secondly, wherever the person dies he must be buried; therefore, if possible, far from their habitations. When a man dies, visits of condolence are paid to the relatives, the visitors bringing a calf or a head of cattle as a mark of sympathy, which is killed and eaten as a kind of consolation. The night after the funeral is passed in tears and cries, A few days later, the doctor comes and makes an incision on the forehead of each of the survivors, and fills it with medicine, in order to ward off contagion and the effect of the sorcery which caused the death. They place on their tombs some souvenir of the profession or vocation of the defunct; for example,-if he had been a hunter, horns or skins; if a chairmaker, a chair; and so on. Over the grave a sacred tree is planted. The tree is a kind of laurel called 'morata.'... A man will kill himself on the tomb of his chief; he thinks, as he passes near by, that he hears the dead man call him and bid him bring him water. These natives believe in transmigration of the soul into animals; thus, the hippopotamus is believed to shelter the spirit of a chief. Nevertheless, they do not appear very clear that the soul can not be in two places at once; else, if a chief has become a hippopotamus in the Zambesi, why should one slay one's self to bring water to his tomb?"

Perhaps Declè was not aware of a widespread belief in a dual soul, consisting of a "spirit," that, as far as known, lives forever in the world of spirits, and a "shadow" that for an uncertain length of time hovers around the mortal remains. Some, as already mentioned in a previous chapter, also name a third entity, the "life,"-that which, being "eaten" by sorcerers, causes the living being to sicken, and which the sorcerer, if detected, can be compelled to return to its owner. Miss Kingsley thought also she had discovered a belief in a fourth entity, the "dream-soul." But this, though doubtless believed in as that which sometimes leaves the sleeping body and goes on distant wanderings, is the same as the "spirit," during whose temporary absence the body continues its breathing and other physical motions, in virtue of the presence of its second and third soul-entities.

The funeral practices of all the tribes, with very few exceptions, over all Africa, however much they may and do vary, contain all of them, as shown by the preceding quotations, a decided belief in, and fear of, the intelligent and probably inimical activity of the spirits of their dead. They include also the custom of the burial with the dead man of more or less of his property, together with the destruction of such things as cannot be conveniently placed in the grave,—clothing, crockery, utensils, wives, slaves, trees of fruitage, etc.

Even among the civilized and enlightened, while of course there would be no excessive destruction of property, nor murder of widow or slave, an extravagant amount of wearing apparel is stuffed into the coffin (which is sometimes made large for that purpose) as a sign of the importance of the dead, and of the sacrifice the love and grief of the living are willing to make.

The residence of the transmigrated spirit is probably not a permanent one. The Wa-nya-mwesi of East Africa "believe in transmigration both during life and after it. Thus, according to them, a sorcerer can transform himself into a wild animal to injure his enemies; but in such cases the change is not permanent, and the soul does not remain in its new habitation."[79]

Leaving out of view the immense difference, caused by the absence of Christianity, in the moral life of native Africa, as compared with that of the United States, there is no one thing that more painfully strikes me, in the low civilization of the former, than their customs for the dead. It would occupy too much space to recount at length all the reasons the natives give for their sometimes apparently heartless ceremonies. The true explanation lies in their belief in witchcraft and their fear of spirits.

From the testimony of travellers, burial customs are much the same all over Africa. What I have written is my personal knowl-

---

79 Declè.

edge of what prevails on the West Coast, in the equatorial regions, and especially in the portion lying along the course of the Ogowe River,—a river that was first brought to public notice through the writings of Paul Du Chaillu, the journeys of a British trader, Mr. R.B.N. Walker, and subsequently by the thorough explorations of Count P. S. De Brazza.

There are in Africa social distinctions of rich and poor, higher and lower classes, just as there are, and always will be, all the world over, the claims of communism to the contrary notwithstanding. These distinctions follow their subjects to the grave,—just as, in our own civilization, one is laid in the sculptured cemetery and another in the Potter's Field.

The African burial-grounds are mostly in the forest, in the low-lying lands and tangled thickets along the sea-beach, or the banks of rivers. Hills and elevated building-sites are reserved for villages and plantations. If a traveller, in journeying along the main river of the country, observes long reaches of uncleared thickets, he will probably be correct in suspecting that these are burial-grounds. His native crew will be slow to inform him of the fact or to converse on the subject, unless to object to an order to go ashore there.

Some of the interior tribes bury all their dead under the clay floors of their houses. The living are thus actually treading and cooking their food over the graves of their relatives.

This mode of burial is reserved as a distinction, in the case of some coast tribes, for a very few of their honored chiefs, or for a specially loved relative.

Over or near the graves of the rich are built little huts, where are laid the common articles used by them in their life,—pieces of crockery, knives, sometimes a table, mirrors, and other goods obtained in foreign trade. Once, in ascending the Ogowe, I observed, tied to the branches of a large tree extending over the stream from the top of the bank, a wooden trade-chest, five pitchers and mugs, and several fathoms of calico prints. I was informed that the grave of a lately deceased chief was near, that these articles were signs of his wealth, and were intended as offerings to spirits to induce them to draw to the villages of his people the trade of passing merchant vessels.

A noticeable fact about these gifts to the spirits is that, however great a thief a man may be, he will not steal from a grave. The coveted mirror will lie there and waste in the rain, and the valuable garment will flap itself to rags in the wind, but human hands will not touch them. Sometimes the temptation to steal is removed by the donor fracturing the article before it is laid on the grave.

Actual interment is generally given to all who in life were regarded as at all worthy of respect. Native implements for excavating being few and small, the making of a grave is quite a task; it is often, therefore, made no deeper than is actually sufficient for covering the corpse. This, according to the greatness of the dead or the wealth of the family, is variously encased, Sometimes it is placed in a coffin made of the ends of an old canoe; or, more shapely, of boards cut from the canoe's bottom and sides; or, even so expensively as to use two trade-boxes, making one long one by knocking out an end from each and telescoping them.

Sometimes the corpse is cast out on the surface of the ground, and perhaps a pile of stones or brushwood gathered over it. Some-times it lies uncovered. Sometimes they are cast into the river.

Many years ago, I was ascending the Ogowe River in my boat, painfully toiling against the current. I had unwisely refused the wish of my crew to stop for our mid-day meal at a desirable ulako (camp-ing-ground), as the hour was too early; and I determined to go on, and stop at some other place. But I regretted presently; for, instead of finding forest and high camping-ground, we came to a long stretch of papyrus swamp; and, after that, to low jungle. We pulled on for another mile, the sun growing hotter, along the unsheltered bank, and we growing faint with hunger as the hour verged to noon. Becoming desperate, I directed the crew to stop at the very first spot that was solid enough for foothold, intending to eat our dry rice without fire. Presently we came to a clump of oil-palms. Their existence showed solid ground, and I seized the rudder and ran the boat ashore. The crew objected, hungry though they were, that "it was not a good place "; but they did not mention why. I jumped ashore, however, and ordered them to follow, and gather sticks for fire. As they were rather slow in so doing, and I overheard murmuring that "firewood is not gotten from palm trees" (which is true), I set them an example by starting off on a search myself.

I had not gone far before I found a pile of brushwood, and, re-joicing at my success, I called out to the crew to come and carry it. While they were coming, I stooped down and laid hold of an eligible stick. But an odor startled me; and the other sticks that I had dislocated falling apart, there was revealed a human foot and shin, which, from the ornaments still remaining about the ankle, I suppose was a woman's.

My attendants fled; and I re-embarked in the boat, sufficiently unconscious of hunger to await it late meal that was not cooked until we reached a comfortable village a short distance beyond. My crew then explained their slowness to obey me at that clump of palm trees, by saying that they knew it looked like a burying-place.

A less respectful mode of burial (if, indeed, the term be not a misnomer) is applied to the poor, to the friendless aged who have wearied out the patience of relatives by a long sickness, and to those whose bodies are offensive by a leprous or otherwise ulcerous condition. Immediately that life seems extinct (and sometimes even before) the wasted frame is tied up in the rnat on which it is lying, and, slung from a pole on the shoulders of two men, is flung out on the surface of the ground in the forest, to become the prey of wild beasts and the scavenger "driver" (Termes bellicosa) ants.

Of one tribe in the upper course of the Ogowe, I was told, who, in their intense fear of ghosts, and their dread of the possible evil influence of the spirits of their own dead relatives, sometimes adopt a horrible plan for preventing their return. With a very material idea of a spirit, they seek to disable it by beating the corpse until every bone is broken. The mangled mass is bung in a bag at the foot of a tree in the forest. Thus mutilated, the spirit is supposed to be unable to return to the village, to entice into its fellowship of death any of the survivors.

Some dead bodies are burned, particularly those of criminals. Persons convicted on a charge of witchcraft are "criminals," and are almost invariably killed. Sometimes they are beheaded. I have often had in my possession the curved knives with which this operation is performed.

Sometimes torture is used: a common mode is to roast the condemned over a slow fire, which is made under a stout bed-frame built for the purpose. In such a case almost the entire body is reduced to ashes. When I was clearing a piece of ground at Belambila in the Ogowe in 1875, for the house which I afterward occupied, my workmen came on a pile of ashes, charcoal, and charred bones, where, they assured me, a criminal had been put to death.

A barely mentionable method of disposal of the bodies of the dead is to eat them. That is possible only in a cannibal country. That it was actual was known among the Gabun Fang fifty years ago, and among my Ogowe Fang twentyfive years ago. None ate of their own dead; adjacent towns exchanged corpses. Women were not allowed to partake. The practice was confined to the old men. One such was pointed out to me at Talaguga in 1882. He robbed graves for that purpose.

Among the coast tribes of the Gabun region of West Africa cremation is not known, nor are corpses thrown out on the ground. Under the influence of foreign example, the dead are coffined, more or less elaborately, according to the ability of the family; and the interment is made in graves of proper depth. In some of these tribes a locality of low, dark, tangled forest, not suitable as site for a village or for a plantation, is used as a public cemetery.

Among the tribes of Batanga in the German Kamerun territory, though the people are civilized, the old unsanitary custom of burying in the kitchen-gardens immediately in the rear of the village, and sometimes actually in the clay floor of the dwelling itself, is still kept up, even by the more enlightened natives. The Christians are not in numbers sufficiently large in any family to control all the burial ceremonies of its dead members. The strange spectacle is therefore presented of a mixture of Christian ritual and fetich custom. In my own experience at funerals of some children of church-members at Batanga, the singing of hymns of faith and hope by the Christian relatives alternated with the howling of half-naked heathen death-dancers in an adjoining house. And when I had read the burial service to the point of beginning the march of the procession to the grave, perhaps only a few rods distant, the heathen remained behind; and while I was reading the "dust to dust" at the grave-side, they would be building a quick fire of chips and dried leaves on the exact spot where the coffin had last stood in the village street. The ashes they would gather and incorporate into their family fetiches, to insure fertility to the mother and other near female relatives of the dead child.

Also, in the Gabun region, there is the remains of a custom, practised especially by the Orungu tribe of Cape Lopez, of a pretended quarrel between two parties of mourners on a question whether or not the burial shall actually be made, even though there is no doubt that it will be, and the coflin is ready to be carried. This contest concluded, a second quarrel is raised on a question as to which of two sets of relatives, the maternal or the paternal, shall have the right to carry it. Very recently this actually occurred at the town of Libreville, and on the premises of the American Presbyterian Mission, the fight being shamefully waged by young men who formerly had been professing Christians. They had been given permission to bury a young man in our Protestant cemetery. The missionary in charge of the station heard a great hubbub on the path entering the mission grounds, as if a fight was in progress. Going to investigate, he found an angry contest was being carried on, under the old heathen idea that the spirit of the dead must see and be pleased by a demonstration of a professed desire to keep him with the living, and not to allow him to be put away from them. The contest of words had almost come to blows, and the victors had set up a disgraceful shout as they seized the coffin to bring it to the grave.

Another custom remains in Gabun,—a pleasant one; it may once have had fetich significance, but it has lost it now, so that Christians may properly retain it. Just before the close of the kwedi, friends (other than relatives) of the mourners will bring some gift, even a small one, make a few remarks appropriate to it and to the circumstances of the receiver, and give it to his or her mourning friend. It is called the "ceremony of lifting up," *i.e.*, out of the literal ashes, and from the supposed depths of grief. For instance, if the gift be a piece of soap, the speech of donation will be, "Sit no longer in the dust with begrimed face! Rise, and use the soap for your body!" Or if it be a piece of cloth, "Be no longer naked! Rise, and clothe yourself with your usual dress!" Or if it be food, "Fast no longer in your grief! Rise, and strengthen your body with food!"

As to the status of the departed in the spirit-world, though all those African tribes from old heathen days knew of the name of God, of His existence, and of some of His attributes, they did not know of the true way of escape from the evils of this present life, of any system of reward and punishment in the future life, nor of any of the conditions of that life.

A Civilized Family. Gabun.

That they had a belief in a future world is evidenced by survivors taking to the graves of their dead, as has been described in the preceding pages, boxes of goods, native materials, foreign cloth, food, and (formerly) even wives and servants, for use in that other life to which they had gone. Whatever may have been supposed about the locality or occupations of that life, the dead were confidently believed to have carried with them all their bu man passions and feelings, and especially their resentments. Fear of those possible resentments dominated the living in all their attempts at spiritual communication with the dead.

As to the locality of the latter, it was not believed that all of them always remained in that unknown other world. They could wander invisibly and intangibly. More than that, they could return bodily and resume this earthly life in other forms; for belief in metempsychosis is a common one among all these tribes. The dead, some of them, return to be born again, either into their own family or into any other family, or even into a beast.

Who thus return, or why they return, is entirely uncertain. Certainly not all are thus born again. Those who in this present life had been great or good or prominent or rich remain in the spirit-world, and constitute the special class of spirits called "awiri" (singular, "ombwiri").

But these awiri are at liberty to revisit the earth: if they choose, taking a local habitation in some prominent natural object, or coming on call to aid in ceremonies for curing the sick. Other spirits, as explained in a previous chapter, are sinkinda, the souls of the common dead; and ilâga, unknown spirits of other nations, or beings who have become "angels," all of these living in "Njambi's Town."

As to Father Njambi Himself, the creator and overseer of all, both living and dead, every kind of spirit-ombwiri, nkinda, olaga, and all sorts of abambo-is under His control, but He does not often exercise it.

CHAPTER XV

Fetichism – some of its practical effects

Depopultation

ONE OF THE EFFECTS OF WITCHCRAFT beliefs in Africa is the depopulation of that continent. Over enormous areas of the country the death rate has exceeded the birth rate. Much of Africa is desert—the Sahara of the north, and the Kalahari of the south—with estimated populations of only one to the square mile. Another large area is a wilderness covered by the great sub-equatorial forest,—a belt about three hundred miles wide and one thousand miles long, with an estimated population of only eighteen to the square mile (among whom are the Pygmy tribes); and these not scattered uniformly, but gathered chiefly on the banks of the water courses, the only highways (except narrow footpaths) through that dismal forest.

The entire population of Africa, including all nationalities,— Copts of Egypt, Moors and Berbers of the north, Arabs of the east, Abyssinians, Pygmies, and Cannibals of the centre, Negroes, both Bantu and Negroid, of the west, south, centre, and east,—probably do not number two hundred million. Of these, the Negroes probably do not amount to one hundred million. German authorities variously estimate the population of their Kamerun country at from two to five million, and they have been vigorously reducing it by their savage punitive expeditions in the interior. The French authorities of the Kongo-Français estimate theirs at from five to ten million.

The population of the great Kongo River was much overestimated after the opening of that river by Stanley. Its people were massed on the river banks, and gave an impression of density which subsequent interior travel has not verified. To walk slowly in an hour over a mile of road that constitutes the one street of a town; to count the huts, and allot such or such a number to each, would give a sufficiently accurate census of one thousand or perhaps two thousand to that town. But that place is the centre of travel or traffic of that region. A half-day's journey on any radius from that town through the surrounding forest would confront the traveller with scarcely any other evidences of human habitation. Towns of the thousands are not the usual sigbt; rather the villages of one hundred, and the hamlets of twenty, excepting in the Sudan, in the Yoruba and other countries of the Niger, and in tbe large capitals of Dahomey and other Guinea kingdoms. There walled cities of from fifty to one hundred thousand inhabitants are known.

These congested districts help to lift the average that would be made low by the paucity in the wilderness and desert portions. Probably the population of the entire continent was much greater two hundred years ago. Depopulation was hastened by the export slave-trade. Livingstone estimated that, on the East Coast, for every slave actually exported, nineteen others died on the way. The foreign slave-trade has long ceased, except from the Upper Nile down through Egypt and Arabia, and from the Sudan across the Sahara to Morocco. But far worse than Arab slave-trade are the diabolical atrocities, committed during the last fifteen years and actually at the present time, in the Kongo, under white officers of the miscalled "Free State," and with the knowledge and allowance of the King of Belgium.

But, aside from all these and other civil and political causes, the fetich religion of Africa has been a large part of its destruction. It has been a Moloch, whose hunger for victims was never satisfied: as illustrated in the annual sacrifice of hundreds and thousands by the priests of the kings of Dahomey and Ashanti; and the burial victims at the funerals of great kings, as in Uganda and all over the continent. If the destruction of such human victims is not so great to-day as it was twenty years ago, due to enlightenment by Christian missions and forceful prohibition by civilized governments, the spirit of and disposition to destruction is not eradicated; it is only suppressed. It is so deep seated and ingrained as a part of religion, that it is among the very last of the shadows of heathenism to disappear after individuals or tribes are apparently civilized and enlightened. Under transforming influences the native has been lifted from dishonesty to honesty, from untruth to truth, from immorality to virtue, from heathenism to Christianity; and yet there still clings to him, though he no longer worships the fetich, a belief in and fear of it. The presence of foreign governments can and does prevent witchcraft murder for the dead; but if these governments were withdrawn from English Sierra Leone, French Kongo-Français, and other partitions of Africa, the witchcraft ordeal and murder would be at once resumed. And no wonder. Inbred beliefs, deepened by millenniums of years of practice, are not eliminated by even a century of foreign teaching. Costume of body and fashion of dress are easily and voluntarily changed; not so the essence of one's being.

Under the assurance that a consecrated charm can be made for the accomplishment of any purpose whatever, it results that almost every native African heathen, in hours of fear or anger or revenge, has made, or has had made, for himself amulets, or has performed rites intended to compass an injury to, and perhaps the death of, some other person. Should that other die, even as long a time as a year afterward, it will be believed that that fetich amulet or act caused the death.

It follows, therefore (although even heathen natives do, in rare cases, say of a death, "Yes, Anzam took this one," *i.e.*, that he died a natural death), that almost universally at any death which we would know as a natural one, surviving relatives and friends make the charge of witchcraft, and seek the witch or wizard, by investigation involving, in the trial, torture, or ordeal by poison, fire, or other tests. For every natural death at least one, and often ten or more, have been executed under witchcraft accusation.

I have pleaded for the lives of accused when I believed them innocent, and whenever I was informed that an investigation was in progress, I said to the crowd assembled in the street, "When you kill these three people to-day, do I see three babies born to take their place in the number of the inhabitants of your village?"

The Balengi on the Benita River, among whom I travelled in 1865-70, were then a large tribe. It is now very small, exterminated largely by witchcraft murders for the dead. The aged, defenceless, and slaves are generally selected as victims. But no one is secure. Relatives of a chief who during his life may have seemed envious of his power, are often suspected and put to death.

For the determination of a doubtful cause of decease postmortems are made, but not on any rational basis or with any knowledge of anatomy. In the autopsy of an ordinary person the object is to find among the bowels or other internal organs some sign which the doctor-priest may declare to be the path of the supposed sorcery-injected destroying spirit. In case of a magician, the object is to see whether his own "familiar" had "eaten" him. Cavities in the lungs are considered proof positive that one's own power has destroyed him. The fimbriated extremities of the fallopian tubes of a uterus are also declared to be "witch." Their ciliary motions on dissection are regarded as a sign that the woman was a witch. In proof, the native doctor said to me, "See! those are the spirit-teeth. Don't you see how they move and extend in desire to catch and eat?" It was in vain that I declared to him that if that was true then every woman all over the world was a witch, and that he was bound to go ahead and kill them all; for that God had made no woman without those things. (Was this "doctor's" idea the same reason for which the old anatomists called those fimbriæ "morsus Diaboli"?)

In Garenganze, among the Barotse,[80] "the trial for witchcraft is short and decisive. If one man suspects another of having bewitched him,—in fact, if he has a grudge against him,—he brings

---

80   Arnot, p. 76.

him before the council, and the ordeal of the boiling pot is resorted to. My proposal is that if they consider it a fair trial of 'whiteness' or 'blackness' of heart, as they call it, then let both the accuser and the accused put their hands into the boiling water. The king is strongly in favor of this proposal, and would try any means to stop this fearful system of murder which is thinning out many of his best men; but the nation is so strongly in favor of the practice that he can do nothing. An old friend of mine, Wizini, who took quite a fatherly care and interest in me, for some peculiar reason of his own, was charged with witchcraft. He pleaded earnestly to be spared the terrible trial, and was reprieved because of his years, but banished from his people and country for life, for no other reason than that a neighbor had an ill feeling against him. Had he, been first to the king with his complaint, he might have gotten his neighbor burned or banished instead of himself.... Their punishments are very cruel. Burning alive is, among the Barotse, a common occurrence; also tying the victim hand and foot and laying him near a nest of large black ('driver') ants, which in a few days pick his bones clean."

But it is well to repeat my own qualification of most statements about "African" customs, which Arnot makes in connection with the above, that, "when manners and customs are referred to, the particular district must be borne in mind. Africa is an immense continent, and there is as much variety in the customs of the different tribes as in their languages. Certain tribes take delight in cruelty and bloodshed; others have a religious fear of shedding human blood, and treat aged people with every kindness, to secure their good-will after death. By other tribes the aged would be cast out as mere food for wild animals."

The testimony of Declè[81] as to the tribes of South-Central Africa is: "You would suppose that the African expected everybody to live forever, since his one explanation of death is an immediate recourse to witchcraft. It is hardly an exaggeration to say that every natural death entails a violent one as its consequence. Along with witchcraft and the inevitable accusation of sorcery when one dies, goes the custom of 'muavi,' the ordeal by poison.... It is plain what complete domination this practice has got over the native mind. The reason is that be thoroughly believes in its efficiency. My own porters have constantly offered to submit to the ordeal on the most trivial charges. Of course, this thorough belief in 'muavi' hands the native over completely defenceless to the witch doctor. The doctor can get rid of anybody he likes to. Besides this, he is a kind of public prosecutor; that is to say, that when he accuses any man or woman of sorcery, he is not obliged, like any ordinary accuser, to take the poison himself."

The "ordeal" or test of the innocence of a person accused of practising witcbcraft or of having caused the death of any one (except in places where Christianity has attained power), is almost the same now as that described by Rev. Dr. J. L. Wilson, and subsequently by Du Chaillu, as existing fifty years ago on the entire West Coast of Africa. On the Upper Guinea coasts it is called the "red water." "It is a decoction made from the inner bark of a large forest tree of the mimosa family." At Calabar a bean was used, an extract

---

81   Three Years in Savage Africa, p. 512.

of which since has been employed in our pharmacopœia, in surgical operations of the eye.

In the Gabun country the bark and leaves of a small tree called "akazya" are used. Farther south, in the Nkâmi (miswritten, "Camma") country, it is called "mbundu."

The decoction itself is supposed to have almost sentience,—an ability to follow, in the various organs of the body, like a policeman, and detect and destroy the witch-spirit supposed to be lurking about.

Accused persons sometimes even demand that they be given the ordeal. This an innocent person could fearlessly do, feeling sure of his innocence, and thinking, as any honest person in a civilized country charged with theft would feel, that it was perfectly safe to have his house searched, sure that no stolen article was secreted there. So here the ignorant native is willing to take this poison, not looking on it as what we call "poison."

People who know that they have at times used witchcraft arts will naturally be unwilling to undergo the test; but if the charge is made after a death, an accused is compelled to drink. "If it nauseates and causes him to vomit freely, he suffers no injury, and is at once pronounced innocent. If, on the other hand, it causes vertigo, and be loses his self-control, it is regarded as evidence of guilt; and then all sorts of indignities and cruelties are practised on him.... On the other hand, if he escapes without injury his character is thoroughly purified.... and he arraigns before the principal men of the town his accusers, who in their turn must submit to the same ordeal, or pay a large fine to the man whom they attempted to injure.... There is seldom any fairness in the administration of the ordeal. No particular quantity of the 'red water' is Prescribed." The doctor, by collusion and family favoritism, may make the decoction very weak; or, influenced by public feeling inimical to the accused, he may compel him to swallow a fatal amount; or he may save his life by a subsequent emetic.[82]

Cannibalism

African cannibalism has been regarded as only a barbarism; but for many years I have strongly suspected that it had some connection with the Negro's religion. It may be a corollary of witchcraft.

Declè intimates the same:[83] "I do not mean such cannibalism as that of certain Kongo tribes, or of the Solomon Islanders, who kill people to eat them, as we eat game. With such tribes I did not come in contact. But there is another form of cannibalism less generally. known to Europeans, and perhaps even more grisly, which consists in digging up dead bodies to feast on their flesh. This practice exists largely among the natives in the region of Lake Nyasa.[84] I know of a case in which the natives of a village in this region seized the opportunity of a white man's presence to break into the hut of one of these reputed cannibals, and found there a human leg banging from the rafters. This incident shows that cannibalism is practised; but also that it is not universal with the tribes among whom it is found, and is condemned by the public opinion of those who do not practise it. But

---

82 Wilson.

83 p. 513.

84 I know of its occurring on the Gabun and Ogowe rivers on the West Coast.—R. H. N.

public opinion in Africa is not a highly developed power.... The real public opinion is witchcraft. And, indeed, in the case of cannibalism, the real public opinion tends to shield the perpetrators, because they are reputed to be sorcerers of high quality."

Rev. Dr. H. C. Trumbull, in his "Blood Covenant" (1893), while gathering testimony from all nations to illustrate his view of the universality of blood as representing life, and the heart as the seat of life, as a part of the religious rite of a covenant, comes incidentally on this same idea of cannibalism as having a religious significance, or at least, as I have expressed above, as a corollary of witchcraft. This will explain why the African cannibal, in conquering his enemy, also eats him; why the heart is especially desired in such feasts; and why the body of any one of distinguished characteristics is prized for the cannibal feast. His strength or skill or bravery or power is to be absorbed along with his flesh.

Trumbull[85] quotes from Réville, the representative comparative religionist of France: "Here you will recognize the idea so widely spread in the two Americas, and indeed almost everywhere amongst uncivilized people (nor is it limited to the uncivilized), that the heart is the epitome, so to speak, of the individual,—his soul in some sense,— so that to appropriate his heart is to appropriate his whole being."

A constant charge against sorcerers in West African tribes is that they have made a person sick by stealing and eating the sick one's "heart," and that the invalid cannot recover till the "heart" is returned.

---

85   p. 107.

Also, see Trumbull:[86] "The widespread popular superstition of the Vampire and of the ghoul seems to be an outgrowth of this universal belief that transfused blood is revivifying. The bloodless shades, leaving their graves at night, seek renewed life by drawing out the blood of those who sleep, taking the life of the living to supply temporary life to the dead.... An added force is given to all these illustrations of the universal belief that transferred blood has a vivifying power, by the conclusions of modern medical science l concerning the possible benefits of blood-transfusion. The primitive belief seems to have had a sound basis in scientific fact."

Histories of our American Indians are full of incidents showing bow the heart of a captive who in dying had exhibited bravery in the endurance of torture, was promptly cut in pieces and eaten, to absorb his courage.

"The Ashanti fetichmen of West Africa, apparently acting on a kindred thought, make a mixture of the hearts of enemies mingled with blood and consecrated herbs, for the vivifying of the conquerors."

"In South Africa, among the Amampondo, one of the Kaffir tribes, it is customary for the chief, on his accession to authority, to be washed in the blood of a near relative, generally a brother, who is put to death on the occasion, and has his skull used as a receptacle for blood."[87]

---

86 p. 115.

87 Trumbull, p. 129.

Secret societies

Another outcome of witchcraft belief is the formation of secret societies, both male and female, of crushing power and far-reaching influence, which, in one aspect of their influence, the governmental, were the only authority, before the intrusion of foreign powers, which could settle a fierce personal dispute or enforce intertribal peace. But their possibilities for good were overbalanced by their actualities of evil.

Among these societies I have, in a previous chapter, mentioned as governmental agencies the Egbo of the Niger Delta, Ukuku of the Corisco region, and Yasi of the Ogowo. There is also in the Gabun region of the equator, among the Shekani, Mwetyi; among the Bakele, Bweti; among the Mpongwe-speaking tribes, Inda and Njembe; and Ukuku and Malinda in the Batanga regions.

A detailed account of the ceremonies of an initiation into Malinda is contained in Chapter XVI.

In a previous chapter I have mentioned my own coming in contact with Ukuku and Yasi.

All these societies had for their primary object the good one of government, for this purpose holding the fetich in terror; but the means used were so arbitrary, the influences employed so oppressive, and the representations so false, that they almost all were evil. Most of them are now discontinued as a tribal power by the presence of foreign governments, the foreign power having actually come in conflict with some of them, as in the case of England recently with the Aro of Nigeria; or, where they still exist, they have degenerated to mere amusement, as Ukukwe, in Gabun; or are kept up as a traditional fashion, as Njembe.

But they all exist, as described by Rev. Dr. Wilson a generation ago, and are at this very present among the tribes of the interior, where foreign government is as yet only nominal.

Mwetyi "is a great spirit, who is supposed to dwell in the bowels of the earth, but comes to the surface of the ground at stated seasons, or when summoned on any special business. A large flat house of peculiar form is erected in the middle of the village for the temporary sojourn of this spirit. The house is always kept perfectly dark, and no one is permitted to enter it, except those who have been initiated into all the mysteries of the order, which includes, however, almost the whole of the adult male population of the village.... When Mwetyi is about to retire from a village, the women, children, un-initiated lads, and any strangers who may be there at the time, are required to leave the village."

"Indâ is an association whose membership is confined to the adult male population. It is headed by a spirit of that name, who dwells in the woods, and appears only when summoned by some unusual event,—at the death of a person connected with the order, at the birth of twins, or at the inauguration of some one into office.... If a distinguished person dies, Indâ affects great rage, and comes the following night with a large posse of men to seize the property of the villagers without discrimination. He is sure to lay bands on as many sheep and goats as are necessary to make a grand feast, and no man has any right to complain.... The institution of Indâ, like that of Mwetyi, is intended to keep the women, children, and slaves in subjection."

"Njembe is a pretty fair counterpart of Inda, but there is no special spirit nor any particular person representing it." Its power resides in the society as a body, and rests on the threat of the employment of fetich medicines to injure recalcitrant persons. Only women are admitted to it. A very considerable fee is demanded for admission to membership. Formerly it was considered an honor to be allowed to be initiated; now, to perpetuate itself, it compels young women to enter it, especially if they have made derogatory remarks about Njembe. The initiation then becomes a kind of punishment. Strange to say, young women thus compelled to enter accept the society, and become zealous to drag others in. The initiation occupies about two weeks, and is accompanied with harsh treatment. Njembe has no special meeting-house. They assemble in a cleared place in the centre of a jungle, where their doings are unseen by outsiders by night or day. Nothing is known of their rites, except that they dance in a nude state, and the songs of their dances are openly heard, and are often of the vilest character.

"They pretend to detect thieves, to find out the secrets of their enemies," to direct women in pregnancy, and in other ways claim to be useful.

"The object of the institution originally, no doubt, was to protect the females from harsh treatment on the part of their husbands."

As a rule, the Mpongwe women say that every woman should be in the Njembe Society; so, at a certain age of a girl, they decide that she shall "go in." But she is not always put through all the ceremonies at once. She may be subjected to only a part of the initiation, the remainder to be performed at another time.

The special occasion for an initiation may be perhaps because the spirit of some recently dead member wants a new one to take her place; or if any young woman has escapea being initiated during her youth or if she is charged with having spoken derisively of Njembe, she may be seized by force and compelled to go through the rite.

The entire process so beats down the will of the novices and terrorizes them, that even those who have been forced into it against their will, when they emerge at the close of the rite, most inviolably preserve its secrets, and express themselves as pleased.

Just before the novices or "pupils" are to enter, they have to prepare a great deal of food,—as much as they can possibly obtain of cassava, fish, and plantains. Two days are spent, before the cere-monies begin, in cooking this food. They make big bundles of ngândâ (gourd seed) pudding, others of ground-nuts and odika (oily kernel of the wild mango), pots of odika and fish boiled, boiled hard plantains, and ripe plantains beaten into rolls called "fufu." This food is to be eaten by them and the older members of the society the first night.

Those older ones, as a part of the hazing which they always practise, deceive the new ones by advising them in advance: "Eat no supper this evening. Save up your appetite. All this food you have prepared is your own, and you will be satiated at the feast to-night." This is said in order to play a hard joke on them. But sometimes a more tender-hearted relative will pity them, and will privately warn them to eat something, knowing that they will be up all night, and that the older members intend to seize and eat what these "pupils" had prepared for themselves, allowing the latter to be faint with hunger.

That evening the society goes into the adjacent jungle, the spot selected including a small stream of water. There they clear a small space for their ceremonies. They dance all night, part of the time in this camp, and part of the time in the street of the town, but always going back to the camp at some early morning hour.

On the second day they come to town, dance there a little while, and then go back to the forest. They beat constantly and monotonously, without time, a short straight stick on a somewhat crescent-shaped piece of board (orega) that is slightly concave on one side. It makes a clear but not a musical note; is heard quite far, and is the distinctive sign of the Njembe Society. No other persons own or will strike the orega music.

In the part of the ceremonies that are public in the village street, a man is invited to assist by beating oil a drum, a matter in which women here are not expert. This drum does not exclude the orega, several of which may be beaten at the same time; at least one must be kept sounding during the whole two weeks by one or another of the candidates, or if these become exhausted, by some other member of the society.

One of the first public preparations is the bending of a limber pole (ilala) as an arch, or two branches, their tops woven together, over the path entering the village. They are wreathed with lycopo-dium ferns, and at their bases are stuck a young, short, recently half-unfolded palm-leaf, painted with Njembe dots of white, red, and black. At the distance of a few hundred feet may be another ilala; indeed, there may be several of them on the way to the camp.

While dancing during the first few days, the society occupies itself with preparations, unknown to the public, for their "work" in the camp. Thither come older members from afar, especially those related to the candidates.

Certain women skilled in the Njembe dances and rules are called "teachers." The first step which an already initiated member takes to become a "teacher" is to find and introduce a new recruit, with whom she must again go through all the rites of initiation more severely than at her first experience. She makes herself perfect in the lessons impressed on her by impressing them on the new pupil. The prospective "teacher" has thus to endure, in this second passage tbrough the rites, all and more than is put on the novice. Little as is known of these rites, it is certain they are severe.

In the singing, each song is known by its own descriptive motions. The motion mentioned is to be actually performed, however difficult or immodest it may be. Generally the immodest portions are reserved for the seclusion of their camp; but the words sung at the camp can be heard at the village, so that all hear them,—men, women, and little children.

One common public song has for its refrain, "Look at the sun"; while that song is being danced, the candidate must gaze steadily at the hot sun, even if it be blinding. Most of the "rules" (and the teacher may invent as many new ones as she chooses) are purposely hard in order to make the candidate suffer, and as part of the process of breaking her will, and ensuring secrecy by a reign of terror.

Also most of the nights the candidate (or several of them if there are a number) must spend hours in keeping a fire burning in some part of the forest. That fire, once started, must be kept burning day and night during the whole two weeks. A girl who in ordinary times would be afraid to go out into the forest alone at night, will, under the Njembe initiation, go out in storin and rain to see that the fire is not extinguished. Sometimes the teacher will lighten the task for her by accompanying her; or some one, pitying, will help to gather the dead wood with which the fire is kept smouldering.

There are also rules for the breaking of which there are fines, *e.g.*, "When you are dancing in public during the initiation, do not laugh aloud." Another rule is that no salutation is to be given or received, nor the person or even the clothing of a visitor touched by a candidate.

The teacher must be quick to imitate, in this her second "degree" or passage through the rites, the rapid motions of the skilled older one who is teaching her and her new recruit.

In order to increase the severity, the pupil, though she may be already wearied, is required to repeat her dance before every newcomer or spectator. The teacher will start the beat of the orega and take a few steps of the dance, and then stop and rest comfortably, the tired pupil taking the orega and continuing the dance.

If pupils are sulky or shy, their teacher and other older members will scold them: "Go on! dance! You may not stand or rest there' Go on! You! this girl with your awkwardness! Do you own the Njembe?" Sometimes a pupil is sulky or stubborn, or, disheartened, begins to cry. No mercy is shown her. Others, in anxiously trying to follow motions, will make absurd mistakes, and bring down on themselves the derision of the spectators. Some pupils really like the dancing, and endeavor to learn quickly. Such as these are praised: "This one knows, and she will some day be a teacher."

It is expected that the relatives of the pupils will be present and encourage them with some little gifts.

It is remarkable how well the secrets of the society are kept. No one has ever been induced to reveal them. Those who have left the society and have become Christians do not tell. Foreigners have again and again tried to bribe, but in vain. Traders and others have tried to induce their native wives to reveal; but these women, obedient to any extent on all other matters, maintain a stubborn silence. Nothing is known outside of the society of their doings in their camp, except that they are all naked, lay aside all modesty, make personal examinations of each other's bodies, sing phallic songs, and indulge in the hardest, severest, and most violent insults and curses heaped up in assumed wrath as jokes on each other. It is really a school in which to learn the fine art of using insults and curses which will be utilized outside the society, upon other persons on occasions of real anger. No man can equal these women in their volubility and bitter tirades when really angry. It is Billingsgate in its glory.

After keeping up the ceremonies for a number of days, the society chooses one for their "last." The day preceding it, they go out in procession with baskets, kettles, and basins, from village to village, still singing, the song being adapted for their errand of begging, and still beating the orega, to get offerings of food, or gifts of rum, tobacco, plates, and cloth. (In a civilized religious worship this would be the taking up of the collection.) At each village on their route any member of the society will direct one of the new pupils to dance, as an exhibition of her recently acquired ability. She does not hesitate, but asks, "Which dance?" The teacher replies, "I will show you," and starting a few steps measured, she stops, and the designated pupil takes it up.

During the initiation the pupils are required to go barefooted; and if they have been wearing dresses, the dresses are taken off and only a native cloth worn. But a slight concession has occasionally been made in favor of some mission-sebool girls when forced into Njembe, who, accustomed to dresses, were allowed to wear them when walking in this public collecting procession.

Njembe. Female Secret Society. Mpongwe, Gabun.

The night of the day on which they come back from this collecting of gifts is the "last night." Dancing is then done by all, both by the teachers and the pupils.

It is not known who is leader. One is spoken of as the "Mother," but it is not known who she is. The chief teacher is seen whenever they come from their camp, and is known by the colored chalk markings different from others.

The next morning, the morning of the "last day," all go out fishing, young and old, along the river or sea beach. This fishing is done among the muddy roots of the mangrove trees. They gather shell-fish of different kinds. But whatever they do or do not obtain, they do not return till each one has caught a small common snake which lives in holes at the mangrove roots. The sound of the orega (which is still constantly beaten) seems to act as a charm, and the snake emerges from its hole and is readily caught; or the hand is boldly thrust into the hole in search of the reptile. In starting out on this fishing the new members do not know that they are to handle snakes. They go as on a happy fishing excursion. Really, it is their final test. They are told to put their hands into these holes, and not to let go of the "fish" they shall seize there. The novice obeys, but presently screams in alarm as she feels a snake-like form wriggling about her hand. Her teacher terribly threatens her; she begs to be excused, dares not let go, and is compelled to pull out the snake twining about her arm. They all then return to the camp, each with her snake in her basket. It is not known what is done with these snakes.

The teacher is to be paid for her services. As the pupils come from different villages, each one has to ask her teacher's permission to go to her relatives to collect the fee. This is done a few days before the final day. They are allowed to go, but with an escort to watch them that they break no rule of the initiation. They do not go into the houses, nor do they speak. They stand in the street. Those who escort them have to do the talking, thus: "We have come to collect our money, as the Njembe will soon be done." If they get a plenty, the pupils are glad; otherwise they have to stand in the hot sun uncovered, except by their crown-like wreath of lycopodium, fern. It is a trying and humiliating position for any girl whose people are poor or unwilling. She must stand there till some one of her people shall contribute what the escort deems sufficient.

Having collected each her fee for the teacher, the pupils go back to her at the village, and seat themselves on the ground under the eaves of the houses on one side of the street, each with her pile of goods near her. The teacher eyes these piles, and selects the girl who apparently has the most, to be the first to begin to pay. Just previous to this, stalks of amomum are laid down in the street, parallel to each other, about eighteen inches apart, in number according with the teacher's random guess of the number of articles in the chosen pile. Then she lays the articles of the pile, one by one, on the amomum stalk. Then another of the teachers seizes the band of the girl who owned these goods, and swinging her from side to side, runs with her rapidly over that line of goods, herself stepping carefully on the interspaces, but apparently trying to confuse the girl into stepping on and breaking some one of the articles, *e.g.*, a mirror or a plate. This ordeal safely passed, the goods of that girl are accepted and put aside near the teacher. The goods of each of the other new girls are treated in the same way, and laid, one by one, on the amomum stalks.

The number of some girl's articles may not equal the standard set by the first, and there may be not enough to cover every stalk. In that case the teacher will allow some article, *e.g.*, a head of tobacco-leaves, to be opened and its separate leaves used to piece out the number. Nevertheless, she will demand that something be added. It is an anxious time for the pupils, watching to see whether their fee is accepted. Sometimes the teacher, seeing that a girl's pile of goods is small, will not even attempt to count or divide it, but, looking at it, sneeringly says, "I see nothing here! Sit you there in the sun till some one brings you more!"

The last act of the "last day," before adjourning, is a public dance called Njegâ (Leopard). For that, the members of the society, and most spectators, dress up in fine clothes. It is performed in the afternoon, and visitors go to see it. The "Leopard" is done by the teachers, two at a time. All these pairs must have their faces painted, each in a different style, no piece of skin left untouched.

In beginning the Leopard dance, one of the pair imitates a leopard sneaking around the corners of the houses; while the other one, waiting, has collected perhaps a dozen of the members as her "children," whom she as their "mother" is to guard from the "leopard." This teacher-mother begins a song, "Children! there is the leopard in shape of a person," adding as a refrain the word, "Mbwero! mbwero! mbwero!" which is repeated rapidly as a warning that the leopard is coming, ending with, "my children!" They sing, and step backward and forward to a drum accompaniment. While these "children" are in great pretended excitement, the leopard is advancing slowly, steadily, and nearer from the ogwerina (rear of the houses) into the street, with extended tongue, and growling. When the mother sees this, her dance step grows quicker, and she backs and motions to her children behind her, they imitating all her steps. The leopard advances with a swaying step in time with the music, and then suddenly dashes forward, and catches one of the children, and sets her aside. This is kept up by the leopard till most of the children are caught, only one or two being left. The mother then seems very much exhausted, with a sad slow step; but the leopard at last catches the others. Now that her children are all dead, the mother is aroused to fury. The conflict remains between her and the leopard. And "mother" must finally kill "leopard." The dance becomes very much more rapid; the two approach nearer and nearer. Mother has a stick like a sword, and finally she kills leopard with a light blow. This coup is received by a shout from the spectators of "o-lo-lo!"

Then another pair are selected to go through the parts of mother and leopard again. Sometimes one will refuse to act, or to be mated with the other one. Then, like a singer in civilized lands, she is met with entreaties from the crowd, "Do act! You know so well how to do it!" And then she yields. If at the last there is remaining only one teacher who has not done the act, one of those who has already performed will mate with her.

At night, the last work of the society is to put out their fire. If the leader has come from a distant village, she wants to go, and she will extinguish the fire that night; or, if she lives near, she may choose to wait several days longer. But during that time the dancing and singing are not kept up, for the society has adjourned.

Whatever else is unknown of the objects of Njembe, it is known that it is a government. It was formerly much more powerful than it is now. At Libreville, Gabun, thirty years ago, no woman dared to speak against it. Mission schoolgirls, feeling themselves secure on the mission premises, sometimes in their school-girl talk foolishly made disparaging remarks about it. When this reached the ear of Njembe, those girls would some day be caught when they were visiting their villages, and forced through the rites. Parents did not dare interfere, and missionaries had no authority to do so.

In one case, however, a missionary did make a successful interference. The girl did not belong to Mpongwe (the tribe of Gabun); she was a slave-waif that had been picked up by the mission, and therefore, in a sense, the mission's daughter. The senior missionary, Rev. William Walker, was a tall, powerful, utterly fearless man, and his custom was always to carry a heavy cane. That day, the Njembe lessons that were being given to the abducted girl had only begun in the village street; she had not yet been taken to their secret camp. Mr. Walker strode among the women and laid bold of the unresisting girl. When some women attempted to drag her away, he brought down his cane heavily at random over any head or shoulder within reach of his long arm; and the girl was glad to be led back to the mission. The rescue was successful. Mr. Walker's use of force was justifiable as against Njembe's forcible abduction of the girl; and his parental position in the case would have justified him if the women had made any complaint against him before the local French magistrate on charge of assault.

In a somewhat similar case, more recently, Njembe sued a missionary, he having assaulted them when they refused to remove their distressingly noisy camp from a too great proximity to the mission grounds. The magistrate dismissed the case, resenting Njembe's existence as a secret society, and its assumption of exercise of governmental authority.

Recently also a native man was successful in thwarting Njembe. A certain native Christian woman had escaped being forced into Njembe during her youth; and by her being very much in mission employ during her adult years, Njembe had ceased to threaten her. Her daughter, of about eighteen years of age, though not a Christian, had also, by her mother's care of her, escaped, though often threatened. A cousin of this daughter had been put through the rite while her father was away on a journey. And now this cousin was trying to induce the daughter to enter. The daughter refused, and perhaps may have made some slighting remark. This remark her cousin reported to Njembe; and some intimations were made that the young woman would be seized. The father of the cousin had formerly been a eburch-member, is educated and gentlemanly. Though he had fallen away from the church, he had no desire to see his niece dragged down. He spoke severely to his daughter about the excitement she was trying to raise, and threatened to call in the aid of the French Chief of Police. The firm stand taken by him and also by the young woman's mother was efficient in preventing her seizure by Njembe. Both these parents are of unusual strength of character and advance in civilization. Without their efficient backing, this young woman would have been forced into Njembe.

Rev. J. L. Wilson,[88] wrote of Njembe almost fifty years ago: "There is no spirit, so far as is known, connected with this association, but all its proceedings are kept profoundly secret. The Njem-

---

88   Western Africa, p. 397.

be make great pretensions, and as a body are really feared by the men. They pretend to detect thieves, to find out the secrets of their enemies; and in various ways they are useful to the community in which they live, or, at least, are so regarded by the people. The object of the institution originally, no doubt, was to protect the females from harsh treatment on the part of their husbands; and as their performances are always veiled in mystery, and they have acquired the reputation of performing wonders, the men are, no doubt, very much restrained by the fear and respect which they have for them as a body."

Most of the above description is, after so many years, true now, except that the power of and respect for the society is lessened by the permeating leaven of a Christian mission and by the dominance of a foreign government; but even in that same region, in portions where these two forces are not in immediate contact with the community, Njembe still is feared.

It is true, also, that there is no special spirit belonging to Njembe, but when the society has occasion to investigate a theft or other crime, it invokes the usual ilaga and other spirits.

It is also still true that in the tribes where Njembe exists women have much more freedom from control by men than in tribes where it does not exist. But even if it has been thus a defence to women against man's severity, it undeniably has been an injury to them by its indecent ceremonies and phallic songs. Such things may make men fear them, but also make it impossible for men to respect them.

Those songs I myself have beard when the Njembe camp was

in a jungle near to a village. The male generative organ was personified, and, in the song addressed to it, the name of a certain man, who was known by the singers to be at that very time in the adjacent village, was tauntingly referred to. Even immoral men were overwhelmed with shame at the shamelessness of the women. And yet those same women, when their Njembe adjourned, resumed in their individual capacities their usual apparent modesty which, as a collective body, they had cast aside. Little has been printed of Njembe's secret proceedings more than Dr. Wilson wrote fifty years ago.

Paul Du Chaillu makes a short statement that he was allowed to witness a part; and he describes a but containing a few almost nude old women sitting around some skulls and other fetiches. Doubtless he saw what be asserts. But, unusual as were his opportunities, and large as was his personal influence with his "Camma" (Nkâmi) native chiefs, it is positive that what was shown him was only a little of Njembe, if indeed it was Njembe at all.

Other white men, with, indeed, perhaps less tact than he, but of greater money power and larger trade opportunities, failed to see anything.

Some twenty-five years ago two Germans (now dead) trading in the Gabun determined secretly to spy out Njembe.

The merchant, the bead of the trading-house, was a welleducated gentleman, and his clerk was an active, intelligent young man. Both knew native customs well, and both spoke the Mpongwe language fluently. Each had a native wife, and being generous—and liberal-handed, had many native friends; but they had been unable to bribe any Njembe women, even their own wives, to reveal anything.

One dark night when the society was in session in a small jungle not far from their trading-house, they went secretly and cautiously through the bushes. They had not approached near enough to the circle of women around the camp-fire to actually recognize any of them (it would have been difficult to recognize their painted faces even by daylight); and they really did not see anything of what was being done. Somehow their approach was discovered, either by information treacherously carried from some one in their retinue of household servants, or by being seen by one of the pickets of the camp, or by the breaking of a branch as they crept through the trees, or, possibly, by their white odor carried on the wind,—odor which to Africans is almost as distinct as is Negro odor to the white race.

Njembe raised a frenzied cry, and started to seize them. The two men fled desperately through the thick bushes. The clerk was recognized, and his name was called out, and the other was assumed to be his employer. They escaped to the safety of their house. Njembe did not dare assault it, French policemen being within call; but next day word was sent by the society denouncing them both, laying a curse on them, and plainly saying that they should die. If the threat had been that the means of death would be magic, these gentlemen would have laughed; but the women did not hesitate to say that they would poison them in their food. This would be entirely possible, even without collusion among the several men and boys that ranged from steward to cook and waiters as their household servants; though, if need were, some of these servants would sooner be treasonable to the white master than dare to refuse Njembe. The case was serious. The older man, as a dispenser of wealth to the entire community, was, even in Njembe's eye, too valuable to be killed; his wife, herself a Njembe woman, interceded for him, and the curse was removed from him on the payment of a large fine. But the curse was doubled over the poor clerk. Njembe would listen to no appeal, nor accept any bribe for him, as they had actually seen him at their camp.

It is a fact that shortly after this this clerk did fall into a decline, with strange symptoms which no doctor understood nor any medicines seemed to touch. He became weaker and weaker, and his life was despaired of. Njembe openly boasted that it was killing him.

I do not know why an appeal was not made to the local French authorities. Perhaps because the merchant did not wish to give more publicity to his escapade; perhaps because it would be difficult to prosecute a society, no individual Njembe woman appearing to be responsible.

To save his clerk, the merchant offered to pay a very large sum. Njembe having had a partial revenge, having demonstrated its power, and standing victorious before the community, was induced to accept. It was never known publicly how much was paid. The curse was withdrawn, and the clerk immediately began to recover; but it was some months before the evil was entirely eradicated from his system.

Beyond Dr. Wilson's and Du Chaillu's short statements about Njembe, I have seen nothing else in print, except the mere mention of the existence of the society by several African travellers. What I have written in the above I have obtained piecemeal at various times from different men and women, Christian and heathen; but all of them spoke with hesitation, and under promise that I should mention no names.

Poisoning for Revenge

There are native poisons. It is known that sometimes they are secretly used in revenge, or to put out of the way a relative whose wealth is desired to be inherited. This much I have to admit, as to charges of "bewitching" and so-called "judicial executions," therefore, that in the case of some deaths they are actual murders, and that the perpetrator deserves to be executed. But it is rare that the proof of guilt is clear. I have to be guarded in my admission of an accused person's guilt, lest I give countenance to the universal belief in death as the result of fetich agencies. I explain to my native questioner: If what the accused has done in fetich rite with intent to kill had any efficiency for taking away life, I allow that he shall be put to death; if he made only fetiches, even if they were intended to kill, be is not guilty of this death, for a mere fetich cannot kill. But if he used poison, with or without fetich, then he is guilty.

But even so, the distinction between a fetich and a poison is vague in the thought of many natives. What I call a "poison" is to them only another material form of a fetich power, both poison and fetich being supposed to be made efficient by the presence of an adjuvant spirit.

Not all the deaths of foreigners in Africa are due to malaria. Some of them have been doubtless due to poison, administered by a revengeful employee. Very many white residents in Africa treat their servants in oppressive and cruel ways. Even those who are not cruel are often autocratic and arbitrary. In a country that has little law to hinder, and no public opinion to shame them, some white men treat the natives almost as slaves, cheating them of their wages, cursing, kicking, striking, beating, and otherwise maltreating and even mutilating them. Some are kind and just; but even they are at times severe in enforcing their authority. So it could occur that even a kindly-disposed foreigner might have his life attempted by an evil-disposed employee whose anger be had aroused.

In general, the Bantu natives of Africa are patient, long-suffering, and not easily aroused to violence, but taking their revenge, if finally their endurance is exhausted, by robbing their master of his goods or otherwise wasting his trade; abandoning him in sickness, so that he dies really of neglect, or, when his boat upsets in the surf of the sea, making no effort to rescue him.

The Bantu tribes are less revengeful and more amiable than the Negroes of Upper Guinea, or the tribes of Senegal and of the Sudan, with their mixture of Arab blood and Mahometan beliefs.

An English traveller recently, in the Igbo, country of Nigeria, in discussing the native belief in occult forces, says: "It is impossible for a white man to be present at their gatherings of 'medicine men,' and it is hard to get a native to talk of such things; but it seems evident to me that there is some reality in the phenomena one hears of, as they are believed everywhere in some degree by white men as well as black. However that may be, the native doctors have a wide knowledge of poisons; and if one is to believe reports, deaths from poison, both among white and black men, are of common occurrence on the Niger. One of the white man's often quoted proverbs is, 'Never quarrel with your cook'; the meaning of which is that the cook can put something in your food in retaliation if you maltreat him.

"There is everywhere a belief that it is possible to put medicine on a path for your enemy which, when he steps over it, will cause him to fall sick and die. Other people can walk uninjured over the spot, but the moment the man for whom the medicine is laid reaches the place, he succumbs, often dying within an hour or two. I have never seen such a case myself; but the Rev. A. E. Richardson says be saw one when on the journey with Bishop Tugwell's house-party. He could offer no explanation of how the thing is done, but does not doubt that it is done. Some of the best educated of our native Christians have told me that they firmly believe in this 'medicine-laying.'"

The most distinct instance of attempt at poisoning which I have met was related to me in March, 1902, by Mr. H. L. Stacey, of the English trading-house of J. Holt & Co. Ltd. I took the following statement from his own lips, and he gave me liberty to use it publicly. He has since died, and his death was sudden.

Mr. Stacey was a gentleman of courteous manner and of good education; fearless, universally kind, and generally just in his treatment of the natives. He was a Christian in his belief, and endeavored to be one in his life. His truthfulness is beyond doubt, thus making his statement entirely reliable.

He had his headquarters at Bata, with native sub-traders scattered north and south and up the Benita River, sorne twenty-three miles south of Bata. There came to him for employment a Lagos man, by name Croly or Crowley. He spoke English well, could read and write, had quite a display of manner, and made himself very useful by his apparent devotion, faithfulness, and honesty. All this deceived Mr. Stacey, who thought he had obtained a valuable servant; and rewarded him by giving him a sub-factory at Lobisa, a few miles up the Benita River. To have a factory of one's own is the goal of the ambition of every white trader's employees.

Mr. Stacey had also a Benga sub-trader on the river at Senje, some ten miles above Lobisa. This Benga went to Bata and reported to Mr. Stacey that Crowley was wasting his goods in riotous living and extravagant giving. While the Benga was away, Crowley falsely told the native Fang, who had been paid in advance by the former to collect india-rubber for him, that the Benga had been dismissed, was in jail, and would never come back, and induced them to sell to himself the rubber they had collected for the Benga. When the Benga returned to his post, and asked his Fang to pay their debt, they told him of the deception Crowley had practised on them. There was, therefore, a triangular quarrel, the Benga suing the Fang for their debt to him, the Fang denouncing Crowley for his cheat, and Crowley angry at the Benga for informing Mr. S. on him.

Just at this stage of affairs Mr. S. came on one of his usual visits of inspection to Senje. The Fang immediately sent secretly a deceptive message down to Crowley, saying that—Mr. S. wished to see him. As soon as he came, the Fang began to fight him. Notwithstanding Crowley's dishonesty to him, Mr. S. magnanimously defended his life, locked him for safety in the Benga's bedroom, and then made the quarrel a quadrilateral by protesting to the Fang against their assaulting his premises. His contention with them was "talked" in public "palaver," and finally was amicably settled. During the "talk" a lad came to Mr. S. excitedly, saying that Crowley was spreading "medicine" in the bed of the Benga, with intent to kill the latter. This aroused again the indignation of the Fang. But Mr. S. laughed down their anxiety, telling them that be was not afraid of "medicine" (he thought it was only fetich); that fetich could not kill a white man; and that, to prove it, he would that night sleep in that bed, and the Benga should sleep elsewhere. When all was settled, be got Crowley quietly away, and sent him down river to his Lobisa house, with expectation of dismissal. At night Mr. S. awoke with a great pain in his abdomen, a great sense of constriction in his chest, skin hot, and body tortured with shooting pains. Only his head was clear and free from any distress. The symptoms were not those of malarial fever. The next day his limbs were paralyzed. The natives said that Crowley had scattered in the bedding and through the mosquito net a poisonous powder.

Mr. S. was taken helpless in his canoe down river, on the way passing very near Lobisa, to a house on the sea-beach near the river's mouth. Believing that Crowley had attempted the life of the Benga, Mr. S., while lying sick, sent word to the adjacent Spanish Government Post for two soldiers to come and arrest Crowley. (Mr. S. had been informed that C. was on his way to him.) For C., when be saw Mr. S. lying sick in his passing canoe, surmised what had happened, and was afraid the Fang would follow him to Lobisa and assault him there. So he had closed his house and fled, following Mr. S. He was coming with a double purpose: first, to plead with Mr. S. against dismissal; second, as be promptly had heard of Mr. Stacey's sleeping in the poisoned bed and being sick, he feared arrest and was ready also to make the murder plan complete, if his plea for mercy was denied. To this end be came prepared with a handful of the powder.

Before he had reached the house where Mr. S. was, the two soldiers had met and arrested him, and were taking him to jail. He asked permission first to be allowed to see his "master." So they brought him to the sick-room, where be made many protestations of friendship and devotion, and plead for mercy. Mr. S. rebuked the soldiers for hesitating in their duty, and for having brought their prisoner there, and bade them take him away to the magistrate; then he fell back on his pillow exhausted, and lay with closed eyes, only semi-conscious. The soldiers went out of the room, leaving C. clinging to the bed. He fell on his knees by Mr. S.'s head, as if still to beg for pardon. Mr. S. felt C.'s hand insinuated under the bed cover near his pillow, and suddenly opened his eyes, to find C.'s closed hand near his face. He struck away the hand. A quantity of dark powder fell on the pillow near his nose. Half suffocated, by an effort he shouted to the soldiers, who came and took C. away. Mr. Stacey's little waiter-boy, who had also come in at the shout, was horrified to see the poison-powder on the pillow. He snatched away the pillow, threw the powder out of doors, and told the soldiers. They, without waiting for official judgment at the Post, gave C. twenty-five lashes at once. Farther blows, twenty-five at a time, were given him while waiting in jail for Mr. S. to get well enough to appear against him. Subsequently the Chef de Poste appointed a day for the hearing; but Mr. S., in his devotion to the trade interests of his employers, asked that the day be postponed, as his sub-traders needed just then much supervision. So the Chef dismissed the matter, seeming to think that if Mr. S. regarded his trade as of more importance than the defence of his life, it was no business of the government to hold the prisoner; and took no farther interest in it.

Having been given, in instalments, an aggregate of two hundred lashes, C. was discharged. He wandered about that region gathering a little food, without friends, feared and hated, and not allowed by some even to enter their villages.

The reputation of the Lagos powder as a powerful agent in destroying life has been known for years among the equatorial coast tribes. Reports of it are well known among white men on the steamers. It is believed in, not as a superstition, nor as a fetich, but as a powerful poison. Clerks and other workmen from Lagos are not welcomed in the Gabun region, as are clerks from other parts of Upper Guinea, for fear of their carrying that poison with them.

Distrust

As a result of the universal employment of fetiches in African tribes, there is no confidence between man and man. Every one is in distrust of his neighbor; every man's hand against his fellow.

"The natives of Africa, though so thoroughly devoted to the use of fetiches, acquire no feeling of security in consequence of using them. Perhaps their only real influence is to make them more insecure than they would have been without them. There is no place in the world where men feel more insecurity. A man must be careful whose company be keeps, what path he walks, whose house be enters, on what stool he seats himself, where he sleeps. He knows not what moment he may place his foot or lay his hand upon some invisible engine of mischief, or by what means the seeds of death may be implanted in his constitution."[89]

Because of this lack of confidence, the natural affections and the duties of the dearest relations are perverted. Wives afraid of husbands, and husbands afraid of wives; children afraid of parents, and parents afraid of children; the chief of the village uncertain of his people; and the entire community that must live and eat and associate together, living and eating and associating with a constant secretly entertained suspicion of each other.

Jugglery

While in some of the rites performed by the native doctor-priest there is real diabolism, *i.e.*, communication with Satan, and certain wonders are performed through the Prince of the Power of Darkness, I am disposed to believe that in most cases the "doctor" is self-deceived, certainly in many cases I believe him to be a deliberate deceiver. The native socalled "prophet" is probably an artful mind-reader; and the fortune-teller, like our own fortune-tellers, a skilful observer of the subject's tones, manner, and unguarded admissions in conversation which give ground for shrewd guessing.

Arnot[90] says: "These professional diviners are no doubt smart fellows, arch-rogues though they be. The secret of their art lies in their constant repetition of every possibility in connection with the

---

89   Wilson, Western Africa.

90   Garenganze, p. 107.

disaster they are called upon to explain until they finally hit upon that which is in the minds of their clients. As the people sit around and repeat the words of the diviner, it is easy for him to detect in their tone of voice or to read in their faces the suspected source of the calamity.

"A man had a favorite dog which was attacked by a leopard, but succeeded in escaping with one of its eyes torn out. To ascertain the reason of this calamity, the owner sent to call one of these diviners. When he arrived, to test him, he was told that a disaster had befallen my acquaintance, and was asked to find out by divination what it was. The diviner with his rattles and other paraphernalia, and dances, and other movements to occupy attention, after the manner of jugglers, asked leading questions of the spirit he was professing to consult, but really he was watching the faces of his audience for their unconsciously given assent or dissent. Thus, in succession, he found that the misfortune, whatever it was, was not to a human being; then not to certain families; then to some object possessed by a certain man; then that it was not about an ox nor about a goat; then that it was about a dog; then, after, certain other possibilities, was it connected with a leopard? So excited were the audience that they forgot that they had been 'giving themselves away,' and when the diviner asked the spirit, 'Was it a leopard?' they shouted with admiration at his supposed skill. After a whole day of such proceedings the diviner triumphed by announcing "that the spirit of the father of one of the man's wives had been grieved at the man's long absence from his town and family, and had employed the leopard to tear the dog's eye as a gentle reminder that it was time he should go back to his own village."

In connection with the Yoruba custom of parents of twins having images carved of their dead twins, "the carving of those images is a flourishing and money-making trade. If the parents of the dead child are in comfortable circumstances, the carvers tell them that they have seen in their dreams the dead twin, and that he or she has asked them to send such and such clothes, articles of food, money, etc.

"Sometimes they say the twins appeared to them in the forest when they went to cut the Ire-wood to be carved, and bade them not to venture it. In such cases special sacrifices must be offered before taking any steps. In this way months pass before the carving is complete; during which time the carvers demand of the parents whatever they feel they are capable of supplying them with."[91]

In the Corisco region, some thirty years ago, I knew a native sorcerer who achieved quite a reputation because he could perform the thimble-rig juggler-trick of making a leaf appear and disappear between two plates.

One of my associates in the Ogowe, the late H. M. Bachelor, M.D., had brought with him from the United States a few tricks of "parlor magic." He quite astonished my schoolchildren by swallowing and subsequently vomiting up a penknife, and by passing a threaded needle through the thigh of one of the boys. Dr. B. did the tricks so artistically that even I did not detect the deception about the penknife; and the boy solemnly asserted that be felt the needle travelling

---

91   Niger and Yoruba Notes.

through his leg. The exhibition was a happy one in revealing to the natives how an evil-disposed sorcerer would be able to deceive them.

A lady of the West African Mission of the American Board says: "I once witnessed the performance of a witch-doctor on one of my visits among the villages. The chief of the country was sick, and the doctor was giving him a massage treatment. By sleight of hand he seemed to draw from the patient's side chicken's claws, feathers, bones, sticks, pebbles, etc. Some "witch," it was supposed, had caused these things to grow in the man's body with intent to kill. It was evident to the astonished crowd which had gathered around, that their king would probably get well, now these things were removed. The doctor's bill was promptly paid,—a thousand balls of rubber, ten pieces of cloth, and a large pig. An ox was slaughtered, and a beer drink indulged in to celebrate the occasion and to appease any offended spirit."

Treatment of Lunatics

The insane being supposed to be physically and mentally possessed by an intruding spirit, their actions are necessarily not considered to be the outcome of their own volitions. This view does not always, in the native mind, relieve a lunatic of the burden of the consequences of his acts.

There is great diversity, therefore, in the treatment of. the insane in different districts and in different tribes. In some regions a tribe holds to the following reasoning: This person is possessed by a spirit. That spirit is. occupying his body and using his voice and limbs for some reason. If we interfere with this person's doings, then we will be interfering with the spirit and may bring evil on ourselves. Therefore it is considered proper to make offerings and some degree of worship to the incarnated spirit. But it is not true that the lunatic himself is an object of worship. The gifts and sacrifices are made solely to and for the spirit; the prayer of the petitioners being that it may refrain from inciting the possessed person to do them evil, and in the hope that it may conclude to depart and leave the patient and them alone.

In other places this same belief of possession leads to a very different logical conclusion. The thought is: This person is possessed by an evil spirit; if we allow him to remain, that evil spirit will do us only evil; let us put this man, who is thus being utilized for evil, out of the way, and perhaps in so doing we may get rid of the possessing spirit also. So the lunatic is put to death. The manner of death sometimes chosen is a cruel one, as if thereby the spirit itself might also be injured or incapacitated to do further evil. Observe that this cruelty is not directed against the demented human being, but against the indwelling spirit. The maniac in being put to death is sometimes beaten with clubs, sometimes burned, sometimes drowned, as if the evil possessing spirit might itself be fractured or charred or sunk.

The forms of lunacy I have seen are mild, rarely maniacal. The lunatics I have met in the Gabun region were both men and women. Among women I have thought a cause was uterine complications; among both men and women, excessive use of tobacco; in two cases of men the cause was hashish-smoking. These last were characterized by a deep melancholy; all the others were marked by absurd hallucinations. Undeniably, in two cases in Gabun, the paroxysms were influenced by the stage of the moon.

The only medication of which the natives know is exorcism by fetich with drum and dance, baths and purgatives. When a person is discovered to be crazy, he is taken to the doctor, who gathers medicinal barks and leaves, makes a very hot decoction, and puts it under a seat on which is placed the patient. Both seat and patient are covered by a cloth, and he is subjected to a severe sweating process. During this time the doctor calls out to the supposed possessing spirit, "Who are you? who are you?" Perhaps the sick man will say (his voice supposed to be under control of nkinda), "I am So-and-so." The doctor replies, "Eh! you So-and-so! leave him, or I will catch you and put you in prison." The prison is a section of sugar-cane stalk with its leaves twined together; and the doctor is believed to be able to confine the nkinda there. And it remains there indefinitely; but it may be released by the will of the doctor, who will choose to free it some day unless he is paid not to do so. Sometimes the crazy person has so many sinkinda that he becomes a maniac, losing all sense of shame or even of hunger. In such a case he is tied till he becomes quiet and the doctor announces that the sinkinda have all gone out. The patient is then washed, and the doctor with song and drum calls on good sinkinda to come and enter, and directs them to take care of the man's body.

The American Negro Voodoo
When the Negro was brought to America as a slave, he brought with him a variety of African things, some good, some bad.

When hurried upon the slave-ships in the Kongo or at Lagos, the slave tied into a little package, hung among his other fetich treasures, seeds of his favorite foods. At least one of these seeds survived, in the West Indies and thence to the United States, with a native name "gumbo." It is the okra (Abelmoschus esculentus), that exists all over Africa, and has spread over the United States.

Ground-nuts—"pea-nuts" (Arachis hypogea), which botanists claim to be a native of South America—have been grown from time immemorial all over Africa, and, in the Loango country bordering on the Kongo River, by the Ashira and some other tribes are used as their staple article of food, rather than the plantain (Musa sapientum), or "manioc," cassava (Jatropha manihot). It is an important export from those regions and from the Gambia to-day. If the nut itself was not carried from Africa to America, its native name was; that name is "mbenda," and it was corrupted to "pindar" in parts of the Southern States.

The evil thing that the slave brought with him was his religion. You do not need to go to Africa to find the fetich. During the hundred years that slavery in our America held the Negro crushed, degraded, and apart, his master could deprive him of, his manhood, his wife, his child, the fruits of his toil, of his life; but there was one thing of which he could not deprive him,-his faith in fetich charms. Not only did this religion of the fetich endure under slavery; it grew. None but Christian masters offered the Negro any other religion; and, by law, even they were debarred from giving him any education. So fetichism flourished. The master's children were infected by the contagion of superstition; they imbibed some of it at their Negro foster-mother's breast. It was a secret religion that lurked thinly covered in slavery days, and that lurks to-day beneath the Negro's Christian profession as a white art, and among non-professors as a black art; a memory of the revenges of his African ancestors; a secret fraternity among slaves of far-distant plantations, with words and signs,—the lifting of a finger, the twitch of an eyelid,—that telegraphed from house to house with amazing rapidity (as to-day in Africa) current news in old slave days and during the late Civil War; suspected, but never understood by the white master; which, as a superstition, has spread itself among our ignorant white masses as the "Hoodoo." Vudu, or Odoism, is simply African fetichism transplanted to American soil.

"It is almost impossible for persons who have been brought up under this system ever to divest themselves fully of its influence. It has been retained among the blacks of this country, and especially at the South, though in a less open form, even to the present day, and probably will never be fully abandoned until they have made much higher attainments in Christian education and civilization. In some of the plantations of the South, as well as in the West Indies, where there has been less Christian culture, egg-shells are hung up in the corners of their chimneys to cause the chickens to flourish; an extracted tooth is thrown over the house or worn around the neck to prevent other teeth from aching; and real fetiches, though not known by this name [perhaps "mascots"?], are used about their persons to shield them from sickness or from the effects of witchcraft." [92]

While on a furlough in the United States in 1891, I visited a town in Southern Virginia, and by invitation of the Negro pastor of

---

92   Wilson.

the African church addressed them on foreign missions. Somewhat at a loss what attitude to take toward a Negro audience in speaking to them of Africa, I candidly asked the pastor what I should say. He bade me speak exactly as if I was addressing an educated white assembly. I did so. In describing native African virtues and vices, I mentioned their fetichism, and remarked that it was the same that obtained in the United States; and lest my hearers might think I was personally attacking them, I added, "down South in Georgia and Louisiana." The bench of elders sitting just in front of me broke out, "And jist around hyar, too."

I had read Cable's "Creole Tales." One of his characters is sick with a strange vague affection whose symptoms medicine had failed to reach. He is superstitious, and one morning he wakes in horror at finding a dead frog secreted under his pillow. That fetich was no novelist's conjecture; it wa's true to life. About 1894 or 1895, while I was alone in charge of Gabun Station, for three successive mornings when I opened the front door, I found a dried frog leaning against the threshold. I did not care enough about it to inquire its significance or to ascertain who put it there. Since then I have found that it is not used as a fetich by people of the Gabun region, but probably by Upper Coast people. I remember that at that time I had three Bassa workmen from Liberia whom I suspected of stealing and who then suddenly deserted my service. I think they placed the frog, there, either to injure me or to prevent my following up their theft.

Folk-lore

An attractive survival of African life in America are "Uncle Remus's" mystic tales of "Beer Rabbit." They are the folk-lore that the slave brought with him from his African home, where in village hut and forest camp often have been told to my own ears similar weird personifications before Harris had actually written them. There being no rabbits in West Africa, "Br'er Rabbit" is an American substitution for "Brother" Njâ (Leopard), or Brother lheli (Gazelle), in Paia Njambi's (the Creator's) council of speaking animals.

CHAPTER XVI
Tales of fetich based on fact

THE VIEW-POINT OF THE NATIVE AFRICAN MIND, in all unusual occurrences, is that of witchcraft. Without looking for an explanation in what civilization would call natural causes, his thought turns at once to the supernatural. Indeed, the supernatural is so constant a factor in his life, that to him it furnishes explanation of events as prompt and reasonable as our reference to the recognized forces of nature. Mere coincidences are often to him miracles.

In the large mass of materials which I gathered from all native sources of information for the formulation of the philosophy of fetichism, as presented in the former part of this work, I found many remarkable tales some of whose incidents were probable, and which to me were explicable on natural grounds, but which my native friends believed were the effect of witchcraft power. I did not dispute them. To do so would either have closed their lips or made them omit the witchcraft element from any subsequent stories they might narrate to me. I thus secured these tales as a purely native product.

I did not use a note-book, fearing that its presence would hamper the freedom of the story-teller, but listened carefully and wrote down the interview immediately at its close. Not all knew that I was writing for publication. That knowledge would have interfered with the simplicity of their utterances. Of my several informants, some were ignorant, some heathen, some Christian, only a few well educated. Of the most intelligent of my informants, two allowed me to take notes as they were speaking, and I really wrote from dictation; they considerately spoke slowly, so that I should miss nothing, while I wrote rapidly and at the same time had to translate their language into English. Of those two, one was able to give part of the interview in English. The thoughts in these stories are entirely native. So are most of the words. I tried to retain the narrators' own structure of sentences, sacrificing a little of English for the sake of native idioms. The prevalence of short words is due to my effort at exact translation of their own words. Occasionally I have used longer words of Latin origin because I had forgotten their word, and in an effort to repeat their idea. The shortness of the sentences is due to the natives' graphic and animated style of speaking. Long sentences are foreign to their mode of speech.

The following two stories are illustrative of the native belief, mentioned in Chapter IV, that we possess not only our physical body, but also an essential or "astral" form, in shape and feature like the body. This form, or "life," with its "heart," can be stolen by magic power while one is asleep, and the individual sleeps on unconscious of his loss. If the life-form is returned to him before he awakes, he will be unaware that anything unusual has happened. If he awakes before that portion of him has been returned, though he may live for a while, he will sicken and eventually die. If the magicians who stole the "life" have eaten the "heart," he sickens at once, and will soon die.

l. A Witch Sweetheart

A certain man loved a woman whom he expected to marry. He visited her regularly. Whenever he intended to visit her, he always notified her thus: "l will be coming such a day" or "such an hour." Then she would say, "Yes." But it happened on a particular day when he told her, "l'll be coming to-night," she said, "No, not to-night, wait till next night." He replied, "No, for l will come to-night." But she refused, "No, l do not want you to come to-night." Then he asked,"What is your objection? Hitherto you have let me come when l pleased. What is the matter to-night?" So she said, "l do not want you to come, because l will be absent to-night." "Where are you going?" he asked. To this she gave as answer only, "Don't come! l don't want you to come!" So the man said, "All right! l will not come. lf you don't want me, then l'm not coming." So he left her, very much surprised at what she had said, and began to think something was going wrong; he thought he would like to know for himself what it was.

This woman was one of those who belonged to the Witch Society, and engaged in its plays. But the man had not suspected this, and did not know that she was one of those who played.

The native belief is that when a witch or wizard has seized some one to "eat" his "life" or do him other harm, if there be a non—society witness hidden or in the open, the odor of that witness weakens the witch power, and the attempt at witchcraft fails.

This man, not suspecting the real state of the case, but in order to know what was going on with the woman, came softly and hid near her house, where he might be able to see whether any one went in or came out. Soon he heard the door of her house open. He saw her come out of the house without any clothing, and she quietly pulled the door to after her and closed it, and then walked away from the place. All this the man saw, but he said nothing. He stood outside waiting, waiting until she should return. After a long while, as be was tired standing, he thought he would go into the house and hide himself somewhere. It was not long after this that he heard a little noise outside, and looking through the apertures of the bamboo wall saw her and others with her, men and women. Some of them were carrying the form of a man on their shoulders. Others spread out on the ground green plantain leaves, and stretched the form on the leaves. Each of the party had a knife, and they began their work of cutting the form into pieces. While thus occupied, they saw that their knives would not penetrate. Some of them began to step around, peeping into recesses as if they were looking for something. Still trying to cut, their knives seemed dulled; no one of them could succeed in cutting out a single piece. So they stopped, and began to sharpen their knives, and again tried to cut, using more force in their efforts. They worked rapidly, for they had to hasten, as there were signs of approaching day.

As they still were unable to make any incisions after the sharpening of the knives, they thought it very strange, and began to suspect that some one was near witnessing what they were doing. So some of them began to search in different directions; they sniffed to detect the odor of a person. This they did over and over again, and came back, and again sharpened their knives, and again they failed. And then they would again go around, sniffing for a human being.

At last, as it was near morning, they had to give up their intention of cutting into this form. So they had to take it up again on their shoulders and carry it back to where they had brought it from, and lost their feast.

Then the woman came back to her house, very much disappointed and excited. Though it was still dark, it was so near daybreak that she did not go to bed, but took a light, and began to hunt all through her house, having at last begun to suspect that perhaps her lover was there. Finally she found him where he was hiding. She was very angry, saying, "Who told you to come here? What brought you? And when did you come? Did I not tell you not to come to-night?" But he turned on her, saying, "But where have you yourself been? And what have you yourself been doing? I came here expecting to find another man here. But that is not what I saw!"

She trembled, saying, "Have you been here a long time?" And he significantly said, "Yes, I have!" Then, furious, she said, "Now you have seen all that we were doing, and you have found me out! And as you have discovered that I am engaged in witchcraft, and lest you tell others about it, you shall see that I will put an end to your life! You shall not go out of this house alive!" So she pulled out her knife. But the man was quite strong, and though he had no weapon, made a hard fight. He was stronger than the woman, was able to get away from her, and left the house just before daylight.

From that day their friendship was broken; neither cared

again to see the face of the other. The man informed on the woman. But she was not prosecuted; for no one was able to make specific complaint that they had lost their "heart-life." That form had been restored to its person unrecognized and uninjured. No one out of the society, not even the victim himself, knew of the attempt that had been made on him.

ll. A Jealous Wife

A man of the Orungu tribe in the Ogowe region had several wives, of whom the chief, commonly called the "queen" or head-wife, had no children. This was a grief to her and a disappointment to the husband. But one of his younger women, who had now become his favorite, had a baby, and the head-wife was jealous of her.

The husband still retained the older one as the bearer of the keys and in direction of the other women, though he was beginning to doubt her, as be suspected her of witchcraft. But he said nothing about it, not being sure.

It is believed that witches can enter houses without opening doors or breaking walls, and can do what they please without other people knowing of it at the time. So one night this man and his young wife were sleeping in the same bed with their little babe. Suddenly, after midnight, the mother happened to wake up startled. She missed her baby from the bed. She looked and looked all over the bed from head to foot, and did not find it. Then she was frightened, woke up her husband gently, and told him in a whisper, The child is missing!

I don't see the child!"

The husband told her to get up and light a gum-torch (for there were coals smouldering on the clay hearth used as a fireplace), that they might look for the child. She did so, and both hunted, looking under the bedstead and elsewhere, but did not find the child. Then they examined the windows and door; for perhaps the child had been taken out by some one. The door and windows were all properly fastened. The mother was very much troubled; but her husband, keeping his own counsel, advised her not to scream or make a noise, but said, "Let us go back to bed, but not to go to sleep; and let the room be dark again." So the wife put out the torch, leaving the room in darkness; and they returned to bed. Then the husband said, "Maybe we can prove or see something before morning" (for be suspected); and he added, "Whoever or whatever has taken the child out so secretly, will secretly bring it back. So we must not sleep, but watch."

So both lay awake in bed for a few hours. Then, just before morning, while it was still dark, they heard a little noise outside near the house, like the rustling of wings and the panting of breath. They were both anxious, and had their eyes wide open. Soon they saw the room flashed full of a bright light from the roof. [Witchcraft people are noted for having a light which they can thus flash.] Then the wife, as soon as she saw the light, quietly nudged her husband; and be returned the pressure, to let her know that he was aware, and also to intimate that she should continue silent as himself; and they pretended to be sleeping soundly.

Soon they saw the figure of a woman descend from the low roof, but with no hole in the roof. The figure came to the bedside and lifted up the edge of the mosquito-net with one hand, in the other holding a child. As soon as she attempted to put the baby back in its place, between the father and mother, the father, as he was the stronger, and nearer to the figure on the outside of the bed, got up quickly, and seized both hands of the woman before she had time to let go of the child and escape from the room. He said aloud to the mother, "Get up! Your baby has been missing. Now light the light, and we will see the person face to face who has taken the child out!"

The young mother did so, and they discovered that it was the head-wife who had brought in the child.

Then, when the father felt the body of the babe, it was limp and burning with fever.

As it was so near daylight the father did not delay, but began at once to make a fuss, and shouted for the people of the village to gather together. And he began a "palaver" (investigation) immediately. When all the people had assembled to hear the palaver, both the father and the mother related what had passed during the night, about their missing the child, and its return.

The head-wife, being accused, was silent, having nothing to say for herself; for she was both ashamed and afraid to confess that she had been eating the life of the baby. But all the people knew that such things were done, and they believed that this woman had done with the, baby whatever she wanted to do while she had it outside that night.

Then the father of the child tied up the head-woman, and said to her, "Now I have you in my hands, I will not let you go until you give back the baby's life, and make it well again." [The belief is that if the "heart-life" has not been eaten the victim can recover.] This she was not able to do, for she had eaten its "heart." So the next day the baby died. And the husband executed that head-woman by cutting her throat.

The above incident was told me at Libreville by a very intelligent Mpongwe as having actually occurred in the Gabun region. It is fully believed that walls are no obstacle to the passage of the bodies of those possessing the power of sorcery. The "light" spoken of I have seen. I do not know what it was. From a small point it would flash with starlike rays. It was carried by a man, who disappeared when pursued. A Christian native told me that he once pursued it, and caught the bearer with a torch concealed in a hollow cylinder; the flashing was caused by his thrusting it in and out of the cylinder.

III. Witchcraft Mothers

(On an itineration in my boat on the Ogowe interior, in 1890, I came to a village of the Akele tribe, whose inhabitants were in an intense state of excitement. All the men were brandishing guns and spears or daggers; women were gesticulating and screaming; the loins of all were girded for fight; and a few only of the older men and some strangers were appealing for quiet.

Among the latter was a native trader of the Mpongwe coast tribe. His trade interests made for peace. I knew him, as he had received some education in our Gabun school.

I saw that in such confusion it would be useless to attempt to ask a hearing for my gospel message. I did not wait to inquire the cause of the day's commotion, and passed on to another village.

Subsequently the Mpongwe man told me the story. Though slightly educated and enlightened, he was not a Christian and believed in fetiches. His account, therefore, was from the heathen standpoint. I cannot repeat his own wording, but the outline of the story is exactly his.)

In that village were two slave women, each married to a free husband. Each was expecting to become a mother,—No. 1 in three months, and No. 2 in six months. They were friends; and, unknown to their husbands, were members of the Witchcraft Society, and were accustomed secretly to attend and take part in the society's midnight meetings and plays. Just what is the nature of those plays is not quite certain, but it is known that wild orgies of dancing constitute a part of them.

These two women, that they might be freer for their dancing and other movements, were accustomed, in going to the meetings, to divest themselves temporarily of their unborn babes. This they were able to do by witchcraft power, in virtue of which the possessor can pass, or cause any one else to pass, uninjured through any material object, as a ray of light passes through glass.

This they did on their way to the meeting-place on the edge of the forest. They laid their babes on the grass in a secluded spot, and resumed them on their return. As they did so, No. 1 observed that hers was a male, and No. 2 that hers was a female. They did this many nights in succession.

Subsequently No. 2 began to be envious of No. 1 in the possession by the latter of a male child. The husband of No. 2 had been very anxious for a son. She knew that if she could present him with a son be would be very proud, and would enlarge her position and privileges in the family. So, one night, she did not wait for her friend No. 1 to return with her, but, excusing herself from the play, came back on the path alone. Coming to where the two babes were lying, she deliberately exchanged her own girl for the boy of No. 1.

The latter stayed very late at the play,—so late that, as she hasted home, fearful lest the morning light should find her on the path (a dangerous thing to a witch-player), on coming to where the babes had been deposited, she snatched up the remaining one without examining it, and, supposing it to be hers, resumed the natural possession of it.

Shortly after this, the nine months of No. 1 were fulfilled, and she bore a child which, to her surprise, she saw was a female. She made no remark, as she immediately suspected what had been done. She waited three months, until the days of No. 2 also were fulfilled. At the birth of the child of No. 2 there was great rejoicing by the husband in the possession of a son. He made a great feast, and called together a large gathering of people. Among them was not invited the woman No. 1; for she and No. 2 were no longer friendly, though neither of them had said anything.

In the midst of the rejoicings No. 1 made her appearance, though uninvited, and striding among the guests, went silently into the bedroom, carrying a three-months-old female babe. She went to the side of the bed of No. 2, laid down the female child, saying, "There 's your baby!" snatched up the male infant, saying, "This is mine!" and strode out of the room into the street and on the way to her house.

A scream from No. 2 startled the crowd of guests; word was passed that the boy was being stolen, and No. 1 was pursued and brought back; but she desperately refused to give up the boy. The whole village was at once thrown into confusion.

That was the state of affairs on the day that I arrived there. My informant told me that he and others induced the crowd to quiet, by saying that the matter could better be settled by a talk than by guns, by sitting down in council than by standing up in fight.

On being brought before the council or palaver, No. 1 was calm and firm. She still held to the boy-baby. She said she was willing to be judged, but demanded that No. 2 should also be made to confront the council. The sense of guilt of the latter made her weak and unable to face the friend she had wronged.

Charged with stealing, No. 1 made a bold speech. She said, "Yes; I have taken my own! If that be stealing, I have stolen!" And then she told the whole truth of the witchcraft plays of herself and No. 2. The latter, overcome with shame for her crime, did not deny; she admitted all. And No. 1 closed her defence by saying, "So this other woman has nothing about which to make complaint. She has her child, and I have mine, and that settles the matter."

The crowd was amazed, and the husbands were ashamed at finding that their wives were witches. The husband of No. 2 was no longer disposed to fight after his wife had admitted that the boy-baby was not her own. The matter was dropped, as no one was really harmed. Neither husband was disposed to fine the wife of the other for her witchcraft., as both were guilty.

The guests ate the feast, but the host had no satisfaction in its now useless expenditure except that it was considered sufficient reparation to the husband of No. I for his own wife's original theft.

IV. The Wizard House-Breaker

(The incidents narrated in the following three stories, The Wizard House-Breaker, The Wizard Murderer, The Wizard and his Invisible Dog, my informant asserted were actual occurrences; Nos. IV. and VI. occurring in the Gabun region, and the parties known. The witchcraft part of the stories consists in the strange light which wizards and witches are said to possess; it is under their control to display or hide, and it gives them power to overcome time and space. The scene of No. V. is on the Ogowe River.)

There were a husband and wife who had been married a number of years. She had a child, a little boy. The husband had a brother; and this brother had taken a strong fancy to the woman, and wanted to possess her. Secretly he was asking her to live with him. But the woman always refused, saying, "No, I do not want it!" Then this brother's love began to change to anger. He cherished vexation in his heart toward the woman, and asked her, "Why do you always refuse me? You are the wife, not of a stranger, but of my brother.

He and I are one, and you ought to accept me." But she persisted, "No, I don't want it!"

The brother's anger deepened into revenge. He possessed nyemba (witchcraft power), and determined to use it.

One day this woman had to go to her plantation; and she arranged for the journey, taking her little boy with her. Before she left the village to go to the plantation, she told the townspeople, "I will remain at the plantation for some days, to take care of my gardens; for I am tired of losses by the wild beasts spoiling my crops." But the other women said, "Ah! your plantation is too far; it is not safe for you to be by yourself." But she said, "I cannot help it; I have to go." She was brave, and persisted in her plan, and made all preparations. On a set day, with her basket on her back, her child on her left bip, and her machete in her right hand, the started. She went on, on, steadily; reached the plantation, and rested there the remainder of that day with her child. After her evening meal she shut the door of the hut and went to bed. The door was fastened with strings and a bar, for the plantation hamlets had no locks.

She awoke suddenly about midnight, and thought she heard a noise outside. She listened quietly. Then she heard the sound again. Presently she discovered by the noise that some one was trying to climb upon the top of the but, for the roof was low. Soon, then, she observed that this person was trying to break open the palm-thatch of the low roof. She still lay quietly. But she remembered a big spear which the husband always kept in one of the rooms of that hut; so she slowly got out of bed, and very softly went to the corner of the room where the spear was standing, and returned to bed with it.

The breaking of the thatch continued. Soon she saw the room filled with a strange light, and then she saw a man trying to enter the roof head foremost. She bravely kept still, and watched his head and shoulders enter. She could not see his face, and did not know who he was. But she did not wait for certainty; she thrust the spear upward at the man's head. Immediately the figure disappeared, and she heard a heavy thud as he fell to the ground into the street outside.

She now began to be frightened; she no longer felt safe, and dreaded what might happen before morning. So she began to get ready to return to town that very night. She girded her loin garment, fastened the cloth for carrying her child, took her machete, hasted out of the hut, and started for her village. In her fear she ran, and rested by walking. Thus, alternately running and walking, she reached the village so exhausted and weak with loss of sleep that when her husband's door was opened shff fell fainting on the floor. He and others were alarmed, and asked, "What? What's the matter?" As soon as she was able to speak, she told the whole story. They asked her, "Did you see the person? Do you know him?" She said, "No; only one thing I know: it was a man, and he fell into the street."

So, when daylight came, the husband and others went to the plantation to see whether they could find the man. When they reached the plantation, they were very much surprised to see that the man was this brother. He was lying dead, with the spear in his neck.

The husband was not vexed at his wife for the death of his brother; he was pleased that she had so well defended herself.

V. The Wizard Murderer

(My informant asserted that this really happened in the Ogowe.)

The parties are a husband and wife, their two little children, and a younger brother of the husband. One of the children, a boy, was a lad old enough to understand affairs.

The brother-in-law loved the woman, and secretly tried to draw her affections to himself; but to all his solicitation she gave only persistent refusal. Thus matters went on, he asking and she refusing; and then his love turned to hatred. It happened one day that the husband and wife had a big quarrel of their own. The wife was so angry that she said she would leave him, take the children, and go to her father's house. But that home'was far away, and could not be reached in one day. Other women tried to prevent her going, as she would have to spend the night in the forest on the way; but she insisted.

Leaving her clothing and other goods, she started off with the two children, a little food, and her machete. Trying to make the journey in one day, she walked very fast. But when the sun had set, and soon darkness would fall, the lad said, "Mother, as we cannot reach there to-nigbt, don't you think we 'd better stop and arrange a sleeping-place before dark, and let the spot be a little aside from the public path?

The mother said, "Yes; that is good!" Then she gave the babe to the lad to hold, while she with her machete began to cut away bushes and clear the ground for a convenient sleeping-spot. After she had cut away some bushes, the lad watching her, saw that she was clearing a space larger than was needed for herself. He asked her, "Do you intend that we all shall sleep in that one place,—you and baby and I?" The mother said, "Yes." But he said, "Why, no! Fix two places,—I by myself, and you and baby in another place." The mother replied, "No, I cannot let you sleep alone in this forest; I want you near me." However, the lad insisted: "But if anything happens to us in the night, then we will be lost all together. I am not willing that we should be all in the same place."

So the lad began to search for a place for himself, and came to a big tree which was not very far from his mother's chosen spot. He called her to him, and said, "I have found a good place. Just you clear for me behind this big tree, and dig a trench for me to lie in, just below the level of the ground." The mother did so.

After the two spots were cleared, they ate their little evening meal, and night came. Then the lad said, "Now I go to lie in the trench, and you sprinkle leaves over me to hide me, and then you go to your sleeping-place. And if anything happens to me at night, I promise I will not cry out; I will remain silent. And you promise that if anything happens to you, you also will not cry out, nor call to me." The mother agreed, and both went to sleep.

Not long after this, both were awakened by a strange flashing light, and the mother saw some one coming to the place where she was lying. Then the light was suddenly extinguished; and she saw a man near her, and recognized that he was her brother-in-law. She was exceedingly alarmed, knowing that he did not come with good intent. In her fright she hoped to gain time by pretending to be friendly with him. So she exclaimed, "Oh! My young husband! Now you have come after me, so that your brother's wife will not have to sleep in the forest alone. Now we will make friendship and be good friends." But he replied in anger: "Friends, you say? You shall see what kind of friends I will make with you to-night! You, the woman who hates me! Where is the lad?" She, determined to shield the child, said, "The lad did not come with me; he preferred to stay in town with—his father." The man replied, "You are not telling me the truth. Tell me where the lad is!" But she persisted in her statement, "He is left in town with his father."

Then the man walked about in search of the lad, going even very near to where be was lying awake in the trench. But the leaves hid him, and his uncle did not discern that the ground had been disturbed. Returning to the woman, he said, "Good! you are telling the truth. I don't see the lad. But now I am ready to attend to you. You shall see." So he approached the woman to seize her. She was so paralyzed with fear that she neither attempted to run away, nor, though her machete was lying near, did she lay hold of it.

Even had she done so, she was too weak with her journey to defend herself. The man snatched up the babe that still was sleeping, and looking around for a rough, projecting root, violently flung the babe against it. It made no cry; and both he and the mother supposed it was instantly killed. Then be drew his machete, which he had made very sharp, and began to cut and slash the woman. She pleaded and cried for help; but there was no help near. She fell, covered with wounds, and died on the spot. All this the lad saw and heard. After killing the mother, the man began again to search for the lad, but did not find him; and, as it was now after midnight, he left the place to go back to town.

Soon after he was gone, the lad, exhausted with terror and fatigue, fell asleep. But be awoke again in the early daylight. Arising from his trench, he went with grief and distress to see the two corpses. Looking at his mother's blood covered form, he saw that she was dead. Looking at his baby brother lying on the root, he took up the little form, sobbing, "Only l am alive. Even this little child was not spared. Am l to go on my journey all alone?" Examining the limp body still. further, it seemed still to show signs of life; and he said to himself, "l think l will try to save it. l am strong enough to carry it to my mother's people, to whom l shall tell this whole story."

So he took up the cloth in which his mother had carried the child, adjusted it for himself, placed the unconscious form in it, and started on his journey. A short distance beyond brought him to a brook. Before be crossed it, he stooped to take a drink of water. Tben examining the little body again, he felt that it was not stiff and was still warm. Said he, "Ah! perhaps it has a little life! l better give it a drink." So he tried; and the baby drank, He rejoiced. "So perhaps it will be alive. l better bathe it." And be did so. Then he crossed the brook, and journeyed on. Before he reached his grandfather's village, he crossed another brook, and bathed the babe, and gave it a drink as at the first brook.

On his arrival at the village the people were surprised to see him without his mother. His grandfather at once wanted to know his story and why he had come there alone. Said he, "Please, before l tell my story, try to save this baby."

After the people had looked to the baby's needs and saw that it might live, they gathered together to listen to what the lad had to say. When they had heard his account, they started back with him to find his mother's corpse. They took it up and carried it to her husband's village, there to hold palaver over the death. As soon as they reached the village, instead of announcing themselves as visitors to the husband, they went straight to the brother-in-law's house. They found him sitting in the veranda. They laid the corpse at his feet. This so startled him that a look of guilt showed on his face. Looking at the party who had brought the corpse, he saw among them the lad; and at once he felt sure that this lad had been a witness of his crime. He lost his self-control, and began to scold, "What do you put this thing at my feet for? Take it away!"

Then all the townspeople gathered around him, being horrified at the news of the woman's death. The husband called them all to a council, and the palaver was held at his house. There the grandfather and the lad told the whole story.

The brother-in-law began to enter a denial; but the husband said, "No, you are guilty! and because we are brothers, and we are one, the guilt is also mine; and I will confess for you. You are guilty. Your actions show it. Why did you become so angry as soon as you saw the corpse at your feet?"

But the wife's family said to the husband, "We have no quarrel with you. We want only the person who killed our sister, and a fine of money for our loss."

Then the husband said, "You are right; this man killed her. Take him, and for a fine take his slaves and other property. He has deliberately deprived me of a wife, and my children of a mother. Take all he owns." It was so done; and the assemblage dispersed.

VI. The Wizard and his Invisible Dog

(This, my informant asserted, actually happened at the town of Libreville, Gabun.)

One night a young woman was alone in her house. She was married; but, that particular night, the husband was absent.

After she had gone to her bed for the night, she slept, but not very soundly. Half awake, she thought she heard something moving in the front reception-room (ikenga). She had lowered the lamp in her bedroom, but it still gave enough light for her to see. She slightly opened the mosquito-net on one side and began to look and listen. But she saw no one nor anything unusual in her room. But as the door between her bedroom and the reception-room was slightly ajar, she looked toward its opening, and thought she saw a figure moving in that room. She felt sure there was some one there. So she stepped softly out of the bed, and peeped through the narrow opening of the door. Sure enough, there was a man.

She was frightened, but controlled herself. She was puzzled to know how he had got into that room, whose outer door she knew she had fastened before she went to bed. She crept quietly back to her bed, and then began to shout, "Who is that? How did you get in? I see you!" There was no answer. The figure ceased moving, and stood still. The woman again cried out, "Who are you? When did you come in? What do you want?" The man replied in a low voice, "It is I!" She rejoined, "Who is 'I'? Are you only 'me'? Who are you? How did you succeed in entering? Go out!" So he apparently opened the door and went out. She was so frightened that she did not immediately. follow him, nor did she make a public outcry.

Awhile afterward she recovered self-control, and arose and went into the outer room, and assured herself that the outside door was fast, as she had left it. She believed he had entered the closed door by witchcraft art.

The next morning she told her village people the story; but she was afraid to mention the man's name (for she knew who he was), because many people thought he possessed power as a wizard, and she feared he would revenge himself on her. She told his name only to her mother.

Not long afterward he came again to her house when she was alone at night, but did not enter. He came to the outside wall against which be knew her bedstead stood. Lying there, she could see his form through the cracks in the bamboo wall. She saw this as she happened to awake from sleep. She saw his figure standing still, and she heard a sound as of the tinkling of a bell moving about, such as natives tie to the necks of their dogs in hunting. The wizard had brought with him this time a small invisible beast to whose neck the invisible but audible bell was attached; and she beard a sound along the bottom of the.wall, as if the animal was scratching a hole for its master's entrance. This time she was so alarmed that she screamed aloud to the people of the village; and then, through the chinks in the wall, she saw passing by in the street the figure of the same man.

The very next day the woman began to be sick of a fever. For several days she was quite ill, and people began to be alarmed for her. Her sickness grew very much worse. Her people sent for a Senegal man, living in Libreville, who had quite a reputation as a doctor in that kind of sickness. When this doctor came, she was able to speak only in a low voice, and she recounted to him what had happened. He asked her to mention the precise spot on which the man had stood outside of the wall of her house. She described to her mother the particular spot, and the mother took the doctor to show him. He scraped up clay from the place and mixed it in a small bowl of cold water. He directed that after she had been given a bath morning and evening this muddy water should be rubbed over her body. She said that when it was thus rubbed over her skin, her flesh temporarily felt as if it was paralyzed.

Her sickness continued more than a month, and then she recovered. Soon after her recovery the man who had attempted to enter her room, and who was suspected of having caused her sickness by witchcraft art, suddenly left Gabun, and went to another country.

VII. Spirit-Dancing

Antyande, a Mpongwe woman of the town of Libreville, Gabun, is a leader of a company of ten or a dozen women in a certain native dance called "ivanga," which is performed only by women. Some dance it only as an exhibition of their gymnastic skill; others mix with it fetich and witchcraft arts, and claim that their movements are under spirit power. Antyande, more than the other women of the company, uses witchcraft in her performances. She seems almost to glide through the air, alighting on the knees of sitting spectators without giving them the impression of weight, gyrating on small stools without moving the stools from their position, and making many other wonderful physical contortions in an exceedingly graceful and easy manner. She even goes to graveyards at night, accompanied by three or four men and women, to get what they call the spirits of the dead. It is said by some of the men who have gone there with her that they do not understand what she does, but that it is so very strange and awful that they are afraid. The reason why she goes for these abambo (ghosts) of the graves is that she may be spry and alert, and able to do with her body whatever she pleases. She claims also to be accompanied by a leopard and a bush-cat that are visible to her but not to others. As these animals are noted for their quick and agile movements, and are under her witch-power control, they are able to impart to her these qualities.

In January, 1902, she was dancing her ivanga, and there was a woman among the spectators who had been drinking to the point of intoxication. In her foolishness she determined to help Antyande by assuming to be directress to keep the spectators in order. But, being drunk, she could not do so; she only made disorder. In attempting to make matters straight she only made them crooked. Antyande asked her to get out of her way. Many, also, of the spectators begged the woman to cease interfering; but she would not, and finally she vexed Antyande by spoiling her movements in getting too close in front of her. Antyande's patience was exhausted, and she suddenly revealed a secret that astonished many even of her intimate acquaintances, saying, "Whoever is related to this drunken woman, please tell her to get out of my way while I am dancing, because my dance is not a mere gymnastic exercise. I have leopards and bushcats about me, and if she comes too near me, and the tails of these animals should twist around her legs, then she will get a sickness: and if that happens, her people must not hold me responsible for it, for I have given you this warning." This surprised many of the people; for they had supposed she was nothing more than an unusually graceful dancer, and that her success was purely physical. Now, publicly, she admitted that the power in her limbs and body causing her graceful undulations was a supernatural one. So some of the women laid hold of the drunken woman, and induced her to get out of the way.

While dancing, Antyande wears a wide belt called "ekope," which is made with white and red stripes, and adorned with fringes of small bells in bands like sleigh-bells. It is known that her ekope has been heard and seen moving as if in the rhythm of a dance in her own room when she was not visibly there. Those who beard the sound of its bells would think she was there practising the dance; but when they went to look, they saw it moving, but did not see her. A few months afterward, a report came at'night to the villages that Antyande was very much excited and could not sleep; that she had gone to her room for the ekope, and that it was not there. So she began to make a great fuss, and begged her associates to keep watch and go with her to search for the missing ekope. Some of these friends were willing; others were not, and these went to their beds. She then went to other villages and told the people there: "My ekope has gone out on a promenade. Have you seen it?" These people were among the chief dancers of her band. But they told her they did not know where the ekope was. So she began to ejaculate a prayer: "Oh, please, you went out for a walk; come back to me, for if you do not return, then I am lost. It will be death to me." Just before daylight, as she was still wandering about with her friends, and singing ivanga songs to attract her ekope, suddenly she and two of her friends heard the tinkling of the bells among the bushes lining a certain road which passes by a Roman Catholic chapel. They all went in the direction of the sound of the bells, and entering a cluster of the bushes, they saw the ekope moving to and fro. She was so—glad to see it, and she bade one of her companions to go and get it. But the woman was afraid, and refused, saying, "Me! Oh, no! Go and get it yourself!" So she went to it, singing her ivanga song, seized it, and brought it to her house.

As she is noted for her grace and skill in that particular dance, another woman, by name Ekâmina, asked her to give her power such as hers, as she also wished to be leader of another band of ivanga dancers. Antyande assented, saying, "Well, do you want spirits with it?" The other replied, "Yes, I want two." So the two women, with a young man to escort them, went at night to the graves and obtained the two desired spirits. It is these which give them spirit power. When under their influence, their bodies are thrilled with a new essence which makes them very light and causes them to act and speak as if insane. The two women came back to Antyande's village, and she performed all the magic ceremonies that Ekâmina wanted.

Some time after this, when Ekâmina had practised much and had danced publicly several times, people began to say to her that she danced very well, and soon she was invited to give exhibitions in various places.

Ekope of the Ivanga Dance. Gabun.

One day it happened that the two women had arranged to dance on the same night, each with her own party, at villages quite distant from each other. Antyande asked Ekâmina to give up her play for that night and join with her, "for," said she, "I want to make mine grand; and you wait for yours another day." But Ekâmina was not willing. Antyande tried to get her to change her mind, and was very much displeased because she refused. Ekâmina said, "I will not give up, for my dance is by special invitation at Añwondo village, so I have to go." (Libreville is three miles long; one end is called "Glass," and Añwondo is at the other end.) Ekâmina lived at Glass, and on her way to Añwondo she had to pass the village of Antyande. The latter said to herself, "As Ekâmina is not willing to do as I wish, and I was the one who gave her this power, I will watch her as she passes, and see what I will do." So, when Ekâmina passed at night with her party to Añwondo, Antyande watched her chance as Ekâmina neared her. She went behind her, and did some magic act which would make the latter powerless to dance and not be aware of—her loss of power. When Ekamina reached Añwondo and commenced her play, she was not able to dance at all. She tried till midnight, and failed. She suspected that Antyande was the cause of the failure, for the latter had not been friendly since their unsatisfactory talk. So she took a portion of her party that same night back to Antyande's village, told the latter her trouble, and begged her, "Please, if you have taken away the power, give it back, so I may finish the dance tonight." Antyande said, "No; you would not listen to me. I am a chief dancer, and you are praised as the same. Go and dance!" Ekamina said, "But please give me back the power; I am not able to dance without it." Antyande replied, "No, go to the graveyard and get other spirits there for yourself." So there was no dance done by Ekamina that night.

VIII. Asiki, or the Little Beings

People believe that Asiki (singular "Isiki") were once human beings, but that wicked men, wizards and witches, or other persons who assert that they have memba (witchcraft powers), caught them when they were children and could not defend themselves, nor could their cries for help be heard when playing among the bushes on the edge of the forest. These wicked persons out off the ends of the children's tongues, so that they can never again speak or inform on their captors. They carry them away, and bide them in a secret place where they cannot be found. There they are subjected to a variety of witchcraft treatment that alters their natures so that they are no longer mortal. This treatment checks their entire physical, mental, and moral growth. They cease to remember or care for their former homes or their human relatives, and they accept all the witchcraft of their captors. Even the hair of their head changes, growing in long, straight black tresses down their backs. They wear a curious comb-shaped ornament on the back of their head. It is not stiff or capable of being used as a comb, and is made of some twisted fibre resembling hair. The Asiki value it almost as a part of their life.

These Asiki will sometimes be seen walking in paths on dark nights, and people meet them coining toward them. It is believed that in their meeting, if a person is fearless by natural bravery, or by fetich power as a wizard or witch, and dares to seize the Isiki and snatch away the "comb," the possession of this ornament will bring him riches. But whoever succeeds in obtaining that"comb"will not be allowed to remain in peaceful possession of it. The poor Isiki will be seen at night wandering about the spot where its treasure was lost, trying to obtain it again.

It happened in the year 1901 that there was a report, even in civilized Gabun, about these Asiki,-that two of them were seen near a certain place on the public road at that part of the town of Libreville known as the "Plateau," where live most of the French traders and government officers. A certain Frenchman, who is known as a freemason, in returning from his 8 p.m. dinner at his boarding-house to his dwelling-place, observed that a small figure was walking on one side of the road, keeping pace with him. He accosted it, "Who are you?" There was no answer; only the figure kept on walking, advancing and retreating before him.

Also, a few nights later, a Negro clerk of a white trader met this small being on that very road, and near the spot where the Frenchman had met it, and it began to chase the Negro. He ran, and came frightened to his employer's office, and told him what had happened. His employer did not believe him, laughed at his fears, and told him he was not telling the truth. The very next night the Frenchman, the trader, and other white men and Negro women were sitting in conversation. The trader told the story of his clerk, whereupon the Frenchman said, "Your clerk did not lie; he told the truth. I have myself met that small being two or three times, but I made no effort to catch it." The women told him of the comb-ornament which Asiki were believed to wear, and of the pride with which Asiki regarded it, and the value it would be to any one who could obtain it. Then the Frenchman replied, "As the little being is so small, the very next time I see it I will try to catch it and bring it here, so that you can see it and know that this story is actually true."

A Street in Libreville, Gabun.

On a subsequent night they two—the Frenchman and the trader—went out to see whether they could meet the Isiki. They did not meet with it that night; but a few evenings later the Frenchman went alone, and met the Isiki near the place where it had first been seen. The Frenchman ran toward it and tried to catch it; but it being very agile eluded his grasp. But, though he failed to seize its body, he succeeded in catching hold of its "comb," and snatched it away, and ran rapidly with it toward his house. It did not consist of any hard material as a real comb, but was made of strands resembling the Isiki's hair, and braided into a comb-like shape. The little being was displeased, and ran after him in order to recover the ornament. Having no tongue, it could not speak, but holding out one hand pleadingly and with the other motioning to the back of its head, it made pathetic sounds in its throat, thus inarticulately begging that its treasure should be given back to it. On nearing the light of the Frenchman's house it retreated, and he showed the ornament to other white men and some native women. (So positive was my informant that the names of these men and women were mentioned to me.) He said to the trader, "You doubted your clerk's story. Have you ever seen anything like this in all your life?" They all said they had not. It was reported that many other persons hearing of it went there to see it.

From that night the little being was often seen by other Negroes. It was always holding out its hand, and seemingly pleading for the return of its "comb." This made the Negroes afraid to pass on that road at night. The Frenchman also often met it; it did not chase him, but followed slowly, pleading with its hands in dumb show, and occasionally making a grunting sound in its throat. This it did so persistently and annoyingly that the Frenchman was wearied with its begging, and determined that the next night he would yield up the "comb." But he went prepared with scissors. He found the little being following him. He stopped, and it approached. He held out his hand with the ornament. As the Isiki jumped forward to snatch at it, the Frenchman tried to lay hold of its body; but it was so very agile that, though it had come so near as to be able to take the comb from the Frenchman's hand, it so quickly twisted itself aside as to elude his grasp. He however succeeded in getting his bands in its long hair, and snipped off a lock with his scissors. The Isiki ran away with its recovered treasure, and did not seem to resent the loss of a portion of its bair. This bair the Frenchman is said to have shown to his companions at their next evening conversation, and l was given to understand that he had sent it to France. lt was straight, not woolly, and long.

These Asiki are supposed not to die, and it is also believed that they can propagate; but so complete has been the parent's change under witchcraft power that the lsiki babe will be only an lsiki and cannot grow up to be a human being.

lt is asserted that Asiki are now made by a sort of creative power (just as leopards and bush-cats are claimed to be made, and used invisibly) by witch doctors.

l am only writing these tales, l am not explaining them. Some of the statements in the above story are too circumstantial to be denied. But there is a wide margin for uncertainty as to what one might see after the conviviality of an 8 p.m. West African dinner. In my sudden leaving of Gabun in June, 1903, l had not time to interrogate the men and women named as having seen the lsiki's tress of hair.

IX. Okove

(The incidents of this story really occurred, and independent of the fetich belief in okove power, are true. At the request of my native informant the names of the two tribes are suppressed, for the sake of the living descendants of the two kings.)

There was an old king of one of the principal tribes of West Equatorial Africa who had great power and was held in great respect and fear; there was none other his equal.

He had brothers and cousins. One of these cousins had a servant, a slave, who had been bought from an interior tribe. It happened that this man had not always been a slave, but in the tribe from which he had been sold he was a freeman. The charge on which he had been sold by his own tribe was that of sorcery and witchcraft murder, the death penalty for which had been commuted to sale into slavery. He was deeply versed in a mystery of a certain fetich or magic power called "Okove." He possessed it so powerfully that no one was able to overcome him in contests of strength, and people were greatly afraid of him.

So his owners intended to get rid of him by selling him out of the country. To do this, they planned to catch him in the daytime; for he exercised his okove power chiefly at night, when he could change himself into a powerful being ready to overcome any one who should resist him.

One night when this great king, who also possessed the okove power (though it was not generally known), went out to inspect, he saw a big tall man walking up and down near his premises. The king said to him, "Ho! who are you?" The man answered, "It is I." The king asked," Who is I?" The man replied daringly, "I have already told you that I am I." So the king asked again, "Who are you? Where did you come from? And what are you doing here?" The man said, "I go everywhere, and do what I please at other people's places, and—so I have come here." The king commanded him, "But, no, not at this place. This is mine. Go back to your own!"

The slave gave answer, "No l that is not my habit. No one can master me!"

The king again ordered him, "Go!" He flatly refused, "No!" The king then said plainly, "Are you not willing to leave my premises?"

He replied," No, l never turn away from anyone. l go away when l please. When l am ready, l will go back to my place." At this the king, restraining himself, slowly said, "Be it so!" and turned away, leaving the slave standing in his yard.

The next day the king sent word for his cousin the owner of the slave to come; to whom, when he had arrived at the house, the king told how he had seen the man at night. And he inquired, "What does he do? Why does he leave his place on the plantation and come to my place at night?" The cousin was surprised to hear this, exclaiming, "So! indeed! he comes here at night?" Then he went back to his house, and calling the slave, asked him about this matter. "Do you go around at night, even to the king's place?" The man said, "Yes." His master said, "Why do you do that? Do you hear of other lower-caste people daring to go to the king's at night?" He answered, "No; but it is l who do as l please." His master told him, "No; you better return to the plantation, and live among the other slaves." He replied "l will go, but not now." His master asked him, "But what are you waiting for?" He only repeated, "Yes; but not now."

The very next night, on the king's going out as usual, be found this slave again at his place, and said to him, "So l you here again?" The man replied, "Yes; just what l told you last night, that l do what l please, and l can master anybody." Then the king said, "l warn you plainly, clear off from my place!" He replied, "No, l do not intend to clear out; but I am ready for a fight."

The king asked, "You really want a fight with me?" The man answered,"Yes, I am ready for it." Said the king, "It is well."

The fight began, each with his full okove power. In such contests, the power is able to change the contestants' bodies to many forms. The slave was quick in his use of them. His first change was to the form of a big gorilla. This also the king met. As the fight went on, the next form was into that of leopards. The fight went on, with frequent changes; the slave always being the first to change. After a while the slave seemed to be growing tired, and the king asked him, "Are yon through?" He answered, "No, only resting." Again the fight was resumed. Finally, the slave took an eagle's form; the king did the same.

Presently the slave seemed to hesitate, and the king said, "You said you wanted a fight. Well, let us go on with it." They continued; but the slave seemed to be exhausted, and the king said, "Now, are you willing to leave the place?" He answered, "No; my fatigue is not yet so great as to make me leave your place." The king had held his power in reserve, and had been tolerant of the man's audacity; but he now resumed his human form, took his gun (the slave had none), and aiming it, off it went, and wounded him. Being wounded, the slave had to acknowledge that he was overcome, and he had to go. When morning came, the slave was not able to get up to go about his work, and remained in bed. The gun-shot wound was a small one, and he was conscious that he was dying of some other cause. He sent some one to the master's house to ask him to come. When his master came, he said, "Ah! master! I have something to say to you. Please plead for me!" The master said, "Plead for you! For what?" The slave then told him, "I went around last night to the king's place. He told me to leave, and I was not willing to do so. So we had a great fight. And I am conquered. But please plead for me, that he may make me well."

The master replied, "Did I not advise you not to go there, but rather to stay at your plantation?" He assented. "But please plead, and I will stay at the plantation."

The master answered, "I do not think the king will be willing to help you." Nevertheless, being a cousin, he went privately to the king, and told him all that the slave had told him. The king refused, saying, "No, I am not going to do anything for him. He must die." The next day the slave was dead.

(Another illustration of that king's okove power was narrated to me.)

There had been ill-feeling between this king's tribe and an adjacent inferior tribe who had killed two of the king's chief men without cause, coming suddenly upon them at night in their fishing-camp. The king's people were very much troubled about it, and asked to be led to war. But the old king said, "You young people'don't know anything. If you go to war, there will be much blood shed on both sides. Leave the matter with me. I will attend to it myself."

So at night he went by himself to the town of the king of the offending tribe, and remained there waiting in ambush on the path. Early next morning four of the women belonging to that town had gone to their gardens with their baskets to get food. The old king followed them secretly. After all of. them had filled their baskets, two lifted them upon their backs and started to return to their town. The other two were just stooping (as is the custom in lifting burdens, leaning forward on one knee in order to place their backs against the basket, with a strap passing around the basket and over their foreheads), when the king came behind them and struck their necks with his okove. They instantly died in that stooping position.

The two women who had gone on ahead reached their town without knowing what had happened to the other two. They waited in town a long time for the two absent ones to come. But when they did not make their appearance, the people began to ask those women about the other two. They said they knew nothing about the delay, only that they had left them ready to come and preparing to lift their baskets. The townspeople, anxious because it was late in the day, went out to search for the women. They found them on the path, dead by their baskets. They examined their bodies for some mark or wound or sign of a blow. There was none. This very much perplexed them, for they did not suspect the cause of their death. They carried the dead bodies to town. The next night the king went again to that same town, and he happened to meet the other king at the boat-landing of the town. So the old king made complaint to the other why the servants of the latter had killed his two chiefs. The other made no reply, having no justification of what his people had done.

Then the old king said, "As your people have done this, there is war between us"; and he struck him with his okove. And he added, "Do you know that I have already begun war with your people? Did you not find two of your women dead yesterday at your gardens? I killed them. But I am not through with you, I want you to pay a fine, and I want the man who killed my two chiefs, for the lives of the two women are not equivalent to those of my two chiefs."

The other king felt he was conquered by some unseen power, and did not resist. He agreed to give up the murderer and pay a fine. The next day he had the murderer caught and brought before a council. He told them that the old king of the other tribe wanted the life of that man and a sum of money for the lives of his two chiefs.

They began to collect on the spot goods and food of all kinds, and many things of little value, with which to make simply the appearance of a full canoe. They tied the prisoner, put him in the canoe, and went with him and the goods to the old king. He received them.

But at night he went again to the other king, and began to rebuke him, saying that what he had sent was not sufficient. The other made a protest: "I have given you enough,—the lives of the two women, the one man, and goods equivalent to two more lives. I have thus given you five for your two."

But the old king, in tribal pride, reckoned the sex and social position of his two men greater than any five of an inferior tribe, and said, "How dare you speak to me like that? You shall surely die!" He struck him with his okove, and went away.

The next day the other king was not able to leave his bed and sent for many of his people to come, saying that be had a special word to speak to them. They came, and he told them all about the death of the two women, and all that had occurred between him and the old king. "And now," he said, "I am dying. We are overcome. It is useless to resist. I want you to remember, as long as the world stands, never to fight or quarrel with the tribe of that king."

Then he turned his face to the wall and died.

X. The Family Idols

(To a village on the St. Thomè or left bank of Gabun Bay, or "River," away up a winding mangrove stream, and on the edge of the forest that was broken by pieces of prairie, I went, in February, 1903, to visit a friend, a sick Christian woman, who was in the care of a relative of hers named Adova.

There were only five huts in the village. At the first one from the edge of the prairie, which was assigned to me in which to sleep, on a bench outside under the low eaves, was a roughly carved wooden idol, about fourteen inches in height. From the dressing of the hair of its head, I supposed it to be intended for a female. Its loins were covered with a narrow strip of cloth. Near it was what could scarcely be recognized as a dog, its head looking more like a pig's, and its tail more like an alligator's. The figures were chalked and painted; and near them were a few gourd utensils for eating and drinking, and some medicinal barks.

Subsequently, at night, in a curtained-off corner of my room, I saw three low baskets, in each of which was a pair of wooden images not six inches high. They were chalked, and adorned with strips of various-colored cloth. In each basket also was a wooden bourglass-shaped article that seemed intended for a double bell. Pieces of medicinal barks filled up the spaces in the baskets. The images were relics of ceremonies held over twins born long ago in the family.

At the other end of the village, in a very small roughly built hut, open on one side, were two other idols,—one, a male, standing and chalked and painted. The female in an ornamented box was not visible; near them was a nondescript animal.

The story of these idols, as told me by my friend (who has since died), is more especially connected with this pair.)

Part l. Okâsi

It was made by a Loango man, a fetich doctor, very many years ago. The Mpongwe family that to-day owns these relics had sent south to Loango, to the Fiât or Ba-Vili tribe, to bring to Gabun for this special purpose this celebrated magician.

When he arrived, the chief of the family who had summoned him went with him off to the forest, with all the medicines, and so forth, which the Loango man had brought. This occurred on that same left side of the "river" where l was visiting.

The magician began to explain everything in the way of directions about the medicines that were to be put into the hollow of the abdomen of the idol (and which to-day is still covered by a small round mirror fastened over it). After explaining all these matters, he gave also all the orunda (prohibitions), *viz.*: The idol must not be allowed to fall on its face; it must have a small hut for shelter from rain and sun: it must be given a light at night, at least of coals of fire. After this, he began to carve the idol. After making the male of the pair, and before making its female, he made a duplicate of the male, exactly like it, except that it was only an imitation without any magic power; and, instead of medicines, only powdered charcoal was put into the hollow in its abdomen, which, however, was to be covered with glass, exactly as the real one.

When these two idols were finished, the two men, the magician and the chief of the family, went with them far into the forest. The Loango said, "I will put these here, and when we go back to your town I will give the power of olâgâ, [a certain kind of spirit] to one—of your women. If she receives it properly, she herself, without knowing our path, will come to this forest, and will make no mistake in choosing the real idol from the imitation; and she will bring it to me in the town." (It is a rule with the native sorcerers that if the one who aspires to the power should make a mistake in this choosing, she must pay a fine of from $60 to $100.)

When all was arranged, the Loango man said, "Now let us go back to town." So they turned back. But when they had gone half of the way, he said to himself, "This Gabun man now knows everything, and where the idols are, and which is the real one. It is his sister who wishes to receive the power; he will go and tell her everything, and she will make no mistake, not by reason of her possessing power, but by his private information." So the Loango said, "Go you to the town, await me there; I will come soon." And he turned back into the forest by himself, took up the two idols from where he had laid them down, went in another direction and hid them there, and then returned to town.

He then gave the power to the woman, and said, "Go and bring the olâgâ." She started, went with only a little power, and was going at random; but before she had gone half-way, she came under the full power. Then she turned her face right and left, and gave an olâgâ yell, seeking to know which way the power would lead her. At once then she knew which was the way; and she went running and shouting frantically, under the influence of this power, to the precise spot, and took up the real idol, making no mistake about the imitation one. Holding it aloft, she returned, shouting and dancing, under the Delphic frenzy. She entered the town singing and dancing in the street, and then laid the idol at the feet of the Loango man. He took it, and knew it was the right one. He then went to the forest and brought also the other, the duplicate. When he returned, he went with it and the real one to the ogwerina (backyard) to show to the Gabun man the slight difference in the two (which he knew by a private mark). In doing this he had to take off the little mirrors and show the difference between the medicines and the charcoal. And he again closed the mirrors. Then, just to test the woman, the magician said to her, "Go and bring me the idol I have left in the ogwerina." She went there, still under the power, and with a frenzied scream seized the right one and brought it to him. He was half glad and half disappointed; for had she mistaken, he would have received more money.

Then the townspeople held a great dance, and the Loango taught them special songs for the olâgâ. The female of the pair of idols had also been made about the same time as the male, but with no special ceremony.

All being finished, the magician named his fee for his services, was paid, and went back to Loango.

This idol was intended as a family fetich, to protect the family at night, and to kill any one who would attempt to injure any of the members. The name of this male of the pair was Okâsi.

The name of the other one, that was under the eaves of the hut in which I slept, was kâkâ-gi-bâlâ-dyambo-gi-bâlâ-ve. These are Shekyani words, and mean "A-great-log-may-rot-but-a-spoken-word-dies-never." That meant that if an enemy came and injured any one in the town, the wrong would never be forgotten and would surely be avenged. That idol might almost stand for a statue of Vengeance.

The above proverb comes from a tale of a cruel old Shekyani chief.

Part II. Barbarity

Once there was a very Powerful Shekyani chief named Ogwedembe. He had many sons and daughters and slaves and slave children and nieces and nephews. He had also a brother. His principal delight was in fighting and killing.

Ogwedembe used to go out on excursions, and would say to his company, "Now we are out of town." That meant that all restraint was cast aside, and that he was ready to kill the first person they might meet, even without a cause.

One day when they were out and were passing through a thick forest, they saw a man up a tree who had come for palm-wine and had filled two of the gourd-bottles used for that purpose. So Ogwedembe shouted to him, "Indeed! what are you doing there? Have you not heard that Ogwedembe and his brother are out of town? Come down quickly and meet us here!"

The man did not dare disobey, and came down. Ogwedembe took the gourds, and said, "You may have one; I and my brother will drink the other." After the drinking, Ogwedembe stripped the man of his clothing, leaving him standing naked and trembling. In his terror the man did not attempt to escape.

Ogwedembe drew his knife, and repeated his questions, "Who told you to come here? Did you not know that Ogwedembe and his brother were out in the forest? Now I will fix you; and you can carry the news to your town that Ogwedembe and his brother are in the forest."

He then seized a portion of the man's body, and with his butcher-knife horribly mutilated him. The man started, bleeding, to go to his town, and died on the way.

The section of country in which Ogwedembe's portion of the Shekyani tribe lived was south of Gabun, toward the Orungu people at the mouth of the Nazareth branch of the Ogowe River. Sometimes he and his brother would travel in their war canoes all the way from their place, and, passing Gabun, would go on northward to attack the Benga of Cape Esterias without cause and in sheer ruthlessness.

Some of his daughters and sisters were married to Mpongwe chiefs at Gabun. At times his daughters and nieces would go and visit him. They would be received with firing of guns and other great demonstrations, and on leaving would be laden with presents.

About twenty years ago one of his sisters, named Akanda, died in the prime of life. She lived at Gabun, her husband a Mpongwe. (She was the mother of Adova, my hostess, who is apparently about sixty years of age, and has a younger brother apparently about thirty years of age.) So, when that sister died, Ogwedembe came to Gabun, on the St. Thomè side, to the funeral. My sick friend happened to be there at the time (for, by family marriage, she is a cousin to Adova) and saw the old chief.

Ogwedembe, according to native custom, demanded of the

husband a fine for his sister's death (as if due to lack of proper care of her). When that was paid, as a sign that no ill-will was retained, Ogwedembe was to give the widower another wife.

During this discussion Ogwedembe kept saying, "I wish my sister had not been married to a Mpongwe, for it is not your custom to shed blood for this cause. But I feel a great desire to kill some one. If this had been a Shekyani marriage, I would have gone from town to town killing as I chose." The Mpongwe replied, "But we have no such custom." He answered, "Yes, I know that. I only said what I would like to do, though your tribal custom will not allow me to do it."

His demand of a fine being finally yielded to and paid, to show his peaceful intentions, he gave the husband one of his daughters, a widow who had with her two children,—a son and a daughter,—and who afterward bore him other children.

Ogwedembe's bloody instincts' were suppressed at that funeral, and he remained awhile after the close of the mourning ceremonies, making friendly visits among his Mpongwe sons-in-law, and then went back to his Sbekyani country.

A short time after that the eldest daughter of that woman Akanda (my hostess Adova) and her husband Owondo visited Ogwedembe. He made a great welcome for them, with dancing and rejoicing of various kinds. Every day be sent his people to fish and hunt, to obtain food for Adova and the children she had with her.

Before Adova left, Ogwedembe called his principal wife and his grandchildren, and said, "When I die, you who are here in Shekyani, do not remain here, but go to Gabun and live with Akanda's children all the rest of your life." When he finally died, they obeyed and came to St. Thomè, of Gabun, bringing their idols with them.

The one female image that was under the eaves of the house in which I slept was for guarding their families; but the three sets of twins were to prevent their mothers from becoming barren.

Part III. The Right of Sanctuary
(It was an ancient and universal custom that a refugee, by clasping the knees of the king of any other tribe, could claim his protection. The king was bound to accept the claim. The obligation he thus assumed was sacred.)

While Adova was there at Shekyani country, visiting Ogwedembe, there came to him an Orungu man with a little slave boy, carrying a box. As soon as they entered the town, both of them came to Ogwedembe, and kneeling and clasping his feet, claimed his protection, and promised voluntarily to be under his authority.

The old chief, without asking the cause of their flight or their reason for coming to him, assented, and summoned the town to make the Ukuku (Spirit-Society of Law) ceremony of installing the man and his slave boy as members of their Shekyani tribe.

Adova and her husband were very kind to this adopted "brother," and he at once became exceedingly intimate with them.

At night this new man had been assigned to the house occupied by Ogwedembe, in a room near him, so that he could watch him that be should not run away, now that he belonged to Ukuku. But it was not known that this man possessed all the power of nyemba (sorcery). Ogwedembe also had power for fighting, and a certain amount of knowledge that warned him not to be deceived by sorcerers.

After two days, on the third night, this man rose, and tried to go to Ogwedembe's room, to put some witchcraft medicine on him. But Ogwedembe saw him coming, rose, seized his staff, walked toward the man in the darkness, and struck him violently on the head. The man fell. But neither of them uttered any word, nor made any outcry.

Very early in the morning Ogwedembe got up, went out, and sat on the veranda of his house. He called to Adova, "Come, I want to tell you something." She came, and be said, "I had a bad dream last night. If any one comes to you to-day to ask you to make medicine for a sore head, do not do it." "Who is it?" she asked. He refused. "No, I will not tell you. But I know that before to-day is over some one will come to you, but do not help him."

The Orungu got up late that day and looked and felt dull. When he left his room, he sent his boy to call Adova. The boy went. She came to him. He said, "Can't you find medicine for a headache? I did not sleep well. My head pains too much." She said, "I do not know a medicine for that kind of headache." The old chief was sitting near, and, looking significantly at the Orungu, said to Adova, "Yes, that is right."

The next night the man said, "I do not wish to sleep here to-night. I will go to an adjacent village, and will be back in the morning." "Well, go," assented Ogwedembe, "but be sure to be back in the morning." And the man said, "Ye."

Scarcely had he left the town to go to the other village, when there came to Ogwedembe three people from a certain Orungu town carrying a message from their Orungu chief, thus: "The chief sent us, saying, 'Please give up this man who came to you and who claimed your protection. Give up the man. You do not know his habits; they are the habits of a worm that in eating spoils only the best. He, with his sorcery, always aims at killing the greatest. If you do not give him up, there will be war; for our chief has had this same demand made on him from a third chief whose people this man has been killing, and our chief will have to make war with you.'"

Ogwedembe laughed. "You say' war' to me? That is nothing to me. You cannot do it. War cannot touch me."

When the message of the Orungu chief was being sent to Ogwedembe, some of the attendants on the delegation had awaited half-way on the route, and only the three had brought the message. Ogwedembe said to these three messengers, "Go and call your chief, and we will talk about it."

The chief came. (All this while the man was away at the other village, not having kept his promise to return.)

Ogwedembe said to the Orungu chief, "It is impossible. The law is sacred. I will not give him up." But in his heart he felt, "I am protecting a sorcerer who has tried to kill me; better I take the money for his extradition, and send him away." He and the chief went on discussing. The point was made that the sorcerer having himself broken his obligation, by attempting to injure his adopted father, relieved that father of his Ukuku duty of protection.

Ogwedembe began to yield, and to name the number of slaves that should be given him as the price of giving up the man. The Orungu chief demurred to the price: "It is too much!" So Ogwedembe brought down the price to six slaves,—three slaves, and three bundles of goods equal to the price of three slaves. And it was so settled. Then the Orungu chief said, "I will go in haste to my town to get you the goods; but as to the three slaves, this man's boy must be counted as one of them."

There was a dispute over this, Ogwedembe claiming that the boy was not guilty of any crime, and that his right to protection still existed. The Orungu insisted that the boy, being a slave, must follow the fortunes of his master, must be extradited as one with him, and then would of their own will be released by them from the penalty of his master's guilt. Ogwedembe consented. So the Orungu chief and his people went to get the goods, on the promise that Ogwedembe would have the man caught and ready to be delivered to them.

At once Ogwedembe sent word to the man to fulfil his promise of returning to the town, and told his sons to be ready early next day to have the man caught and tied, ready for delivery on arrival of the goods.

Next day Ogwedembe, seeing the man coming to him, came out of his house to meet him, and speaking ewiria (bidden meaning), called out to his people, "Sons, have you tied up the bundle of bush-deer meat?" "Oh yes, father, we'll have it ready just now," as they came running to him. Then they suddenly fell upon the man, dragged him inside the house, began to strip off his clothing, and tied him. He at once knew that there was no mercy, and he did not resist; but he said to his boy, "Call me Adova and her husband."

But she knew he was naked, so she told her husband to go and hear what the man had to say. Owondo went, and the man said,

"Owondo, I have no friends here; only you and Adova have been kind to me, so I call you my friend. Untie this small strip of cloth I have about my waist. I have four silver dollars there. I am going to die. These dollars are of no use to me; you and your wife take them. My box is in Adova's care; she must have the few things in it." So Owondo untied the girdle, took the money, and went out.

Shortly afterward the Orungu people came, bringing the goods and slaves, and took away the man. He was taken by the three messengers to the half-way camp, where they had left their attendants. There were no houses there for shelter, and only their mosquito-nets as tents. They stopped there with the intention of passing the night, and next day of going on to their Orungu town.

When it came evening they began to prepare their sleeping-places, and at bedtime one by one they went to lie down. A large branch from an overhanging tree fell very near the bed of one of the Orungu leaders, which was adjoining that of the sorcerer. So they all said, "Ah! we see what is being done by his arts. If this has begun so soon, who knows what will happen before morning? Let us start at once."

So they all made ready that very night, and went out of the forest, down to the beach, and got into their boat (as they had come part of the way by sea).

Not long after they had started the sea became very rough. Soon the boat capsized, broke to pieces, and all their goods were lost. They all escaped ashore, but the sorcerer was missing. They waited on the beach until daylight, and then found his loin cloth washed ashore. (His hands had been tied.) They believed that he had caused the storm, and was willing to die with them in the general destruction rather than survive to be put to death by the torture to which sorcerers were usually subjected.

So these people sent back word to Ogwedembe and to the nearer villages to let them know what had happened to them, and they returned to their Orungu country by land.

The little slave boy, who had been left with Ogwedembe as one of the three to be given as the price of extradition, was shortly afterward given by him as a present to the sick friend I was visiting that day. She stated that he was a most faithful servant and affectionate attendant on her infant daughter. He stayed with her, and died in her service a few years later, about 1883; and she mourned for him, for she had treated him, not as a slave, but as a son.

XI. Unago and Ekela-Mbengo

(In the presence of theosophy, telepathy, thought-transference, astrophysics, and wireless telegraphy, the following Benga legend has at least a standing-place. It was written more than forty years ago by an educated native in the Benga dialect. I translate it into English, preserving some of the native idiom.)

Unago and Ekela were great friends. They lived, Unago at Mbini in Eyo (Benito River); Ekela at Jeke in Muni (the river Muni, opposite Elobi islands in Corisco Bay. The two rivers are at least forty miles apart; Ekela is supposed to make the journey in two hours.)

They were accustomed, if one killed a wild animal, to send for the other. One day Unago killed a hog. Then he sent for his friend Ekela. He at Mbini said, "Oh, Chum Ekela I start you out very early in the morning hither. Come to eat a feast of pig." And his children would say, "Father, your friend at Jeke, and you right here, will he hear?" Said he, "Yes, he will hear." And so Ekela, off there, would say to his children, "Do you hear how my friend is calling to me?" His children answered, "We do not hear." Says he, "Yes, my friend has called me to eat pig there to-morrow."

Before daybreak Ekela takes his staff and his fly-brush and starts. When the sun is at the point of shining at Corisco, he reaches Mbini. Unago says to his children, "Did I not say to you that he can hear?"

And so they eat the feast; the feast ended, they tell narratives. In the afternoon Ekela says, "Chum, I 'm going back." Unago says, "Yes."

Having left him after escorting him part of the way, this one goes on, and that one returns. When Ekela, going on and on, reaches clear to Jeke, then day darkens. When his children see the lunch which he brings, then they believe that he has been at Mbini.

A Proverb: Manga Ma Ekela
(Manga means "the sea"; secondarily, "the sea-beach"; thirdly, by euphemism, "a latrine," or "going to a latrine." For the sea-beach is used by the natives for that purpose, they going there immediately on rising in the morning. They stay, of course, but a short time. If one should stay very long, this proverb would be used of him, be-

cause Ekela, when he went, stayed and made a journey of fifteen or twenty miles.)

Ekela was accustomed, if he started out early to the seaside in the morning, to say, "I am going to manga"; then he went on and on, clear on to Hondo (a place at least fifteen miles distant). Passing Hondo, his "manga," would end only wherever he and his friend Unago met. There having told their stories, they then each returned. This one went to his village, and that one to his village. When Ekela was about to go back to his village, then be would leave his fly-brush at the spot where he and his friend had been; and when he would arrive at home, he would say to his children, "Go, take for me the fly-brush which was forgotten of me, there at the sea, on the place where I was. Follow my foot-tracks." When the children went, it was step by step to Hondo, and the foot-tracks were still farther beyond.

The children, wearied, came back together unto their father, and said, "We did not see the brush." When be went another morning, then he himself brought it.

XI. Malanda
– An Initiation into a Family Guardian-Spirit Company

(Manjana was my cook at Batanga in 1902. He is a young married man with several small children. He is of a mild, kindly disposition, obliging and smiling, without much force of character, slightly educated, civilized in manner and dress, but without even a pretence of Christianity; at heart a heathen, though a member of the Roman Catholic church, into which he consented to be baptized as the means of obtaining in marriage his wife, who had been raised in that church.

His Romanism sat lightly on him, for be voluntarily attended my Protestant evening-prayers, taking his turn with others in reading verses around in the chapter of Scripture for the day; then be liked to take part in the general conversation which followed about native beliefs and native customs.

Yâkâ, or family fetich, is no longer, at Batanga, a matter of dread, even to the heathen; so Manjana was not afraid to tell me freely what happened when he was initiated into it as a lad. I wrote down his story hastily, as soon as he left that evening. I later wrote it out in full, while it was all fresh in my memory. I could not exactly reproduce his graphic native words, so I did not attempt them. The description is my own. But I followed exactly the line of his story, and used only his thoughts. He said:

"I knew that a house was being built on the edge of the forest, a short distance from our village. I and other lads and young men assisted the strong adult men who were building it. But I did not then know for what purpose or why it was being built. I remembered afterward that no girls or women were either assisting or even lounging about it, watching the process of building and chatting with the workmen, as when other houses were built. I did not know that they had been told not to look there. I remembered afterward that the house was located separately from the other houses of the village, but that did not just then strike me as strange. Somewhat similar houses had been built, as temporary sheds in making a boat or canoe. Such houses are built rapidly, and not with the same care as is used in the erection of dwellings. So it did not occur to me as noticeable that this house was finished in the short time of two weeks. One gable of it was left open.

Nor did I connect its erection with the fact that a prominent man of our family had died just two weeks before. I know now that, in the manner of his death, or in things that happened immediately afterward, the elders of the family had seen inauspicious signs that made them fear that evil was being plotted against us. As I now know, some six or eight of our leading adult male members of the family had had a secret consultation, and had decided that Malanda should be invoked.

I did not then know much about Malanda. I knew the name, that it was a power, that it was dreaded; but how or why I had not been told.

I know now that while this house was being built one or two other men were carving an image of a male figure; also, that when the house was completed, that very night some of those elders had secretly disinterred the corpse that had been already two weeks in its grave, and had brought it to that house. There they had extracted two teeth, and had fastetened them in the hollowed-out cavities representing the eyes and had hidden them there by fastening over them, with a common resinous gum of the forest, two small pieces of glass. And they had stood the image, painted hideously, on the cover of a large box, made of the flexible inner bark of a tree, at the closed end of the house.

Then they had cut off the head of the corpse and had scooped out its rotten brains. These they had mixed with chalk and powdered red-wood and the ashes of other plants, and had tied up the mixture carefully in a bundle of dry plantain leaves. I already knew and had seen such things regarded as very valuable "medicine," used to rub on the forehead or other parts of the body. Then they had tied the headless corpse erect against a side wall of the house, keeping its arms extended by cross pieces of wood.

The first that I knew that anything unusual was about to occur was early one morning, just after the completion of the house, when the voices of the elders were heard in the street, "Malanda has come!" The women and girls were frightened. They knew they were not to look at Malanda. And we lads were oppressed with a vague dread that subdued us from our usual boisterous plays. We knew the name "Malanda." It was a power, it was mysterious. Mystery is a burden; it might be for good or for evil.

Immediately all the adult men went into the forest. In about an hour they returned, bearing on their shoulders a long, large log of a tree. They cast it into the middle of the street, facing the sun. The hour was about 8 a.m.

They sternly ordered about twenty of the young men and lads to sit down on the log. The mystery that had burdened me now fell heavier. Our mothers and sisters were afraid to look on us, even with sympathy. These men were our fathers and uncles and elder brothers, but their voices were harsh, their faces set with severity, their eyes had no light of recognition as relatives, and their hands handled us roughly. I was dazed and helpless in my own village and among my own relatives, but not a word of pity nor a look of even kindness from a single person! Each of the twenty also was too occupied with his own destiny to speak to a fellow victim. As far as our treatment was concerned we might have been slaves in another tribe. With no will of our own we blindly did as we were bidden.

We were told to throw our heads back, bending our necks to the point of pain, and to stare with unblinking eyes at the sun. As the sun mounted all that morning, hot and glaring, toward the zenith, we were sedulously watched to see that we kept our heads back, arms down, and eyes following the burning sun in its ascent. My throat was parched with thirst. My brain began to whirl, the pain in my eyes became intolerable, and l ceased to hear; all around me became black, and l fell off the log.

As each one of us thus became exhausted or actually fainted, we were blindfolded and taken to that house. On reaching it still blindfolded l knew nothing that was there. l smelled only a horrible odor. The same rough hands and hard voices had possession of me. Though blindfolded, l could feel that the eyes that were looking on me were cruel. lt was useless to resist, as they began to beat me with rods. My outcries only brought severer blows. l perceived that submission lightened their strokes. When finally l ceased struggling or crying, the bandage was removed. The horror of that headless corpse standing extending its rotting arms toward me, and the staring glass eyes of the image overcame me, and l attempted to flee. That was futile. l was seized and beaten more severely than before, until l had no will or wish, but utter submission to the will of whatever power it might be, natural or supernatural, into whose hands l had fallen. When all twenty of us had been thus reduced to abject submission, we were treated less severely. Some kindness began to be shown. Our physical wants were looked after and regarded. Food and drink were supplied us. I observed an occasional look of recognition.I began to feel that I was being admitted into a companionship. There was something manly in the thought of being entrusted with a secret to which younger lads were not admitted and from which all of womankind were debarred. This gave me a sense of elevation. There were some people whom I could look down upon! It began to be worth while to have suffered so much. I began to be accustomed to the corpse of my relative. True, I was a prisoner; but the days were relieved by a variety of instructions and ceremonies practised over us by the doctor.

At first we were, in succession, solemnly asked whether we were possessed of any witchcraft power ("o na jemba?" Have you a witch?) Elsewhere we all would have indignantly denied having any such evil doings. But in the face of that corpse, under the presence of the unknown power to which we were being introduced, in the hands of a pitiless inquisition, and with the obliteration of our own wills, we did not dare lie. Would not the power know we were lying? We told what we imagined to be the truth; some admitted, some denied.

The Yâkâ bundle was opened; some of its dust was added to the brain-mixture (already mentioned). Of this compound an ointment was made. On the breasts of those who denied were drawn commendatory longitudinal lines of that ointment. On the breasts of those who admitted were drawn corrective horizontal lines with the same mixture. Instructions appropriate to our respective condition, as witch possessed or non-possessed, were given by the doctor.

We were interested also in watching the digging of a pit in the floor of the house. When this had reached a depth of over six feet, a tunnel was driven laterally under one of the side walls, and opening), out, a rod or two beyond, where a low hut was built to conceal it. Into this tunnel the doctor and three or four of the strongest of the elders carried the corpse, and left it there for about ten days, the doctor passing much of that time with it.

After we had been in the house almost twenty days, although still confined, I did not feel that I was a prisoner; I was deeply interested in seeing and taking part in this great mystery. I no longer dreaded the dead. Even if physical pain were yet to be inflicted on me, I would take it gladly as the price of a knowledge which ministered to manly pride. I was being made a sharer in the rights and possession of the family guardian-spirit.

A few days after this the corpse, now reduced almost to a skeleton, was brought up from the tunnel, and bisected longitudinally. The halves were laid a few feet apart, parallel and a short distance away from the two sides of the house. We were gathered in two companies against the walls, and were told to advance toward each other, carefully stepping over, and by no means to tread on, our half of the remains. And the two companies met in the centre.

We now felt we were free, though not formally told so. We had made a fearful oath of secrecy. We preferred to remain and assist in the final order of the house. The doctor and elders now disarticulated the skeleton (for such it was, the man being dead now at least five weeks, and the decomposed flesh having almost all fallen away). The bones were put into the bark box on which stood the image. They were an addition to the contents of the Yâkâ, or family fetich. Then, at the close of three weeks' confinement in the house, we emerged in procession, the elders bearing the box and the image on the top, and proceeded to the village street. There the box and image were set; and a joyous dance was started with drum and song, with all the people of the village, male and female. A sheep or goat was killed, and a feast prepared. While the dance was going on, the elders around the box were bowing and praying to the image on their knees. From time to time a man would parade by, lifting his steps high and bowing low, and as suddenly erecting himself and strongly aspirating, "Hah! hah!" And the village was glad, for it felt sure no evil could now come to it. I was safe, and ready, at the next time of danger, to assist in torturing the next younger set of lads, for was I not a freeman of the family guardian-spirit?

The box and image were stowed away in a back room of the village headman's dwelling, who would often take a plate full of food to it, as a sacrifice, and sometimes an offering of cloth or other goods; and the village felt safe.

Nevertheless, the house was not torn down; it stood empty and unused. But if, even a year later, evil still fell on the village, the elders knew that something about the Malanda had not been rightly performed. And it must all be done over again with the next dead adult male (never a female) and with a new lot of neophytes.

A woman may be subjected to a part of the above ceremonies if she is suspected of witchcraft, or if, on examination, she confess to using black art. To purge her of this evil, and to counteract the consequences of what she may have done, she is taken to the little hut over the end of the tunnel, and some of the above described ceremonies are performed over her; but she is never taken into the house, nor into the presence of the corpse.

XIII. Three-Things came back too late

(The following narrative was told me by a Batanga native Christian woman who, herself less than thirty years of age, is a great-granddaughter of the man one of whose wives was the witch of this story. I bade her, in giving me the account, to speak, not from her present Christian standpoint and her only slight superstitious bias, but from the full heathen view-point. The confusing mixture of singular and plural pronouns referring to the witch is an exact reproduction of my informant's words.)

The great-grandfather was a heathen and a polygamist. He had four wives. One of them was a member of an interior tribe, the Boheba, more heathenish and superstitious than his own Batanga coast tribe. Unknown to him, she was a member of the Witchcraft Society, had power with the spirits, and they with her, attended their secret night meetings, and engaged in their unhallowed orgies.

The husband, though not a member of the society, had acquired some knowledge of witchcraft art, and, though without the power to transform himself, as wizards did, was able to see and know what was being done at distances beyond ordinary human sight.

One night she arose from her bed to go and attend a witchcraft play. She left her physical "house," the fleshly body, lying on the bed, so that no one not in the secret, seeing that body lying there, would think other than it was herself, nor would know that she was gone out. In her going out she willed to emerge as Three-Things, and this triple unit went off to the witchcraft play. The husband happened to see this, and watched her as she disappeared, saw where she went, and, though distant and out of sight, knew what she was doing. So he said to himself, "She is off at her play; I also will do some playing here; she shall know what I have done."

Among the several things of which followers of witchcraft are afraid, and which weaken their power, is cayenne pepper. So this man gathered a large quantity of pepper-pods from the bushes growing in the behu (kitchen-garden), and bruised them in a mortar to a fine soft pulp. This he smeared thoroughly all over the woman's unconscious body as it lay in her bedroom. He left not the smallest portion of her skin untouched by the pepper,—from her scalp, and in the interstices of her fingers and toes, minutely over her entire body.

Meanwhile, with the woman at her play, the night was passing. The witches' sacred bird, the owl, began its early morning warning boot. She prepared to return. As she was returning, the first morning cock-crow also warned her to hasten, lest daybreak should find her triple unit outside of its fleshly "house." So the three came rushing with the speed of wind back to her village. Her husband was on the watch; he heard this panting sound as of a person breathing rapidly, and felt the impulse of their wind as she reached her hut and came in to re-enter their house.

He saw her approach every possible part of the body, seeking to find even a minute spot that was not barred by the pepper. She searched long and anxiously, but in vain; and in despair they went and hid herself in a wood-pile at the back of one of the village huts, waiting in terror for some possible escape.

All this the husband saw silently. When morning light finally came, be knew that this wife was dead, for her life-spirit had not succeeded in returning to its body within the specified time. It was therefore a dead body. But he said nothing about it to any one, and went off fishing.

As the morning hours were passing while be was away and the woman's door of her hut was still closed, his children began to wonder and to say, "What is this? What is the matter? Since morning light our father's wife has not come out into the street." After waiting awhile longer, their anxiety and curiosity overcame them, and they broke in the door. There they saw the woman lying dead. They fled in fear, saying, "What is this that has killed our father's wife?" They went down to the beach to meet him as be returned from fishing, and excitedly told him, "Father, we have found your Boheba wife dead!" The man, to their surprise, did not seem grieved. He simply said, "Let another one of my wives cook for me; I will first eat." Still more to their surprise, he added, "And you, my children, and all people of the village, do not—any of you dare even to touch the body. Only, at once, send word to her Boheba relatives to come."

This warning he gave his people, lest any of them should sicken by coming close to the atmosphere that the witch had possibly brought back with her from her play.

By the time he had fmished eating, the woman's relatives

had arrived. They were all heavily armed with guns and spears and knives, and were threatening revenge for their sister's death.

The man quietly bade them delay their anger till they had heard what he had to say; and took them to the woman's hut, that they themselves—might examine the corpse, leaving to them the chance of contamination.

They examined; they lifted up the body of their sister, and searched closely for any sign of wound or bruise. Finding none, but still angry, they were mystified, and exclaimed, "What then has killed her?" And they seated themselves for a verbal investigation. But the man said, "We will not talk just yet. First stand up, and you shall see for yourselves." As they arose, the man said, "Remove all those sticks in that wood-pile. You will find the woman there." So they pulled away the sticks; and there they found Three-Things. "There!" said the husband, "see the reason why your sister is dead!" At that the relatives were ashamed, and said, "Brother-in-law! we have nothing to say against you, for our eyes see what our sister has done. She has killed herself, and she is worthy to be punished by fire." (Burning was a common mode of execution for the crime of witchcraft.)

In her terror at being unable to get back into her mortal body, the Three-Things, all the while she was hidden in the wood-pile, had shrivelled smaller and smaller until what was left were three deformed crab-sbaped beings, a few inches long, with mouths like frogs. These, paralyzed with fear, could not speak, but could only chatter and tremble.

So the relatives seized these Three-Things, and also carried away the body; and, followed by all the people of the village, they burnt it and them on a large rock by the sea.

That rock I pass very often as I walk on the beach. At high tide it is cutoff from the shore a distance of a few yards; at low tide one can walk out to it. It is only a few hundred yards from our Batanga Mission Station.

CHAPTER XVII
Fetich in Folk-lore

THE TELLING OF FOLK-LORE TALES AMOUNTS, with the Afri-can Negro, almost to a passion. By day, both men and women have their manual occupations, or, even if idling, pass the time in sleep or gossip; but at night, particularly with moonlight, if there be on hand no dances, either of fetich-worship or of mere amusement, some story-teller is asked to recite. All know the tales, but not all can recite them dramatically. The audience never wearies of repetition. The skilful story-teller in Africa occupies in the community the place filled in civilization by the actor or concert-singer.

This is true all over Africa. In any one region there are certain tales common to all the tribes in that region. But almost every tribe will have tales distinctive to it. It is part of native courtesy to ask a visitor to contribute his local story to the amusement of the evening.

Some of these tales are probably of ancient origin, as to their plot and their characters. I am disposed to give the folk-lore of Af-rica a very ancient origin. Ethnology and philology trace the Bantu stream from the northeast, not by a straight line diagonally to the southwest, but the stream, starting with an infusion of Hamitic (and perhaps Caucasian) blood in the Nubian provinces, flowed south to the Cape, and then, turning on itself, flowed northwestward until it lost itself at the Bight of Benin. That blood gave to the Bantu features more delicate than those of the northern Guinea Negro.

That stream, as it flowed, carried with it arts, thoughts, plants, and animals from the south of Egypt. The bellows used in every village smithy on the West Coast is the same as is depicted on Egyptian monuments. The great personages mentioned as "kings" are probably semi-deified ancestors, or are even confounded with the Creator. It may not be only a coincidence that the ancient Egyptian word "Ra" exists in west equatorial tribes (contracted from "rera" = my father) with its meaning of "Lord," "Master,"Sir." In these tales the name Ra-Mborakinda, is used interchangeably with the Divine Name, Ra-Nyambe.

But it is true that a doubt can be raised against the antiquity of some of the tales, in which are introduced words, *e.g.* "cannon," "pistol," articles not known to the African until comparatively modern times. And in the case of a few, such as No. V., the origin is in all probability modern. In No. V. the reader at once turns in thought to "Ali Baba and the Forty Thieves." There the internal evidence is positive, either that the story was heard long ago from Arabs (or perhaps within the last hundred years from some foreigner), or there may have been an original African story, to which modern narrators have attached incidents of Ali Baba which they have overheard within the last fifty years from some white trader or educated Sierra-Leonian.

But it would not necessarily condemn a tale's claim to antiquity that it had in it modern words. Such words as "gun," "pistol," "stairway," "canvas," and others may be interpolations. It was probably true long ago, as is now the case, that narrators added to or changed words uttered by the characters. Where in the plot some modern weipon is named, long ago it was perhaps a spear, club, or bow and arrow. When Dutch and Portuguese built their forts on the African shore three hundred years ago, some bright narrator could readily have varied the evening's performance by introducing a cannon into the story. Such variations necessarily grew; for the native languages were not crystallized into written ones until the days of the modern missionary.

In recitation great latitude is allowed as to the time occupied. Brevity is not desired. A story whose outline could be told in ten minutes may be spread over two hours by a vivid use of the speaker's imagination in a minute description of details. A great deal of repetition (after the manner of "This is the house that Jack built") is employed, that would be wearisome to a civilized audience, but is intensely enjoyed by the African, *e.g.*, where the plot calls for the doing of an act for several days in succession, we would say simply, "And the next day he did the same." But the native lover of folk-lore will repeat the same details in the same words for the second and third and even fourth day. In my reporting I have omitted this repetition.

I have purposely used some native idioms in order to retain local color. African narrators use very short sentences. ... One of their daily recognized idioms finds its exact parallel in the speech of our own children. Listen to a civilized child's animated account of some act. They repeat. The native does so constantly. He is not satisfied, in telling the narrative of a journey, by saying curtly, "I went." His form is, "I went, went, there, there," etc. His dramatic acting keeps up the interest of the audience in the twice-told tale.

I. Queen Ngwe-Nkonde and her Manja

A king, by name Ra-Mborakinda, had many wives, but be had no children at all. He was dissatisfied, and was always saying that he wanted children. So he went to a certain great wizard, named Ra-Marânge, to get help for his trouble.

Whenever any one went on any business to Ra-Marânge, before he had time to tell the wizard what he wanted, Ra-Marânge would say, "Have you come to have something wonderful done?" On the visitor saying, "Yes," Ra-Marânge, as the first step in his preparations and to obtain all needed power, would jump into fire or do some other astonishing act.

So, this day, he sprang into the fire, and came out unharmed and strong. Then he told Ra-Mborakinda to tell his story of what be had come for.

The king said, "Other people have children, but I have none. Make me a medicine that sball cause my women to bear children." Ra-Marânge replied, "Yes, I will fix you the medicine; and after I have made the mixture, you must require all of your women to eat of it." So the wizard fixed the medicine, and the king took it with him and went home.

His queen's name was Ngwe-nkonde; and among his lesser wives and concubines were two quite young women who were friends, one of whom lived with the queen in her hut as her little manja, or handmaid.

As soon as Ra-Mborakinda arrived, he announced his possession of the medicine, and ordered all his women to come and eat of it. But Ngwe-nkonde was jealous of her young maid, and did not wish her to become a mother. So, early in the morning, she purposely sent the manja away to their mpindi (plantation hut) on a made-up errand, so that she might not be present at the feast.

At the appointed hour the king spread out the medicine, and called the women to come. They each came with a piece of plantain leaf as a plate, and assembled to eat, and Ramborakinda divided out the medicine among them. Then the other of the two young women remembered her friend the manja, and observed that she was absent. So she quickly tore off a piece of her plantain leaf, and divided on it a part of her own share of the medicine, and hid it by her, to keep it for the manja, so that she could have it on her return from the mpindi. In the afternoon, when the manja returned, her friend gave her the portion of the medicine, and she ate it. Soon after this, all these women told Ra-Mborakinda that they expected to become mothers.

After a few months he announced to them that he was going away on a long trade-journey and that he would not return until a stated time. He gave them directions that in the meanwhile they should leave his town and go to their parents' homes and stay there until his return.

Now it happened that all these women had homes except the little manja; her parents were dead, but she remembered the locality of their deserted village.

So Ra-Mborakinda left to go on his journey, and all the expectant mothers scattered to the homes of their parents, except the manja, who had to follow with the queen to her people's village. But soon after their arrival at Ngwe-nkonde's home, the latter began to treat her maid cruelly; and finally, in her severity, she said, "Go away to your own home and sojourn there," the while that she knew very well that her manja had no home. Her thought and hope were that the manja would perish in the wilderness.

As the maid knew the spot where her home had been, she left Ngwe-nkonde's village, and started into the forest to go to her deserted village. On arriving there, she found no houses nor any remains of human habitation. But there was a very large fallen tree, with a trunk so curved that it was not lying entirely flat on the ground. Under this enormous log she sat down to rest, and it gave her shade and shelter. She accepted it as her place at which to live and slept there that night. When she awoke in the morning, she saw lying near her food and other needed things; but she saw no one coming or going. A few days later on awaking in the morning she saw a nice little house with everything prepared of food and clothing and medicines and such articles as would be needed by a mother for her babe. She stayed there, and in a few days gave birth to a man-child. Each day in the morning she found, prepared for her hand, food and other needed things lying near.

So she stayed there a long time till her baby was able to creep. When the baby had grown strong, she knew it was the time that Ra-Mborakinda had appointed for the return of his women to his town. She finally gathered together her things for the journey next day. That night, before she had gone to sleep, suddenly she saw a little girl standing near her, and she heard a voice which she remembered as her mother's saying, "I give you this little girl to carry the babe for you. But when you go back to Ra-Mborakinda, do not allow anyone but yourself and this girl to carry the child; if you do, the girl will disappear." So the next morning they started on their journey, the young mother and baby and the girl-nurse.

During this while each of the other women had also born her baby, and they were now preparing to return to Ra-Mborakinda's town. But of them all none had born real human beings, except the manja and her young friend. All the others had born monstrosities, like snakes, frogs, and other creatures. Ngwe-nkonde had born two snails, of the kind called "nkala." (It is a very large snail.)

So that day Ngwe-nkonde was coming along with her nyamba (a long scarf) hung over her right shoulder, and her two snails resting in the slack of the scarf, as in a hammock, over her left hip, and supported by her left arm. When the manja reached the cross-roads, she found the queen waiting there. Her object in waiting there was to know whether her maid was still in existence.

On seeing the manja, Ngwe-nkonde pretended to be pleased and said, "Let me see the child you have born;" and she stepped forward to take the baby away from the little girl-nurse. Manja, in her fear of her mistress and accustomed to submit to her, forgot to resist. Ngwe-nkonde saw that the babe was healthy and attractive, and she coveted it. She exclaimed, "Oh, what a nice child you have born! Let me help you carry it!" The moment she took the baby, the girl-nurse disappeared. Ngwe-nkonde deposited the babe in her scarf, and gave the two snails to her manja, saying, "You carry this for me!" She did this, intending to cause Ra-Mborakinda to think that the baby was her own; she had no intention to return it to its real mother; and the manja did not dare to complain.

So they went onward on their journey to the king's town. All the women, as they arrived there, saluted each other, "Mbolo!" "Ai! mbolo!" "Ai!" and each told her story and showed her baby. Then they all brought their babies to the King Ra-Mborakinda, that the father might see his children. In the king's presence Ngwe-nkonde took out the baby boy from her scarf and placed it at her breast to nurse. But the child turned its bead away and would not nurse, and did nothing but cry and cry. Poor little manja did not dare to claim her own, and she took no interest in the snails to show them to the king. For a whole day there was confusion. The baby boy persisted in rejecting Ngwenkonde's breast and kept on crying, and the snails were moaning.

Not knowing what to make of this trouble, Ra-Mborakinda went again to Ra-Marânge. The wizard laughed when he saw the king coming with this new trouble, for, by his magic power, he already knew all that had happened. "So!" he says, "you have come with another trouble, eh?" And at once he jumps into the fire, and emerges clean and strong.

Then the king informed the wizard what his difficulty was. And Ra-Marânge told him, "This is a small thing. It does not need medicine. Go you and tell all your women each to cook some very nice food; then, sitting in a circle, each must put the nice food near her feet. All the babies must be put in a bunch together in the centre, and you will see what will happen."

So Ra-Mborakinda went back to his town and told the women to follow these directions. They all did so, except the queen and her manja. The former did not put the baby boy in the bunch of the other babies, but retained him on her lap, and tried to make him eat of her nice food. But he only resisted, and kept on crying, and the manja, in her grief and hopelessness, had not prepared any nice food, only a pottage of greens, which she thought good enough for her present unhappiness.

The king seeing that the wizard's directions were not fully followed by the queen, compelled her to put the baby down in the company of the other creatures, and then he and all the mothers sat around watching what would happen.

Soon all the children began to creep, each to its own mother. The two snails went to Ngwe-nkonde, and began to eat of her nice food. The little baby boy crept rapidly toward the manja, and began with satisfaction to eat of the poor food at its mother's feet.

That was a revelation to the king and to all the other mothers. They were surprised and indignant that Ngwenkonde had been try-ing to steal the baby from the manja; Ra-Mborakinda deposed her from being queen. And the other women shouted derision at her, "Ngwe-nkonde! O! o-o-o!" and drove her from the town. She went away in her shame, leaving the two snails behind, and never returned.

And the king made the manja queen in her place. And the story ends.

ll. The Beautiful Daughter

There was a married woman, a king's daughter, by name Maria, who was very beautiful. She had a magic mirror that possessed the power of speech, which she used every day, particularly when she desired to go out for a promenade. She would then take this mirror from its hiding-place, and looking at it, would ask, "My mirror! is there any other beautiful woman like myself?" And this mirror would reply, "Mistress! there is none."

This she was accustomed to do every day until she became jealous at the very thought of ever having a rival.

Subsequently she became a mother, and bore a daughter. She saw that the child was very beautiful, more so than even herself. This child grew in gracefulness; was amiable, not proud; and was unconscious of her beauty.

When the daughter was about twelve years of age, the mother dreaded lest her child should know how attractive she was and should unintentionally rival her. She told her never to enter a certain room where she had her toilet. And the mother went on as formerly, looking into her mirror, and then going out to display her beauty.

One day the daughter said to herself, "Ah! I'm tired of this prohibition !" So she took the keys, and opened the door of the forbidden room. She looked around, but not observing anything especially noticeable, she went out again, locking the door. And the next day, the mother went in as usual, and then went out for her walk. After the mother had gone, the daughter said again to herself, "No! there must be something special about that room. I will go in again and make a search." Looking around carefully, she noticed a pretty casket on a table. Opening it, she saw it contained a mirror. There was something strange about its appearance, and she determined to examine it. While she was doing so, the mirror spoke, and said, "Oh, maiden! there is no one as beautiful as you!" She put back the mirror in its place, and went out, carefully fastening the door. The next day, when the mother went as usual to make her toilet and to ask of the mirror her usual question, "Is there another as beautiful as I?" it replied, "Yes, mistress, there is another fairer than you."

So she went out of the room much displeased, and, suspecting her daughter, said to her, "Daughter, have you been in that room?" The girl said, "No, I have not." But the mother insisted, "Yes, you have; for how is it that my mirror tells me that there is another woman more beautiful than I? And you are the only one who has beauty such as mine."

During all these years the mother had kept the daughter in the palace, and had not allowed her to be seen in public, as she dreaded to bear any one but herself praised. Then the enraged mother sent for her father's soldiers, and delivering the girl to them, she commanded, "You just go out into the forest and kill this girl."

They obeyed her orders, and led the girl away, taking with them also two big dogs. When they reached the forest, the soldiers said to her, "Your mother told us to kill you. But you are so good and pretty that we are not willing to do it. You just go your way and wander in this forest, and await what may happen."

The girl went her way; and the soldiers killed the two dogs, so that they might have blood on their swords to show to the mother.

Having done this, they went back to her, and said, "We have killed the girl; here is her blood on our swords." And the mother was satisfied.

But in the forest the girl had gone on, wandering aimlessly, till she happened to reach what seemed a hamlet having only one house. She went up its front steps and tried the door. It was not locked, and she went in. She saw or heard no one, but she noticed that the house was very much in disorder; so she began to arrange it. After sweeping and putting everything in neat order, she went upstairs and hid herself under one of the bedsteads.

But she did not know that the house belonged to robbers who spent their days in stealing, and brought their plunder home in the evening. When they returned that day, laden with booty, they were surprised to find their house in neat order and their goods arranged in piles. In their wonder they exclaimed, "Who has been here and fixed our house so nicely?"

So they prepared their food, ate, drank, and slept, but they did not clean up the table nor wash the dishes.

And the next day they went out again on their business of stealing.

After they were gone, the girl, hungry and frightened, crept out of her hiding-place, and cooked and ate food for herself. Then, as on the first day, she swept the floors and washed up the dishes. And then she cooked a meal for the men to have it ready against their return in the late afternoon; and again she occupied herself with the arrangement of the goods in the rooms. Then she went back to her hiding-place.

When the robbers returned that day and laid down their booty, they were again surprised to find not only their house in good order, but food ready on the table. And they wondered, "Who does all this for us?"

They first sat down to eat; and then they said, "Let us look around and find out who does all this." They searched, but they found no one.

The next day they armed themselves as usual to go out, leaving the table and their recent load of stealings in disorder.

When they had gone, the girl again emerged from her hiding-place, and, as before, cooked, ate, washed up, swept, arranged, and prepared the evening meal.

Again the robbers, on their return, were still more astonished, as they exclaimed, "Whoever does this? If it is a woman, then we will take her as our sister. She shall take care of our house and our goods, but none of us shall marry her; but if it is a man, he must be compelled to join in our business."

The next day, when they were all going out on their ways, they appointed one of their number to remain behind, hidden, who should watch, and thus they should know who had been helping them.

When they had gone, the girl, ignorant that one had been left to watch, came out of her biding, and began to do as on the other days. When she went outdoors to the kitchen [kitchens here are all detached] to cook, the watcher came in sight. She was frightened, and began to run away; but he called out, "Don't be afraid! Don't run, but come here! What are you afraid of? You are not doing anything bad, you have been doing us only good. Come here!" She stood and said, "I was afraid you would kill me!"

He came to her, saying, "What a beautiful girl to look at! When did you come here, and who are you?" So she told him her story. And when she had finished all the housework, she sat down with this man to await the coming of the others. When the others came and saw the two, they said to him, "So you found her?" He replied only, "Yes." Looking on her, they exclaimed, "Oh, what a beautiful girl!" To calm her excitement, they told her, "Do not be alarmed! You are to be our sister."

So they took all their goods and put them in her care, and herself in charge of the house. Thus they lived for some time,—they stealing, and she taking care for them.

But one day, at the palace, the wicked mother began to have some uneasy doubts whether her soldiers had really obeyed her orders to kill her daughter, and thought, "Perhaps the child was not really killed." She had a familiar servant, an old woman, very friendly to her. To her she revealed her story, and said, "Please go out and spy in every town. Look whether you see a girl who is very beautiful; if so, she is my daughter. You must kill her." The old woman replied, "Yes, my friend, I will do this thing for you." So she went out and began her spying.

The very first place at which she happened to arrive was the robbers' house. There being no people in sight, she entered the house, and found a girl alone. On account of the girl's great beauty, she felt sure at once that this was her friend's daughter. The girl gave her a seat and offered hospitality. The old woman exclaimed, "Oh, what a nice looking child! Who are you, and who is your mother?" The girl, not suspecting evil, told her story.

Then the old woman said, "Your hair looks a little untidy. Come here, and let me fix it." The girl consented; and the old woman began to braid her hair. She had bidden in her sleeve a long sharpened nail. When she had completed the hair-dressing, she thrust the nail deeply into the girl's head, who instantly fell down, apparently dead. Looking at the limp body, the old woman said to herself, "Good for that! I have done it for my friend." And she went away, leaving the corpse lying there, and reported to the mother what she had done. The mother felt sure her friend had not deceived her.

When the robbers returned that day, they found the girl lying dead. They were very much troubled. They began to examine the corpse, to find what was the cause of death, but they found no sign of any wound; and instead of the corpse being rigid, it was limp; there was perspiration on the head and neck. So they decided, "This nice life-looking face we will not put in a grave." So they made a handsome casket, overlaid it with gold, and adorned the body with a profusion of gold ornaments. They did not nail on the lid, but made it to slide in grooves. Supposing the body liable to decay, they placed the coffin outdoors in the air; and to keep it out of the reach of any animals, they hung it by the halliards of their flag-staff. Every day, on their going out and on their return, they pulled it down by the halliards, drew out the lid, and looked on the fresh, apparently living face of their "sister."

One day while they were all out on their business there happened to stray that way a man by name Eserengila (tale-bearer), who lived at the town of a man named Ogula. Coming to the robbers' house, he saw no one; but he at once observed the hanging golden box. Exclaiming, "What a nice thing!" he hasted back to his master Ogula, and called him. "Come and see what a nice thing I have found; it is something worth taking!" So Ogula went with him, and Eserengila pulled down the gilded box from the flag-staff. They did not enter the house, nor did they know anything of its character; and they carried away the box in haste, without looking at its contents, to Ogula's, and put it in a small room in his house.

Some days after it had been placed there Ogula went in to examine what it contained. He saw that the top of this coffin-like box was not nailed, but slid in a groove. He withdrew it, and was amazed to see a beautiful young woman apparently dead. Yet there was no look or odor of death. As she was not emaciated by disease, he examined the body to find a possible cause of death; but be found no sign, and wondering, exclaimed, "This beautiful girl! What has caused her to die?"

He replaced the lid, and left the room, carefully closing the door. But he again returned to look at the beautiful face of the corpse; and sighed, "Oh, I wish this beautiful being were alive! She would be such a nice playmate for my daughter, who is just about her size." Again be went and shut the door very carefully. He told his daughter never to enter that room, and she said, "Yes "; and he continued his daily visits there.

After many days Ogula's daughter became tired of seeing him enter while she was forbidden. So one day, when he was gone out of the house, she said to herself, "My father always forbids me this room; now I will go in and see what he has there." She entered, and saw only the gilded box, and exclaimed, "Oh, what a nice box! I'll just open it and see what is inside."

She began to draw the lid out of its grooves, and a human head was revealed with a splendid mass of hair covered with gold ornaments. She withdrew the lid entirely, and saw the form of the young woman, and delightedly said, "A beautiful girl, with such nice hair, and covered with golden ornaments!" She did not know why the girl seemed so unconscious, and began to say, "I wish she could speak to me, so we might be friends, because she is only a little larger than I." So she gave the stranger's salutation, "Mbolo! mbolo!" As no response was made, she protested, "Oh, I salute you, mbolo, but you do not answer!" She was disappointed, and slid back the cover, and went out of the room. Something about the door aroused the suspicions of her father on his return to the house, and he asked her, "Have you been inside that room?" She answered, "No! You told me never to go there, and I have not gone." Next day Ogula went out again, and his daughter thought she would have another look at the beautiful face. Entering the room, she again drew out the lid, and again she gave the salutation, "Mbolo!" There was no response. Again she protested, "Oh, I speak to you, and you won't answer me!" And then she added, "May I play with you, and fondle your head, and feel your hair? Perhaps you have lice for me to remove?" [one of the commonest of native African friendly services among both men and women]. She began to feel through the hair with her fingers, and presently she touched something hard. Looking closely, she found it was the head of a nail. Astonished, she said, Oh, she has a nail in her head! I 'll try to pull it out!

Instantly, on her doing so, the girl sneezed, opened her eyes, stared around, rose up in a sitting posture, and said, "Oh, I must have been sleeping a long time." The other asked, "You were only sleeping?" And the girl replied, "Yes." Then Ogula's daughter saluted, "Mbolo! and the girl responded, "Ai, Mbolo!" and the other, "Ai!"

Then the girl asked, "Where am I? What place is this?" The other said, "Why, you are in my father's house. This is my father's house." And the girl asked, "But who or what brought me here?" Then Ogula's daughter told her the whole story of Eserengila's having found the gilded box. They at once conceived a great liking for each other, and started to be friends. They played and laughed and talked and embraced, and fondled each other. This they did for quite a while.

Then the beautiful one was tired, and she said, "It is better that you put back the nail and let me sleep again." So the girl lay down in the box, the nail was inserted in her bead, and she instantly fell into unconsciousness.

Ogula's daughter slid back the lid, and went out of the room, carefully closing the doox. She now lost all desire to go out of the house and play with her former companions. Her father observed this, and urged her to play and visit as she formerly had done. But she declined, making some excuses, and saying she had no wish to do so. All her interest lay in that room of the gilded box and beautiful girl. Whenever her father went out, she at once would go to the room, draw out the lid, and pull out the nail; her friend would sit up, and they would play, and repeat their friendship. Ogula's daughter, seeing that her friend's desire for sleep was weakness for want of food, daily brought her food. And the girl grew strong and well and happy.

This was kept up many days without Ogula knowing of it.

But it happened one day, when the two girls were thus sitting in their friendship, they continued their play and conversation so long that Ogula's daughter forgot the time of her father's return; and he suddenly entered the room, and was surprised to see the two girls talking. She was frightened when she saw her father. But he was not angry, and quieted her, saying, "Do not be afraid! How is it that you have been able to bring this girl to life? What have you done?"

She told her father all about it, especially of the nail. Then Ogula sat down by the girl of the gilded box, and asked the story of her life. She told him all. Then he said, "As your mother is the kind of woman that sends people to kill, and I am chief in this place, I will-investigate this matter to-morrow. I will call all the people of this region, and there will be an ozâzâ (palaver) in the morning; and you shall remain, for you are to be my wife."

The next day all the country side were called,—the wicked mother, the soldiers, the old woman, and everybody else (except the unknown robbers). The palaver was talked from point to point of the history, and, just at the last, this beautiful girl walked into the assemblage, accompanied by Ogula's daughter.

As soon as Maria saw her daughter enter, she started from her seat, looked at the old woman, and fiercely said to her, "Here is this girl again! not dead yet! I thought you killed her!" The old woman was amazed, but asserted, "Yes, and I did. I kept my promise to you!"

Then the girl sat down, and Ogula bade her tell her entire story in the presence of all the people. So she told from the very beginning,—about the magic looking-glass, about the soldiers, about the robbers' house, and on till the stay in Ogula's house.

Then all the people began to shout and deride and revile, and threaten Maria and the old woman. This frightened the cruel Maria and her wicked friend, and they ran away to a far country, and never came back again.

So the beautiful young woman was married to Ogula, and was happy with his daughter as a companion.

But the robbers, in their secret house, not having heard of the ozâzâ , kept on mourning and grieving for their lost sister, not knowing where she had gone or what had become of her. And so the story ends.

(The above story is probably not more than two hundred or two hundred and fifty years old; the name "Maria" doubtless being derived from Portuguese occupants of the Kongo country.)

III. The Husband who came from an Animal

Ra-Nyambie in his great town had his wives and sons and daughters, and lived in glory.

He had a best-beloved daughter, by name Ilâmbe. There is a certain fetich charm called "ngalo," by means of which its possessor can have gratified any wish he may express. Ngalo is not obtainable by purchase or art; only certain persons are born with it. This Ilâmbe was born with a ngalo. While she was growing up, her father made a great deal of her and gave her very many things,—servants and houses, according to her wishes. When Ilâmbe had grown up to womanbood, she said, "Father, I will not like a man who has other wives. I shall want my husband all for myself." And the father said, "Be it so."

As years went on, llâmbe thought it was time she should be married, but she saw no one who pleased her fancy. So she took counsel with her ngalo, thinking, "What shall I do to get a husband for myself?"

She decided on a plan. Her father's people often went out hunting. One day, when they were going out, she said to them, "If you find some small animal, do not kill it, but bring it to me alive."

So they went out hunting, and they found a small animal resembling a goat, called "mbinde" (wild goat). They brought it to her, asking pardon for its smallness, and said, "We did not find anything, only this mbinde." She took it, saying, "It is good." Then turning to one of the men, she bade him, "Just skin this very carefully for me"; and to another of the servants, "Bring me plenty of water, and put it in my bathroom for a bath." Each of these servants did as he was bidden,—this one flaying the animal, that one bringing the water. When the one had finished flaying, and brought the entire flesh to her, she said, "Just put it into this water for a bath." She left it there two days, soaking in the water., The skin she put in a fire, burned it to black ashes, and carefully saved all the ash. This she did not do herself, but told a servant to do it, cautioning him to lose none of it. When it was brought to her, she wrapped it up with care, and put it safely away so that none of it should be lost.

On the third day she spoke to her ngalo, "Ngalo mine, ngalo mine, I tell you, turn this mbinde to a very handsomelooking man!" Instantly the mbinde was changed to a finely formed man, who jumped out of the bath-tub, dressed very richly.

Then llâmbe called one of her servants, and bade, "Go to my father, and tell him I wish the town to be cleaned as thoroughly and quickly as possible, because I have a husband, and I want to come and show him to you; so my father must be ready to greet us."

The father summoned his servant Ompunga (Wind), who came, and at once swept up the place clean.

llâmbe went out from her house with her husband, be and she walking side by side through the street on the way to her father's house. All along their route the people were wondering at the man's fine appearance, and shouting, "Where did llâmbe get this man?" When she reached her father's house, he ordered a salute of cannon for her. He was much pleased to see the man with the crowd of people, and received him with respect.

Having thus visited her father, llâmbe returned to her own house with her husband, the people still shouting in admiration of him. The news spread everywhere about llâmbe's fine-looking husband, and there was great praise of them. They lived happily in their marriage for a while, but trouble came.

llâmbe had a younger sister living still at her father's house. One day llâmbe changed her mind about having a husband all to herself, and thought, "I better share him with my younger sister." So she went out to her father to tell him about it, saying, "Father, I 've changed my mind. I want my younger sister to live with me, and marry the same man with me."

Her father, though himself having many wives, said, "You now change your mind, and are willing to share your husband with an-other woman. Will there be no trouble in the future?" She answered "No!" He repeated his question; but she assured him it would be agreeable. So she took her sister (without consulting the husband, as he was under her control, by power of her ngalo), led her to her house, and presented her as a new wife to her husband.

They remained on these terms for some time without any trouble. But as time went on, the report about that handsome man went far, and finally reached Ra-Mborakinda's town. Another woman lived there, also named Ilâmbe, of the same age as the other, and she was unmarried. This Ilâmbe said to herself, "I am tired of hearing the report about this handsome man. I will go, though uninvited I be, and see for myself." So she tells her brother and some of his men, "Take me over there to that town, and I will return to-day." She told her father the same words: "I am going to see that man, and will return." When this Ilâmbe got to the other Ilâmbe's house, the hus-band was out, but the wife received her with great hospitality; and the two sisters and their visitor all ate together. Soon the husband came, and the wife introduced the visitor. "Here is my friend Ilâmbe come to see you." "Good," he said. Then it was late in the day, and the visiting Ilâmbe's attendants said to her, "The day is past; let us be going." But she refused to go, and told them to return, saying that she would stay awhile with her friend Ilâmbe.

But really, in her coming she was not simply a visitor and sightseer; she intended to stay and share in the husband.

As her brother was leaving, he asked, "But when will you re-turn? and shall we come for you?" She said, "No; I myself will come back when I please." When the evening came, the hostess began to fix a sleeping-place for her visitor, showing her much kindness in the care of her arrangements.

The second day the hostess observed something suspicious in the manner with which her husband regarded the visitor; he said to his wife, "Here is your friend. Speak to her for me. Are you willing to do that?" She looked at him steadily, and slowly said, "Yes." So at evening she spoke of the matter to her visitor, who at once assented.

When llâmbe parted with her husband before retiring, she said to him, "Go with this new woman, but do not forget your and my morning custom." [That was their habit of rising very early for a morning bath.] He only said, "Yes." They all retired for the night.

The next morning the hostess was up early as usual, and had her bath, and was out of her room, waiting. But the man was not up yet, nor were there any sounds of preparation in his room. So llâmbe, after waiting awhile, had to call to waken him. He woke, saying, "Oh, yes, yes, I'm coming!"

The next day it was the same, he staying with the new llâmbe and rising late in the morning. The fourth day his wife said to him, "You have work to do, and you do not get up to do it till late." He was displeased at her fault-finding. When she saw that, she also was displeased.

So when he went to the bathroom she followed him there. On the way she had secretly taken with her the roll of black powder she had kept from the day of his creation.

While he was bathing, she turned aside, without his noticing it, and opening the roll of the powder, took out of it a little, and held it between her finger and thumb.

While he was dressing, she came near, stooped down, and rubbed the powder on his feet. They suddenly turned to hoofs. He began stamping his hoofs on the floor, surprised, and saying, "Wife, what is this?" She said, "It is nothing. You have finished dressing. Go out." He began to plead; she relented, and by her ngalo's power changed the hoofs back to feet. They both went out of the room and had their breakfast, and that day passed. But at night he again abandoned his wife for the new llâmbe, and next morning he was up later even than on the previous days. He had to be called several times before he would awake. He began to grumble and scold, "Can't a person be left to sleep as long as be desires?" And when he and the new llâmbe came from that bedroom, she joined in the man's displeasure at his having been disturbed. He went for his bath. The wife followed, and used the powder as she had done the day before, turning his feet to hoofs. He begged and pleaded. She again forgave him, and fixed the feet again. And they two came out of the bathroom and had their breakfast as usual. He went to his work, and the day wore on. At night he again deserted his wife. The next morning there was the same confusion in arousing him as on the other days.

His wife accompanied him to the bathroom as usual. While be was in the bath, and before he was done bathing, she left the room, and told the new llâmbe, "You sit down near the bathroom door. You will see him come out." The visitor replied, "It is well"; and she sat down. And llâmbe went into the bathroom again.

When the man got out of his bath, as soon as he attempted to dress himself, llâmbe, without saying anything or making any complaint, went behind him, and having the whole roll of powder with her, she opened the bundle, flung it on his back, and said, "You go back to where you came from!" Instantly he was changed to a mbinde, and he began to leap about as a goat. Then llâmbe cried out to the other llâmbe at the door, "Are you ready to receive him? He's coming!" and she opened the door. Out ran the mbinde, leaped from the house, dashed through the town and off to the forest, the people shouting in derision, "Hâ! Hâ! Hâ! So, indeed, that handsome man was the mbinde that was taken to llâmbe's house!

Then the wife said to the other llâmbe, "Did you see your man? Call him! That's he running off there!" The next day llâmbe said to the visitor, "Send word for your people that they may come for you."

The following day they were sent for, and they came to ll-âmbe's house. After they had arrived, llâmbe sent word to her father, "Have your place cleaned, I am coming to enter a complaint." The father replied, "Very well!" Ompunga came and swept the place. Seats were prepared in the street. llâmbe summoned the visitor and her people, saying, "Let us all go to my father's house."

So they went there, and llâmbe made her complaint, telling all from the beginning: how she obtained a husband; how the other llâmbe had come; how she received her kindly; how she even had been willing to share her busband with her, but how the new llâmbe had monopolized instead of simply sharing; and how things had become so bad that she had to send the man back to his beast origin. Turning to the visiting people, she said, "I have nothing more to say except that your sister llâmbe is not going back to your town, but has to be my slave all the days of my life."

So the king's council justified her, and pronounced the judgment just. The people scattered to their homes. And the two sisters went to their house, with the other llâmbe as their slave.

IV. The Fairy Wife

In his great town, King Ra-Mborakinda, or Ra-Nyambie, lived in glory with all his wives and sons and daughters. Some of his great and favored sons had large business and great wealth. But there was one of the sons, named Nkombe, whose mother was not a favorite wife of the king, so this Nkombe was poor. Everything went against him, and his life was quite miserable; only, he had a gun, and he knew bow to shoot; that was all. So he thought, "I'm tired of this kind of life. I better leave and go off by myself."

He gathered together the few things that belonged to him,—a few plates and pots, and his gun and ammunition,—and went away. He went far into the forest, and with his machete began to clear a little place for a camping-ground (olako).

He fixed up his camp, and next morning went out hunting. When he began to feel hungry, he turned back to cook his food. On his return be had fresh meat with him; this he cooked, set it on the table, and ate. After eating, be cleared off the table, washed the dishes, brushed up the floor, and the new meat that was left he put on the orala (drying-frame) for next day's use. So that day's work was done.

Next day he again leaves the camp, and with his gun is off again to his hunting. At noon he comes back with his meat,—antelope, or wild pig, or whatever it may be. He cooks his food, eats; and that day's work is done just as the day before.

So he did many days. After each day's work he was so tired and felt so lonely he wished he had a mother or some one to do for him.

Unknown to him, since he had come to that olako, there was a woman named Ilâmbe, who belonged to the awiri (fairies), who secretly had observed, all that he did. One day she thought to herself, "Oh, I am sorry for this man; I think that as I have the power I will turn myself into a human being and help him, for I do not like to see him suffer." So she said to herself, "To-day I will cause Nkombe to be unsuccessful, so that he shall kill only ntori (a big forest rat), and I will bide myself in ntori."

So Nkombe hunted long and far that day, and saw nothing worthy of being shot. He was getting hungry, and murmured, "Ah! I have not been able to kill anything to-day." But presently he saw ntori pass by, and he said, "Well, I'll have to take this small animal, utori!" He shot it, and took it with him to his camp. When he reached the olako, as he had other meat on the orala, and was in a hurry, after singeing and cleaning ntori, he threw it on the orala, and took the older dried meat, and began to cook it for his supper. He, went on with his usual day's work, as it took only a little while to arrange ntori on the orala.

Next day be went out as usual on his hunting journey. While he was away, and before be returned, Ilâmbe had crept out of the head of ntori. She brushed up the camp, and made everything neat and clean. She began to cook, taking meat from the drying-frame.

She cooked it very nicely, and ate part,—her share, just enough to satisfy her appetite. Then she crept back into ntori's head, as she knew Nkombe must be about starting back.

Late in the afternoon Nkombe returned with some wild meat. He took down dried meat from the orala, leaving his fresh meat unattended to, for be was in a burry to cook, being hungry. He went to his little hut to get plate, kettle, and so forth. To his surprise, on the table was everything ready, food and plate and drink. He exclaimed, "What word is this? Where did this come from? Is this the work of my mother's spirit? She has pitied me and has come and done this. I wish I knew where she came from."

This occurred during three successive days, just the same each day. Nkombe was puzzled. He wanted to find out, and decided to go to the great prophet, Ra-Marânge. The prophet saw hiin coming, and greeted him, "Sale! (Hail) my son, sale!" "Mbolo," replied Nkombe. Ra-Marânge continued, "What did you come for? What are you doing?" "I come for you to make medicine, that you may prophesy for me about a matter I want to find out."

Ra-Marânge said, "Child, I am old, and do not do such things now. I have given the power to Ogula-ya-impazya-vazya" [so called because his body was all-covered-by-a-disease-of-pimples]. "Well, where shall I go to him?" The prophet replied, "He is not far."

Nkombe starts to go to Ogula-ya-impazya-vazya, who presently sees him coming. As soon as Nkombe reached him, Ogula-ya-impazya-vazya said, "If you come to me for medicine, good, for that is my only business; but if for anything else, clear off!" "Yes, that is what I came for."

So Ogula-ya-impazya-vazya began to kindle his big fire. Nkombe was surprised, not knowing what was to be done with the fire. The next minute he sees Ogula-ya-impazya-vazya throw himself into the flames. Nkombe was startled and afraid, thinking, "Is this man going to kill himself for me?" The prophet rolled himself several times in the fire in order to get the power. Some of his pimples on his body burst in the flame; and he jumped out, ready with his power to do the medicine. He said, "Hah, repeat your story; I am ready!" Nkombe told all his story,—how be had worked for himself, and how for a few days past he had been helped by some one, and wanted to know who it was, if Ogula-yaimpazya-vazya would please tell him. "Hah, that's a small matter for me!" So the prophet told him, "You killed ntori for yourself a few days ago, and this being is a woman who has come to be your wife, and has hidden herself in ntori." "But," said Nkombe, "how shall I be able to catch her, so that she shall be a real woman, for I do not see her?"

"I'll let you know how. Go back and hunt all the same for three days. On the fourth day go out as usual, but do not go hunting. Hide near the olako,—near, but not where you will be seen." Then the prophet gave Nkombe a prepared powder, and told him to keep it carefully. He gave him also a small cornucopia (ozyoto) full of a bruised medicinal leaf, and told him, "Go and put these two medicines in a secret place near your olako. On the fourth day have these two medicines with you where you hide. When you see her come out, and while she is doing your work, you will run and seize her, and say to her, "You are my wife." She will not understand your language, and will niurmur and shake her bead and resist. But when you hold her fast, sprinkle the powder all over her body. Then take the ozoto, and squeeze some of the juice in her nostrils, eyes, and mouth. She will begin to sneeze. Repeat the words, 'You are my wife, my wife!' Then she will understand you, and will yield."

So Nkombe took the medicines, and obeyed directions; hid the medicines and hunted the three days, his heart bursting with anxiety to get the days done that seemed so long. At last the three days were over and the fourth day came.

Now the woman, by the power that was with her, knew all these things; she knew she would be caught that day.

After Nkombe had left in the morning with the medicines, had hidden himself, and was waiting for the hours to pass, the woman, hesitating on her fate, did not come out quickly as on the other days. But finally Nkombe saw the pieces of meat on the frames shake. And out of ntori's head came a beautiful woman with clean soft skin. He could hardly restrain himself. She went on with all the usual work,— cooking, and so forth. But that day she did not divide nor partake of the food, but put all of it on the table. When be saw she had finished, and was washing her hands preparatory to jumping back into ntori on the orala, he came out of the bushes, and stepping cautiously but rapidly, rushed to seize her. He caught her. She began to resist, and he followed the prophet's directions. The woman at first was murmuring and sobbing, and Nkombe was trying to calm her with the words "My wife." Finally, under the powder, she quieted. When the juice was dropped into her mouth, she was able to speak his language. She told him all her story,—how she had pitied him, and had entered into ntori, and everything else. "But," she said, "there is one more thing I must tell you. I have come indeed to be your wife, and I have the power to make you rich or poor, happy or unhappy. I will give you only one rule: Be good to me, and I will be so to you; but never say to me that I came from the low origin of a rat's head." Nkombe exclaimed, "No, no I You have done so much for me, I could never so humiliate you." "You speak well, but be very careful not to break your promise." So they ate and finished the day's work.

Next day the woman wanted to build a town by word of her power. She said, "Mwe [Sir] Nkombe, surely you will not live in an olako all your life. Look for a site for a town, and mark it with stakes for its length and width." Nkombe was puzzled. He had a wife, but where would be get materials for a house; for be was as poor of goods as he was before? Being troubled, he made no reply to his wife, and did not go to mark a site. At night they retired, Nkombe still troubled about the building of a town; but Ilâmbe was smiling in her heart, for she knew what she would do. So she made him fall into a deep sleep. She went out at night a short distance, and chose a good town-site. She spoke to her ngalo (a guardian-spirit charm), "Ngalo mine, before morning I want to see all this place cleared, and covered with nice houses, and all the houses furnished—and supplied with men and maid servants." And she returned to bed.

Before daybreak everything was ready, as Ilâmbe desired. The ngalo had made the olako disappear, and. Nkombe and wife were sleeping inside their nice house. When morning came, Nkombe did not know where he was, nor even on which side to get out of bed. He exclaimed, "What is this word?" "You are in your own house and in your own town." So both went out to inspect their town and their servants. Nkombe did not know how well to thank her, so glad was he.

Later the wife became a mother, and a son was born. Nkombe called this first-born Ogula. Again, a daughter was born. Then the wife told her ngalo to bring ships of wealth. The next day ships were seen coming. Nkombe went on board and had a conversation with the captains. They stayed a few days, and then sailed a-way, leaving Nkombe a cargo of wealth. Another time ships came, and Nkombe went off on board as before; and these ships sailed away, also leaving wealth. Other children ivere born to them. Children of a fairy mother are called "aganlo"; they grow very fast, and are very wise.

Other ships came. One day one comes, and Nkombe, having gone on board, has there a convivial time, stays all day, and returns nearly drunk. The wife says to him, "Nkombe, often you come from ships looking in this way, and I do not like it. I have spoken with you often, that if a food or a drink is not good in its effects, it is better to leave it off. But you do not care for my words." Nkombe, under the influence of liquor, was vexed with her, rebuked her, and began to use hard words with orâwo (insult): "You—you—this woman who— but I won't finish it." Soon, however, he took up the quarrel again, saying, "A person can know from your manners that you came out of—" The wife said, "When you are drunk, you say half sentences; why hold back? Say what you want to say."

He shouted angrily, "Yes, if I want to say it, I will say it! It was my own ntori that I killed. If I had not killed it, would you have come out of it?" Then Ilâmbe said, "Please repeat that; I do not quite un-derstand you." He repeated it. She exclaimed, "Eh!" but said no more, and waited until morning, when he would be sober.

So early in the morning she told him to get up, so that she could do her housework. She did the morning's work, washing things neatly. but rapidly. Then she called her sons and daughters, and in their presence said to their father, "You said so-and-so yesterday; now I am off and with my children."

Nkombe knew he had said the forbidden words. He pleaded for mercy; but she replied, "No, you broke your promise." The two elder children pleaded for their father: "It was only once. Though a bad thing, it cannot break a marriage. Forgive it." But the mother persisted, "No!" Then the two elder ones said they would not leave their father.

So she said to him, "Now be thankful you have these two. If it was not for them, I would put you back where you were just as I found you; but for the sake of these two children, I leave some of my power with them." Then to those two she said, "You will call on me for help when you have need, and I will be near to help you."

So she took the two younger ones, and said to their father, "As this place is quite open, Nkombe, sit you here and see me depart." Nkombe did so. He and the two older children watched the mother and the two younger ones walk down the path from the town. They went to the bank of the river, and, wading in, disappeared in the river depths.

V. The Thieves and their Enchanted House

Ra-Mborakinda had his big town of men and women and children, all in good condition. But a kind of plague came upon the people suddenly, killing many. In a short time it destroyed most of the inhabitants, and finally but few were left.

So one of the elder sons said to a younger one, "Let us flee for our lives!" This elder brother's name was Ogula, and the younger brother's name was Nkombe. When Ogula had thus said, "Let us flee for our lives," Nkombe agreed. Ogula took as his servant a boy, and together with Nkombe they went out. They went aimlessly, not following any particular plan, but vaguely hoping to happen on any place.

They went, went, wandering on, on, till they came to a small hut, almost too miserable for a dwelling. But in their extremity they said, "Oh! there is a house! Let us go to it; maybe we'll find shelter there." So they walked up to it, and, to their surprise, saw there. an old man mending a piece of canvas.

He saluted them, and asked them where they came from. They told their story, and Ogula asked the old man whether he would, of his kindness, give them shelter. He said, "Yes, if you are willing to do as I tell you; for living here is hard, and there is nothing to eat. I have to cut firewood and carry it to the city (osenge) far away, and sell it there. That city belongs to a big merchant."

Ogula said, "Yes; we are willing." So the next day Ogula himself and Nkombe and their servant set themselves ready for work. After they had cut their firewood, they asked the old man the way to the city. He directed them. They went, sold their firewood, and brought food. This they did many times, cutting firewood and going to the city and buying food; and they each built a house of their own near the old man's hut.

But after a while Ogula began to tire of this kind of life so he said to himself, "If I only had a gun, I could go hunting. But even without the gun, I will go out and see what I can see." So he went out alone, not calling his brother or his servant to go with him. He went and went, on, on, for a half-day's journey, till he happened to come to a large house built in a very strange style, having no door at its side and with a flat roof. The place looked clean, as if kept in order by people. He approached cautiously; but looking around, he saw no one at all. He said to himself, "Who owns this place? Surely some one owns it, for it is so clean; but I see no one here. I won't leave this place to-day till I know who lives here." He decided to retire a little and climb up a tall tree overlooking the house and watch from there. He was very hungry, having had no food that day, but he still decided to wait and see what was about the house.

After he had been up the tree a long while, late in the after-noon he saw a number of men coming. He saw one of them climb up the side of the house to the roof, where was a trap-door. All of the men had bundles of goods. The first one who had climbed to the roof spoke a few words to the door as he stood before it, and the two parts of the door flew open of themselves. Then the other men climbed up with their bundles, and went into the house.

All this Ogula could see from his tree-top. He said to himself, "Now I am hungry, and must go, for I have seen enough to-day. I see that this house is occupied, and by men, and how they enter; it is enough for to-day." He thought it time to move before any of the people should come out of the house. He came down rapidly, and went back to the little hut of the old man.

When he got to his own house, his brother Nkombe asked, Where have you been all day?" Ogula said, "I was tired of working, and took a walk to the forest, and missed my way." But he did not tell his brother the story of what he had seen.

Ogula then ate a little and went to bed, though it was not very late. He went thus soon to bed, for he wanted to go early next day to inspect the big house again. So, very, very early, before daylight, Ogula was up and off, for he did not wish his brother to ask him where he was going.

He remembered the way to the big house, and went directly there. He climbed his tree. He looked and saw that the door of the house was open. He waited a little while, and then saw the men climbing out of the door. Their leader was the last; he spoke a cabalistic word, pressed his foot on the threshold, as the two sides of the door folded together, and it was closed.

After they had been gone quite awhile, Ogula thought he would try to enter the house, first seeking what was the way to open it. He said to himself, "I know they have goods there, for I have seen them carried in." So he descended from the tree, and going to the house, climbed up the side. When he got to the top, he searched for something by which the door could be opened. He saw nothing like a key or lock or handle. Then he remembered the words he had heard the leader use, and thought, "Perhaps they were the means by which the door was opened." So he uttered the words, "Yâginla mie, kâ nungwa, aweme!" (Obey me, and thyself open!) and, to his surprise, the door flew open. Then he went down the flight of steps leading below to the interior of the house. He was startled when he saw the room full of all kinds of money and goods and wealth that any one could wish to have. One could have taken away a great deal without its absence being noticed, so abundant was the amount.

Ogula thought, "Isn't this fine! But I must be quick, lest the owners of this house catch me here." So he took a cloth, and put into it a few small articles and a quantity of cash. He tied up the bundle, went up the stairway, and walked out of the door which he had left open. At the top he remembered the word "Nunja!" (Shut!) which the leader had used for closing. He spoke it; and the door shut. He hasted away, and back to the hut of the old man. He did not—enter it, but went to his own house and there hid the bundle. He told no one anything, neither the old man nor his servant nor even his brother. Soon the brother came over from his house, saying, "Brother! I looked for you this morning; you must have gone out very early." "Yes, I went out early, for I am tired of seeing so little; so I went out to see what I could see."

The next day he did the same. On this trip be took not only money from the house, but some fine clothing for himself to wear. As before, on emerging at the top of the house, he spoke the word "Nunja!" the door closed, and he was away again, no one having seen him. When Ogula got back to his house, Nkombe asked him the same question of the day before, "Where have you been?" and he made only the evasive answer. But Nkorobe began to be troubled. He feared something was wrong, and be determined to find out what was the matter. So he decided to get up next morning just as early as Ogula. The reason that Ogula did not tell Nkombe was because the latter had a had jealous heart, and was very covetous of money. So early in the morning Ogula was off. He did not know that Nkombe had any thought of following him. But as soon as Nkombe saw Ogula start, be followed him cautiously, so that he might find out what his brother was doing.

Ogula walked on straight and rapidly, and never looked behind, for he had no suspicion that he was being followed. When he got to the house, as usual he ordered the door to open, and descended inside. While he was beginning to select the things he wanted to take, to his surprise he saw Nkombe also descending the stairway. Ogula said, "Nkombe! what is this? Who showed you the way? Who told youto come here? I am troubled to find you here; for this will be the end of you! I knew it was not safe for you to come here. What I took was for us both."

Nkombe said, "No! you hid it from me. I have found it now. I will be rich for myself." By this time Ogula had tied up his bundle ready to go out. But Nkombe was snatching up a large quantity from every side. Ogula said, "Nkombe! be quick! You do not know how to shut that door, and it will not be safe for us to be found here by those people." But Nkombe was not satisfied with one bundle, he was still gathering up other bundles. Ogula wearied of waiting and begging of Nkombe to come, so he said he must go and leave him, saying, "Now, Nkombe, it is not safe to wait longer. I have waited for you and begged you to leave with me; so I go alone. You cannot get out with all those bundles."

But Nkombe would not listen. So Ogula went out, and spoke the word that closed the door, leaving Nkombe in the house. However, being anxious for his brother, Ogula did not go away, but climbed his tree to see what would happen.

When Nkombe had entered the house, he had with him a big, sharp knife.

Ogula waited outside till those people should come. Soon they came. The leader did as usual, being the first to climb to the house-top and to order the door to open. The door flew open, and the leader descended. As soon as he entered, he found another man, Nkombe, in the house. The leader asked, "Who are you, and how did you get in here?" Nkombe did not reply, but drawing his knife, plunged it into the leaders neck. With one outcry the man fell dead. By this time some of the other men had climbed up and were about to enter. When they got inside, they saw their leader lying dead, and this stranger standing armed. One of the men drew his pistol and shot Nkombe. [Observe the pistol; all these folk-lore stories disregard anachronisms or even impossibilities.] They carried his dead body to the roof, and threw it off to the ground. All this Ogula saw, looking from the treetop down into the house.

Then those people began to be perplexed and suspicious, say-ing, "This is not the work of only one, for we found the door closed on our arrival. So this person inside must have had some associate outside. How shall we find it out?"

They began to plan, each one with his proposition. One said, "Let us go and bury the dead body." Another, "Let us leave it and go on with our business, and if on our return the body is missing, that will be a proof that a partner has taken it. Then we will get on the track and find where the body was taken." And they agreed that he whose plan proved successful should be their new leader. So they closed the door, left Nkombe's dead body lying, and went off on their usual business.

After they had been gone quite a while, Ogula came down quickly from the tree. He tried to carry the body of his brother without dragging it so as not to leave any sign of a trail. And he did not follow the path, but walked parallel with it among the bushes. He hid the body, and then went away to his house. He called his servant, telling him that Nkombe was dead, and that he wanted him to come help bury the body. He did not call the old man, but only told him that his brother was dead.

He and the servant went to the spot where he had left his brother's body. They carried it far into the forest, buried it, and then went back to their house.

When the thieves came again to their house, they missed the dead body, so that part of their plan had proved true; and they said to the one who had proposed it, "You were right. You are our leader. What is your next order? "He said, "To-morrow we will not go out to do our business, but we will go out to hunt for this other man."

The next day they went, and scattering searched on all paths to see whether they would meet with some one or see some house. Some of them who were on a certain path came to the huts of the old man and Ogula. The first person they saw was the old man sitting in his doorway. They stopped and saluted. They asked him a few questions, and then consulting together agreed to return to their house and come back next day, hoping to find out something from the old man. They went back to their house. Previous to this, from the time that Ogula had been stealing goods he had built with his servant a little village of his own some distance from the old man's hut. On this first coming of the thieves, Ocula, hidden in his house, had seen them, and he said to himself, As they now know of this place, I better go away, for fear this thing be found out, and they kill me as they did my brother." So at night he left that house and went off to his village.

In the morning of the next day, when the thieves came, they brought liquor, for they had planned that they would make this old man drunk, that he might talk when he was foolish with liquor.

They came to the old man's and saluted him. They sat and conversed, asking him,"How many people are here? Are you always living alone?" At first be replied, "Yes, I live alone." "But you are so old, how do you get your food by yourself? Would you like to taste a nice drink? We are sorry for you in your lack of comforts." "Yes, I would like to taste it."

So they opened their liquor, drank a little themselves, and gave to him. After he had drunk he became talkative, and began conversation again: "Oh, yes, you asked me if I lived alone. But not quite alone. There is a young man here." The thieves were glad to hear him talk, and gave him more liquor. He drank; they asked more questions, "You said there was another man with you; where is he?" Then the old man repeated the whole story of the coming of the brothers, to the death of one of them; and added, "A few days ago one of them came to tell me he was going to bury his brother; but I do not know when or how he died." So they asked the old man, "You know where be was buried?" "No." "But where is that living brother?" "Oh, he has just left me, and is gone to his new place not very far away. I have not been there, but you can easily find it."

They consulted among themselves. "As this other man may hear of what we are about, we will go away to-day, disguise ourselves, and to-morrow seek for his place." So they all left.

Next day two or three came disguised, and found Ogula's new house in the afternoon. He did not recognize their faces. He welcomed them as strangers and treated them politely. They asked, "Is this your house? Do you live alone?" He answered straightly, but did not mention his brother. But they felt they had enough proof of who he was, and left. But before they left they had observed the number and location of the rooms and the shape of the house. In the house was a large public reception and sitting room, and from it were doors leading to the servant's room and to a little entry opening into Ogula's room.

The next day Ogula and his servant were doing their work of refining the gum-copal they had gathered for trade; it was being boiled in an enormous kettle. When this copal was melted, the kettle was set, with its boiling-hot pitchy contents, in that little entry. In the afternoon came the whole company of thieves, all disguised. They said, "We have come to make your acquaintance, and to relieve your loneliness by an evening's amusement." Ogula began to prepare them food. They sat at the food, eating and drinking; had conversation, and spent the evening laughing and playing. At night most of them pretended to be drunk and sleepy, and stretched themselves on the floor of the large room as if in sleep.

Ogula also had been drinking, and said he was tired and would go to bed. But his servant was sober; he saw what the men were doing, and suspected evil. He thought: "Ah! my master is drunk, and these people are strangers. What will happen?" So when the lights were put out and he was going to bed, he left open the door of the little entry and locked the door of his master's room. After midnight the thieves rose and consulted. "Let us go and kill him." They arose and trod softly toward Ogula's room. Not quite sober, they missed the proper way, stepped through the open door of the little entry, and stumbled into the caldron of copal. It was still hot, and stuck to their bodies like pitch. They were in agony, but did not dare to cry out. They all were crawling covered with the hot gum, except the last man, who had jumped over the bodies of those who had fallen before him; and he ran away to their house.

But Ogula was sleeping, ignorant of what was going on.

In the morning the boy, who also had slept, on opening the house, found the kettle full of tarred limbs of dead human bodies. He knocked at Ogula's door and waked him. But Ogula said, "Don't disturb me, I am so tired from last night's revel." "Yes, but get up and see what has happened." Ogula came and saw. Then he told the lad that but for him he would have been dead. Ogula thenceforth took him as a brother. Then he and the boy had a big work of throwing out the bodies of the thieves. Ogula was not afraid of a charge of murder, for the thieves had tumbled themselves into the scalding contents of the kettle. He had enough wealth, and did not go again to the thieves' house.

But that one man who had escaped was wishing for revenge, yet was afraid to come to Ogula's house by himself. Time went on. Ogula remained quiet. But his enemy still sought revenge, waiting for an opportunity.

Gradually, too, Ogula had forgotten his enemy's face; for the thieves were many, and all disguised, and he would be unable to distinguish which one had escaped.

On a time it happened that this thief went far to another country; and while he was there, Ogula also happened to journey to that very town. The lad had said, being now a young man, "May I go too?" "Yes, you may, for you are like a brother. You must go wherever I do." On the very second day in the town the two, Ogula and the thief, met. The thief recognized Ogula; but Ogula did not recognize him, and neither spoke; but the young man, with better memory, said to himself, "I have seen this man somewhere." He looked closely, but said nothing.

The next day the thief made a feast. He met Ogula again on the street and saluted him, "Mbolo! I am making a feast. You seem a stranger. I would like you to come." "Yes; where?" "At such-and-such a place.","Yes, I will come. But this attendant of mine is good, and must be invited too." "Yes, I have no objections." Next evening the feast was held, and people came to it. The thief placed Ogula and his servant near himself. There was much eating and drinking. The thief became excited, and determined to kill Ogula at the table by sticking him with a knife.

All the while that the thief was watching Ogula, the servant was watching the thief. Presently the latter turned slightly and began to draw a knife. The servant watched him closely. The thief's knife was out, and the servant's knife was out too. But the thief was watching only Ogula, and did not know what the servant was doing.

Just as the thief was about to thrust at Ogula, the servant jumped and thrust his knife into the thief's neck. The man fell, blood flowing abundantly over the table. The guests were alarmed, and were about to seize the servant, who pointed at the drawn knife in the man's hand that had been intended for his master; and then he told their whole story.

So the guests decided that there was no charge against Ogula and his servant, and scattered. The next day Ogula and his servant left. As he knew that that man was the last of the company of thieves, he said, in gladness, "Now! Glory!" Then he thought, "All that wealth is mine, since this last one who tried to take my life is dead."

As he had seen enough of the world by travel, he decided to stay in one place. He would call people to live with him in a new town which he would build for them around that enchanted house of the thieves, which he took as his own with all its wealth. And he lived long in that house in great glory, with wife and children and retainers and slaves.

VI. Banga of the Five Faces

Ra-Mborakinda lived in his town with his sons and daughters and his glory. One son was Nkombe, and another Ogula, whose full name was Ogula-keva-anlingo-n'-ogendâ (Ogula-who-goes-faster-than-water); but they were not of the same mother.

Ogula grew up without taking any wife. He became a great man, with knowledge of sorcery. One day his father said to him,

"Ogula, as you are a big man now, I think it is time for you to have a wife. I think you had better choose from one of my young wives." Ogula replied, "No, I will get a wife in my own way." So one day be went to another osenge (clearing) of a town which belonged to a man of the awiri (spirits; plural of "ombwiri"), *i.e.*, one who possessed magic power, and obtained one of his daughters. Her name was Ikâgu-ny'-awiri.

He brought the girl home to his father's house, where she was very much admired as "a fine woman! a fine woman!" She was indeed very pretty. Then Ogula said to her, "As you are now my wife, you must be orunda (set apart from) to other men, and I will be orunda to other women, even if I go to work at another place." And she replied, "It is well."

At another time Ogula said, "I think it better for us to move away from my father's town, and put my house just a little way off." After the new house was finished they moved to it, and lived by themselves. Ogula had business elsewhere that compelled him to be often absent, returning at times in the afternoons. Whenever Nkombe knew that Ogula was out, he would come and annoy Ikâgu with solicitation to leave her husband and marry him. Ogula knew of this, for he had a ngalo (a special fetich) that enabled him to know what was going on elsewhere. The wife would say, "Ah, Nkombe! No, I know that you are my husband's brother; but I do not want you!" Then, when it was time for Ogula to return, Nkombe would go off. That went on for many days; Nkombe visiting Ikâgu whenever he had opportunity, and the wife refusing him every time. It went on so long that at last Ogula thought that he would speak to his wife about it.

So he began to ask her, "Is everything all right? Has any one been troubling you?" She answered, "No." He asked her again, and again she said, "No." Thus it went on,—Nkombe coming; Ogula asking questions; and the wife, unwilling to make trouble between the two brothers, denying. But one day the trouble that Nkombe made the wife was so great that Ogula, with the aid of his ngalo, thought surely she would acknowledge. But she did not; for that day, when he came and called his wife into their bedroom, and asked her, she only asserted weakly, "No trouble." Then he said, "Do you think I do not know? You are a good wife to me. I know all that has passed between you and Nkombe." And he added, "As Nkombe is making you all this trouble, I will have to remove again far from my father's town, and go elsewhere." So he went far away, and built a small village for himself and wife. They put it in good order, and made the pathway wide and clean.

But in his going far from his father's town be had unknowingly come near to another town that belonged to another Ra-Mborakinda, who also had great power and many sons and daughters. One of the sons also was named Ogula, just as old and as large as this first Ogula. One day this Ogula went out hunting with his gun. He went far, leaving his town far away, going on and on till be saw it was late in the day and that it was time to go back.

Just as be was about returning he came to a nice clean pathway, and he wondered, "So here are people? This fine path! who cleans it? and where does it lead to?" So be thought he would go and see for himself; and he started on the path. He had not gone far before he came to the house of Ogula. There he stood, admiring the house and grounds. "A fine house! a fine house!"

When Ogula saw Ogula 2d standing in the street, he invited him up into the house. They asked each other a few questions, became acquainted, and made friendship; and Ogula kept Ogula 2d for two days as his guest. Then Ogula 2d said, "They may think me lost, in town, after these two days. Thanks for your kindness, but I had better go." And he added, "Some day I will send for you, and you will come to visit me, that I may show you hospitality."

Ogula 2d went back to his place. He had a sister who was a very troublesome woman, assuming authority and giving orders like a man. Her name was Banga-yi-baganlo-tani (Banga-of-five-faces). Though her father, the king, and her brother were still living, she insisted on governing the town. When any one displeased her, or she was vexed with any one, she would order that person to lie down before a cannon and be shot to pieces. The father was wearied of her annoyances, but did not know what to do with her.

As Ogula 2d had left word with Ogula that be would invite him on another day, he did so. Ogula accepted; but as the invitation was only to himself, he did not take his wife, but went by himself, and was welcomed and entertained.

When it was late afternoon, he was about to go back, but Ogula 2d said, "You were so kind to me; do not go back to-day. Stay with me." And Ogula consented.

In asking Ogula to stay, Ogula 2d thought, "As his wife is not here, perhaps he will want another woman. I have my sister here; but if I first offer her, it will be a shame, for he has not asked for any one" [an actual native African custom, to give a guest a temporary wife, as one of the usual hospitalities. The custom is not resented by the women].

All this while Ogula had not seen the sister. When they were ready for the evening meal, Ogula 2d thought it time to call his sister to see the guest. She fixed herself up finely, clean, and with ornaments. She came and sat in the house, and there were the usual salutations of "Mbolo!" "Ai, mbolo!" and some conversation.

While they were talking, Banga had her face cast down with eyes to the ground. And when she lifted her eyes to look at Ogula, her face changed. From the time she came in till meal-time, she made a succession of these changes of her face, thinking that Ogula would be surprised, and would admire the changes, and expecting that he would ask her brother for her.

She waited and waited; Ogula saw all these five changes of her face, but was not attracted. They went to their food, and ate and finished. And they talked on till bedtime; but Ogula had said nothing of love. Banga was annoyed and disappointed; she went to her bed piqued and with resentful thoughts.

The next morning Ogula said it was time to go back to his wife. When he was getting ready to go, Banga said to him, "Have you a wife?"

He answered, "Yes." She said, "I want her to come and visit me some day." And Ogula agreed. He went, and returning to his house, told his wife that Banga wanted to see her.

After Ogula was gone, Banga asked her brother about Ogula's wife. "Is she pretty?" And he told her how finely the wife had looked. Banga was not pleased at that, was jealous, and waited till

Ikâgu should come that she might see for herself. "I will see if she is more beautiful than I with my five countenances." Subsequently Banga chose a day, and sent for Ikâgu. She dressed for the journey, and Ogula, not being invited, took her only half-way.

When Ogula's wife arrived, Banga saw that it was true that she was pretty, and of graceful carriage in her walking, and she did not wonder that her husband was charmed with her. But she hid her jealousy, and pretended to be pleased with her visitor. Ogula's wife did not spend the night there; when she thought it time to go, she said good-bye, and turned to leave.

When she had gone, Banga was planning for a contest with her. She said to herself, "Now I see wky that man made me feel ashamed at his not asking for my love,—because his wife is so beautiful. She shall see that I will have her killed, and I shall have her husband."

So after a few days she sent word to Ogula's wife, "Prepare yourself for a fight, and come and meet me at my fatber's house."

But the wife said to Ogula, "I have done nothing. What is the fight for?" Nevertheless, she began to prepare a fighting dress, and before it was finished another messenger came with word, "You are waited for."

So she said, "As it is not a call for peace, I had better put on a dress that befits blood." So she dressed in red. After she was dressed she started, and Ogula went with her, to hear what was the ground of the challenge.

As soon, as they got to the town, they found Banga striding up and down the street. Her cannon was already loaded, waiting to be fired. When Ogula wanted to know what the "palaver" was, Banga said,

"I do not want to talk with you; I only want you to obey my orders."

But Ikâgu wanted to know what the trouble was, and began to ask, "What have I done?" Banga only repeated, "I don't want any words from you; only, you come and lie down in front of this cannon." Ikâgu obeyed, and lay down, and Banga ordered her men to fire the cannon.

By this time Ogula, by the power of his ngalo, had changed the places of the two women. When the cannon was fired, and the smoke had cleared away, the people who stood by saw Ikâgu standing safe by her husband, and Banga lying dead. All the assembled people began to wonder, "What is this? What is this?"

So Banga's father called Ogula, and said, "Do not think I am displeased with you at the death of my daughter; I too was wearied at her doings. So, as you are justified, and Banga was wrong, it is no matter to be quarrelled about."

And Ogula 2d said to Ogula, "I am not vexed at you. You had done nothing. She wanted to bring trouble on you, and it has come on herself. I have no fight with you. We will still be friends. But do not live off in your forest village by yourself; come you and your wife to live in this town."

So Ogula and his wife consented, and agreed to remove, and live with Ogula 2d. And they did so without further trouble.

VII. The Two Brothers

Ra-Mborakinda has his great town, and his wives, and his children, and the glory of his kingdoin. All his women had no children, except the loved head-wife, Ngwe-nkonde (Mother of Queens), and the unloved Ngwe-vazya (Mother of Skin-Disease). Each of these two had children, sons, at the same time. The father gave them their names. Ngwenkonde's was Nkombe, and Ngwe-vazya's was Ogula. Again these two women became mothers. This time both of them had daughters. Ngwe-nkonde's was named Ngwanga, and Ngwe-vazya's was llâmbe. A third time these two bore children, sons, on the same day. These two sons grew up without names till they began to talk, for the father had delayed to give them names. But one day he called them to announce to them their names. What he had selected they refused, saying that they had already named themselves. Ngwe-nkonde's child named himself Osongo, and Ngwe-vazya's Obengi. And the father agreed.

These two children grew and loved each other very much. No one would have thought that they belonged to different mothers, so great was the love they had for each other. They were always seen together, and always ate at the same place. When one happened to be out at mealtime, the other would not eat, and would begin to cry till the absent one returned. Both were handsome in form and feature.

When Ngwe-vazya's people beard about her nice-looking little boy, they sent word to her, "We have heard about your children, but we have not seen you for a long time. Come and visit us, and bring your youngest son, for we have beard of him and want to see him."

So she went and asked permission of Ra-Mborakinda, saying that she wanted to go and see her people. He was willing. Then she made herself ready to start. As soon as Osongo knew that his brother Obengi was going away, be began to cry at the thought of separation. He said, "I am not going to stay alone. I have to go too, for I am not willing to be separated from my brother. And Obengi said the same: "If Osongo does not go with us, then I will not go at all." Then Ngwe-vazya thought to herself, "No, it will not,do for me to take Osongo along with me, for his mother and I are not friendly." And she told Osongo that he must stay. But both the boys persisted, "No, we both must go." So Ngwe-vazya said, "Well, let it be so. I will take care of Osongo as if he were my own son." And Ra-Mborakinda and Ngwe-nkonde were willing that Osongo should go.

So they started and went; and when they reached the town of Ngwe-vazya's family the people were very glad to receive them. She was very attentive to both the boys, watching them wherever they went, for they were the beloved sons of Ra-Mborakinda. She was there at her people's town about two months. Then she told them that it was time to return home with the two boys. Her people assented, and began to load her and the boys with parting presents.

They went back to Ra-Mborakinda's town, and there also their people were glad to see them return, for the children had grown, and looked well. The people, and even Ra-Mborakinda, praised Ngwe-vazya for having so well cared for the children, especially the one who was not her own.

This made Ngwe-nkonde more jealous, because of the praise that Ra-Mborakinda gave, and because of the boys' fine report of their visit and the abundance of gifts with which Ngwe-vazya had returned. So Ngwe-nkonde made up her mind that some day she would do the same, that she might receive similar praise. She waited some time before she attempted to carry out her plan. By the time that she got ready to ask leave to go the boys had grown to be lads. One day she thought proper to ask Ra-Mborakinda permission to go visiting with her son. Ra-Mborakinda was willing, and she commenced her preparations.

And again confusion came because of the two lads refusing to be separated. Osongo refused to go alone. But afterward he, knowing of his mother's jealous disposition, changed his mind, and said to Obengi, "No, I think you better stay." But Obengi refused, saying, "No, I have to go too." Osongo then told him the true reason for his objecting. "I said this because I know that my mother is not like yours, So please stay; I will be gone only two days, and will then come and meet you." But Obengi insisted, "If you go, I go." And Ngwe-nkonde said, "Well, let it be so; I will take care of you both."

So they went. When they reached the town of Ngwe-nkonde's family, the people were glad to see them. She also was apparently kind and attentive to the lads for the first two days. On the third day she began to think the care was troublesome. "These lads, are big enough to take care of themselves like men."

She did indeed feel kindly toward Obengi, liking his looks, and she said to herself, "I think I will try to win his affections from his mother to myself." She tried to do so, but the lad was not influenced by her. When she noticed that he did not seem to care for her attentions, she was displeased, began to hate him, and made up her mind to kill him.

All the days that the lads were there at the town they went out on excursions to the forest, hunting animals. As soon as they came back they would sit down together to chat and to eat sugar-cane [with African children a substitute for candy].

Ngwe-nkonde knew of this habit. After she had decided to kill Obengi, on the next day she had the sugar-cane ready for them. She rubbed poison on one of the stalks, and arranged that that very piece should be the the first one that Obengi would take. He had taken only two bites, and was chewing, when he exclaimed, "Brother, I begin to feel giddy, and my eyes see double! Please give me some water quickly!" Water was brought to him. He took a little of it. Others, spectators, became excited, and began to dash water over his face. But soon he fell down dead.

Then Ngwe-Nkonde exclaimed to herself, "So I've been here only five days, and now the lad is dead. I don't care! Let him die!"

By this time Osongo had become greatly excited, crying out, and repeating over and over, "My brother! Oh, my brother! Oh, my same age!" His mother said to him, "To-morrow I will have him buried, and we will start back to our town." Osongo replied to her, "That shall not be. He shall not be buried here. We both came together, and though he is dead, we both will go back together." The next morning Osongo said to his mother, "I know that you are at the bottom of this trouble. You know something about it. You brought him. And now he is dead. I charge you with killing him." She only replied, "I know nothing of that. We will wait, and we shall know."

They began to get ready for the return journey, and some of the people said, "Let a coffin be made, and the body be placed there." But Osongo said, "No, I don't want that, I have a hammock, and he shall be carried in it." So they prepared the hammock, and placed in it the dead body.

As to Ngwe-Nkonde, Osongo had her arrested, and held as a prisoner, with her hands tied behind her, and he took a long whip with which to drive her. And they started on their journey.

On the way Osongo was wailing a mourning-song, and cursing his mother, and weeping, saying, "Oh, we both came together, and he is dead! Oh, my brother! Oh, my same age! Obengi gone! Osongo left! Oh, the children of one father! Osongo, who belongs to Ng-we-Nkonde, left, and Obengi, who belongs to Ngwe-Vazya, gone!" And thus they went, be repeating these impromptu words of his song, and weeping as he went. As they were going thus, while they were still only half-way on their route, a man, Eserengila (tale-bearer), one of his father's servants, was out in the forest hunting. He heard the song. Listening, he said to himself, "Those words! What do they mean?" Listening still, he thought he recognized Osongo's voice, and understood that one was living and the other dead.

So he ran ahead to carry the news to the town before the corpse should arrive there. When he reached the town, he first told his wife about it. She advised him, "If that is so, don't go and tell this bad news to the king; a servant like you should not be the bearer of ill news." But he still said, "No, but I'm going to tell the father." His wife insisted, "Do not do it! With those two beloved children, if the news be not true, the parents will make trouble for you!" But Eserengila started to tell, and by the time he had finished his story the company with the corpse were near enough for the people of the town to hear all the words of Osongo's song of mourning.

Obengi's father and mother were so excited with grief that

their people had to bold them fast as if they were prisoners, to prevent them injuring themselves. The funeral company all went up to the king's house, and laid down the body of his son; and Osongo's mother, still tied, was led into the house.

The townspeople were all excited, shouting and weeping. Some began to give directions about the making of a fine coffin. But Osongo said, "No, I don't want him to be put into a coffin yet, because when my brother was alive we had many confidences and secrets, and now that he is dead, I have somewhat of a work to do before he is buried. Let the corpse wait awhile." So be asked them all to leave the corpse alone while he went out of the town for a short time.

Then he went away to the village of Ra-Mârânge, and said to him, "I'm in great trouble, and indeed I need your help." The prophet replied, "Child, I am too old; I am not making medicine now. Go to Ogula-y'-impazya-vazya, and repeat your story to him; he will help you."

Ra-Maranue showed him the way to Ogula-y'-impazya-vazya's place. He went, and had not gone far when be found it. Going to the magician, Osongo said, "I'm in trouble, and have come to you." As soon as he had said this, Ogula-y'-impazya-vazya made his magic fire, and stepped into it. Osongo was frightened, thinking, "I've come to this man, and he is about to kill himself for me"; and he ran away. But he had not gone far, when he heard the niagician's nkendo (a witchcraft bell) ringing, and his voice calling to him, "If you have come for medicine, come back; but if for anything else, then run away." So Osongo returned quickly, and found that the old magician had emerged from his fire and was waiting for him. Osongo told his story of his brother's death, and said be wanted direction what to do. Ogula-y'-impazya-vazya gave him medicine for a certain purpose, and told him what to do and bow to do it.

When Osongo came back with the medicine, he entered his father's house, into the room where his brother's corpse was lying, and ordered every one to leave him alone for a while. They all left the room. He closed the door, and following the directions given him by Ogula-y'-impazya-vazya, be brought Obengi to life again.

Now came a question what was to be done with Ngwe-nkonde, the attempted murderess. It was demanded that her throat should be cut, and that her body, weighted with stones, should be flung into the river. "For," said Osongo, "I will not own such a mother; she is very bad. Obengi's mother shall be my mother." It was decided so. And Ra-Mborakinda said to Ngwe-vazya, "You step up to the queen's seat with your two sons" (meaning Osongo and Obengi).

And Ngwe-vazya became head-wife, and was very kind and attentive to both sons.

And the matter ended.

VIII. Jeki and his Ozâzi

Ra-Mborakinda had his town where he lived with his wives, his sons, his daughters, and his glory.

Lord Mborakinda had his loved head-wife, Ngwe-nkonde, and the unloved one, Ngwe-lege. Both of these, with other of his wives, had sons and daughters. Ngwe-nkonde's first son was Nkombe, and she had two others. Ngwe-lege also had three sons, but the eldest of these, Jeki, was a thief. He stole everything he came across,—food,:fish, and all. This became so notorious that when people saw him approach their houses they would begin to hide their food and goods, saying, "There comes that thief!"

Jeki's grandfather, the father of his mother, was dead. One night, in a dream, that grandfather came to him, and said to him, "Jeki, my son, when will you leave off that stealing, and try to work and do other things as others do? To-morrow morning come to me early; I have a word to say to you." Jeki replied, "But where do you live, and how can I know the way to that town?" He answered, "You just start at your town entrance, and go on, and you will see the way to my place before you reach it."

So the next morning Jeki, remembering his dream, said to his mother, "Please fix me up some food." [He did not tell her that the purpose of the food was not simply for his breakfast, but as an extra supply for a journey.] The food that was prepared for him was five rolls made of boiled plantains mashed into a kind of pudding called "nkima," and tied up with dried fish. When these were ready, he put them inside his travelling-bag. Then be dressed himself for his-journey.

His mother said, "Where are you going. He evaded, and said, "I will be back again." So he went away.

After he had been gone a little while, be came to a fork of the road, and without hesitation his feet took the one leading to the right. After going on for a while he met two people named Isakiliya, fighting, whose forms were like sticks. [These sticks were abambo, or ghosts. In all native folk-lore, where spirits embody themselves, they take an absurd or singular form, that they may test the amiability or severity, as the case may be, of human beings with whom they may meet. They bless the kind, and curse the unkind.] He went to them to make peace, and parted them; took out one of his rolls of nkima and fish, gave to them, and passed on. They thanked him, and gave him a blessing, "Peace be on you, both going and coming!" He went on and on, and then he met two Antyâ (eyes) fighting. In the same way as with the Isakiliya, he went to them, separated them, gave them food, was blessed, and went on his way.

Again he met in the same way two Kumu (stumps) fighting, and in the same way he interfered between them, made peace, gave food, was blessed, and went on his journey. He went on and on, and met with a fourth fight. This time it was between two Poti (heads), and in the same way he made peace between them, gave a gift, was blessed, and went on.

He journeyed and journeyed. And he came to a dividing of the way, and was puzzled which to take. Suddenly an old woman appeared. He saluted her, "Mbolo!" took out his last roll of nkima, and gave it to her. The old woman thanked him, and asked him, "Where are you going?" He replied, "I'm on my way to an old man, but am a little uncertain as to my way." She said, "Oh, joy! I know him. I know the way. His name is Re-ve-nla-gâ-li." She showed him the way, pronounced a blessing on him, and he passed on. He had not gone much farther when he came to the place.

hen the old grandfather saw him, he greeted him, "Have you come, son?" He answered, "Yes."

"Well," said the grandfather, "I just live here by myself, and do my work myself." And the old man made food for him. Then next day this grandfather began to have a talk with Jeki. He rebuked him for his habit of stealing. Jeki replied, "But, grandfather, what can I do? I have no work nor any money. Even if I try to leave off stealing, I cannot. I do not know what medicine will cause me to leave it off." Then said the grandfather, "Well, child, I will make the medicine for you before you go back to your mother." So Jeki remained a few days with his grandfather, and then said, "I wish to go back." The grandfather said, "Yes, but I have some little work for you to do before you leave." So Jeki said, "Good! let me have the work."

The grandfather gave him an axe, and told him to go and cut firewood sufficient to fill the small woodshed. Jeki did so, filling the shed in that one day. The regular occupation of the old man was the twisting of ropes for the lines of seines. So the next day he told Jeki to go and get the inner barks, whose fibre was used in his rope-making. Jeki went to the forest, gathered this material, and returned with it to the old man.

The next day the grandfather said to Jeki, "Now I am ready to start you off on your journey." And he added, "As you gave as reasons for stealing that you had neither money nor the means of getting it, I will provide that." Then the old man called him, took him to a brook-side, and reminded him that he had promised that he could make a medicine to cure him of his desire to steal.

The grandfather began to cut open Jeki's chest, and took out his heart, washed it all clean, and put it back again. Then they went back to the grandfather's house. There be gave Jeki an ozâzi (wooden pestle), and said, "Now, son, take this. This is your wealth. Everything that you wish, this will bring to you. Hold it up, express your wish, and will get it. But there is one orunda (taboo) connected with it: no one must pronounce the word 'salt' in your hearing. You may see and use salt, but may not speak its name nor hear it spoken, for if you do things will turn out bad for you." "But," the old man added, "if that happens, I will now tell you what to do." And he revealed to him a secret, and gave him full directions. When the grandfather had finished, he led him a short distance on the way, and returned to his house. He had not prepared any food for Jeki for the journey, for he with the ozâzi would himself be able to supply all his own wishes.

Jeki goes on and on, and then exclaims doubtfully, "Ah, only this ozâzi is to furnish me with everything! I'm getting hungry; so, soon I'll try its power." He went on a little farther, and then decided that he would try whether be could get anything by means of the ozâzi. So be held it up, and said, "I wish a table of food to be spread for me, with two white men to eat with me." Instantly there was seen a tent, and table covered with food, and two white men sitting. He sat down with these two companions. After they had eaten, be spoke to the ozâzi to cause the tent and its contents to disappear. They did so. This proved for him the power of his ozâzi, and be was glad, and went on his way satisfied.

Finally he reached his father's town, whose people saw him coming, but gave him no welcome, except his mother, who was glad to see him. But most of the people only said, "There! there is that thief coming again. We must begin to hide our things. After Jeki's arrival, in a few days, the townspeople noticed a change in him, and inquired of each other, "Has he been stealing, or has he really changed?" for shortly after his return be had told his mother and brothers all the news, and had warned the people of the town about the orunda of "salt." In the course of a few days Jeki did many wonderful things with his ozâzi. He wished for nice little premises of his own with houses and conveniences, near his father's town, supplied with servants and clothing and furniture. These appeared. Soon, by the wealth that he possessed, be became master of the town, and ruled over the other children of his father. He obtained from that same ozâzi, created by its power, two wives,—Ngwanga and llâmbe, who were loving and obedient. He also bought three other wives from the village, who were like servants to the two chief ones. He confided his plans and everything to the two favored ones who had come out of the ozâzi.

In the course of time he thought he would display his power before the people, and for their benefit, by causing ships to come with wealth. So he held up the ozâzi, and said, "I want to see a ship come full of merchandise!"

Presently the townspeople began to shout, "A ship! a ship!" It anchored. Jeki called his own brothers and half-brothers, and directed," You all get ready and go out to the ship, and tell the captain that I will follow you." They made ready, and went on board, and asked, "What goods have you brought?" The captain told them, "Mostly cloth, and a few other things." They informed him, "Soon the chief of the town will come." And they returned ashore, and reported to Jeki what was on board. He made himself ready and went, leaving word for them to follow soon and discharge the cargo. The ship lay there a few days, and then sailed away. Then Jeki divided the goods among his brothers and parents, keeping only a small share for himself.

Thus it went on: every few months Jeki ordering a ship to come with goods. As usual, he would send his brothers first, they would bring a report, and then he would go on board. Sometimes he would eat with the ship's company, sometimes he would invite them ashore to eat in his own house.

All this time no one had broken the orunda of "salt." But, to prove things, Jeki thought be would try his half-brothers, and see what were their real feelings toward him. So the next time he caused ships to come with a cargo of salt only. At sight of the ships there was the usual shout of "A ship! a ship!" The brothers went aboard as usual, and found what the cargo was. The half-brotbers returned ashore immediately, and began to shout when they neared Jeki's house, "The ships are full of salt!" He heard the word, and said to his mother and to his two chief wives, "Do you hear that?"

The half-brothers came close to him, and exclaimed, "Dâgula [Sir], the ships are loaded with nothing but salt, salt, salt, and the captain is waiting for you." Jeki asked again, as if he had not heard, "What is it the captains have brought?" And they said, "Salt." So he said, "Let it be so. To-day is the day. Good! You go and get ready, and I will get ready, and we shall all go together."

Then the two chief wives looked very sorrowful, for they felt sure by his look and tone that something bad was about to happen.

First be ordered a bath to be prepared for himself. It was made ready, and be bathed, and went to dress himself in the other room, where his goods were stored. When he had entered, be called his own two brothers and the two wives, and closed the door. He began to examine a few of his boxes. Opening a certain one, he said, "Of all my wealth, this was one of the first. Now I am going to die. But as it is always the custom, a few days after the funeral, to decide who shall be the successor and inheritor, when that day arrives, come and open this particular box. Do not forget to take the cloth for covering the throne of my successor from this box."

Inside of that box was a small casket, holding a large black silk handkerchief. He kept the secret received from his grandfather, and did not tell them what would happen when they should come to get cloth from the box. They understood only that on the throne-day they were to open the big box and the little casket it contained. Then he told them, "Now you may go out." They went out. Jeki shut the door, and began to dress for the ships. But, before dressing, he took out the black silk handkerchief from the small box, and rubbed it over his entire body; and, carefully folding it, put it back again in the casket and closed it. Then be was ready to start. And they all went off to the ships, be with the ozâzi in hand. He, with his own brothers, was in a boat following the boat of his half-brothers.

He raised a death-song, "Ilendo! Ilendo! give me skill for a dance! Ilendo! Ilendo! give me skill for a play!" This he sang on the way, jumping from boat to boat. He said be would go on board the ships, but ordered all his brothers not to come. His plan was that they were to be only witnesses of his death. He boarded one of the ships, and went over the deck singing and dancing with that same Ilendo song. Then he jumped to the deck of the next vessel.

As be did so, the first one sank instantly. On the second ship he sang and danced, and jumped thence to the third, the second sinking as the first. On the third ship be continued the song and dance; he remained on it a long while, for he caused it to sink slowly. When the water reached the vessel's deck, the brothers in the boats were looking on with fear. His own brothers began to cry, seeing the ship sinking, for they knew that Jeki would die with it. When it sank, the boats went ashore wailing, and took the news to the town.

But the half-brothers were not really mourning; they were planning the division of Jeki's property. All the town held the kwedi (mourning); but after the fifth day the half-brothers told their father that it was time for the exaltation of a successor to Jeki, the ceremony of ampenda (glories). Ngwe-nkonde's first-born son, Nkombe, said, "I will be the first to stand on the throne, and my two brothers will be next." Jeki's two brothers refused to have anything to say about the division. They determined they would remain quiet and see what would be done. And the two wives of Jeki said the same.

When the half-brothers came to the house of mourning, they began to discuss which of these two women they would inherit. Then one of the two wives said, "Oh, Ngwanga, we must not forget what Jeki told us about the box, now that the people are fixing for the ampenda!"

So the two brothers of Jeki and the two women went inside the room, shut the door, and began to open the big box to take out the little casket. By this time the people outside had everything ready for the ceremony of the ampenda. The two women now opened the casket, took out the black handkerchief, and unfolded it. And Jeki stood in the middle of the room, with his ozâzi in his hand. Their surprise was great; their joy extreme. In their joy they ran to embrace him.

The people outside were very busy with their arrangements. Nkombe already had taken the throne, having painted his face with the little white mark of rule, and given orders to have the signal-drum beaten; and the crowd began to dance and sing to his praise.

Jeki sent his youngest brother, Oraniga (last-born), saying, "Just go privately and tell my father about me, that I have come to life. And I want him to have the whole town swept, and to lay bars of iron along the streets for me to step on from this house to his. Say also that Ntyege (monkey) must continue his firing of guns and cannon; then I will come and meet my father."

Oraniga did so; and the father said, "Good!" and Oraniga returned. The father gave the desired orders about the sweeping and the iron bars and the firing of cannon; but the people at the throne-house did not know of all this.

Then Jeki and his two wives and two brothers dressed themselves finely to walk to the father's house, and marched in procession through the street. A few of the people saw them, wondered, and asked the drums to stop, exclaiming, "Where did they come from?" The procession went on to the father's house, and Ntyege kept on with the cannon firing.

On reaching his father's house, Jeki told him he had something to say, and the father ordered the drum to cease. All the people were summoned to the father's house to hear Jeki's words. He said, "Father, I know that I am your son, and Nkombe is your son. You, all know what Nkombe has done, for he was at the bottom of this matter; so now choose between him and me. If you love him more,

I will go far away and stay by myself; but if you love me, Nkombe must be removed from this town."

So the father asked the opinion of others. (For himself, he wanted to have Jeki.) Nkombe's own brothers said he ought to be killed, "for he is not so good to us as Jeki was." So they bound Nkombe, and tied a stone about his neck, and drowned him in the sea.

And everything went on well, Jeki governing, and providing for the town.

Glossary

A.

Abuna, abundance.

Aganlo, children of mixed mortal and fairy birth.

Akazya, a poisonous tree.

Amie, do not know.

Anlingo, water.

Antâ (sing. **intyâ**), eyes.

Anyambe, the Divine Name.

Aweme, yourself.

Ayenwe, unseen.

B.

Bâbâkâ, consent thou.

Behu, kitchen garden.

Benda, a kind of rat.

Biaň, medicine.

Bobâbu; soft.

Bohamba, Boka Bokadi, Bokuda, a certain medicinal tree.

Bolondo, a poisonous tree.

Bongâm, a certain medicinal tree.

Botombaka, passing away.

Buhwa, day.

Bwanga, medicine.

D.

Dâgula, Mr., a title of respect.

Diba, marriage.

Diyâ, the hearth; a household.

Diyaka, to live.

E.

Ebâbi, a male love philtre.

Egona, a small antelope.horn.

Ehongo, a cornucopia.

Ekongi, a guardian-spirit fetich.

Ekope, a girdle.

Elâmbâ, a certain medicinal tree.

Elinga, a basket.

Etomba, tribe.

Evove, harlot.

Ewiria, words of hidden meaning.

F.

Fufu, mashed, boiled ripe plantains.

G.

Go, to, in, at.

Greegree (gria-gris), fetich amulet.

Gumbo, okra.

Gwandere, a medicine for worms.

H.

Haye, will not do.

Hume, a certain fish.

I.

Ibambo (pl. **abambo**), ghosts.

Ibâtâ, a blessing.

Iga, the forest.

Iguga, woe.

Iheli, a gazelle.

Ijawe (pl. **majawe**), blood relative.

Ikaka (pl. **makaka**), family name.

Ilala, an arch; a stairway.

Ilina (pl. **malina**), soul.

Ina, my mother.

Ilina (pl. **malinla**), soul.

Injenji, a certain leaf; fault

Isakiliya, kindling-wood.

Isiki (pl. **asiki**), a dwarf changeling.

Itaka, a kitchen hanging-shelf.

Itala, a view.

Ivaha, a wish.

Ivenda (pl. **ampenda**), glory.

Iyele, a female love philtre.

J.

Ja, of.

Jaka, to beget.

Joba, the sun.

Jomba, meat cooked in a bundle of plantain leaves.

Juju, an amulet.

K.
Kâ, and you.
Kasa, a lash.
Keva, to surpass.
Kilinga, a kind of bird.
Kimbwa-mbenje, native bark-cloth.
Kna, a kind of bird.
Knakna, a large kind of bird.
Koka, a large kind of bird.
Kombo, a superstitious ejaculation.
Konde, queen.
Kota, a certain tree.
Kulu, a kind of spirit.
Kumu, a stump.
Kwedi, time of mourning.

L.
Lale, my father.

M.
Mabili, an east-wind fetich.
Mba, not I.
Mbenda, ground-nut.
Mbi, I.
Mbinde, a wild goat.
Mbolo, gray hairs; a salutation.
Mbulu, a wild dog.
Mbumbu, rainbow.
Mbundu, poison ordeal.
Mbwa (pl. **imbwa**), dog.
Mbwaye, a poison test.
Mehole, ripe plantains.
Miba, water.
Mie, me.
Monda, witchcraft medicine.
Mondi (pl. **myondi**), a class of spirits.
Mpazya, skin disease.
Mulimate, a small horn for cupping.
Musimo, spirits of the dead.
Muskwa, a medicinal brush.
Mutira, a medicinal stick.
Mvia, a kind of bird.
Mwana, a child.
Mwanga, a plantation.

N.
Na, with.
Ndabo, house.

Ndembe, young.
Nduma, a kind of snake.
Ngalo, a guardian-spirit charm.
Ngâma, a water plant.
Ngândâ, gourd seeds.
Ngânde, moon.
Ngofu, an iron fetich bracelet.
Ngunye, a flying-squirrel.
Nguwu, hippopotamus.
Ngwe, mother.
Njabi, a wild oily fruit.
Njegâ, leopard.
Nkâlâ, a large snail.
Nkânjâ, a marriage dance.
Nkendo, a magician's bell.
Nkinda (pl. **sinkinda**), a class of spirits.
Nsânâ, Sunday.
Nsinsim, a shadow.
Ntori, a large forest rat.
Nyege, a monkey.
Nungwa, open thou.
Nunja, shut thou.
Nyamba, a scarf slung over the right
shoulder, in which to carry a babe.
Nyemba, witchcraft.
Nyolo, body.

O.
Odika, kernel of the wild mango.
Oganga, doctor.
Ogendâ, a journey.
Ogwerina, rear of a house.
Okove, a powerful fetich.
Okume, African mahogany tree.
Okundu, a kind of fetich for trading.
Olâgâ (pl. **ilâgâ**), a class of spirits.
Olako, a camping place.
Ombwiri (pl. **awiri**), a class of spirits.
Ompunga, wind.
Orala, a hanging shelf over a fire place.
Oraniga, last-born.
Orâwo, insult.
Orega, the Njembe secret society drum.
Orunda, a prohibition; taboo.
Osenge, a cleared place in the forest.
Ovâvi (pl. **ivâvi**), messenger.
Owavi (pl. **sijavi**), a leaf.
Ozyâzi, a pestle.

Ozyoto, a cornucopia.

P.
Pala, my father.
Pavo, a knife.
Peke, ever.

R.
Rera, my father.

S.
Saba, **Sabali**, an oath.
Sale, hail!

T.
Tamba, the womb.
Tube, a certain leaf.
Tuwaka, bless; spit

U.
Udinge, a great person.
Ukuku (pl. **mekuku**), spirit; secret society.
Ukwala, a machete.
Untyanya, a medicinal bark.
Unyongo, a medicine tree.
Upuma, a period of six months.
Utodu, old.
Uvengwa, a phantom.

V.
Veya, fire.

Y.
Yâginla, *imperative*, hear thou.
Yâkâ, a family fetich.

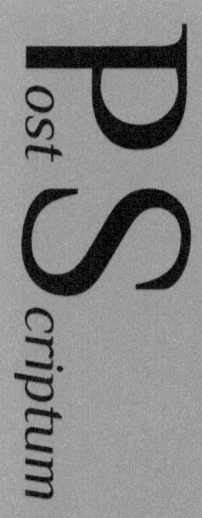

About Robert Hamill Nassau

VAMzzz Publishing

Biography Nassau

Robert Hamill Nassau (1835-1921) was born in Newtown Square, Pennsylvania. He went to the Lawrenceville School in Lawrenceville, New Jersey, continuing his education at the College of New Jersey. From 1856 -1859 he moved on to the Princeton Theological Seminary and obtained a medical qualification from Pennsylvania Medical School in1861.

Nassau was an ordained minister and a medical doctor. On the instigation of the Presbytery of New Brunswick he joined the Presbyterian Board of Foreign Missions as a missionary, with his first posting being to the African island of Corisco off the coast of present day at Equatorial Guinea. He and his wife Mary Cloyd Latta served there and at Benito on the mainland until her death in 1870.

Throughout his career, he served as a missionary in places as Benita, Belambla, Kangwe, Talaguga, Baraka (Libreville) and Batanga. In 1874 the Presbyterian U.S.A. Board of Foreign Missions determined to press into the Ogowe interior, and Nassau established a station in Balimbila, about 200 miles inland. That work was later moved to Kangwe. In 1879 the Ogowe church was organized at Kangwe, the beginning of his missionary work among the Mpongwe people. Nassau's second wife, Mary Brunette Foster, who died in 1884, and his sister Isabel Nassau, where the first white women to live in the Ogowe region.

In 1892 and 1893 France claimed Gabon and Ogowe as a colony. The Presbyterians transferred their work in those areas to the Paris Evangelical Mission Society. In 1894 Nassau and sister were assigned to Batanga station in German Kamerun, where they serve until their retirement in 1906.

After serving churches in Florida for several years, Nassau died in Ambler, Pennsylvania. With his first wife, who was a fellow missionary, Nassau had three sons, William Latta, George Paull and Charles Francis. His second wife left him a daughter, also named Mary Brunette Foster.

His original writings are kept as part of the The Burke Library Archives, held at the Columbia University Libraries, New York. ■

'Nassau was an ordained minister and a medical doctor.'

Paper books

VAMzzz Publishing is located in the very centre of old Amsterdam, in The Netherlands. Our publishing company creates high quality revised editions of five star occult, witchcraft, Gothic and esoteric classics, mostly written in the Fin de siècle-period and early 20th century.

As a publisher, we deeply respect the writer of any book we choose, so we join our forces (top level graphic design & thirty years of occult studies) to produce enchanting volumes which maximize the reading pleasure and inform, often with extra added information. In contrast to the current trend of digital screen addiction, we think, this variety of literature needs to be presented on paper. *No e-books, but real books!*

Apart from republications of valuable but forgotten books, we are also in the preparation of new publications on topics such as self-healing, magic, new astrology and more.

Previews of all books including a complete table of contents can be viewed on www.vamzzz.com. More books will be added to the list. *VAMzzz Publishing* strives to publish new volumes every month. Please visit our website regularly for the latest updates.

VAMzzz Publishing
P.O. Box 3340
1001 AC Amsterdam
The Netherlands
contactvamzzz@gmail.com
www.vamzzz.com

VOODOOS and OBEAHS
Phases of West India Witchcraft

Joseph J. Williams

Recommended

Voodoos and Obeahs
*Phases of West India
Witchcraft*
by Joseph J. Williams
374 pages, Paperback,
ISBN 9789492355119

Voodoos and Obeahs: Phases of West India Witchcraft by the Jesuit anthropologist Joseph J. Williams (1875-1940) offers a careful documentation of the history and ethnography of Voodoo and reveals the connection of both Haitian Voodoo and Jamaican Obeah to snake worship (ophioletreia). In Jamaica, Obeah is the general term to denote those Africans who in the island practice witchcraft or sorcery. Williams includes numerous quotations from rare documents and books on the topic. This work goes into great depth concerning the New World-African connection and is highly recommended if you want a deep understanding of the dramatic historical background of Haitian and Jamaican magic and witchcraft, and the profound influence of imperialism, slavery and racism on its development.

Williams is best known for his anthropological writings about African and Caribbean people, which include *Whispering of the Caribbean, Whence the "Black Irish" of Jamaica?, Psychic Phenomena in Jamaica* and *Africa's God.*

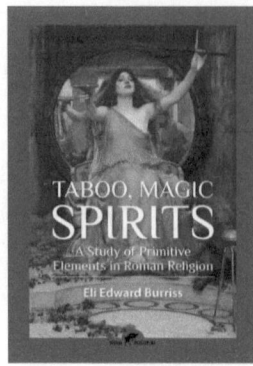

Taboo, Magic, Spirits
A study of primitive elements in Roman religion
by Eli Edward Burriss
200 pages, Paperback, ISBN 9789492355034

In Ancient Rome Mana was the term used for a mysterious, magical medium, which could be helpful or harmful (Taboo). Just like the Chinese qi, it could empower the positive and the negative. Contents: Mana, Magic and Animism – Positive and Negative Mana (Taboo) – Miscellaneous Taboos – Magic Acts: The General Principles – Removing Evils by - Magic Acts – Incantation and Prayer– Naturalism and Animism.

Chaldean Magic
It's Origin and Development
by François Lenormant
454 pages, Paperback, ISBN 9789492355027

The essentials of magic in Chaldea are presented inside a context of comparison or contrast to Egyptian, Median, Turanian, Finno-Tartarian and Akkadian magic, mythologies, religion and speech. Interesting is the Chaldean demonology, with its incubus, succubus, vampire, nightmare and many Elemental spirits, most of them coalesced with the primal powers of nature.

Amazons - Two publications in one book -
I. The Amazons by Guy Cadogan Rothery
II. Religious Cults Associated With the Amazons
by Florence Mary Bennett
328 pages, Paperback, ISBN 9789492355089

Contents I: The Amazons of Antiquity – Amazons in Far Asia – Modern Amazons of the Caucasus – Amazons of Europe – Amazons of Africa – Amazons of America – The Amazon Stones. Contents II: The Amazons in Greek legend – The Great Mother – Ephesian Artemis – Artemis Astrateia and Apollo Amazonius – Ares.

Là-Bas
A Journey into the Self
by Joris-Karl Huysmans
378 pages, Paperback, ISBN 9789492355058

The plot of *Là-Bas* concerns the novelist Durtal, who is disgusted by the emptiness and vulgarity of the modern world. He seeks relief by turning to the study of the Middle Ages. Through his contacts in Paris, Durtal discovers that Satanism is not a thing of the past but alive and kicking in turn of the century France. The novel culminates with a description of a black mass.

Devil-worship in France
Or The Question of Lucifer
by Arthur Edward Waite
240 pages, Paperback, ISBN 9789492355065

In *Devil-Worship in France,* Waite attempts to discern what is genuine from what is fake in the evidence of 19th century Satanism. To get the answers he spends a great deal of time investigating the French Masonic echelon, debunking a "conspiracy of falsehood" and determining what should be understood by Satanism and what not. Huysmans' diabolical novel *Là-Bas* (1891) inspired Waite to write this sceptical analysis.

Testament of Solomon
A First Century AD Grimoire
76 pages, Paperback, ISBN 9789492355041

A first century AD grimoire, and therefore the oldest, and least known, of all grimoires (magical instruction books) in the occult tradition. The book describes health inflicting demons of zodiacal decans, summoned by King Solomon, and how he controlled them to use their forces to build his temple and more. Translated by F. C. Conybeare, appeared first in the *Jewish Quarterly Review* of October, 1898.

Fairy Mythology *(Volume 1)*
Romance and Superstition of Various Countries 1
by Thomas Keightley
404 pages, Paperback, ISBN 9789492355096

Fairy Mythology *(Volume 2)*
Romance and Superstition of Various Countries 2
by Thomas Keightley
404 pages, Paperback, ISBN 9789492355102

The term Fairy covers all kinds of nature spirits, not just the tiny sugarsweet creatures hovering around flowers. A unique and impressive book on this subject, published in a revised 2 volume-edition. No wiccan or pagan can afford to leave these books unopened. About Elves, Dwarfs, Kobolds, Trolls, Changelings, Meremaids, Nisses, Fairies, Brownies, Puck and other Elemental spirits all over the world.

Etruscan Magic & Occult Remedies
(Two volumes in one book)
Charles Godfrey Leland
628 pages, Paperback, ISBN 9789492355003

Part One of the book gives us a complete and detailed insight in the Etruscan and Roman rooted pantheon of the Tuscan Streghe (witches). Part Two describes many of their spells, incantations, sorcery and several lost divination methods. Much information in this book, Leland received first hand from the Tuscan witches Maddalena and Marietta.

Aradia
Gospel of the Witches
by Charles Godfrey Leland
174 pages, Paperback, ISBN 9789492355010

This wonderful book describes the creation according to
Italian witch-lore. We also read about the witch-meeting
or sabbath (treguenda) and the book contains many
original magical recipes, like spells for love and good
fortune. Diana is further connected to the Moon and
the fairy world.

Demonology and Devil-Lore (Volume 1)
by Moncure Daniel Conway
490 pages, Paperback, ISBN 9789492355157

Demonology and Devil-Lore (Volume 2)
by Moncure Daniel Conway
518 pages, Paperback, ISBN 9789492355164

Within the demonology scope, this rare and mostly
forgotten, almost 1000 pages thick masterpiece, remains
unsurpassed in quality and completeness. Even in the
21st century the works offer fascinating missing links
for both the academic and student of occult traditions.
Moncure Daniel Conway divides Volume 1 in three
parts and deals mainly with the evolution and thematic
classification of ex-gods, demons and nature creatures.
Volume 2 deals primarily with the diabolic and with the
Devil himself, his ethnic history and connected topics.

Ophiolatreia
Rites and Mysteries of Serpent Worship
Author: Hargrave Jennings
186 pages, Paperback, ISBN 9789492355126

An account of the rites and mysteries connected with the origin, rise and development of serpent worship in various parts of the world, enriched with interesting traditions, and a full description of the celebrated serpent mounds & temples, the whole forming an exposition of one of the phases of phallic, or sex worship.

Anansi
Jamaican stories of the Spider God
Author: Martha Warren Beckwith
494 pages, Paperback, ISBN 9789492355171

Anansi is both a god, spirit and African folktale character. He often takes the shape of a spider and is considered to be the spirit of all knowledge of stories. He is also one of the most important characters of West African and Caribbean folklore..

Recommended

PAN Magazine
by VAMzzz Publishing
Free Online
www.vamzzz.com/pan.html

In Greek religion and mythology, PAN, the companion of the nymphs, is the god of the wild, shepherds and flocks, wild mountains and rustic music. He has the hindquarters, legs and horns of a goat, in the same manner as a faun or satyr. He is also recognized as the god of fields, groves and wooded glens; connected to fertility, the joy of life itself and the season of spring.

Though a mortal god in antiquity and an underground witch-god in medieval times, the last decades PAN has become a patron of both modern occultism, Wicca, paganism and the green guerilla – enthroned again as the one and only God of the Earth and Nature. PAN is the vibe touching those who refuse to become part of a machine, and who remain loyal to Mother Nature, the visible and hidden one. Therefore PAN is the most suitable icon we could chose for this quarterly periodical.